You Never Try,
You Never Know

Six Years in Liberia

Ruth Jacobson

Ruth Jacobson (signature)

Court Street Press
Seattle, Washington

Editing and book design: Judith Yarrow
Cover design: Ciam Sawyer
Editorial assistance: Patricia Lichiello, Neil Banta-Blacker

Printed by Gorham Printing, www.gorhamprinting.com

Cover photograph: Ruth and Harold Jacobson in Liberia, 1971
(photographer unknown)

Court Street Press
3707 37th Avenue South
Seattle, Washington 98144-7110
jayarrow@gmail.com

ISBN 978-0-9647444-2-4
First printing: January 2001
Second printing: March 2011

Printed in the United States of America.

To our Liberian family and friends.

PROLOGUE

You might wonder what would motivate a couple in their fifties to become Peace Corps volunteers and serve in a totally unfamiliar part of the world. The Liberian saying "You never try, you never know" captures our decision to store away our belongings, leave our family and friends, and spend what turned out to be six memorable years in Africa.

After a long career as a registered nurse and then as an instructor of practical nursing at Tacoma Vocational Technical Institute and several community colleges, I had risen to a management position in the state vocational education/community college system. Most of my work involved helping to establish practical nursing and other health occupations training programs. Harold, on the other hand, after years of work as a maintenance mechanic, had been trying without much success to start a small saw-sharpening business.

We had always warned our two daughters that when they had completed school and left home, we didn't plan to sit around and wait for them to come to visit nor did we expect to be available as baby sitters. Our daughters were now well out of college and on their own. And we, in our mid-50s, were ready for some kind of adventure.

A combination of circumstances influenced our decision about our future. The first was meeting some returned Peace Corps volunteers, friends of our daughter Judith, who talked enthusiastically of their experiences in Africa and the South Pacific. Their stories inspired us. The second influence was an interview in the *Tacoma News Tribune* with a couple like us, newly returned from service in South America and now serving as recruiters for Peace Corps. Harold and I looked at each other and said, "We could do that." This was followed by serious discussion and stocktaking. Finally we said, "Why not give it a try."

About that time, Peace Corps had shifted its recruitment focus from new graduates to older people with more life experience. One of Judith's friends telephoned the national recruiting office and recommended us.

Harold and I discovered that we had the perfect combination of experiences and skills for an overseas assignment. The Great Depression had been a formative period in our lives and prepared us for the life of austerity we were warned of. In fact, we learned in telephone conversations with Peace Corps officials that our life experiences would be assets in the work we anticipated.

Peace Corps wanted us right away and immediately offered us an assignment in the Marshall Islands but I couldn't leave my job so quickly. Also, although we were renting at the time, we had two vehicles to dispose of, as well as arrangements to make for storing our household furnishings, clothing, and accumulated clutter of a long life together. We had to decline that assignment, but we were soon offered another, this time in Liberia, West Africa.

Note about the letters

These letters were saved by my daughters and my mother, Signe Hanson. For space or privacy issues, we have removed travel arrangements, financial instructions, family-related comments not relevant to our African experience, redundant paragraphs (same thing written to different people), and letter closings.

Acknowledgments

First, and foremost, I have to thank my mother for saving so many of my letters, which made this book possible. I would also like to thank everyone who assisted by typing letters and reading the manuscript. I especially want to thank our friend Laurie Guzoto, who spent so many hours typing more than half of these letters.

Finally I want to thank my daughter, Judith Yarrow. I would never have completed this project without her loving admonition to publish these letters and her tireless work editing them.

Original map: http://en.wikipedia.org/wiki/File:Un-liberia.png

Brief History of Liberia

Liberia is about two-thirds the size of Washington State. As of 2010, about 3.5 million people live there. They speak English and 25 native languages.

In 1822 freed US slaves began to settle in what is today Liberia. By 1847, they had established the Republic of Liberia and over the years slowly expanded government control throughout the country. Bong, Lofa, and Nimba counties, where Ruth and Harold lived, were formed in 1964.

In 1980, a military coup led by Samuel Doe began almost a decade of authoritarian rule. In 1989, Charles Taylor rebelled against Doe's regime, leading to prolonged civil war. A movement called Women of Liberia Mass Action for Peace helped bring peace to Liberia after the 14-year civil war and, in 2005, helped elect President Ellen Johnson Sirleaf, the first African female head of state.

Ruth and Harold shortly after beginning their Liberian assignment.

THE PEACE CORPS YEARS

Dearest Mother,   **March 10, 1971, Philadelphia**

Our training period has begun, and so far things look OK. We checked in here at the hotel yesterday afternoon and met the other members of our "team," about 30 people. Six are married couples, two with two little boys each. Each has a one-year old. There are two couples older than we are and one man in our age bracket. The rest are fairly youthful, some just out of college—civil engineers, horticulturists and community development people. This week will be spent getting acquainted with Liberia through slides, movies, talks, and lots of opportunities to ask questions. There are also arrangements for people who need physicals and dental work, and we all had to have more shots. We will take off on Monday eve from Kennedy airport and will arrive, non-stop, in Monrovia the next morning.

Some of the orientation team is from Liberia. One is the secretary of Internal Affairs and the other is the director of Agriculture of Liberia. So we have an opportunity to talk with the people who are actually familiar with life there. I probably won't have any assignment until we get into the country and we see where Harold is to be stationed.

Dear Mother,   **March 15, 1971, Philadelphia**

This will be our last night in the USA for quite a while. We'll leave on the 7:45 PM plane tomorrow. It doesn't seem possible that we're here and taking off on such a jaunt. So far, things have been going well. It seems like a nice group that we'll be with and the people from Liberia, including our Peace Corps leader for this project really impresses us.

It's been a quiet Sunday. We had a final meeting this morning and then dashed out to go to church. The only one we could find with the time close to 11 AM was an Episcopal church. It's a very old huge building called St. Marks—lots of stained glass and very ornate, gold fittings around the altar. But it was one of the friendliest groups we've been in, in a long time. In fact, at one point in the service, everyone greeted the persons next to them—shook hands and smiled and spoke to each other. We also took communion and they used the common cup—a silver goblet. It was a bit hard to follow the service since it was very formal and an unfamiliar form—reminded me of the Catholic service. At any rate, it was an enjoyable experience.

We've enjoyed hunting different restaurants this week. Tonight, we went to a Japanese one, one night Greek, and another Italian, and also, a Chinese place. We also enjoy having lunch in a little Jewish delicatessen. There are so many unusual kinds of things to buy. We've learned that our most common kind of food in Liberia will be chicken and rice and no fresh vegetables or salad greens since there is no way really to get them clean.

Our training period will be for two months, part of which will be living with a volunteer, or with a Liberian family. Our first week will be in the capital city, Monrovia, and then we will be taken to a smaller town "up-country" for the rest of the training period. We can expect to receive mail about once a week. There is a strong possibility that we'll be stationed in Monrovia, and I'll be involved with the hospital there.

Thursday evening Monrovia. We've just finished our third day in Monrovia, and it's difficult to know where to begin. We have been very much on our own since we arrived about 10:30 Tuesday. We were so late getting out of Philadelphia because of weather that the plane for Liberia had to wait. It was really a fast shuffle through customs with everyone intent on pushing us through. "Peace Corps" were magic words at that point, but I'll admit some of the young airport guys took a second look when Harold and I said it!

We stopped for about an hour in Dakar, Senegal, and then about an hour later landed in Monrovia. Hot and humid. They really went through everything very thoroughly. We were taken in a little bus and some PC vans to our hotel, casually assigned rooms, and from then on, we were on our own until we were to report for our first meeting, free to do whatever we wanted.

The city itself is fantastic. About 100,000 people, a third of whom leave the city during harvest time and go up-country to their tribal village, for several months. The poverty and squalor are unbelievable, but it's been such a way of life, that life continues to go on. Our hotel is considered to be fairly good by these standards, but I haven't stayed in one like it since we stayed in that hotel in Cashmere, so long ago. On top of this is the question of whether you can drink the water. You can't depend that the running water is uncontaminated because while it is supposedly purified at the source, there are such frequent breakdowns in the system that it is more than likely unsafe to drink. I'm such a water drinker, and on top of that we perspire so freely that on the first day I was just desperate for a drink of enjoyable and safe water. One volunteer would say never drink water unless you've broken the seal yourself, or you know for sure it's been boiled. Another said "Ask if it's boiled." Another would say, "Ask if it's boiled and if they say yes, believe them."

Just finding a place to have a meal was pretty hairy at first—being understood, understanding the people, strange concoctions, etc. We have quite a nice bunch of people to work with, and everyone tries to help the next person, and by now, we're feeling quite comfortable. We've met so many people both in the government and in PC, seen so many strange things, heard so many foreign tongues; even Liberian English [*a local dialect of English mixed with old southern US expressions*] is becoming more understandable. We had three more shots and oral polio vaccine. Still have two more shots and gamma globulin (every four months) for hepatitis.

We have walked many, many miles. The other mode of travel is by taxi—25 cents each way, or by "money bus" on which the fare is 10 cents. Tomorrow at 6 AM we all leave, again by mini bus, for a town inland called Gbarnga, pronounced "bonga," where we will all split up and continue on by taxi for a "live in" experience. We are to go to a town called Fissibu, pronounced like it is spelled. We'll live with a married couple, both PC teachers, until Tuesday. The idea is for us to learn, on a one-to-one basis, all about village life and the work of volunteers. Each volunteer or volunteer couple will be in a different village or town. Ours is a total of six hours driving time from the capital, about 150 miles, all dirt roads.

Today we had a long session with an Anglican priest who is an expert on tribal dialects and on Liberian English. You may remember I told you this is an English-speaking country. A minority of the educated class speaks good English, some speak with a pronounced accent, and the majority of those who live in Monrovia speak Liberian English, which is practically unintelligible to the uninitiated like us. Imagine a combination of Southern terms and Southern accents and dialect, pidgin or Cajun type, and tribal words—a vocabulary that doesn't have many of our everyday words but has phrases that may mean the same thing or, in some cases, may have almost the opposite meaning, all combined with a tonal emphasis different from English. We will have three weeks of intensive language study during our training period, both in Liberian English and in the tribal dialect of the community where we are to be assigned.

The people who are responsible for our training are very versed on the country. Most have lived here a long time or are Liberians themselves. Everyone likes it here so much that they hate to leave. At least a third of the volunteers here have re-enrolled or extended or taken jobs here. The country, the government as well as individuals, think highly of Peace Corps and of the volunteers. For example, on this project, we are called Liberian employees, not PCVs [*Peace Corps volunteers*], and are supposed to be responsible to the Liberian government personnel. This apparently is a new approach and is being looked at with a great deal of interest both by the government and by PC.

I can't get over the kinds of homes we see all around us here. Many of the people do all of their living, cooking, eating, sleeping, bathing in tiny huts or in the yard or in the streets all around the downtown or central part of the city. It's a terribly crowded noisy colorful city. People are constantly moving about, trying to sell you something or taking care of their own needs. Everyone carries their things on their heads, even tiny tots, barefoot or wearing sandals and very colorful dresses or shirts. There are beautiful batik and tie-dye materials as everyday wear. If any of you have read *Zinzin Road*, it is very authentic, except for the political aspect that it describes, according to our trainers.

Dear Mother,   **March 20, 1971, Fissibu**

Since we landed in Monrovia, we have been kept so busy or else I've been so exhausted when there has been time so that I haven't written any letters yet. I'll try to get this finished so that I can send it with the PC mail person this morning before another full day. We have seen so many new and strange things and had so many new experiences since leaving the United States that it's hard to know where to start.

This little town, Fissibu, consists of about 450 houses—no idea how many people, all or most of whom speak their tribal dialect only. There's no electricity or running water, and all the people "make farm" to support their families. We will be here for four days or so. The young PC couple we will be with teach in a teacher training institute here. Today we are leaving early to go to another village to their market. Market day in the interior villages is apparently a big social event, too, along with the time when people come in to sell their wares.

Yesterday was my birthday [53]; what a different one. We traveled from the city where we had been staying in a hotel. We were driven for three hours in a mini bus—12 of us, on a very dusty road, and went about 75-100 miles. I had "Happy Birthday" sung to me as we drove and bounced along. There were two flat tires along the way. Then we got into taxis, seven people in a vehicle about the size of our Corvair, and drove another 60 miles. Dusty. Then into another taxi, which included a chicken for a passenger.

I was so dirty when we arrived at our hosts' home, you can't believe. In the evening our hosts took us to the home of two other volunteers for a visit. There are six in this village, all teachers. It was absolutely pitch black. No moon. We walked about a mile, with flashlights, through the woods and the town. Their house was lit with candles. One of the boys had baked a pineapple upside down cake and served us each a wedge of cake and mine had a lighted candle stuck in it. They all sang "Happy Birthday" for me.

Sunday afternoon. (We had to leave for the market before I could finish my letter.) The market was fantastic. Some of the unusual things for sale were fried grasshoppers, smoked rat, bamboo worms, and armadillo

meat, along with papaya, rice, bananas, oranges, and more common produce. We bought, or rather our hosts bought, enough fruit and vegetables
for several days, for 25 cents. Most cost just a few pennies each. A pineapple was 3 cents.

In the afternoon we took a taxi, literally the only mode of travel since
no one has a car, to a town about five miles away called Zorzor where
there is a Lutheran mission hospital, Curran Lutheran Hospital, which has
been there since 1926. It too, was indescribable, different from anything
I've ever experienced before. If you've ever read anything about Dr. Albert
Schweitzer's work in Lambourene you'll have some idea. The conditions
they have to treat and the methods and equipment that are available are
pretty unfamiliar. I'll never have a casual attitude about mission contribu-
tions again.

This morning we got up very early and hiked through the "bush" (the
jungle) for about 45 minutes to where some town people were beating
palm nuts. Palm oil is one of the Liberian staples. It is extracted from palm
nuts in a very clever but primitive fashion. They are cooked in a huge iron
pot, many, many pounds of them, carried to a huge rock-and-cement vat
formed into a big hole. There they are beaten into a mush-like mass with
long poles. The oil comes out into a hole made in the center of the mass.
Counting babies and children, there were at least 30 people there. It was
an all-day job, and while it's hard work, they sang and joked, too.

We think we will get along fine, even though we still don't know what
part of the country we will be in, or exactly what we will be doing.

Dear Ellen [Ruth's sister],   **March 24, 1971, Monrovia**

Happy Birthday from Africa! My birthday was different from yours—in a
mud-block house, lit only with candles, about 150 miles up-country. We're
back in Monrovia about a block from where this picture was taken. Harold
is getting some training at the Caterpillar Co., so I finally have some time
to do some letter writing.

It will be about six weeks yet until we have a place to live, since
during the training period they move us around every four to five days
for different experiences. Everything is different for us here. It reminds
me of how we used to live when we were kids, except that the language is
different and the customs so different. We've eaten so many different foods
and encountered so many different ways of doing things. Most things in

homes up-country are handmade. Farming is done with a machete and stick. It's called making farm and means new land has to be cleared each year to plant rice and whatever else will be planted. We like whatever we've seen and done and hope we will get work we can do.

Dear Mother,   **March 25, 1971, Fissibu**

We are in Fissibu on a "live in," staying with a PC couple who are in their third year, and who teach in a teacher training institute here. There are four more volunteers here, all teachers. They have all been very nice to us.

This is a small town, houses all made of mud and sticks with thatched roofs. Apparently, the old tribal ways have been retained almost completely here. The PCVs say that there is a lot of "devil business" in the town, and there are many times that the people must stay in their houses with their shutters closed [*because those uninitiated to the Porro Society cannot look at the "devil," who is very powerful*]. The purpose of our visit here is to give us an experience with Liberian country ways, and it's been good. We went to a market yesterday in a town about eight miles away.

It has been very hard to stay with letter writing. The light is very poor at night, either candles or, if electricity, it's perhaps with a 25 watt bulb. Usually it too goes off at 10 PM, if not before because of lightning storms. So far, the only rain has come at night and then in torrents. On a tin roof, it's so loud you can hardly talk to each other.

We checked into another hotel yesterday in Monrovia. Our room is air conditioned but very tiny. Our lights are three small bulbs in a ceiling fixture that look like large Christmas tree lights. This AM I saw a huge cockroach in the bathroom. I expect to become quite nonchalant about bugs eventually, although the girls tell me there are absolutely huge black spiders in their houses up-country—with a three-inch spread, including their legs. The thought of them makes me shudder, although the girls say they are harmless and really shy of people. Snakes apparently are not a problem—they are afraid of people and if you walk slowly and make noise, you never see them. When walking at night you always use a flashlight.

One night in Fissibu we walked from our hosts' home about 8:30 to that of another volunteer, through the town and on about another half mile through an unpopulated area. It was pitch dark, no moon or stars. We came upon a group of town people, maybe 50, standing in a close throng, chanting and singing and doing a kind of dance. There was a very dim light from the fire. It was all quite eerie, but apparently quite commonplace. Fissibu is a fairly large town—about 450 houses and about 5,000 people—no one actually knows how many [*because there is no accurate census*]. All the houses are whitewashed with mostly palm thatched roofs, some galvanized zinc but they are red because of the dust which covers everything during dry season. The people are friendly, and we struggle to talk to each other. We're finding it easier to understand their English and do a lot of listening. The four days we spent in Fissibu were packed with new experiences.

There are so many different and beautiful locally made and used things. Some of the lappa [*a wrap-around skirt, similar to a sarong*] cloth, hand-woven country-cloth, tie-dye, and wax print materials are lovely, and also some of the woven and carved items. We have already bought some pieces of cloth so we can have some country shirts made for Harold. The girl we stayed with liked to cook and made Liberian food for us each day—things like palm butter soup and eggplant and bitter ball soup. These are served over rice and called country chop, very good and highly spiced with red peppers.

Travelling in Liberia is indescribable. The only way is on foot or packed into an overcrowded taxi or money bus, which may be anything from a pickup truck with a canopy on the back and seats (boards) on the sides, to a large van-like bus such as the high school activity buses. They have very little springs because most of the roads are dirt and very "washboardy." I felt like I was riding in a vibrator for five hours on our return to Monrovia yesterday. The cost is usually $1 an hour, which is the way they figure rather than by the distance. You can usually count on covering 30–35 miles in an hour if there are no complications, such as flats and breakdowns. Taxis don't go until they are full and that means stuffed with people and animals and produce. We shared a taxi on our way up with a chicken that seemed quite used to riding in a car. You're red with dust right away.

We think we will like it here although we have no idea where we will be assigned. We hope it will be up-country, rather than in the city. Life is very simple here but tasks are time-consuming. Harold has to go to some training sessions so I have a little time for myself. He will be gone three days, and then we will go up-country again.

Dear Mother,   **March 27, 1971, Monrovia**

We are sitting on the balcony of our hotel (second floor). It's noontime, and throngs of people in groups of twos and threes, etc., are constantly moving. The same scene goes on, early in the morning until late at night.

We find it fascinating to sit and watch, "just like the cinema," one of the Lebanese hotel guests commented to me. Costumes of every style are commonplace—lappas, long, short, and variations of the lappa, from just a casual wrap around and tucked in at the waist to very beautifully styled combinations. Headdresses, too, are many shapes, styles, and colors. Western dress, mainly in very colorful cottons, is pretty common. Most men are in loosely fit sport-type shirts in beautiful tie dye and wax-print lappa cloth. Wide bands of intricate stitching designs decorate a lot of the shirts.

There are many Mandingo people here, who are Muslim, and their costumes are unusual—long, rather straight robes always in plain colors, sometimes white. They, too, may have intricate stitched designs on the edges. Sometimes, they wear long, tapered trousers and a little cap like a fez. Other men wear a suit that looks like tailored pajamas, usually in a pastel color. The people I've been describing are generally Liberian. There is also a large population of Lebanese who seem to be the economic backbone of the country. They operate and own nearly all that has to do with selling and things like restaurants, bars, movies. I never see the men wearing anything but dark trousers and white shirts.

I meant to mention that the scene below our balcony that I just described is of restaurants, bars, delicatessens, beverage store, and many little hole-in-the-wall eating shops and tailor shops. So the movement is continuous. Everyone talks loudly; they're cheerful and friendly. Taxis go by constantly, honk and screech brakes, and there is a constant parade of peddlers of every sort, mostly carrying their wares on their heads—piled high or hung over their shoulders or arms or attached with safety pins. They are very insistent when trying to sell something. The only way you buy anything here is by haggling. You never pay the first price. I'll have to learn that because it makes me very uncomfortable to do it. Little children constantly ask you for pennies, saying, "I have hungry belly." Sometimes they grab Harold's leg and look at him beseechingly, and you know Harold and kids.

Behind us in the lounge of our hotel is a group of Mandingo men some of whom stay here in the hotel. They are carrying on what sounds like a very excited conversation, which apparently is quite a normal way of communicating. It's totally unintelligible to us. This tribe comes from the northern part of Liberia and generally are traders, very clever people, we are told.

We have had a fascinating time so far, although living in a hotel and out of a suitcase, and eating in restaurants is getting a bit tiresome. Tomorrow we leave by Land Rover to go up-country again for two weeks of on-the-job training for Harold. He will work with a British man who is in charge of a rice project and with four Liberian mechanics for a week and then work with another group of PC mechanics in another town for a week of training on the job. We will live in a house they've rented for us with another PC couple. They are from Florida, about 28. I have realized by now, that nothing is planned for the women PCVs. We are strictly on our own. In a way, this is good, but when we are so impermanent, it's kind of a strain.

This week, while Harold was at his meetings, I did a lot of exploring in the markets and got ideas for furnishing our home. I also spent some time visiting hospitals. JF Kennedy is a 250-bed modern facility that should open sometime this year. No one seems to know where the staff or operating money is coming from. I visited with the head of the school of Medical Science there and had all kinds of offers for a teaching position. If we are stationed in Monrovia, I'll try to get PC to let me work there. I sat in on a nursing curriculum session and decided I could make a contribution there. I also visited the Liberian Government hospital. It's an old ramshackle building where they care for hundreds of patients. They too, need staff nurses and would be glad to have me. I still want to look into the voc-ed situation, too.

We decided to stop watching the people and instead, join them. We went to a Liberian restaurant for lunch and had rice, with palm oil soup and with flower soup. The first had beef, chicken, and shrimp in a kind of gravy made from palm kernels and highly seasoned with red peppers. The second is a sauce made from some kind of greens that look like pigweed, with beef in it, also very hot. Then we walked on to a tailor shop in a little shack that was about eight feet square. It almost looked like a box, where two men were sewing clothes. I had ordered two shirts for Harold and two dresses for myself on Thursday, and they were ready today. Harold looks like he belongs here now. One shirt is a tie dye in blues and kola nut brown, and the other one is a Java print, bright blue with a design kind of like a man's colored hankie. My dresses are also tie dye in kola nut brown with a bit of dark blue, the other made of a bright orange red print lappa. I will be looking for some lappas for you too. We will be able to go to Sierra Leone, which joins Liberia, where tie dye and wax print lappas cost about half of what they are here. There are big markets there.

I've gone to the market here in Monrovia and found it fascinating. It would have been fun to buy some of the produce but with no cooking facilities yet, it was kind of frustrating. This particular market was under a roof, rather than in the open air. It covers about the size of city block, maybe a bit less.

Produce is displayed on tables, all kinds of things that people raise. The butcher shop had big cow feet, hair, and all displayed right out front as well as a big, un-skinned, cow head. People cook their rice there, play checkers, wash dishes, make biscuits, have their babies nap beside their displays, visit, crochet, weave baskets, all the time noisily visiting and trying to sell to anyone who comes near. We've walked miles and miles. Actually, we are better off without a car because we can see so much more.

When we return from up-country on the 9th, we begin cross-cultural and language training and, again, will go and stay in the area where we will be assigned so we can begin learning the appropriate one. If it's Monrovia we won't have to learn a language, only Liberian English. It will be difficult to mail letters for the next few weeks since our mail has to be brought to Monrovia by someone in order to mail it. And people avoid taking a trip in a taxi or a money bus if they can help it. It's hot and dusty, and the drivers always think there is room for one more. Our mail from you will be delivered to us up-country when one of the staff is coming up or when a PC volunteer is coming our way. I plan to do my usual letter writing from day to day and send it when I can.

Judith [*their daughter*], I read a book here that I think Ciam [*Judith's son*] would enjoy because it gives a very authentic picture of Liberia. It's called *Five Cent, Five Cent*. I think you all would enjoy it because of the accuracy both in pictures and story. I've been trying to get another book about Liberia—ordered it too late in the US before we left Tacoma. It is not approved by the Liberian government, so I can't get it here. Perhaps you'd send it to me if you can find it. It is called *Liberia, Evolution of Privilege.* If you do send it, wrap it so it doesn't look like a book and just mail it by regular mail—airmail is too expensive. Judith, you might like to read *ZinZin Road,* too.

Dear Ingwer [Ruth's brother],   April 1, 1971, Gbedin

This town is about 200 miles up-country from Monrovia. We came Sunday eve and are staying with a young Peace Corps couple for a week, for Harold to get some on-the-job training. We've just learned that we will be assigned here, where there is a fairly large rice project, with quite a bit of machinery. Harold will be responsible for keeping it going, with the help of four Liberian mechanics, and teach them to do it alone when he finally leaves. I'll have lots to do with health problems, but don't know yet what it will be. There are no nurses in the area.

Gbedin (pronounced "baydin") is a tiny town, really a village, that is here because of the rice project. There are no stores. Gbedin is between two larger, but actually small towns, 10-12 miles each way. There are no stores in Gbedin, you must go by taxi or bus (25 cents each way) to the other towns to shop. Ganta, to the south, has a market on Thursdays, Sanniquellie, to the north has market day on Saturdays.

We will have a tiny house here, electricity of sorts, running cold water (we will have to boil our drinking water), and inside plumbing. The house is pretty bad, but they say they will have it fixed by the time we come, around the first of May. We still have three weeks of language and cross-cultural training at another town about 12 miles north of here.

This is beautiful country. It looks something like the North Bend, Washington, area. The Nimba Mountains are near, and except for leafy trees rather than evergreens, it looks like the Cascade foothills. It is much cooler here than in Monrovia, although with the humidity so high, it's hot. But I'm sure we will like it here. Harold really likes the job he is to do, and the people are friendly. We are getting so we can understand people better. Most of the women only speak their tribal dialect, so I plan to keep on with language study. Peace Corps will pay for that so I plan to take advantage of it.

It has been interesting to experiment with Liberian foods. So far, wherever we have stayed, the people have served some kind of Liberian food. It is quite hot, since everyone uses a lot of hot peppers. Last night though, we went to a volunteer's birthday party here in Gbedin and had pizza, beer, and chocolate cake!

We haven't seen TV, heard a radio, or seen an American newspaper for so long that we are really out of touch. Mail is only delivered and picked up once a week, but today our project director flew in so I can send this back with him.

Dear Mother and Uncle Emil,   **April 2, 1971, Gbedin**

Almost a week has gone by since we came to this little town, way up-country. Gbedin is near the Guinea border. In fact, it is separated from Guinea by the Nimba Mountains, which look quite like the foothills of the Cascades—minus the evergreens, of course. These mountains are covered by bush.

There are about 240 different varieties of trees in Liberia. Some are very tall and some are bush-like. The logging companies (none around here), can harvest only one tree per acre; the others aren't suitable or large enough. There is a lot of coffee grown here, and cocoa trees are being encouraged, and of course, there are lots of rubber trees. Fifty miles NE from here is the Lamco iron mining operation—the fourth largest iron mine in the world. Bethlehem Steel is one of the major investors. We went there today to see it and found it to be just like a big operation in the US. There is quite a contingent of Swedish, Danish, and English, plus some Americans who are in supervisory positions. This is the major industry in Liberia, besides the rubber companies.

Gbedin isn't a typical town, since it is made up of people who have come here because of the rice farming. A co-op is being developed by a PCV too. Consequently, there is not the typical tribal town activity, no town chief, and things really revolve around the rice project.

We will have a tiny house, made of wood and corrugated tin. It has running cold water, a bathroom with a shower, and electricity from 6 AM until noon and from 6-9 PM, except when there is lightning or a storm, then there is no electricity.

There is a Methodist Mission Hospital 12 miles away with a Leprosarium. They do some very interesting reconstructive surgery there. The doctor told me they would welcome me there. I may spend a couple days a week there. There is also a clinic here for the project, where they really need someone to get it cleaned up and operating right, and they would like me to do something there, too. There is also a lot of health teaching needed in the homes, so I don't think I will have any trouble working something out. When I have a plan, I will just have to talk to the Peace Corps director about it. Harold is very pleased with his assignment. They have really praised him for his work and attitude, etc., which does a lot for him.

Our diet is different from at home, rice every day with some kind of "chop," or soup as they call it to serve over the rice. We had eggplant and tomato tonight. We've had palm butter soup, bitter ball soup, sweet potato greens soup. They always add some bits of meat or fish and, of course, always hot pepper. This is their entire meal. Fruits and vegetables are very cheap here. We bought bananas today for 1 cent each and 5 cents will buy us enough greens for our soup.

If you're willing to eat the Liberian way, you can eat very inexpensively. If you want to buy the usual American supermarket type of food or other imported things—canned or frozen—it's quite expensive and also hard to get. Frozen food is only available in Monrovia or Lamco. We're over 200 miles from one and 40 miles from the other and don't have a car. A trip to Monrovia takes all day and costs $5 each way. Fortunately, we like foreign food so we're enjoying the new things.

We haven't seen any wild animals yet, except an elephant on the President's farm and a civet cat, something like a raccoon, that someone had for a pet. Today, we saw our first snake. It was dead on the road, killed by a car.

The people are very welcoming and we are beginning to feel at home.

Dear Mother,   **April 4, 1971, Monrovia**

Thanks so much for your letters. Yesterday and today were a real treat, with four letters today and four yesterday. It was the first mail we've received in two weeks, since we've been up-country, with no mail delivery.

We are spending our last night here in Monrovia before leaving for a three-week stay up-country for the last of our training. This will be language and cross-cultural training, and an introduction to the Mano dialect, and learning more about the people in the villages where we will work for the next two years. A teacher or informant as they call him here will live with us, also a young man, another PCV. We will study the Mano dialect about six hours a day with a tape recorder, too. He will take us to the markets in the villages. We are to stay overnight in a village, meet the paramount chief and other "big people," and try to start communicating with the people in their dialect.

We will be in a town called Sanniquellie, in the NE corner of Liberia near the Ivory Coast border, about 12 miles from Gbedin, the town we are to live in permanently, about 240 miles from Monrovia. Because of the road conditions, it will be a six-hour trip at best. We are getting a little used to the travel. This will be by chartered taxi and will cost the three of us $20, all together. This way, we'll be sure to get there, unless the car breaks down, a fairly common occurrence. Sometimes, you can get half way there, and the driver decides he hasn't enough fares, so he foists you off on another driver. Gas costs 53 cents a gallon, and drivers usually buy only a gallon or so at a time. You'll see little stands way up-country, with a few gallon jugs of gas. Taxis will stop and buy one and chug on. Buses do the same thing.

We came to Monrovia last Friday for more meetings here and had quite a nice Easter weekend. Had our last shots—so far we've been immunized for cholera (two shots), rabies (two), hepatitis (this is gamma globulin every four months), small pox, yellow fever, polio, plus have to take anti-malaria pills every week, oh yes, tetanus, too.

On Saturday, we were invited to a beach party at the home of our PC project director. He has lived here with his family for 13 years. He came originally as an Episcopal missionary.

The city is right on the beach. It is truly a beautiful beach. However, the undertow is very treacherous, and swimming is safe only in certain areas. We enjoyed the surf and spent a lot of time in the water, but I didn't go out very far because of the undertow. The water was just the right temperature, and the sandy beach is lovely. The people served two kinds of Liberian rice and a huge tray of fruit—pineapple, avocado, grapefruit, which are available all year and at such little cost most of the year.

On Easter Sunday we went to church, and since we couldn't find out when the service would be, we just took a chance and found ourselves in a service preached entirely in the Loma dialect. The American pastor preached in English and the Liberian pastor interpreted it into Loma. The liturgy was totally different as far as the music was concerned, although

I'm sure the words were the same as we use. None of the liturgy was in English. The choir was all women, and the music was more like a chant, with certain words repeated over and over, and much hand clapping in rhythm.

The men sat on one side, and the women on the other. I wish you could have seen the dresses. Most of the women were in colorful lappas, of every color and print. The ankle-length lappas are wrapped around their waists, with the ends tucked in. None of the lappas are just plain colors. They wear tops that are usually sleeveless, sometimes matching the skirt, but are more likely of another color and pattern. Their heads are wrapped in scarves, like a turban, and again, vary in the way they are wrapped, but all are swirled around, and usually are quite high. They all wear dangly earrings—pierced ears are common, and most little girls, even two year olds are already wearing a little earring of some sort. Most of the lappas are made of tie-dye cotton Java prints although some are made of silk. In fact, I plan to use some of them for curtains, bedspreads and table cloths.

Getting back to Sunday: After church, we took a money bus (fare 10 cents) and took a long ride to the end of the line, and saw parts of the city we had never seen before. The contrasts are unimaginable, from tiny tumble-down shacks, with people cooking over open fires in an iron pot, to luxurious big mansions with iron grilles, called "rogue bars" and meant to keep out thieves, on every window and door. When we got back to the downtown section, we walked several blocks to the Ducor Hotel. It is on the highest hill in Monrovia, in fact of the entire country, built right on the beach, and from the roof, gives a magnificent view of the city, and lots of the water, way out to sea.

The Ducor is nine stories high and compares favorably with fine hotels in the US. It is like living in another world from where we have been living. They have a beautiful pool, nightclub, and all the usual amenities. Rooms are about $25 a day. Contrast this with the fact that most Liberians' income is about $150 a year. We finished the day by going to a Swiss restaurant by the beach and having cheese fondue, our last splurge before going up-country.

Monrovia is the only real city in Liberia, where all the money is, and there are many millionaires, but all are Americo-Liberians, descendants of the original black settlers here. Another interesting thing is that the

Lebanese are about the only merchants. They are very astute business-men, not really liked by the Liberians, but very necessary for the economy of the country. One of the critical books I read said that the government prefers to have these aliens responsible for most of the business instead of Liberians because they don't want a strong Liberian economic group to grow because they would have too much political strength. The Lebanese do not pose a threat to the party in power, which is the only political party here. It is called the True Whig party.

The government is pretty much controlled by the few who have been in control for a very long time. They are friends of the President, and nearly all Americo-Liberians. There is much "money eating," as they call it, but most people just shrug it off. We do hear talk though, of changes to be made when the President dies. He is now 78 and has been in office since 1946. He is enormously popular with the people.

Life isn't easy for the people in the villages in the bush, where most of the people live. They work very hard just to live—plant their rice and cassava, have a few scrawny chickens and goats running around. Malnutrition is so obvious. Many of the children have greatly enlarged abdomens, a sign of lack of protein. The diet is predominantly rice.

Women have no status. They have to take care of the family and work in the rice fields all day. All work is done by hand, using a cutlass to cut the bush to clear the land (a new place every year). Then they use sticks to scratch the soil to plant the rice. They have to beat the rice to remove the hulls—this means many hours of pounding with a four-foot pole in a big hand hewn wooden mortar usually about two and a half feet high. Women seldom go to school. People appear to be happy, though, often singing as they work, and all have been friendly and welcoming to us.

Last week, one of the men Harold had been working with brought him a bottle of palm wine. They tap a palm tree near the top, and it produces about a bucket of palm wine a day for about one month, and then dies. Remember, there are millions of palm trees here. The men like to gather under the palm tree at night, and after a while, you can hear singing and joking and merry making.

Every day since we have been here there has been a new thing, or rather, several new things to experience and learn. We have eaten so many different foods. I've learned how to cook some, both Liberian and Lebanese. Last week a young house boy where we were staying brought home three bullfrogs. He proceeded to clean them just like a chicken and fried them and shared them with Harold. I wasn't quite ready for them. He left the feet on them, even the little toes! Another night he cooked a chicken with palm-butter soup and, of course, rice. It was a little startling to discover the feet in the soup, too. It just took the appetite away from one of the new PC boys we had invited for dinner. Another night we had sweet potato greens and fish soup and rice, the head included. They don't waste anything

Another thing we are learning is how to bargain. I'm rather uncomfortable with trying to get a lower price, but it seems that is the only way things are bought and sold here. Nothing is marked, and the price is anything the traffic will bear. Street peddlers will follow you a block begging you to buy if it appears you may be even a bit interested. You can buy absolutely anything on the street—a live chicken, a goat, a pig, underwear, slippers, zippers, lappas, food of all kinds, and on and on. People walk around with their wares on their heads or draped on their shoulders and arms, usually piles of lappas, and will whip one open to show you at the slightest hint of interest.

We have really had a great time just walking along the streets, and watching the people, sometimes stop to talk with some we find easier to converse with, but that is still a struggle. Even though English is the official language, it's a strange kind of English. But we haven't yet had a bad experience while we've been here.

Harold has found the people he is to work with to be very glad to have him. Already, they call him "mine boss." The hard thing for him will be to get supplies and parts. So many things are broken down already, and either no one knew how to fix it or parts were never delivered. So it just sits and rusts away. There is no phone in the little town (village) we are to live in but there is a radio used to call in to the Dept. of Agriculture in Monrovia. Mail is delivered and picked up once a week.

Often times, things that are needed on the Project are diverted to some official's farm, instead, so you wait, sometimes for months. Things, like the caterpillar that is used to clear land for the rice project, have been ordered to the Vice President's farm for some project of his, and of course, it has to go there. It sounds hard to believe, doesn't it? However, Harold says he will make it if he can't get it new, and you know how he can manufacture something when he has to.

I've spent some time at the local clinic and will be able to do almost anything I want to. It's mainly a matter of what needs to be done first. There is nothing done in Gbedin for pre-natal care, prevention of illness, any kind of basic sanitation. I expect to get acquainted with some of the women and gain their confidence before I try to do much.

Thursday night, one of the school boys brought his little brother with huge cutlass wound on his forearm. He said someone had swung at a mouse in the field, and hit the boy instead. I managed to pull it together and bandage him with my first-aid supplies. I don't think it will be long before people will be looking for this kind of care. Then, maybe, I can begin with how to keep well. There is so much malaria and dysentery, both of which can be prevented. Getting people to change is another matter. People tell us that the changes that have occurred in Liberia in the past ten years are remarkable. So, with change being accelerated elsewhere, perhaps we will see some in the two years we will be here.

I wanted to tell you about "rogueing," too. This means burglarizing. A rogue rogues. It is a terrific problem, especially in the cities. Houses have iron rogue bars on their windows, big padlocks on their doors, stores all have heavy metal grating over their windows and doors, and still there is much thievery. You can't leave your house empty at night—must have someone staying in it while you're away. We will have to have a house boy who will stay in our house when we are away in the evening and especially, over weekends. Apparently, in any developing country, where people have so little, and they see others who seem to have so much, rogueing is rampant.

When anyone catches a rogue in action, he hollers, "Rogue, Rogue," and everyone around joins in a chase. Then, if they catch him, they beat him up. No one bothers to call the police, because it doesn't do any good, since they can be bought off for just a few dollars. And besides, I think people really seem to love to chase rogues.

Another thing about wearing apparel, little tots go naked as often as not, with little girls wearing a string around their middles, as "medicine." Kids go to the bathroom any place, any time. People don't seem to mend their clothes even if they might know how to sew. Sometimes it's amazing how their clothes can stay on, they are so tattered. Sleeves just hang by a few threads, shirts are sometimes half gone, and trousers may be only a waistband, front, and cuffs. You wonder sometimes why they even bother.

Many women go bare on top, especially old women, but even some young girls. The topless look isn't what you might imagine, though, because breasts are pretty saggy and flat, in most part because of many pregnancies and hard work. So many women are pregnant and carrying an infant on their back, held on by a lappa wrapped around their middle. And still the population remains constant. So many infants die before they're two.

Yesterday and today were red-letter days—the first mail we have had in two weeks since there was no mail delivery while we were up-country. It's hard to know what to write about, with so much happening to us. This past month has been a fantastic experience. It's just a month today since we arrived here. It seems like twice that because of all the new things. We're getting used to the weather, I think. By next month the rains will start, so it will be cooler, damper though. We have been so fortunate not to have had even as much as a tummy ache. We are reasonably careful though, boil our drinking water, avoid foods that might be contaminated, eat well-cooked meat, etc.

Dear Ingwer,   **April 13, 1971, Gbedin**

We have lost all track of time. The past two weeks up-country in Gbedin, we had no newspaper, radio, or telephone. I had to make a special point to remember what day it was.

I still have a hard time realizing we are actually in Africa. The scenery could actually be LA or in the south, that is until you look around and see mud and thatch houses and people in their native dress. Most of the women are in colorful lappas and head dresses, but the men are in the usual shirts and shorts. Men's shirts are more likely bright, like the women's, in a different style from American shirts—very attractive.

There are some good carpenters, but we see very little fine cabinet work. It's usually pretty rough, clobbered up and all one style. Harold will make cupboards and shelves, etc. in our house since there is nothing in it. Lumber is cheap, mahogany, teak and the like, solid mahogany, not just with a skin on plywood. Plywood is $8 a sheet.

You would get a kick out of the money system. You can't manage without small money—pennies, nickels, dimes, and quarters, and then paper money. Anything over $1 is very hard to get change for, and a $10 bill throws them into a panic. A $20 is the largest bill they have. I asked for 10 ones yesterday in the bank and had to take silver dollars. Paper money is very scarce, since they have to have it printed in the US at great cost. [*Liberia uses US currency.*] The bills are dirty and limp—the kind that would be withdrawn in our country.

One of the Chinese fellows in Gbedin, where we will live, told me about a snake he shot a few months ago about a mile from Gbedin, along the road. It was black, about the size of his leg above the knee and was 17½ feet long. He shot it five times, the last shot in the head, and finally killed it. He'd been hunting and had a rifle with him. I don't know what kind it was.

When I asked him what they did with it, he said they ate it, and it was good. Kind of surprised me, but I've seen some funny things eaten here. Some of the kids dig in the big ant hills and get the grubs—they call them bug-a-bugs. They are about two inches long, lots of times tiny ones about a half inch long, and they gobble them up. I can hardly stand to watch them.

Dear Mother,   **April 18, 1971, Sanniquellie**

We are finishing our first week here, trying to learn the Mano dialect and more about the culture. I spent one afternoon visiting the baby clinic and one afternoon visiting a village with one of the nuns. She takes medicines and about once a week tries to teach ABC type classes.

So many of the little children have no way to go to school, because if the government puts a teacher there, there is no way for kids to get out to where the schools are. This town is about eight miles from Sanniquellie, the nearest school. The only transportation is by taxi, which is 25 cents each way, if they even come there. The town is about a mile from the main road. The kids have to pay for uniforms and books when they to go school, so even that makes school impossible for most.

Right now, I'm hoping to start a well-baby and prenatal clinic in Gbedin, through help from the government and some from CARE, I hope. I'll try to do health classes in villages and in the schools for the kids, give immunizations and work with women to feed their children properly. Also, do an outpatient clinic for people who are sick or need wounds dressed.

Unless I am able to get sponsored by the PHS [*Liberian Public Health Service*], I won't have any source of supply for medicines and other necessary supplies. It will be a slow process but I'm kind of excited about the possibilities. Someone came last night and asked if I could pull teeth! He has a terrible cavity, and the tooth can't be saved. Maybe I'll have to learn how! I'm sure I'll be doing a lot more than that from the looks of things so far.

The first night we arrived here a Peace Corps guy came by and asked me to look at some red swellings on his arm and back. They were red and swollen and looked infected, so I decided to open them. Guess what— they were botfly bites. I removed the larvae from them, and the next day he was improved. I'd only read about such things before.

So far, we've had no health problems. Malaria and "runny belly" (diarrhea) are the two main health hazards. Hepatitis, too, is something we have to be careful about so we don't eat raw things without either peeling or soaking it in iodine water.

It is really nice to get your letters, Mother, quotes and all. Not seeing familiar people takes some getting used to, but we haven't been homesick, yet. There have been quite a few volunteers wherever we have been, so that's a link with home. But when we get to Gbedin there will be only Harold and me and one other young couple, Larry and Mary, and Marcia, a young woman who is a home economics volunteer. Also four Chinese men who are rice specialists, and the British project engineer, and all the rest are Liberians. I'm looking forward to being in Gbedin because I think it will be better to be really involved with the people we came to help. They are asking when we are coming back, which is gratifying

Dear Vikki and Gill,   April 18, 1971, Sanniquellie
[their daughter and son-in-law]

We've just finished our first week of language and cross-cultural training. It goes so slowly, trying to learn a new language. It's hard anytime and this one has so many tonal variations, kind of like Chinese. How you shape your lips affects it, too. There are so many words that start with GB and KP and MB, the first letter is almost silent, but not quite. For instance, the town of Kpain is pronounced almost like "bang," kind of explosively. The town of Gbarnga is pronounced "bonga," but with a very soft-sounding G, and so on. Accents are on the first and last syllables, unlike so many of our words, for instance Tacoma would likely be pronounced "Tácomá." In Liberian English the accent is the same way.

It is fun getting involved in it. I went with one of the nursing nuns to a village where she takes medicines and could ask people how they were feeling. When they said, "Min kong kong," I knew they were saying, "I'm feeling bad," so maybe there is hope for me. It will take a long time.

We are living here with a fellow named John Mitchell, a 25-year-old fellow, from Yonkers, NY. He graduated from Cornell in '69 in Agriculture Economics and is here to help set up co-ops with the farmers. We enjoy him a great deal, do our language classes together, visit the markets, and "walk about." We also cook together, even brush our teeth out the back door together!

We have a houseboy who cooks our evening meal, does the dishes, washes our clothes, and keeps the house half-way tidy. We pay him $5.50 a week. With the rather primitive living conditions, carrying water, boiling it, washing clothes on a scrub board, ironing with a charcoal iron, it takes a lot of time just to do your housework and meals with little time left over to do the job you're supposed to be doing.

The other thing is that the boys need work if they are to go to school. They need money for uniforms and books, and Peace Corps volunteers are the only ones who can hire them. We also have a boy who asked us for a job as soon as we arrived in Gbedin. He's about fourteen, in the 6th grade, which is average here. He will help with our house work and laundry and stay in our house whenever we are away on weekends or in the evening. Rogueing is so prevalent here, it's a must. I'll also do the cooking since I like to do it.

Apparently, you're considered very "mean" if you won't give a boy a job. For his work we will pay him $10 a month, or $7.50 plus his dinner daily, or take care of his school costs and clothes and keep him in pocket money, or "small money" as they call it here. We will probably do the latter, since we want to help the kids who want an education, and this sounds like the best way.

A little kid about six years old has attached himself to us. He is at the door every morning about 7 AM looking through the screen and inching his way in the door. When we go out to go to the market, or visiting here, he is right at our heels. When we got out of church yesterday, about a half mile from here, all of a sudden he was walking along beside us. We can converse with him a little.

Dear Vikki and Gill,   **April 25, 1971, Gbedin**

Our suitcase living makes it very hard to be at all organized. We packed up again on Friday and took a money bus to Gbedin for the weekend.

We are house-sitting for the project engineer while he is in Monrovia. We wanted to come anyway so we could check up on our house. They have poured the concrete floor in the living room—the former one had rotted through in several places. They also made another window in the kitchen. Now if they will get the plumbing done in the kitchen, install a sink, and build a block wall on one side of the kitchen so we can screen the upper part, we will be able to move in. It will be May 4 or 5 before we are ready to move, so I'm optimistic.

People keep saying, "Remember you're in Liberia," whenever you want things to happen on time. So we will just have to wait and see. We don't really want to keep on living with someone else, so we are willing to rough it if we have to in our own place. There is a lot of painting needed, but at least we will have lots of time, if nothing else.

I wanted to tell you about a meal, called "Gaypah," we had yesterday with some Peace Corps friends. It's very popular with Liberians. It is made from cassava, a root similar to a sweet potato. It's peeled, then cooked, and then beaten in a mortar until it is all pulverized and mashed kind of like potatoes. All strings are removed. When it is served, it is placed in a bowl and looks like a loaf of bread dough. It is eaten with the hands—break a small wad, form it into a ball, dip it in your soup and roll it around to get it slippery, and then pop it in your mouth and swallow it without chewing it. They laugh if they see you chewing it.

Fufu and *dumboy* are similar, but they are handled differently in their preparation. For example, one is fermented. I haven't tasted either one of these. The soup we were served was made of groundhog. They told us it was similar to our nutria. They clean it, burn the hair off it in the fire, cut it up, and then cook skin and all in a pot of water with seasonings. It was really quite tasty. The only thing is that with a lot of things we've eaten here, you can't think too much when you're eating. It will be good to start cooking again. There are so many things available that we like and that are inexpensive.

Actually, with the allowance that they give us, we should be able to save money since we like the foods that are available in the markets.

Some of the foods that we are used to having are expensive since they are imported. We'll do without them. Paper towels are 65 cents a roll and paper napkins are 50 cents for a small pack. We will use cloth ones that I will make. I will bake our bread. There is no store in Gbedin, and the bread that is available in Ganta dries out right away. We will have to plan ahead since getting to a town isn't easy although it can be a fascinating experience. Most small towns have a Lebanese store that usually stocks a little bit of everything. However, Gbedin is too small for even one store so you can't run out and get something like we were used to doing.

Friday we experienced our first real storm. We could see it coming in the distance for about half an hour. The sky became black, the mountains disappeared, the lightning and thunder became more intense, and then the wind blew very hard. We could see it as it came close, because the trees waved crazily, and the rain would fall so heavily that it partially dimmed the trees. We quickly put our buckets outside under the eaves—as did the people in the houses around us. Since most of the water in Sanniquellie must be drawn from wells, and carried home, when rain water is available, it's welcome. When the rain hit us, we could hardly hear each other talking—on a tin roof it was very loud.

We stood on our screened porch and watched people scurrying to get under cover. We had to shut all of our shutters because the rain blew in so badly. Consequently, our house was so dim we could hardly see. Electricity is turned off during the day until about 5 or 6 and we haven't a lamp. Candles or lamps are essential here with the sporadic, and often absence of, electricity.

It's amazing how quickly one can adapt. I'm already taking for granted the hand washing of laundry, for instance. I was thinking the other day about the electric appliances that we used daily and how I haven't really missed them. I will have an electric iron though.

I forgot to say that the storm lasted about an hour and ended about as suddenly as it started. Our three buckets were two-thirds full—regular-size water pails. So you can see how much it comes down. We do have running cold water in our house in Gbedin, but must plan on an erratic supply. So Harold will get a 50 gallon drum and fix a trough on our roof so it will direct the water over the drum. This way we'll have a pretty constant supply of water anytime, since rainy season is about to begin. I will enjoy having rainwater to wash my hair. Such luxury!

Our Mano is coming along slowly. We plan to keep up with it when we get settled. It pleases people so much when you say something in their language.

Did I tell you that we have a kitten? It belongs to a Lebanese store-keeper in Sanniquellie. He has a new litter. When we get moved, he will bring the kitten so we can keep the mice, rats, and cockroaches under control. He said we'd have to bring a small boy to catch the kitten, though. We got another kitten last week, but decided to give it to Marcia, the Home Economics girl here in Gbedin, since she has so many mice in her house. We brought it down in the taxi with us and surprised her with it. Now the cat is right at home there.

Did I tell you that mangoes and tangerines are green here? The tangerines are very good but the oranges this time of year are sour with a tough membrane. Grapefruit, pulp and all, are out of this world, though, and are very sweet. When things are really good here, people say they are sweet, or "too sweet, for true," if they are really good.

Dear Mother,   **April 25, 1971, Gbedin**

It's Sunday again, another full week has flown by. We are in Gbedin again, staying in Harold's future boss's home. He took his wife, Anna, to Monrovia to put her on a plane for Denmark. She and their six-month-old baby will stay with her parents there for the next 10 months, until his tour here is completed. She has hated it here.

He works for the Ag Department as the project engineer and is the typical colonial-type Englishman—"all Africans are bloody fools, etc." It will take a lot of cool for Harold to work closely with him, as Harold will have to do.

We will return to Sanniquellie this PM for the next week—will be glad when training is over because it's so inconvenient to be packing and unpacking and never having what you need with you because it's in the suitcase you didn't bring with you. This week in Gbedin, we had a very unusual experience, one that we might never have another chance to see in the next two years. This was the return of the boys from "bush school."

Bush school is when young boys and men go through training and various rituals to become members of the tribal society. It's very secret, divulged only to men. No women can see it, not even men from another tribe, and especially not white people. They say the boys "go into the devil's belly," and when they come out of bush school, they are different persons. Even have different tribal names. These boys stayed in bush school since last November, somewhere out in the bush. They are circumcised if not already done, and often small cuts in intricate designs are made on their bodies, chest, thighs, arms, face. These cuts leave little scars, and are very important to the people.

The town chief took us to the town where we waited for an hour, in a small hut. When the shouts and chants and music were heard, everyone had to go into their houses and close their doors and shutters, except men who had already had the experience. It was another hour before they had completed all the necessary ceremonies, all the time walking around the town and singing, etc., leaving a group of boys, all dressed up in fine new clothes, seated on mats all in a row, with a new lappa completely covering their heads and faces. There were four such groups. It was sweltering in the house, no ventilation, half dark, and women and kids sitting quietly.

They were all terrified. When the "devil" is in town any time it's frightening for them. They say that if anyone, the uninitiated, looks on him, they will die soon. He has fantastic power as far as they are concerned—certainly, a way people are controlled. Very few, at least of the women, know who he is. The devil is always dressed in an elaborate costume with a mask, etc. When we could finally come out of the house, there was a great deal of singing and dancing and cavorting about, gun shooting and merrymaking. The women especially, were happy, not having seen their kids in all the time they were away.

It was about 6 PM before we got out of the house, and nightfall comes about 6:30. So, when we left about 7 PM, it was pitch dark. We had about a mile of trail to walk so didn't want to wait too long. However, the merrymaking went on for hours and will continue every night for at least a week. It wasn't the least bit frightening to us, just a bit eerie at times, when you realize how powerful such ancient rites are for people.

The term "country devil" is a missionary term and not accurate. The Mano word is *Geh*. The boys were still covered with the lappas. They sat without moving or speaking the entire time. Sometime later in the night they would be revealed.

There were little boys as well as grown men in the group. Since bush school takes place only once every four years, people might send their boys before starting school, or sometimes wait so it won't interfere with regular school.

All of these experiences are helpful in getting better understanding of the culture, which is so different from ours in almost every way.

The people have been working on our house. The house itself belongs to the department of agriculture so the project employees are doing the fixing. Our house is the Dept. of Ag's contribution, so we won't pay any rent. Harold will build some shelves for the kitchen, and we will paint everything because it is so dark and grimy.

Dear Ingwer and Kay,   **April 25, 1971, Gbedin**

We attended a Catholic Mission Church last Sunday in Sanniquellie. The priest is Mano. He preached in English, and then an interpreter gave it in Mano. The liturgy was in Mano. The young man who is living with us is Catholic. He is from New York, and told us the service was identical to those at home. This church is 12 miles from Gbedin where we will live. A Methodist church is 10 miles in the opposite direction from Gbedin. To get there we will have to take a taxi or money-bus, both of which are undependable as to time, so we may not get to either one very often.

Harold will be starting to build shelves for our kitchen. You should see most of the carpenter work, Ingwer. Nothing is level or even. Doors and windows are crooked, floors, even in new houses, slant any old way. Harold decided he could do as good a job as the so-called carpenters. We won't have doors on our shelves. I want everything open in order to keep bugs out easier. I think things will be very much like they were when we were kids. Clothes are washed on a washboard. A carpenter will make us a washboard out of a solid piece of mahogany. They are almost works of art and cost $1.50. Have you heard of Whismore lumber? It's a little lighter color than what we are used to seeing. Here, it's used a lot for making furniture.

Incidentally, if you have any way to tape some of your records or Mary Lou's organ playing on a cassette, once in a while, we would love to have it. We can't always get anything good on the radio, so some nice music would be welcome. With all of our moving around, we've just kept our radio packed away. In both Sanniquellie and Monrovia there is so much stealing that you have to take so much care or you will lose everything. In Gbedin, there is very little problem, so they say, although you must make your house burglar-proof. We have been told that thieves don't hurt anyone, and often just take silly things, like a cigarette lighter, rather than money.

Apparently a lot of the rogues are students; they live in a larger town, are on their own, have to pay tuition for both grade and high school and buy books and uniforms, and jobs are hard to get. Most villages and little towns, if they have a school, only go to the sixth grade. By this time, kids are sixteen or more. Their parents either can't or won't help them because they aren't in favor of their getting "book." Very few girls ever make it past second or third grade.

It's very hard for people to get an education here. Classes are very large, generally 50 or 80 in a class. One of the PCVs, who teaches tenth, eleventh, and twelfth grades, says she has 60 in the tenth, teaching them three subjects, 60 in the eleventh with three subjects, and 30 in the twelfth, with three subjects. Imagine the papers she has to correct, plus so many of the kids speak poor English, which they are supposed to use in school exclusively. Many of the Liberian teachers have only an eighth- or ninth-grade education.

Dearest Mother,   **May 1, 1971, Monrovia**

We are finally Peace Corps volunteers, officially. We were sworn in yesterday here in Monrovia. It was really a formality only, and then a big party at an interesting place with Dept. of Agriculture "big people," too. The party was at the Liberian Cultural Center, a place near the beach where a typical village has been built and is inhabited by representatives of several different tribes. The houses are all palm-thatched, with white washed walls. In one of the houses were native crafts for sale.

The children did their native dances in typical tribal costumes and make-up, to music played on their native instruments. It was quite fascinating to watch. The food was Liberian too, with lots of pineapple and guava and grapefruit. They also served snails in a sauce, or "soup," made of some kind of greens. The snails were quite tiny—the shells are about one and a half inches long—black and white spotted ones. I couldn't make myself eat them but Harold enjoyed them. You have to suck them out of the shells, with a kind of kissing or smacking movement of your lips.

We came to Monrovia Friday. We spent the entire day making the 200-mile trip by taxi. We're staying in a house with another PC couple and their two little boys. It's a nice change from our rather primitive living in Sanniquellie and from the hotel life, which is far from luxurious here. Tomorrow, we receive our final shots and then must buy all of our household goods and Harold's tools. We also have to stock up on groceries, since there is no store in our town. By the time the vehicles are filled with passengers, there is little room left for baggage.

We will be very busy for a while getting our house livable—painting, building shelves and cupboards, screening windows. However, Harold will be starting to work next week, and I'll start visiting in the village.

We expect to leave Monrovia for Gbedin this Friday, and will be glad to stop traveling around. Rainy season will soon begin, and we've been told that the roads are often impassable. Water floods the roads, bridges wash out, or it's just too muddy to drive. So we don't plan to go too far very often for a while.

Our mail should be addressed as usual. All PC mail is delivered by a PC driver since there is no regular mail service outside of Monrovia. So our mail goes to Monrovia PC office, and on Mondays is taken to Gbarnga, the up-country PC office, and on Mondays another driver picks it up and brings it up our way and takes any of our mail to Monrovia to be mailed. So you can see, although it only takes four days for your letters to reach Liberia, it takes at least another week for anything to reach us.

The people who are staying in this house with us take the *Christian Science Monitor*. They just received about a two-week supply of them, so we have been devouring them. They are the first newspapers we've seen for a long time. We can buy the *New York Times* here, about a day late, for 35 cents, and we do that whenever we are in the city. Incidentally, one thing we would enjoy would be a magazine subscription, such as the *Saturday Review* or *Newsweek*. We do have time to read, now that life is less rushed.

We live in a house this week that is several miles out from the city center, and usually take a money bus for 10 cents. We've learned which ones are more comfortable. The people are jammed into the seats, but no one is standing because the vehicles aren't high enough. There are jump seats however, for extra people, that fill the narrow aisles. And usually the person who wants out at a stop is in the back of the bus. This means that a whole bunch of passengers have to get out first, folding up their seats on the way.

It's really quite hilarious, and people rarely get upset at the inconvenience. You finally get there, and even if you might be late, nothing seems to start on time, so it's all right anyway.

Dear Judith and Vikki,   **May 6, 1971, Monrovia**

Your letter, mailed on April 6, reached us here yesterday. Actually, it would have reached us by the 4th, but it was Election Day here, a national holiday. If anyone is caught selling anything or operating their business before 6 PM, they could be jailed, except restaurants can operate.

There is only one main road out of Monrovia for the rest of the country. It leads to Gbarnga, which is a crossroads. One leads to Sanniquellie, near Guinea and Ivory Coast, about 100 miles. One leads NW to Foya, next to Sierra Leone, about 125 miles. One leads SE, to the coast, another 125 miles. There are no coastal roads. Each of these trips takes much longer than the mileage would indicate, because of the road and vehicle conditions. When you ask anyone how far it is to anyplace they never tell you how many miles. Rather, they tell you how long it takes, or often, how much money, both of which are more to the point.

We are so pleased you will be sending us some Tupperware, which I really can use [to protect food items from bugs and humidity]. Also, please take the cover off of the book I asked for, and replace it with something innocuous. Also, I could use a plain paperback cookbook. I can't find one here. There are lots of gourmet and specialty ones, but I really need one that has recipes for breads and biscuits, and pies, and everyday things. I'll be baking bread and cookies. Our little gas stove works fine, and it's kind of fun to have the time. Regarding the newspaper, we think the *Christian Science Monitor*, Sunday Edition, would be great. We should be getting the *Progressive* one of these days. I changed the subscription just before we left, but those things take forever. We hope to save quite a bit while we're here and then have funds to do quite a lot of travelling during our leave time.

Last week, David Lee, the psychologist from the University of Florida who has been one of our training officers, took us to dinner at a really fancy place here in Monrovia. His wife had come over for his last three weeks, so she and Dave, and Harold and I had a pleasant evening together: filet mignon, cocktails, wine, etc. It was a very different evening from our last two months. He said it was in honor of our swearing-in, and our becoming full-fledged PCVs. This occurred on Monday, followed by a big party at the Cultural Center.

We came into Monrovia last Friday evening—finished up our language and cross-cultural stuff in Sanniquellie, stopped in Gbedin to check on our house, and then on to the big city. For the last two days we've been trying to buy all of the household items we need, like pots and pans, dishes, cleaning supplies, and groceries to last a couple of months. We bought things like soap, powdered milk, spices, peanut butter, and sugar. It meant grubbing through the little Lebanese stores. There is no such thing as a department store or second-hand store. We've gone through $200, without even trying. (We were given a housing allowance.) If you want furniture you have to have it made—quite cheap, though. We will just sell everything when we leave, since nothing is good quality. Many household items come from Red China.

We think of you all so much but don't ever feel homesick. We miss people, but only fondly.

Dear Vikki,   **May 8, 1971, Monrovia**

We have finally completed our household shopping. It has been a job, but kind of fun. For so many of the things, you have to dicker on, which takes time, and of course, even finding them takes time.

We looked for a double boiler in nearly every Lebanese store, dusty, piled with all sorts of things. No-one had a double boiler. Finally, yesterday we saw a shop on a side street, run by a girl from India, wearing a sari. We told her what we were looking for, but she just looked blankly at us. Then I saw one sitting on a shelf in the back of the store. I said, "Oh, you have some," and went and got one, all covered with dust. She beamed and said, "I don't know what they are, so when people ask, I just say no." Just then, a friend walked by. I called her and she came in and bought the other one. Everyone was happy; the shop lady even took 50 cents off of the $4.50 price.

We have chartered a taxi to haul us today with all the house stuff we've accumulated, no furniture, and two months of groceries. Quite a load. It will cost us $25 for the five- to six-hour trip, barring flat tires, broken wheels, etc. It is really a free-for-all when you go to a taxi-stand to get a ride for such a trip. Everyone converges on you, jabbering and gesturing, trying to grab your bags. Harold has a great time, trying to get a decent price and a car that looks like it will hold together. It appears to be great fun for the drivers, too. Everyone is slapping each other on the back and laughing and yelling. Of course, in Liberian English, it's just that much more complicated.

We are so glad to be leaving the city. It's fascinating and there are lots of things to do, but just too many people, noise and confusion. Gbedin will be totally opposite, with lots of time to do what we want.

If you could ever find a small book on bamboo carpentry we could use one. We plan to use bamboo quite a bit in our house. It's plentiful and free.

Our time is gone now, so I'll have to close so I can drop this in the mail before we leave. It seems like I'm always meeting a deadline with the mail! However, that is the only deadline we have in this country. No one hurries. They just say, *"Neh my, ya"* ("Never mind, ya.")

Dearest Mother,   **May 10, 1971, Gbedin**

We have finally moved into our little house—arrived Saturday afternoon. Even though it's a pretty sad sight, it is our home, and we're really glad to be into our own place, and we can start fixing it up. Actually, other than the fact that it is so dirty, from standing empty for so long, and having only men living in it who haven't been concerned about cleaning, and in a state of disrepair, it isn't so bad.

Things wear out and fall apart easily in this country, and they are put together so poorly in the first place. We do have running water—have discovered that we are one out of three houses that have warm water! We have electricity a few hours in the evening, and in the morning until noon. (Harold has to keep the light plant functioning.) The water comes from a spring in the hill above our house and should be pretty pure. We do have to boil and filter it though, to be sure. Many of our PC friends have to have all of their water carried, so we really feel fortunate.

We also have an inside bathroom—sink, toilet, and shower that he can fix, too. There is a plumber, carpenter, and mason who work for the rice project, and the project director has told them to do the fixing for us. Peace Corps is furnishing the needed materials, like boards, cement and paint, since they don't have to pay any rent for us to the Agricultural Department. The Department is furnishing the house, and Harold will work with the men in order to get the work done sooner.

No one here hurries, which is kind of nice for a change. People here always have time to stop and talk. Instead of just giving directions to some place, they take time to go with you so you will find it.

As I've said, there is no store here in Gbedin, so we will have to go to the market in Sanniquellie. It is held every Saturday where we can buy fruits and vegetables, meat, and fish. Our house-boy can catch fish for us, too. Harold bought him some hooks and line. He can get greens for us by just going out and picking them. They are free, so are palm nuts, two kinds of staple foods here. He can also find pineapple, grapefruit, guava, and bananas, very cheaply, plus rice is available in the rice mill, here, for 10 cents a pound.

We eat rice nearly every day, seldom see potatoes, and don't miss them. Eddoes [*a variety of taro, a tropical root vegetable*] and cassavas are very plentiful and inexpensive and you can use them like you do potatoes. We use powdered milk and canned cheese, so actually, with good planning, nutritionally, there is no problem. I hope you won't worry about our health. We know how to keep healthy as far as diet and cleanliness are

Ruth and Harold's house in Gbedin.

concerned, and are using precautions that are recommended. It is very easy to become careless, we have found. So far, there are no problems, and in our own house, it should be easier.

The weather is still hot and humid, much like Texas, but of course, no air-conditioning up-country. Things are green all the time, trees in bloom, sky so blue, cloudless most of the time. It's really beautiful country.

I meant to mention about our house, that we have paint, brushes, and a borrowed paint roller, and this week I plan to paint all of the rooms. School boys keep coming, asking for jobs, so two of them will help me. We have a kitchen, which is only an empty room right now, two bedrooms, dining room and living room, and the bathroom. (Everything is in a small scale.) There is also a good-sized porch, which the men will screen in this week, since it is really the only cool place in the evening, and we have to keep the mosquitoes out as much as possible. I have been able to buy a hand-operated sewing machine from the Danish girl I told you about, so I will be able to make curtains, dish towels, etc. We won't try to start on our assignments until next week because of the house repairs.

Tonight we are having dinner with the PC couple we stayed with here before. They will serve us palm butter with snails—at least I'm going to try. Palm butter is a kind of sauce they call soup, served over rice. Every day is new!

Dearest Mother,   **May 16, 1971, Gbedin**

I just had to stop and make us a calendar so I could figure out what the date is. It doesn't seem to matter since we never seem to have deadlines, or places we have to hurry to. We've been in our house for a week now, and it's coming along quite well. I have to keep reminding myself that I'm not back in time about 20 or 30 years, especially when we are washing clothes in the washtub, writing letters by kerosene lamp, walking every place instead of driving a car, and so on. Actually, with running water, electric lights some of the time, a gas stove, and kerosene refrigerator, we're very fortunate. However, the lights went off tonight in the storm, and our water supply stopped yesterday afternoon until noon today due to a broken pipe near the source. Our modern conveniences aren't all that dependable!

Harold will get a big 50-gallon drum we can collect rain water in (from the roof run-off), so we will always have water available. The water pipe does get plugged up with leaves, or the pipe breaks, both rather common. This past week we've had the carpenter, mason and plumber working in our house—all are employed by the rice project. Harold has worked along with all of them, showing them how to make do with what they have. One of the men said to another one, "That ol' man can do ever' t'ing, can't fool him." We have also painted, so things look much cleaner. They have built a nice counter in the kitchen, and installed a sink that Harold bought for $5. The lumber is rough (it's hardwood), but very solid. They put linoleum on the counter and on the floor. We still have to paint the bathroom and dining room, which is doubling right now as a kitchen until the real one is finished.

I tried out my "new" hand-operated sewing machine yesterday on some curtains for the bedroom. It's amazing how easy it is to operate. Over here, a treadle machine is a luxury. They cost from $45 to $75. I paid $25 for my hand-operated one and will no doubt sell it when we leave. I feel very fortunate to have it, with all the sewing I will have to do, including, curtains, place mats, napkins, dish towels, even shirts for Harold from the pretty African fabrics available so inexpensively. It's amazing how one's sense of values can change, to be happy with such a simple thing as my hand-operated sewing machine, and feel luxurious with linoleum on the living room floor!

Harold killed his first snake, right by our front steps. The Liberians call it a Yah snake. It is poisonous. It was just swallowing a frog when Harold saw it. He killed it with his cutlass, a very basic, all-purpose tool and weapon here.

In the week that we have been here, so many people have come to the door wanting medicine, very sick babies, too. One was unconscious, with a 105 temp. I gave it a cool sponge bath, with everyone standing around watching. The fever started down, and he became conscious. Apparently, the infant had malaria. There is so much of that here. Now people can't wait until I start working at the clinic. Unfortunately, I have so few medicines, and don't know how soon I'll get the support of the PHS. I'm also trying to get a microscope so I can check stool specimens for worms. There is also so much of that, too. Hookworm and others, with a different medicine needed for each. A doctor isn't available so if I don't do it no one else is here to do it.

We went to a fun party Friday eve at the Pearmines', the young Oregon couple we met here earlier. They invited some of the farmers who Larry works with, and some of the teachers that Mary works with, and the PCVs in the area. Their house boy and his friend cooked pawpaw (papaya) and pork soup and palm butter and pork soup. They cooked a wash tub of rice. Of course, there was plenty of palm wine, the common Liberian alcoholic beverage.

There was native music, played on homemade instruments, and dancing, around and around the room, in single file, kind of a three-step. As always at any gathering, there were a lot of speeches. Some of the men wore country robes. It was very colorful and gay. The next day, we went to the school football game (actually soccer) against a team from another town. This was a big social event. Nearly everyone turns out. Afterward, they all go to the community hall, where the school girls have cooked rice and soup. There was dancing and music, and more speeches, given by people in the order of their importance. As always they are very flowery, detailed, and repetitious, accompanied by much clapping and applause

The people are so nice here, very friendly and considerate, and seem genuinely glad that we are here, as well as grateful for our help. Even though they have so little, they are generous with what they have and even though we think we ourselves have very little here, we have so much compared to them. For instance, we have dishes and cups for each of us; they have only one bowl, from which everyone eats, with their hands, at the same time. Children learn to shift for themselves at an early age and to take care of each other.

We are planning on planting a garden soon—have some parsley, onion, chives, and lettuce seeds, so far. The Chinese here, three rice specialists from Taiwan, grow beautiful vegetables. We expect to get more seeds from them.

Dear Mother,   **May 23, 1971, Gbedin**

The school term is different here. It begins in March, and then a short break and the second term begins, and ends at Christmas. Then their summer vacation goes from January until March.

The cool time of the year is just beginning. People say the rains are just two weeks away, now. We've had a couple of really hard rains, so far, in the evening and during the night. So far, it's been very welcome, because of the heat during the day.

In the two weeks that we've been here, we've been very busy with house repairs, and now have done enough to kind of ease off, and do a little each day. With the help of the carpenter and mason, and Harold, we've just about foiled the mosquitoes. They put screens on all the windows. Harold has stuffed cracks and holes with paper and masking tape. Now they will make a 2x4 frame around the upper part of our front porch (it's about 9x11) and screen that, too. That will give us a fairly cool place to sit in the evening, since the house gets pretty warm inside at that time.

Harold has laid linoleum in a somewhat patched up manner in our dining and living rooms and the kitchen. What a difference that makes in keeping the house swept up. This week, I will get material hemmed for curtains in the living room. We're quite open to passers by, and people stop and stare in all the time. In fact, so many stop in and greet us, sometimes sit, and after a while say, "Excuse, ya. I go now," and get up and leave. I'm trying to get used to having someone here all the time.

Right now, two early-teenaged boys are sitting and visiting with Harold. They are talking fishing. These boys are so knowledgeable about everything around them, catching fish, planting and harvesting rice, cooking all kinds of things (native foods), making mats. Some are very quick to catch on to mechanical things once they're shown, although they seldom have any contact with anything mechanical in their daily life, even telling time. They haven't had much opportunity to learn. These two boys are 16, and are in the sixth grade.

We seldom see girls here. They stay home all the time. However, one of the mechanics asked me if he could have his sister come and spend some time with me regularly because he wants her to learn how to do things she will need to know when she gets married. I suppose she is 14 or so, and in the fourth or fifth grade. These people are just as intelligent as others their age, I am sure, but haven't had the educational advantage, plus school is taught in English, a second language for them, which they must learn when they do start school. And they start school much later than American kids do.

Our closest neighbors are three Chinese rice specialists from Taiwan. They have been here a couple of years, providing the technical know-how in paddy rice growing. Their English is pretty bad. I think I will start working with one of them who speaks the least English, and wants to learn more. They brought us a huge bag of rice, at least 25 lbs., and said, "Tell us when you want more." They also bring me beautiful fresh vegetables from their garden. I gave them some parsley and lettuce seeds that I bought in Monrovia, which they've planted for me in their plot. Our soil here is very poor. The topsoil was bulldozed off when the buildings were originally put up. The Chinese guys plant about a mile away by the rice fields, and they use commercial fertilizer.

I baked them some bread, which really tickled them. The next day they brought us a little bowl of what looked like a little filled dumpling. It contained meat cut in small bits—tasted like pork—and some kind of chopped up green vegetable. When I said to Harold, "I wonder what is in it," he said, "Don't ask, just eat it," which I guess is the safest thing. These are the same fellows who killed a python that was 17 feet long, and about 8 inches in diameter near here, and they ate it!

We are enjoying all the different nationalities we meet here. There is something interesting about all of them, and so many new things to learn. For instance, Saturday we had a ride to Ganta with John Chambers, the Project Engineer (the British man). We shopped in the Lebanese store there for provisions. When we were through, the owner invited us to his home for coffee. He is from Beirut and speaks French better than English. He has stores in three small towns near Ganta, one for each young son. He has lived in Ganta for 21 years. He has a very fine house around the corner from his store, furnished like a Western-style home—stereo, ping-pong table, etc.

He served us Turkish coffee in tiny cups, very strong and sweet, and seemed honored to have us visit his home. He said, "If you need something on Sundays or holidays when the store is closed, come to my house, and I'll get it for you." I think I've mentioned the Lebanese merchants before. They do all the trading, and are very sharp business men. They don't associate with the Liberians very much. Some do marry Liberian women, since it's the only way they can own property—in their wives' names. You can't own land here unless you're a citizen, and you have to be black to become a citizen.

Harold has begun to get the shop organized, so they can systematically repair the tractors, one at a time. Apparently, they have seven tractors, but only three are in operation. Each of the others are "spoiled" as they say, probably because only one little thing is wrong. Harold began last week to make what he didn't have. He made a gasket, a very intricate little thing, for a hydraulic pump on the tractor that had been sitting around "spoiled."

Tomorrow, I expect to start spending some time at the clinic, at least in the mornings. Then in the late afternoon when people come in from the fields, I'll visit in the village and try to learn more about what can and needs to be done. I made an inventory of medicines last week.

Every day, though, I have a new experience. Last night, just as we were about to sit down to eat, the director brought an old man to the house. He had cut the end of one finger off just by the first knuckle, with his cutlass, while cutting sticks. I cleaned it and dressed it and told him he had to go to the doctor to have it repaired. They said he didn't have any money, and besides, it would be OK. I haven't seen him today and shudder to think about what it looks like, and feels like, especially if it gets infected.

John said, "You don't know these people, or what it's like here." I'm sure he's right. I woke up last night thinking about that finger, and had a hard time getting to sleep again. The cutlass is the people's all-purpose tool. They use it to dig, hack, cut, chop, pry, hammer, plant, and harvest. It has a thick handle about 6 to 8 inches long, and a blade about 3 inches wide and 18 inches long. They sell for 50 to 75 cents in a Lebanese store. More wounds are caused by them than I ever imagined. No one has a saw or hammer or axe, or as a general rule, even a shovel or hoe. When they cut bush and clear land, they plant rice, which most of the people in the villages grow (not the swamp rice like that grown here). Here in this government project, rice-growing is mechanized, with government-owned vehicles.

We also went to the Leprosarium at Ganta Mission on Saturday to see about buying some chairs for our dining room. The residents there make rattan-seated, mahogany chairs and sell them for $2.00. So far, we are still using borrowed chairs.

They also do some fantastic carvings, such as masks, statues, etc. I bought a marriage chain for a wedding present. It is a chain carved from a single piece of wood, with a head on each end, one a man, one a woman. This one is carved from camphor wood, a very heavy wood. It's quite an experience to buy something there. About a dozen people converge on you, saying, "Missy, buy please," pushing a carving at you. Their prices are always about three times what you finally pay.

Dear Mother,   **May 30, 1971, Gbedin**

Here it is another week gone by. So much happens every week that the days just speed by. All week, I think I will sit down and write to you, and the days are so full I don't get at it. We get up early, Harold goes to work by 7, and by night we're so tired, we're ready for bed early. I didn't ever think I'd get to that kind of schedule.

This past week I've been visiting various places and people, trying to make some plans for my work. I spent one day at the Ganta Methodist Mission Hospital and Leprosarium. I had lunch with the doctor and his wife who teaches in the school there, and I attended one of his classes for leprosy health assistants. The doctor does some very interesting rehabilitative surgery for leprosy victims, such as tendon transplants, tendon lengthening, and nerve transplants. He makes some novel orthopedicappliances, such as artificial legs out of 2x4 lumber and scrap metal. Today, I visited with the county health doctor, also a mission doctor. I think through him, I'll be able to get a maternal and child health clinic started here in Gbedin. It is badly needed.

Harold working in the maintenance shop with Eddie Robinson.

I've also been spending some time at the clinic here, which is operated by Daniel, a "dresser," which is like a health assistant. Dressers are basically untrained, and their entire practice consists of treating with penicillin or chloroquin, both by injection. When he gives oral medicine, liquid or tablets, the patients all use the same cup, never washed between patients. He does boil the needles, but covers them with an un-sterile lid. I will try to avoid working there as much as possible; instead will spend time in the village, with the people in their homes, or when they come to the house and ask for my help, a very common thing, even when the clinic is open.

I've been cooking and preparing so many different things that we or our houseboy gather, such as a variety of greens. I suppose it's like you used to do, with dandelion and pigweed greens. There are about five kinds of greens that are free for the picking, or for only 5 cents for a large bunch in the markets. We have rice every night, with a greens "soup" of some sort, made with a little fish or meat, maybe "cow meat," beef from cows brought from Guinea, tough as leather, but OK if tenderized with a little papaya; added to this are some tomato sauce, a chicken bouillon cube, and always red peppers. This is called "chop," a standard meal. All restaurants, if you can call them that up-country, are called "chop houses."

We also fry plantain for breakfast, have eggplant plentifully, which makes a good soup. Limes are only 5 cents for about 30 limes, grapefruit, two for 5 cents, oranges four for 5 cents. Both are full of seeds but very sweet. Pawpaw and pineapple grow wild. We have several in our yard. So, with this kind of thing for lunch, and rice and soup for supper, we fare quite well and inexpensively. Fortunately, we like rice, and so far, our Chinese friends grow it and keep us supplied.

We really enjoy the fellows, exchanging foods with them, talking about Taiwan, and teaching them English, learning about growing paddy rice, and so on. We also have many visitors. The people come in and sit and visit or to have me help them with some complaint. We have a great time trying to understand each other. There are always some school boys here, looking at books or studying. They try to help me with Mano; we get a lot of laughs out of it.

Our houseboy, John, is Gio, from a tiny village far from here by motor car and then at least a two-mile walk on a path into the bush. He lives with an uncle, who makes him work in the rice fields and then takes the money he earns. John eats with us at night and at noon, otherwise, he would have very little to eat. The uncle doesn't buy either his clothes or pay his school fees. John, who is 15, has to manage some way. He's lived here with his uncle for seven years, in order to go to school. His father was killed by a snake. He begged us to hire him, and his teacher did too. We pay him $7.50 a month, plus his meals. He'd like to stay here all the time—we can hardly chase him home at night. So many boys need jobs just to stay in school.

Harold keeps quite busy with his job. There is always a tractor or a vehicle of some sort that needs his attention. The Liberian mechanics know very little about trouble-shooting, and things keep breaking down, over and over. He's also been busy working on our house, but now, has only painting to finish. Of course, he still has furniture to make. He will make seats for our screened porch, and some book cases, both out of bamboo, and some sort of palm "stem," split, for seats. He bought a hen last week, to see if he can raise some chickens for eggs and meat. Eggs cost $1.00 a dozen, and chicken is tough as well as expensive.

Dear Vikki,   **June 4, 1971, Gbedin**

Rainy season is coming on, what they call winter. It's not really cold, just cooler when it is raining. People tell us they need a sweater occasionally. We are still sleeping with only a sheet on and no clothes at all. Twice, we've had only a light blanket. Actually, the mornings are nice and cool, but the afternoons warm and humid. If it rains in the evening or night, drying clothes the next day is a problem. We don't notice the humidity— must be used to it now, but realize it when clothes stay damp on the clothesline all day.

We had a very bad storm two nights ago, and had rain coming in half the windows, since they are just screened. The wind blew in almost like a hurricane. We now have woven mats for the windows, and Harold will get them hung this weekend. Then we can roll them down when it begins to storm. So far, it's just a big adventure, and kind of exciting to get things battened down, watch the lightning and light the lamps. We could hardly keep them lit, candles either, because the wind blew in so hard.

While I'm writing this, a Liberian lady, Lucy Toe, is ironing for me. She is dressed with a head-tie, a turban-like wrap, and a lappa around her from waist to the floor. She has an18-month-old baby on her back, tied there with another lappa. The child has fallen asleep now, so we will put it on the bed. Her husband works here in the mechanic shop and is on hourly wage, paid by petty cash. He probably earns less than $1 a day. But most of the men on petty cash pay have not received any salary for at least six months—this is from the government, remember. He plants rice and cassava to feed the family. She isn't too strong—has anemia, so I've given her iron and vitamins.

She came to see me last week, speaks very limited English, but we manage. (Her tribe is Grebo, totally different from Mano.) I gave her a cup of coffee, and we sat together. Finally, she said, "Mah. Mah, I have no lappa, I have no money. Do you have some work I can do so I can earn some money?" I told her I would talk to Harold, but we already had two boys who worked for us.

Anyway, Harold and I decided she could do some ironing, and we could pay her a little. It's a problem sometimes, having some of the women work for you, because they have had no contact with a house like this. They iron with a charcoal iron, cook over a fire in an iron pot, wash dishes and do their meal preparation squatting on the ground. Much of the time, even with John, I have to spend time with them, showing how to do it and then supervising for a while. Much simpler to do it myself, I'm sure, but hard to say no.

John is so interested in learning so many new things. I made rice pancakes yesterday, and he was fascinated. He loves rice anyway, but seeing it in pancakes was completely new. He said when he had finished eating, "Thanks for a good breakfast. I can fight anyone today."

Incidentally, yesterday, Mrs. Toe saw your picture on the table. It is your college graduation picture. She picked it up, and looked at it for a long time, studying it so carefully. Finally, she raised it to her lips and kissed it. Then she looked at it some more, kissed it again very softly, and then set it down. It was as though she saw your picture as a living person and was moved by it. These people are really nice.

I'm having my usual morning. People stop in for a visit, medical help, or just to say hello. I've just come back from the clinic. The man who runs it sent a message that they had an eye emergency, so I grabbed my first aid kit and dashed down the hill. Fortunately, I could help him—a welder who had been chipping metal had got a piece in his eye. It was so much like my Voc. School kids that it was no problem, and the eye wasn't damaged. I feel that all these "successes" help build the confidence of the people I will be working with as we get our clinic plans going.

Mrs. Toe's mother-in-law has just arrived. She is a very attractive Liberian lady, who smokes a little pipe, and here comes my mail deliverer, so I must close.

Dear Mother,   June 6, 1971, Gbedin

It seems that the first thing I have to do when I want to start writing a letter is to go look at the calendar, to see what the date is. We never seem to need to know the date, and the days go by, and it is easy to lose track.

It is about three months to the day since we left home, and the time has gone so fast. So much has happened in that time that it is hard to believe it's really us and we are really in Africa.

Our days have settled into a routine of sorts. Harold goes to work each day, and our home has reached the stage where we both have more free time to do some of the things we want to do. But our routine is as changeable here as it always has been. There are so many things to interrupt. I guess you could say our usual day is unusual, and things seldom go as planned.

Our life is much less private here than at home. For example, when we lived in Dallas, we seldom knew people who lived around us. And at Parkland, we knew only our next-door and across-the-street neighbors. We lived inside our house and had little contact with the neighborhood, and our friends lived miles away. Here, we live in the midst of the community and find it hard to be by ourselves. So much of the people's activities are outside. They cook outside over a fire or in a separate little cook house. They carry water, gather greens, do the washing, and visit outside their houses. Consequently, people go by our house all the time, and frequently stop and sit a while. Life starts early in the morning here, and we often have people stopping in by 7 AM; sometimes, late in the evening, too, and often at meal times.

Many of the women come by for health reasons, and now, school girls do, too. So many of the school girls already have babies, and they may be only 13 or 14 and may be only in the fourth grade, having started school so late. I see more of the women at my house than at the clinic, just now. I don't want to create problems, but don't want to become part of the clinic, as it's now run. I go for a short time each day, visit with the dresser, see a few patients, and give them some medicine, and then he calls me when he has someone he needs help with.

Last evening I saw the man whose eye I treated and asked him how his eye was. He said, "Fine. I poured some cane juice in it." Cane juice is distilled from sugar cane, and I think it is straight rum.

I've begun the first steps toward getting an under-fives clinic started here and hope, in this way, to be able to influence the quality of the treatment in the clinic. This evening, Elizabeth a Liberian friend who lives here, stopped in with her baby—a five-day-old little girl. She is a beautiful woman, about 35 at least, and has had two babies that died and doesn't seem to have any other children. Friday, a man from up by Sanniquellie came by taxi with the baby and asked Elizabeth if she would keep it. His wife had died when the baby was born, and there were no women to care for the baby. Someone told him about Elizabeth and her husband, so he came to her.

She was tickled to get the baby and will give it a good home. Both she and her husband have jobs here at the project, so they have an income. And besides, they are good managers, not true of so many of the people here. (Most people make very little money and seem to blow it right away, as a general rule.)

She had already had the baby's ears pierced this morning and had a little thread tied through them. In about a week, she will put little gold earrings in and in a week or so probably give her a little gold bracelet. Many of the babies wear an ankle bracelet, too, and a string of some sort around their waist that is supposed to be some sort of "medicine." Often times we see teeny little girls walking around with nothing on but their medicine.

Last week, I saw an interesting scene. I was waiting for a taxi by the side of the road here. Several people were already there—a lady with three big bags of corn ears and of greens, probably taking them to the market. There were also five to six men. One had a chicken he was trans-porting, that had a string tied to its leg to keep it from running away. Suddenly I realized that the woman was changing her clothes. She had stripped to the waist, and opened one of her bundles in which she had a stack of freshly ironed clothes. The men were carrying on a conversation and appeared to not be noticing the woman, since for them it was quite a commonplace sight. She donned a brassiere, pulled a clean blouse over her head, and appeared unaware of anyone around. She put on a fresh lappa, a fresh head tie, and looked like a new woman. No doubt, she had walked miles to get to the taxi stop, and now was ready to change and go off to town to make market.

Our Chinese friends were here again this evening and brought us two golden melons, small yellow melons shaped like a watermelon. They have planted lot of them in their garden, and this was their first picking. While they are here, we spend a lot of time learning about each other's country. They are so interested in learning English, and are a lot of fun. We had them over a few nights ago for banana cream pie that I made with bananas they had given us. They have given us so much Taiwan tea that we won't have to buy tea all the time we are here.

We became full-fledged chicken farmers this past weekend. Harold has wanted to get a hen and try to raise a setting of chickens, because meat is so scarce, and eggs are very dear. We have to pay $1 a dozen, and they aren't always fresh. To buy meat, we can buy a country chicken, a scrawny, tough bird, for at least $1 for a small one, buy a piece of wild meat, like bush deer—a very small animal—a groundhog, or a ground squirrel. All of these we could get occasionally here or we buy "cow meat" at the Saturday market. These are beef cows that look like Brahmas and are hauled or driven here from Guinea or Ivory Coast to the market, and are they tough!

So, back to chicken farming. Harold bought a hen for $1.75 from a lady who has a small farm near here. He built a little pen out of odds and ends. When he first got it home, he kept her tied by one of her legs with a piece of string, which she didn't seem to mind at all. This was Saturday AM. Saturday at 9 PM, a man knocked on the door with a rooster and asked Harold if he wanted it. So, Harold gave him $1.25 for it. The next day, one of the women we had met here and visited with—in fact we had helped her when she was fanning her rice, sent her little boy to our door with an American Leghorn pullet, as a "dash." Now, just a bit ago, our house-boy's uncle "bock bocked" at our door, and here he was with a half-grown chicken for us for our soup. So, now we have four chickens, one just about ready to lay. And we had planned on having only one hen and having her run loose after a while to find a papa.

You can't imagine the things people come and ask us to buy. Yesterday a man came with two kittens, and asked us to buy them. One of the men who works in Harold's shop asked him if we would take his nine-year-old son and raise him, so he can go to school. The boy lives farther up-country that has no school.

Did I tell you I have been making our bread? I also made Mango jam this week and will try to make orange marmalade, and pineapple jam, too. To buy something like that is out of the question, but the fruit is very inexpensive. And I have the time, which is needed for most of our cooking.

I'll have to tell you about Mrs. Toe, who was here this week. She is from the Grebo tribe and speaks very little English. Grebo is very different from the language I'm learning. She is very hard up and wanted to earn some money. I told her she could do some ironing for me. After she finished ironing, we were having coffee together. Your picture was sitting on the table, and while we were "talking small," because of our communication difficulty, she looked at your picture, and said, "Hello, Ma," very quietly. The day before, she had been looking at Vikki's picture, then raised it up and kissed it, looked some more, then kissed it again, and set it back down. Someone told me later that the Grebo people are very superstitious and believe that the person really is there if their picture is there. It was quite touching, I thought. It appeared that to her, the pictures were real people.

You would really enjoy these people, mother, and seeing how they live and work and play. They are very nice and very knowledgeable, about their way of life, tribal customs, and their environment. They are so ignorant of life anywhere else. Their moral and ethical attitudes are completely different from those in the Western world. We realize how important it is to not judge or condemn others because they are different. And it makes us examine our own standards very seriously, as to whether they are the only ones or the right ones. We have much to learn. We do know we are very fortunate to have this opportunity to be here in such a developing country.

Dear Mother,   **June 14, 1971, Gbedin**

We were thinking lately, that the last few months have been like an extended visit, except unlike former vacation trips, we don't seem to go home.

Actually, this seems like home to us now, even though it's far away from our families. People have been so kind to us, and seem to be genuinely glad to have us here. It's a very nice feeling. We are surprised that it doesn't seem strange at all to be the only white persons in most situations. I can be in a tiny village, surrounded by a bunch of little black kids and adults, all wearing the strangest assortment of clothing, with very limited communication capability, yet feel quite at home and not the least uncomfortable. I'm picking up each day in my ability to communicate in both Mano and Liberian English, which is a big help. In fact, my very limited French comes in handy, since there are some people from Guinea here, and they speak French rather than English, and of course a dialect which I can't understand.

This week, I started giving English lessons to one of our young Chinese neighbors. It's going to be interesting trying to keep everything sorted out!

Every day brings a new situation for me to deal with as far as health problems are concerned. The kinds of things I have to deal with, without medical supervision, would astound you. Women come to me with sick babies, babies with the worst kinds of skin infections, women problems, men with gonorrhea, and of course, malaria. The man with the very sick baby I wrote about before, came Friday and dashed me two big pineapples. Another girl whose baby is improving now—I've been hot-packing an abscess—said Saturday, "I will bring you some bitter ball and eggplant when I bring baby Monday." People are very appreciative and generous, even when they have so little. And it is unthinkable to refuse such a gift, even though you know they haven't very much.

Yesterday, we went a short distance into the bush to watch a group of people, called a *ku*, scratch a farm. They have cut the bush with their cutlasses, burned the sticks, and sowed rice. All this is on a very hilly terrain. The next step was to scratch the rice in with hand-forged, short-handled hoes, which are about 14 inches long, a job for the women, who bend double and hoe all day to a rhythm set by a drum. The drums are made of hollowed-out logs, about eight inches in diameter, and two feet long, played by men. There were three drummers. They play a very snappy beat that sets the pace. Everyone had been drinking cane juice, so they were hoeing and dancing and having a great time, despite the dust and hot sun.

The women all wore a lappa from the waist down, and most were bare above. Some wore a bra, some a top of some sort, and all wore a head tie. This was a fascinating thing to watch. Some of the men were from here, and all were watching and enjoying it. We wanted to take pictures, but the people were offended by our suggestion, so we didn't try. They could have made us pay quite a bit of money for offending them if we had persisted. This ku is typical of how their farm work is done, kind of like our old threshing crew days, I guess.

Our house has become quite nice, even though it's really such a shack. Harold has put reed mats at the windows now, which we keep rolled up until it rains. Our next rainstorm will give them a good test. We also have similar mats for the floor, baskets, etc., so we're looking quite homey.

I'll have to tell you about my last week's bread-making experience. I started it in the morning and produced a lovely looking ball of dough. I covered it and went to the clinic for a while. When I came back, the dough had raised beautifully. I punched it down, waited a while, and started to make loaves, planning to make biscuits for a friend, too. Then I saw a little bug, and thought it had just flown in, so I took it out and kept on making my loaf, such nice dough. But there was another bug, which made me curious, so I began to examine the dough. I'm sure you can imagine what I found—little worms that had been in the flour, which I hadn't seen. It almost made me sick, especially when I realized I had made baking powder biscuits for breakfast.

When Harold came home, he told me to bake it and feed it to the chickens. I decided to let John do it so I wouldn't have to look at it anymore. When John came from school, he said, "Not the chickens. I'll make biscuits and sell them at school tomorrow, 1 cent, 1 cent," and that is what he did. I said, "Oh, John, no." And then he said that kids eat worse than that—bamboo worms, bug-a-bugs, etc. We really had a big laugh about the whole episode but now I certainly sift the flour every time. It's amazing what you can get used to, isn't it?

Dear Mother,   **June 20, 1971, Gbedin**

There are always people in our house—groups of little school kids who come to sit and look at books, farmers and their wives, and kids who have some health problem or other. Many come just out of curiosity, and even though we don't speak the same language, we manage. But it is hard to follow through on a project, because of the interruptions.

My Mano is progressing, but slowly. Three days a week, I walk around the village with Bea, visiting with people, and two days a week we sit at home and work on the language, about two-hours at a time. People are so pleased when they hear you use some of their dialect, and I'm so pleased when we can understand each other. The majority of the women speak only their dialect, and using an interpreter is far from satisfactory.

Did I tell you we have five chickens now, one a rooster. Two hens have begun to lay, and when we have enough eggs, Harold will try to set two of them. Maybe, we can raise some meat! This week we were given a piece of groundhog meat, which we used to make soup. Actually, it doesn't taste bad, especially when meat is so scarce.

Cooking is a novel experience, especially with so many new things to try. We have fried plantain. I made peanut butter from ground peas, or "grou' pea" as they're called, roasting them first, and then grinding them in a mortar. I make bread using palm wine for leavening, mango jam, papaya jam, collard greens, sweet potato greens, fried eddoes, palm butter soup, and many more. However, getting food isn't as simple as going to the supermarket. You can hunt some, and gather things freely. You must haggle over prices in the market. Then preparing it takes so much longer. I try lots of new things and enjoy it.

Harold and John, our house boy, are planting a garden, which will be really nice to have. We already have pineapple plants in it, which will bear next year. Our latest find, in a bunch of old parts, was an old-fashioned clothes stamper, like you used to have. What a welcome addition. John does our washing, and he was grinning from ear to ear when he used it this week. It's much better than the washboard and easier on our clothes and on him.

This week, Harold cut my hair, can you imagine that? I didn't think I'd ever let him try, but he did a pretty good job. He used a little hair trimmer that has a razor blade in it. I told him I was going to try to get a ride to Lamco to get a haircut, but wanted him to try to trim my neckline. He just kept on, and now I don't have to pay for a haircut.

Dear Mother,   **June 27, 1971, Gbedin**

Winter has begun here, although it's more like summer at home. It rains some every day, but so far, not for long periods at a time. However, when it does rain it comes in torrents, and sometimes the wind blows like a gale—uproots trees and blows roofs off. The corrugated zinc roofs are just tacked on, so it isn't surprising. When the rain stops, the sun comes out and it's quite warm again. Yesterday it was 85 degrees.

The main problem during rainy season is that the roads wash out and bridges go out, so that travel is questionable. We plan to go to Monrovia for a few days after the 4th, but will go with John Chambers in his truck; shouldn't have problems. So far we haven't worn a sweater, but have slept with a light blanket sometimes. Actually, the cooler weather is very welcome, mud and all.

Our days go by very fast. Harold keeps busy at work, with something to solve every day. He is in his element there. He also helps some of the people after work do some kind of farm project, or he's doing more on our house. Things fall apart fast here, so there is constant upkeep needed— the weather deteriorates things, termites destroy them, and then in the first place, things are put together so poorly.

I'm busy every day with people, either here or at the clinic, who are sick or who have hurt themselves. So far, I haven't been able to get the wheels turning to get PHS sponsorship, but will contact people on my own when I'm in Monrovia. There is no immunization program here at all for babies, and there are 100s of babies. Measles are a serious problem in Liberia. Last week, in a neighboring village there were two deaths from measles.

People are so used to getting sick and then having a shot of penicillin for almost any complaint. They can buy penicillin and streptomycin from the drug store and bring it to the clinic and ask you to give it to them. I didn't bring any syringes with me, thank goodness, so have a reason for not giving it. And at the same time, I try to get them to realize how dangerous it is to take penicillin for just anything. However, the dresser here encourages it. He makes money on every injection he gives. So I try to teach prevention of illness, better sanitation, to keep from getting sick. It's interesting, to say the least.

Yesterday we walked to a village one and a half miles away where we had been invited to church. It's a Mano village, and all was in Mano. Very informal, with most of the people there doing some of the talking. They invited us to tell about God and to offer prayers. John was with us, so he translated for us. They seemed to be so happy to have us. There were only a few people attending, although there are at least 600 living in the village.

We've found everyone to be friendly to us. They are surprised when they learn that we are Peace Corps volunteers. Can't understand that any-one our age will give up a "soft life" in the US to come here and help them. So they are very grateful, and want to help us get adjusted. I'm coming along fairly well with my language study, and this really pleases people. When I stumble along in their dialect, they laugh and try to help me say it right.

Weddings here aren't much, no ceremony at all. The man usually pays the girl's father 25 cents to $25, and the girl goes to live with him, as often as not, as his second or third or fourth wife. It is usual for a man to have more than one wife, although they say that the "civilized" ones aren't as apt to. Funerals, or rather deaths, involve much more, wailing and crying, and carrying on for several days, during which time all kinds of relatives gather. You can hear them far into the night, although we haven't been present at one yet.

The entire way of life here is so different from the American way of living. Fortunately, we are able to fit into it well, being curious and interested in knowing more about it rather than looking at it critically. I mentioned that the people here are so friendly and welcoming. A strange thing though, is that they always need to *juke* you, that is, take advantage of you in a business deal. They do this even with their best friends. Everyone knows what is going on. If you can get the best of them in their efforts to *juke* you, it's fine, no one thinks anything of it. They're always "jammed" for money and ask for more than they should. And of course, white people always mean money to them, and they always jack up the prices. We're learning fast! John usually watches out for us, and doesn't let anyone overcharge us.

We acquired a little kitten this week, a tiny, calico one. Cats aren't easy to find, and then, Liberians want Americans to buy them, rather than give them away. We decided a cat was a necessity because of the rats and mice and huge cockroaches. So far we haven't seen either rats or mice in our house, but some of our friends have. I can't say the same for cockroaches though, big ones, too, two to three inches long. They really make me shiver. Surprisingly, as yet, we've seen very few spiders.

Dear Mother,   **July 9, 1971, Gbedin**

Here it is, well into July already. I've never seen time go by so fast, and we are not in a constant rush. However, every day seems to bring something new, although it seems like our life is so routine, now.

We spent Sunday, Monday, and Tuesday in Monrovia, our first trip away in two months. We stayed with a couple who had come to Liberia with us. They are from Seattle and about our age. We were the only "mature" ones in the group. Whenever you visit or rather, travel in Liberia, you have to make arrangements to stay with someone, because there are no hotels or motels except in Monrovia. These people were so lonesome. They don't have much in common with the younger PCs, have no kids of their own, for one thing, and were very homesick. So when we knocked on their door on Sunday evening, they welcomed us like long-lost buddies, and assured us we could stay any time.

He has a VW bus for his job, so was able to take us all around to take care of our business, which was a big help. Otherwise, the only alternative is taking a taxi, plus much more time.

I had made appointments to try to get things moving for the well-baby clinic here, but the red tape isn't any different here than in the US. In the meantime, I keep busy here with a varied clientele. The man I told you about who cut his finger off is now completely OK. I would never have believed that it would do so well, not even a bit of inflammation at any time. He thinks I can do anything, now.

People keep bringing me things, cabbage, pineapple, chicken, a snake skin, cassava, you name it. I keep telling them I don't need any pay, but this is just a *dash*, and I can't refuse lest I offend them.

We thought of all of you on July 4th. There was nothing different here, although our Chinese friends brought us a Chinese dessert in honor of our Independence Day. It was made with dried fruits and rice. We have a lot of get-togethers here, both with our PC friends and with our Liberian neighbors, so we're not lacking in entertainment. But, it isn't like families and old friends.

Incidentally, when we were in Monrovia, we had to go to the PC doctor's office for more shots—an every three month thing. While there, we weighed in. Harold has taken off 20 lbs. without trying and looks quite fit. I've lost 6 lbs. I'm sure we'll continue to lose for a while, with more exercise, less rich food, and, I suppose, the heat. Anyway, we're glad we aren't gaining, which a lot of the girls do here.

We have been enjoying the clippings you send, Mom. Some of the people do, too. They don't know what comic strips or cartoon characters are. Some ask me if that is what most white people look like. They don't know what to think about Snoopy typing letters and some of the other things he does. One of the funny things that Liberian people believe is that a rooster can lay eggs—once a year, a tiny one. So, when the clipping came telling about a male ostrich laying an egg, we really had a laugh.

I haven't had much time to write. We seldom have a morning or afternoon without people coming in, and of course, at night with the lights off so early, letter writing is not easy. Close to the lamp, there are too many bugs, and away from it you can't see to write. I'm still having mosquito problems—just about get cleared up and another mass of bites come along.

We do learn patience here, though. Nothing is ever done in a hurry. I'm actually enjoying the leisurely pace, but wonder if I'll be able to keep up with the rat race when we come home.

Dear Jenny [Harold's sister],   **July 15, 1971, Gbedin**

I think I wrote before about Harold's chickens. Two of his hens started to set—on one batch of eggs. One finally gave up, but the other one stayed with it.

Two days ago they started to hatch, and by evening, there were five little ones. The next day, all of them had disappeared. Another hatched yesterday, and by evening, it was gone. Only a shell was left. She still has three eggs, but Harold thinks they aren't fertile. Now, he's trying to decide what could have taken the chickens, a snake, rat, a big, rather wild house cat, a hawk, or even a big rooster that he's been taking care of for a neighbor. So our plans for some nice, tender fryers ended in a hurry.

He will try buying a setting of eggs next, and put the hen in a place by herself. Most chickens just run loose and forage for their food and are thin and tough. He wanted to keep his penned up and feed them and make them fat.

You know, Jenny, one time you asked me, "What will you do about your hair in Africa?" What a change! I keep it cut short, wash it in the shower, fluff it up with a towel, and that is it. No permanent, no hair spray, and seldom any rollers. Harold even cuts it for me sometimes, but last week, when we went to Monrovia, I went into a beauty shop and had it cut right. I'm kind of an oddity here, because no one has "silver hair," as they call it. People are always commenting about it, wondering if I made it this color and wanting to touch it.

Most of the women keep their head covered most of the time, and nearly always it is braided in a series of little French braid rows all over their heads. Most little girls have their hair braided that way, too. Men and boys have their heads shaved, "cleaned" they say. And of course, everyone's hair is black.

There is an iron mine about 50 miles north of here on the Guinea border. It's a Swedish operation, with mostly Scandinavians there. It's a shock to go there and see just blondes, after being with only black people here. It makes me feel like I've been transported to another world. The people there keep very much to themselves, no socializing with Liberians, and live quite a luxurious life. Our life is so different here! Remember your life when your kids were very little, and you can visualize us now, except it doesn't get cold.

Dear Mother, July 18, 1971, Gbedin

This is the week when the school term ends for semester break, which will be a two-week period. Then second term begins and ends around Christmas. Summer vacation begins then and lasts until about March. It's hard for us to remember that it is about summer vacation at home. Many of our PC friends are teachers so they are getting ready for semester break vacations and trips to neighboring countries.

I don't know if I've mentioned the trip we hope to take at the end of the year. While that is quite a while from now, time does go fast. So we're making plans and saving our pennies to take a trip to East Africa. We hope to see as much of Africa as we can in the next two years.

We have finally completed our house repairs, decorating, and acquiring furniture. We have been quite ingenious about furnishings. Used cement blocks covered with mats for stools, cement blocks and a foot board from the bed for a book case, all kinds of woven straw things that people sell in the markets very cheaply, such as wicker chairs, rattan-seated chairs, baskets, big gourds for bowls, the native cotton material for everything from sheets, curtains, and wall hangings, to placemats, napkins, shirts and dresses, and bedspreads.

I'm so thankful for the $25 sewing machine I bought (hand operated). I've made so many things. Have mended Harold's clothes and John's, as well as fairly regularly mend shirts and trousers for some of the school boys. I help some of the women and girls sew dresses for themselves. A school boy might "bock bock" (they say "bock bock" at the door instead of knocking), then sit for an hour and then finally say "Yes, Ma, will you mend this for me, and reduce it in size so it will fit me?" It will be a man's shirt someone has given him. So I mark it with a felt pen, and off he goes. Then I start whacking away at it.

Sometimes, they sit for a long time, and we finally say, "Did you want something?" and then they tell us, or else say, "No. I just came to visit." In the meantime, they haven't said a word, maybe looked at a maga-

zine. Some days we just hope no one will come to our door. This morning (Sunday), one man came with his sick baby, and got us out of bed at
7 AM. Last Sunday, it was 6 AM. Thursday night, it was 2:30 AM. What an
interesting life.

I've hung some of the pictures of the family on a cloth-covered board
in our dining room. Everyone who comes in is fascinated with them. John,
our houseboy, gives everyone a run-down on each person pictured, when
they come in. It's quite amusing to listen.

Dear Mother,   **July 26, 1971, Gbedin**

This is Liberian Independence Day, usually a big day of celebration.
Everybody gets new clothes; there is singing and dancing and visiting and
celebrating. However, Friday, President Tubman died in London, following surgery. So the whole country is in mourning. Consequently, it was a
very slow day here in Gbedin. Many people have gone to Monrovia to view
his body, which is lying in state in the Executive Mansion. Apparently, no
business will be carried on until after his funeral, which will take place on
Thursday. Stores have been closed since his death. We don't know when
they will be open.

People have been visiting us off and on all day "for their 26th," they
say. It's customary to dash them something, so I baked a big batch of biscuits yesterday, and a pineapple upside down cake, with fresh pineapple.
People also have brought us presents. One man, the one who lost his finger, came about 7 AM, and gave me a live chicken. I stood there, visiting
with him, with the chicken in my arms.

I think I've mentioned Beatrice, the Mano girl who is teaching me
Mano. We spend a couple of hours together each morning, learning the
language and teaching each other new things. She shows me how to make
Liberian things, and I show her how to do things like baking and cutting
out clothes for sewing. Today, she dressed her two little girls up in new
clothes, and herself in a new lappa suit she had just sewn (helped me
make myself one, too), and came to have their pictures taken. It's a treat
for them to have their picture made, since seldom does anyone here have
a camera. I promised her pictures if they turn out OK.

A new thing I've learned this week is to make country rope. John
and another school boy took me far out in the bush on Saturday and cut
bamboo palm branches from high in the trees. They went up them in their

bare feet, just like monkeys. We carried the branches home, and they showed me how to strip the raffia out and plait it so it makes a tough fiber, or rope. I'm going to try making some macramé with it. The people here make bags and mats from it.

A new group of volunteers has arrived in country. We learned today that five of them will stay with us for a week. Since President Tubman's death everything has shut down, and remains closed until after his funeral. Consequently, all the activities that had been scheduled for the group had to be cancelled. So they are bringing them up-country—50 of them, all teachers. We're glad to have them, although five is quite a bunch for us at one time. We are reimbursed for the food, so that is no problem. Actually, we kind of enjoy the variety, and it's nice to return the hospitality that was shown to us when we first came. It also makes a good break in this little village. Also, there are always school boys who want to work, so it's easy to get extra help for a reasonable amount.

The weather is really nice now. It usually showers—or pours—at least once a day, around 4 PM, and not for too long a period at a time. Then it may rain some at night, but the days are much cooler, and the nights comfortable for sleeping. Getting clothes dry is somewhat of a problem, because even if it isn't raining the air is so damp. Unless the sun comes out, clothes just won't dry. Last week, I hung things out and took them in five times in three days, trying to get them dry.

We've found the afternoon showers to be welcome and refreshing. Since my hair is so short, and I don't have a perm any more, I don't even mind if I get wet. My clothes soon get dry and so does my hair. I usually wear rubber thongs so there is no problem with wet feet. It's a nice, casual life, and it seems to agree with us.

It's hard to realize that employment is so bad at home. All that seems very far away to us, now. In fact, the thought of coming back to the hectic life again, is not the least appealing. We have such a nice, casual way of life here, that we will be spoiled.

This week, we have been quite creative, actually, out of necessity. Harold sawed two salt-pork barrels in half. He had bought them for 75 cents each in Monrovia last week. I made cushions from a $1 lappa, stuffed it with 15-cents-worth of country straw, and we ended up with two nice stools and a coffee table for our porch, also, a rice storage container, as well, plus I made two other cushions for our living room chairs. Now, with the rope hammock a friend gave us, our porch is nicely furnished. It's such a neat place to sit and visit, and at a cost of $2.65!

You would hardly recognize Harold. He hasn't had a haircut since the first of May except for some trimming I've done. He looks like he has a lot of hair now; it's curling on the ends around his ears. And mine is shorter than ever. It looks better than it ever has, according to Harold. And when it rains, *neh my, ya* (never mind, yah). It dries and looks just fine.

Dear Richard, David, and Lois [Ruth's siblings],   August 4, 1971, Gbedin

You know, birthdays are something unique for people here. Seldom do people know their age, let alone, the month or day. If anyone in the family knows a child's age, it is the father. Some of them now keep track of their young children's birth dates, "born day," they call it. When I ask a woman her baby's age, she says, "I will ask its Pa." We just asked a young boy we are helping to go to school what his age is. He smiled and said, "One man came to live in their village in 1952, and he tells me I was just born then. So I think I was born in 1952." Sometimes, when I give medicine to babies, the dosage is according to age, so I check their teeth, under six months, close to a year, or a year and a half, etc., and decide according to their dentition. Something like determining the age of a horse, isn't it?

The rainy season, winter season, is here now. Actually, it only rains for part of a day at a time—most likely in late afternoon. But sometimes, it rains all night. The temperature is definitely cooler now. Yesterday, it was 68 in the house, which was a bit too cool. We have only screens on our windows, and when there is a breeze, which is frequently, it really blows in. I had to finally hunt up a sweater I had stored away and expect to use it a lot now. Harold thinks the temperature is just about right. When the sun comes up, it is soon in the 80s.

We have both gotten quite tan, me more than Harold, since I walk about in the villages so much during the day. We never seem to sunburn, which surprised me, being so close to the equator. Some of the school boys here, 14 and 15 year-olds, believe that American Negroes turn white when they live in the North, where it is cold, and when they wear over-coats. I don't think we convinced them that it isn't true.

The contrasts between young boys here and American boys of a similar age are fascinating. I think I wrote some time ago that here kids start school late, and then have three years of pre-elementary school before starting first grade. This is for the majority of the kids, who don't know English. And even by the time they start first grade, their English is still limited. Anyway, by the time a kid is in the fourth, fifth, or sixth grade, he is at least 13, more likely 15, as is John, our houseboy. They have had no exposure to anything *kwi* (civilized), and are so unfamiliar with things we think are routine.

For instance, John came home with homework for math that had to do with square and cubic measurements. In helping him, I found his concept of feet and inches was nil. He couldn't say how many inches were in a foot. In fact, he couldn't say how many eggs were in a dozen. But put him in his own environment, and he's very knowledgeable. I walked last week in the bush with him and another school boy to find the palm tree from which raffia is made. It was about a four-hour hike, and they showed me so many things and told me about so many things that an unfamiliar person would take a long time to learn.

Another real problem here is that so many adults don't want their kids to "know book," that is, to get an education. They want him to stay home and be a country man, and help them on the farm. Consequently, a great number of kids have to earn all their own way, beginning in their early years, if they really want to go to school. If John were not able to live with us here and earn a little bit, he wouldn't be in school this term. And actual costs for elementary school are really only about $1.50 a term for registration and supplies, plus their clothes and food. There are many, many boys and a few girls living here with relatives or friends so they can attend school. So many little villages in the bush have no schools at all. High school costs are considerably higher.

One young fellow, the first one I mentioned, is the son of a village quarter chief, in a nearby town. The family lives in the chief's quarter, which is a kind of compound with a few houses clustered around it. There are 35 men and boys in the family. (They don't count the females.) He told me that he and his brother and one cousin are the only ones who are getting educated, and that the family gives no help toward their education, even though they are able to.

The family, instead, urges the boys to stay home and work on the farm. This young man, David, is now a junior inhigh school. He is about 20, a really bright kid. In order to go to high school, he has to live in another town, earn money for his fees and uniforms, books, etc. Jobs are scarce, and the pay so low. For instance, some of the men here earn only 33 cents day. At any rate, we decided to help him get through the next two years of high school. It seems like such a waste for kids like this to be unable to get an education. And we've concluded that until more people are educated here, the lot of the ordinary Liberian will continue to be very hard.

Things are going fairly well for us. Living here isn't that different in many respects. We're so used to being the only white people here, that we don't feel all that different. The terrain is so similar to home, and until we look at the details it's kind of easy to forget that we are living in Africa. And it's rather nice having so few belongings to take care of, plus most of them the kind we'll leave with people here when we do come home.

Harold keeps busy all the time, both on the job and off. There is always something for him to do, either repair or improve our house. Or, there is someone who needs him to help fix something. He's had the best time with bamboo, which is so plentiful. They call it cane. Harold has used it to make towel racks, benches, napkin rings, ashtrays, candle holders, room dividers, and picture frames, after going into the bush to gather it, of course.

We are always looking for things that people here can make and sell to earn a little money. We have started a couple of school boys making rings from palm nuts, to sell to PC visitors. They make a shiny, dark brown ring and don't take a lot of work to make. So many of the people here are so used to just eking out a bare living, making a country farm, growing upland rice and cassava, and having so little. At the same time, most don't seem interested in learning anything different. The younger people though, have a different attitude, and they are the ones, I expect, we will be working with more.

Dear Mother,   **August 8, 1971, Gbedin**

We don't have any electricity now, due to a broken generator, so it means kerosene lamps quite early. Actually, it isn't too bad, since the only electric appliance we have is an iron, and I can manage without that for a while. At home, I didn't ever think I could get along without a vacuum cleaner, electric coffee pot, and washing machine, etc. And now, I don't even miss them, most of the time, that is. Most of the people here have never heard of such things. You can't describe them so they would even understand what you're talking about.

We have been hearing on our radio (battery), about Nixon's recent announcement about opening trade with Red China, and about getting them in the UN, also, about the different reactions of people in the US. We would be interested in hearing such comments. Our Taiwanese friends here feel it would be a great mistake. They say "Big China," as they call it, will only make trouble for the UN, and that Taiwan will likely pull out of the UN if Red China comes in. They don't hear Radio Taiwan, and their newspapers are always months late.

Incidentally, we haven't received any magazines yet. However, mail has been very irregular and undependable, so much so that some of the volunteers made an official request to PC headquarters to look into the problem of missing mail.

After the President died, the official PO was closed for nearly a week, and no mail moved in the country. In fact, nearly all businesses shut down until after the funeral. At first, the notice came out that no stores could open until after the funeral, which was on Thursday, and Tubman died the previous Friday. However, someone finally realized that people wouldn't eat if they couldn't buy food, so they finally let stores open Monday forenoon, and then close again on Thursday.

We have had quite a few guests in the past week or two. They were four new volunteers who came for a "live-in," such as we had when we first came, and the parents of one of the older volunteers. They were visiting from Kansas, and having a great time visiting the country—real home folks, who we really enjoyed having. Everyone expects to put up people all the time. Some people bring their sheets and towels, which is a big help. I finally got extra sheets, so we can make up two more beds. We enjoy the company, anyway, and expect to be staying with people when we take trips.

We plan to take a trip to Foya soon. This is a town in the NW part of Liberia, on the Sierra Leone border. There are big cloth markets just across the border in SL, where I want to get some material to send home. They have a large variety of beautiful hand-done tie dye and wax print cottons, which I think the "girls" in the family would enjoy, you too. They are much less expensive there, and if we have a ride it will make it worth it to go.

It's a long way from here—close to 200 miles, which on Liberian roads, during rainy season, really takes a long time. Sometimes it can take two days, depending upon the roads and the durability of the car. It's almost like going to Eastern Washington from Tacoma in the old Fords, I guess.

Dear Judith,   **August 22, 1971, Gbedin**

Another day gone by, so fast, it seems. We've had a busy, busy time, but not the hectic rush like we always had at home. It's just that there are so many things going on and so much to do. Actually, some days are trying.

I spend six or seven hours at the clinic every day. I'm trying to get a patient registration system going. Then before and after, and often into the evening, people are here for some kind of request. Perhaps a child who needs its eyes washed out, and treated with medicine, a baby with a skin infection, or all kinds of bodily complaints, plus wounds and sores of all kinds. I've even seen two syphilis chancres (male patients), something I had never seen before. Sometimes, I feel like closing the curtains and locking the doors. Sometimes too, I can persuade the people to go to the hospital to be seen by a Dr.

Yesterday was Harold's birthday [*56th*]. I baked three cakes, and invited some of his colleagues and some friends. It was a nice day, and in the evening, several were here for dinner. Even though we were far away from family, it was a good day. One of the girls baked him a cherry pie, which we put candles on.

John, our houseboy, doesn't know the month he was born, only the year. So we told him he could choose his own birthday, and we would make him a birthday cake. So between him and Harold, they decided he could have Grandpa Jacobson's birthday, September 9, and we will have a modest birthday celebration for him.

Joseph Blatchford, head of US Peace Corps, will be in Liberia at the end of the month and will make a trip to Sanniquellie, so we will plan to go there and meet him. Today, Dale Gilles, the Washington, DC, Liberian Desk Officer who signed us up, came by and had lunch with us. It was fun to see him again over here.

The other night we had an exciting time. Around dinner time we discovered a rat behind our refrigerator—saw his tail sticking out, if you can imagine. I was petrified, and started to leave, but before long, I was armed with a cutlass, as were Harold and John, and helped to catch it. The kitten just wanted to play with it, just romped after it, so we had to catch it for her. Now Harold is checking to see where it might have come in, so he can plug any holes. It's a constant battle against pests—cockroaches, mice, etc., and of course, always mosquitoes.

Dearest Mother,   **August 29, 1971, Monrovia**

We are in Monrovia again for a few days. Our life has been horribly torn up this past week. One of our PC friends at Gbedin, Marcia, was murdered with a cutlass, in her bed, Tuesday night. Harold and I found her the next day. We had to take care of her and all the other details for the next 24 hours.

It was the most gruesome experience we have ever had. To make it really bad, the two suspects are men very close to us, John Chambers, the British engineer, and Robert Toe, a Liberian tractor driver, whose wife, Lucy, works for me and is in our house a lot. (She is the lady I told you about, who says hello to your picture whenever she comes in to work.) Robert finally confessed yesterday.

We came to Monrovia day before yesterday for a memorial service for Marcia and expected to go right back to Gbedin. However, the secretary of Agriculture has called a meeting of Ag volunteers and especially wants Gbedin volunteers to be there, tomorrow morning. They also feel at both the DA and PC that we shouldn't go back until things settle down. The PC director told us yesterday that they don't know how they would have managed during the tragedy without someone like us to keep things calm, and get the necessary things done. However, it was very hard for us. We are still feeling the after effects—just numb.

We are staying with the Weirs, the couple from Seattle, who came to Liberia with us. They're lonesome here and always glad to have us. Today we went to church. Their apartment is about six blocks from the only Lutheran church in Monrovia. It's nice to attend a familiar service. We do miss church.

One thing we wanted to say about this tragedy is that you shouldn't be concerned that we are in danger. This is the first time a white person has been killed by a Liberian. This man was mentally deranged, I'm sure. He gave me the creeps, but you could find such a person in the US, much more than you'd find here.

I've never been frightened here. I often go out at night with some man whose wife or child is sick. Our house boy, John, and Bea, my Mano friend, always tell me I shouldn't go out at night, and certainly shouldn't answer the door at night. I just laugh and say nothing will happen to me. Now, I have changed and will be very careful. We will also rogue-proof our bedroom windows.

The whole country is just sick over what happened to Marcia and say this just doesn't happen in Liberia. Hopefully, things will settle down soon, and we can go home. I still have to help one of the PC staff go through all of Marcia's things and get them packed to send home. We were so concerned that the newspapers at home would have had something in them about this, and you would have been worried.

Our weather has definitely changed. It's hard to remember that it is summer at home when it is rainy and cloudy here. I've been wearing my pant-suit quite a lot to keep warm. The weather in Monrovia is warmer than up-country.

I'm still sewing a bit, helping school kids with their sewing. I am making shirts for Harold and John. My sewing machine is worth its weight in gold.

Much of my patient work continues to be done at my house or in the village when I visit. You should see the steaming set-up I've worked out for babies with bronchitis—heating water in a pot over a fire, etc.

Dear Mother,   **September 5, 1971, Gbedin**

Please note the date—our 30th wedding anniversary. It is a bit unusual to spend it in Africa, isn't it?
Our plans for a big time in Monrovia were abruptly changed with Marcia's death. We didn't have the heart for anything after that. Mary and Larry invited us over last night for pizza and beer, and we had a pleasant time with them. Later, we walked home in the moonlight. Earlier in the day, Mary had come over to make pumpkin pie with me. She wanted to learn how to do it. We had a country pumpkin. Actually, it looks like a long, pale green squash and is delicious. It made a good pie.

We're still recovering from the horrible experience of last week. We still have to sort and pack all of her things, so until all of that is done, it will be hard to get it out of our minds. Everyone is so tense here yet, even though the guilty person is in jail. As soon as it gets dark, people stay in their houses. The project director made everyone move from the barracks that are near us. That is where the murderer lived. So now, only the four Chinese men and we are living in this area. Oh yes, three school teachers are still here. Consequently, where before we saw people walking by our house all the time, now there are very few. I'm sure the next couple of weeks we will see more changes, and perhaps things will relax a bit and get back to normal.

It's interesting to see how the Liberians react to something like this. Most of the country people believe the US will retaliate in some way, like a war. When Mr. Blatchford was flown to Sanniquellie on Tuesday, they circled Gbedin to show him the rice project. Many people here thought they were US planes coming to bomb them, and they ran out in the bush. They also have strong feelings about what should be done to the murderer. Hardly a person I've talked to thinks they should have a trial, since he's already confessed. They all think he should be killed, but not quickly. He should be made to suffer, like he made Marcia suffer, such as burying him alive, or cutting off both hands with a cutlass, or burning him. We realize that these people are not long from a tribal society, in which a wrong-doer was dealt with quickly and strongly by village "big men."

Our garden is coming along nicely and is really a treat. We now have some lovely parsley and some cucumbers. We will have zucchini in about a month, I think, and also our cabbage is close to being ready. We also will have sweet potato greens soon. These are the leaves of a kind of sweet potato, very good and a mainstay of our diet. So far we've never eaten the potato, just the leaves. They are kind of like spinach or chard when cooked. We put meat or fish and onions with them (and hot pepper), and eat them with our rice.

One of Harold's chickens has finally begun to set again. This time, he's made a separate place for her to set, so perhaps he won't lose her babies again. These chickens lay very small eggs. They look like a Banty egg and are a pale brown.

Other than this business we've had to go through, our life is just fine. Harold is very busy and enjoys what he is doing. Some of the PC kids call him "Mr. Wizard." He has a reputation for being able to do anything. The big people in the Dept. of Agriculture are very impressed because he's gotten machinery working that has been down for more than a year. We are hoping that since he is here now, they will support the place better, as far as supplying parts, etc., for keeping the machines going.

It's Monday morning now. Last night we had the worst rainstorm since we've been here. Our living room ceiling leaked so much we had to mop the floor this morning. The water supply (pipes) must be flooded; at least, there is no water coming out. Our electricity is out; all the fields are a sea of mud. I'm just about to start for the clinic, quite an undertaking when it has rained so much. Fortunately, when the sun comes out, things dry off pretty fast.

Dear Mother,   **September 12, 1971, Gbedin**

We've spent another busy weekend, from early in the morning until late, with few dull moments. Today, we celebrated our African son's first birthday. Even though he is 15, this is his first actual birthday he's ever had—a date we picked out, September 9th— but that was too hectic a day to do anything about birthdays. We decided Sunday was a better day for visitors.

Today, I baked two cakes, and put candles on one. Actually, they were the kind we use at Christmas, with little angel chimes on them, since birthdays are unknown up-country. We told John to invite some friends. He borrowed a record player and some records, and they all danced and had cake and cokes. We gave him a new pair of tennis shoes—his were threadbare—and one of the shirts Harold had brought from home that John really coveted, and one of Harold's cowboy string-type leather ties. Your birthday card arrived yesterday, and was he ever pleased and surprised. I think it was the first time he ever received a letter in the mail.

The two Chinese men, Mr. Chiang and Mr. Chang, just left after eating the last two pieces of birthday cake. In between the party, getting dinner, getting up this morning, I had several people in for medicine, etc. One lady with a cutlass wound, a child with infected eyes, a couple of kids with fevers, and some others with tummy aches and so on.

Some days are particularly wearing because people come at all hours. I will have to establish some hours that people can come, unless it's a real emergency and of course, most people think theirs is a special situation. Sometimes they are quite sick. One man in Monrovia who owns a drug supply house gave me a bunch of medicine samples and, also, a big bag of balloons, which I've been giving to little kids when they get medicine. Now I think they find all kinds of things wrong so they can come get a balloon.

This week was really difficult. We have all been under such a strain since Marcia's death. We had to finally go into her house and sort and pack all of her things. Mary, Larry, Harold and I, and Daniel Goe, the PC field officer, spent all Thursday in the process. Then we had to sort and price all her household things and furniture and such and start to sell them.

Mary had suggested that we sell all the things her parents didn't want sent home and create a scholarship in her name for sixth graders who will go on to seventh grade next year. They will have to leave here and go to school in Sanniquellie and will have to pay for fees, uniforms and books. Daniel was relieved to have things taken care of like this, because he had no idea what to do with them. Yesterday, we finally finished pricing things and tomorrow will have a sale in her house. Just going into her house is awful.

Harold and Ruth celebrating their 30th anniversary.

Having to make decisions on what to do with this and that, and then running across something we knew meant a lot to her or something that reminded us of some episode with her was hard to take. For instance, she had a big Pan Am calendar on her bedroom wall. I took it off the wall and then noticed she had July 26 marked in red, with Flag Day written in (a National holiday here). That was the night she was killed.

Then on top of that, her house was rogued on Friday night. Someone went through a window screen and took some of the canned goods and perhaps some of the small things. What an eerie feeling. I really get the creeps when I go there and will be so glad when we finish tomorrow. One of the bad things for us is that her house is just down the hill from ours— like across a city street. Whenever we go on our porch, there it is, with all its reminders. I suppose in a few weeks it will be different, but for now, it's not too much fun.

The murderer is being held in Sanniquellie at the soldier's compound. Prisoners here are beaten routinely as a matter of punishment, and people just expect it. For example, prisoners are beaten on market day at the public market, so everyone can watch. The difference with a criminal such as Robert Toe is that he is beaten at the soldier's compound, but it is still public, each Saturday, until the trial, supposedly in October. He is stretched out on the ground and tied and then two soldiers beat him with heavy whips, at least 25 lashes, but usually many more, since they give two or three for each count.

I was so sickened when I was told about it that I almost burst into tears, but Liberians, even civilized ones, say, "Of course, he has to be beaten. He must be made to suffer like he made Marcia suffer." We certainly realize we're in a foreign country when we experience something like this, even though it's hard to understand.

Families have to feed the prisoners or they don't get food. Lucy, Robert's wife, took him some rice, and when she got back to Gbedin, everyone was angry with her for feeding a murderer. The project manager (a Liberian) told her to pack her things and get her children (all small ones), and he took her immediately to Ganta. He said anyone who feels sorry for Toe isn't wanted in Gbedin. Most of the people felt he had done right.

While he is in jail, Robert is kept immobilized by having one foot hobbled in a heavy piece of log, with an iron bar through it to keep his foot from pulling out. One educated woman told me and said, "Oh, you haven't seen our country way of punishment?" and felt they were doing the right thing to keep him from escaping.

Some of these things will give you an idea of the emotional state we've been in lately—since July 27. We are really nervous about what could happen next, although we know we are safer now than when Robert was walking around before.

However, there has been so much rogueing all around, so we know it's just a matter of time before we get hit. Harold is going to put rogue bars on the windows in our bedroom and kitchen, the most vulnerable ones. They are standard on most houses in Monrovia, but we never thought we would need them here. I hate bars or iron mesh on windows, but lately I'm afraid if we don't, someone will break in. John stays in our house whenever we're away after dark, but he's such a sound sleeper I'm not sure he would hear anyone. People tell us that if someone is in the house, rogues seldom come in. In fact, I'm sure if Marcia had had her house boy sleep in, Robert wouldn't have come in.

I may have mentioned before that one of the problems in Gbedin is that it is what is called a transitional town and, consequently, is caught between civilized and tribal ways. Many tribes are represented here, instead of a one-tribe village, where there is much control by the village or town "big people" in the bush society. There is much animosity between tribes, very little trust of each other, and often of people of their own tribe.

There is no sense of community here, and while there is a chief, he's very weak and is responsible only for the farmers who live in one of the "camps" and not the project support staff, who live in another "camp." These are the mechanics, etc., with whom Harold works. He knows them the best, although he is getting acquainted with the farmers.

I spend a lot of time in the farmers' community, and in their homes, and know many of the wives and kids. I also visit a lot with the families of the mechanics. Some of them speak fairly good English, so it's easier to communicate with them. I'm fortunate that Bea fits in well in both places. Her mother is a farmer, and her husband works in the office. The people know her and like her, so most doors are open to me as well.

No one knows what will happen here now. With a new presidential administration, there could be drastic changes—either lots more support or practically none. One of the Liberian PC officers told us this week that the Dept. of Agriculture would ask Harold to take charge here when John, the present engineer, leaves in February. They want Harold to stay on when his PC stint is ended and sign a contract with the government. They're very impressed with what he has accomplished so far and are particularly dissatisfied with Chambers, who is mostly talk and little else, as well as terribly hard to get along with.

We will probably move into his house at any rate. It is larger, and we have so many visitors, we are often jammed for room to put them up. Also, it is safer, since it has glass jalousie windows, is higher off the ground, and is situated by other houses, which our present house is not. Hopefully, we will also get his truck, which would be a real boon, since traveling is such a hassle. Harold isn't at all interested in a contract with the government, too many problems with the government. As a PCV, it's a much better relationship.

As I look this over, I realize it is mostly negative—probably a reflection of the current state of affairs and will pass. We certainly aren't discouraged about Liberia. It's just too close to the tragedy to throw it off immediately. One of these days I'll tell you about my work at the clinic. I always fill up the pages before I'm through with everything.

Last evening, we went to the Pearmines'. Another young couple from Sanniquellie, who are in their third year here, were there too. We had popcorn and beer and a lively discussion about the status of women, about who *is* God, and several controversial topics. It was good for all of us. We really enjoy the young people, and they seem to enjoy us. Did I tell you we have begun to learn to play bridge? Later, we'll teach Larry how to play Pinochle.

The generator broke down about two weeks ago, so not only are we back to kerosene lamps, but also to cold showers and ironing with a charcoal iron. School girls do this for me in return for my helping them pay for their uniforms and school fees.

Dear Vikki,   **September 18, 1971, Gbedin**

I'm sitting in a little palm-thatched hut at the edge of a rice paddy, while Harold works on a rice thresher for one of the farmers. These little low, open huts are called kitchens. Chickens wander in and out, and several small children play and stand around, watch me and laugh. They're just toddlers, and maybe nine or ten years, in various stages of dress or rather undress. Some are naked. One little girl wears just panties, another just a little vest, most are in tattered shirt and shorts. But they all seem happy and laughing, and most of them have a job to do.

From the time kids start school, they are expected to take care of their clothes—wash them, press them. Most of the kids, until eight or so, don't speak English, but I'm "hearing" Mano more and more, and they can understand my Mano more and more. Some of the ladies are so pleased when I answer them or ask them something in their language. They put their arms around me and say, "Oh, Mah," and laugh and shake my hand. It really makes the effort seem worthwhile.

Monday the 20th. I didn't get very far with this letter. Harold finished his job, and showed the farmer how to run the thresher—he had installed a motor in it, where ordinarily the threshers are turned by hand. It was more than a two-mile walk to the farms; we really had a long walk. Actually, I walk that much most days, going to the villages, visiting and taking medicine. We are both thriving on it, though.

The weather has begun to turn warm. I didn't think rainy season was bad at all. In fact, we'd like it to last a bit longer, before the weather turns hot. Our garden has already begun to produce. We have lovely cucumbers, and the cabbage will be ready in a week. Zucchini and eggplant will be ready within a week. It's such a treat to have fresh vegetables, especially those you know are safe to eat. Generally, vegetables get wormy so soon, so Harold got some lime to dust them with. So far our cucumbers have no worms. I plan to make some dill pickles—found some dill seed in Monrovia.

Harold met with Department of Agriculture people today. They told him he would soon have a vehicle because of all the running around he has to do on the project. This is welcome news, since we can use it to go to Ganta or Sanniquellie to the markets.

Dear Vikki,   **September 21, 1971, Monrovia**

We are back in the "big city," getting some business taken care of. Harold has had tonsillitis, and I think some rheumatic pains, so he wanted to see the doctor and also needed to see some Dept. of Ag. people. I needed to see some people in Public Health about my work. So since we found a ride from Gbedin, we threw our things together Sunday and took off on about 15 minutes notice. Anything to avoid a taxi ride. We're staying with the Weirs again. They came to Gbedin Friday and stayed with us. This is the first time they have been up-country.

They are such strange people, close to 60, childless. He is very dissatisfied here, doesn't like the people, or the food, or the climate, or his job, and is counting the days until he gets home. She isn't very enthusiastic about things, but isn't unhappy. I asked her last eve how they happened to come into PC. Incidentally, he doesn't really like young people, thinks all the PC kids here are hippies. She said they didn't want to work for wages any more and weren't quite ready to retire, and this was just to fill time. They like to have us come and visit them—say we are about the only ones they can talk to; that really depresses me. We like living here, like the people, the food, and the new things we see and do, and also, enjoy the

PC kids. I keep thinking we will hear that they have gone home, but she says he won't go back on his word and that he wants to stay long enough to get a vacation!

I was finally successful today in seeing the head of the Liberian Public Health Department, who told me the Dept, would support the well-child clinic I've been trying to get started in Gbedin. Up until now, I've been so frustrated because the person in the PC office here, who is in charge of the health program, refused to consider me as a health volunteer in her program. She is very insecure, I'm sure, an RN from the US, and was miffed, I think, that someone else brought me here and didn't clue her in.

After trying every way in the right channels, and being nice about it, I went to the PC country director, associate director, and finally to Dale Gilles, the Liberian desk officer in Washington, DC, and told them I was ready to go to Blatchford when he comes in country. My approach was that they had been dishonest with me, in that they had recruited mature people with hard-to-find skills, and then assigned Harold to an area and ignored me.

They finally started to give me some attention and advised me to go directly to the top in PHS, which I did. He immediately called the Liberian PHS person responsible for these clinics for a meeting this morning, with me. He really pinned her down as to the next steps to be done, so I'm hopeful. We will meet again on Thursday to work out details. There may be some antagonism from the PC staff person, who gave me the run-around, but I'm sure I can handle that.

Next day. Last evening we went to a movie, *The Sicilian Clan,* the first real movie since we've been here. It was kind of enjoyable after so long and in a nice theater. While we were in Sanniquellie, we went to an awful spaghetti western in a Lebanese store building, with benches for seats. The people love them, yell and scream when the fighting and shooting start. Harold liked it, but oh my. I went home at intermission. Sometimes, they show them at Harry Bar, the local pub in Gbedin. Everyone sits on the floor, and the sound is turned up loud, quite exciting for Gbedin since it's the only entertainment except for what people make for themselves.

Dear Mother,   **September 26, 1971, Gbedin**

Another week gone by. Every week brings something new. Our friends, the Weirs, the couple from Seattle that I told you about before, are very bored, and don't like much of anything here. We can't understand it, because we are finding nearly everything, if not really enjoyable, at least interesting. Some things, like finding a rat in the kitchen, and having to chase it with a cutlass, I'd just as soon do without. However, I learned I can cope with something like that and not run screaming from the house, which is what I wanted to do!

You'll be pleased to learn that I've finally been successful in getting PC staff here and the Liberian Public Health Service to give me the necessary support for a well-baby clinic here in Gbedin. I spent most of the week in Monrovia "talking it." I have to spend all of this week and part of next week in Monrovia, getting "oriented" to the way clinics are run. It will be the first time Harold and I have been away from each other since we arrived here. I'm sure he will manage OK with John here.

Yesterday, I gave Harold a haircut, his first in over three months, so you can imagine what he looked like. I did such a bad job, that Mr. Chiang came over with his hair cutting equipment—he cuts all the Chinese guys' hair in typical Chinese style—and finished the job. Harold says it's like you'd put a bowl on your head, but I think it's better than before we started. I finally resorted to a professional hair cut last month, so my hair doesn't look too bad. Harold can touch it up now and then. We're still losing a little weight, but think its fine for a while. Harold is down to 178, over 20 lbs. loss, and I'm under 120. We'll be back to our early marriage weight, before too long. We both feel fine.

You asked why Robert Toe killed Marcia. He was a weird man, seemed to have a persecution complex and a lot of repressed hatred for many people. She was raped too, so we think there was a sex motive, as well. He never made a statement as to why, to our knowledge. His wife came to see us yesterday, with the little girl, and looks much better than before and seems happy, now. She is living with her mother and some other relatives in another part of the country, several hours away from here. I think she will be all right. I'm very fond of her and her kids, and she feels Harold and I are very special.

September 30. I didn't get this mailed so carried it down to Monrovia on Sunday, and have been busy ever since. I've been staying with Norton Berman and his wife Susan. He's deputy director of PC, in line to be country director in a few months. We met him in Philadelphia. He is Jewish, a lawyer, around 40. Susan, his second wife, is 26, a former English teacher, not Jewish. They visited us up-country a couple of times and seemed pleased that I could stay with them. They have a beautiful, big house on the beach, and have lots of hot water, what a luxury! They live far out of the city, so I have to walk a mile before I can get a taxi, two to get the bus. But actually, I'm so used to walking, it's no problem.

Tomorrow, I'll try to get a taxi around noon, when we will be through for the week, and head back to Gbedin, hopefully by 6 PM. Have to come back for two days next week. Taxi fare from here to Gbedin is $4.25. It usually figures out to be $1.00 an hour. Roads are bad now, so it takes longer, and of course, it's always an experience to get a taxi for the price and the time you want it. We went to see *Mash* Tuesday eve. Bermans are movie fans and see everything. Will go out to dinner this eve and then to another movie. Harold saw one last week too—three movies in two weeks is something I haven't done in years.

The political situation here is really interesting. Tolbert, the new President, will be inaugurated in January. It sounds like between now and then he is going to institute reforms that will put him in solid with the people. For instance, he's been sacking top cabinet people for inefficiency and for "money-eating." Yesterday, two top security people who have eaten $85,000 plus this year (each) were told they would be prosecuted if they didn't pay the money back immediately. The newspaper is very interesting lately.

Dearest Mother,   **October 6, 1971, Gbedin**

I'm sitting in a restaurant in Monrovia where you can get an American-style hamburger, which tastes good once in a while. I'm leaving in an hour or two for Gbedin, after spending two days winding up the details for the well-baby and ante-natal clinic. It's really been tough going, getting people to do something they hadn't planned on doing.
I will be giving immunizations and limited medications and tests to pregnant woman, "belly women," as they are called. They say, "She got belly," when a woman is pregnant. At the clinic, we will do a lot of health education, also at the homes, as to foods they should eat to have a healthy baby, etc. I will have to find a midwife to work with me, as well as try to retrain the health workers, remodel the building or get another one, keep on learning Mano, visit people in their homes. So many things, but a real challenge.

I'm also working on a project with the associate PC director. He has a group of health people assigned to JFK Hospital—doctors, nurses, X-ray techs, etc., all PCVs. He's appointed me project evaluator for the group. I'll work with them on an intermittent basis for the next two years and try to determine how effective this program is. It will be a nice contrast to Gbedin and give us a reason to come to the city once in a while.

Citrus fruit season is starting. Oranges, grapefruit, and tangerines are really delicious here, although they are very full of seeds. Our garden is producing well now, so we have a fair variety of vegetables.

So far, things have settled down in Gbedin. A dependable night watchman has been hired. He makes rounds at night, and really watches our house. Harold has made our most vulnerable windows secure, and John

Ruth demonstrating how to give a medicine to a clinic mother.

stays in our house if we are away. So we are really safe enough. It's quite hard to keep on being so careful, because we feel so much at home here, actually safer than in the streets at home.

When I came back home Friday from a week in Monrovia, people came to the house and said, "Thank God you are back. Thank God for coming back. You have to stay here a long time," and so on.

Dear Mother,   **October 15, 1971, Gbedin**

It is seven months today, since we left the US. How fast the time has gone by. Even though we never seem to be rushed, we are always busy and the weeks go by before we know it.

Rainy season is "coming to finish," as they say here, and the weather is warmer. We are still having rain showers every day or so, but usually not for too long a period. Actually, they are very welcome, because they cool things off nicely. Hopefully, we will be more used to the weather this year, so shouldn't notice the humidity quite so much.

I've been off-schedule for the past two weeks while I was in Monrovia becoming oriented to the well-baby/maternal health program. After spending nearly two weeks there, they sent me home with enough supplies to get me started. In the meantime, we made a request for Marcia's house for a clinic building, and the Dept. of Agriculture came through with that yesterday. The present clinic building is very unsatisfactory. Also, no one knew what they could do with Marcia's house, since none of us could imagine anyone living in it. It is a long trailer that belonged to an American construction company. It has a good-sized house built along one side of it. We will use the house part.

Right now, Bea and I are walking about the town, taking a census of kids under five. Wednesday evening, we met at the chief's house with a lot of the people to tell them about our plans, and why they should come to the clinic. It is going to be interesting to see how things will work out. Part of the work I'm supposed to do is health education. Each day you hold a clinic you are to teach something, everything very basic, about keeping clean to avoid sickness, eating right, and so on. Changing people's living habits is a long-time effort any time, and here, where habits of generations are ingrained, it will be harder. I'm making posters, flip charts, and such teaching aids. It's a real challenge to try to tell a story without the printed word. The people can't read so everything has to be pictures that they can understand.

Lately, people have been swamping me with produce. I tell them that the medicine I give them or things I do for their children are not for money. But they say, "It not for pay, you have good way and I want to give you something from the country." They've brought me, in the past week or two, dozens of grapefruit and oranges, bitter ball, pumpkin, tangerines, plantain, pawpaw, eggplant, and bananas. Probably, in terms of dollars, it isn't more than $2 worth; they get it from the bush or from their farms. We use a lot of these things, so they are quite welcome. We would ordinarily get them from the market, so it's nice they are available here.

We now have a car, or rather, Jeep (a Toyota Land Cruiser). Harold is still working on it to get all the bugs worked out. It has been sitting here for about five years because some small thing was wrong. The assistant secretary in the Dept. of Ag., who is responsible for this project, is very impressed with Harold's work here and decided he needed transportation around the project. He told Harold to fix up the Jeep, and he would send him what he needed to get it in running order.

While it's been kind of nice not to have to worry about keeping up a car, it has also been a nuisance with travel such a hassle up here. They will furnish our gas, too, and while it is theoretically for government business, we can use it for our own convenience. I haven't driven a car since we left home, so it will be strange to drive again.

The President is expected to come up as far as Sanniquellie before the month is over, so we expect him to stop here, too. Consequently, the roads are in fairly good shape, in anticipation of his visit.

We have another guest this week, a farmer from San Joaquin Valley in California. He's about 40. His wife and two small daughters have just arrived as Peace Corps volunteers.

When you send us a letter in a plain envelope, perhaps you could tape a few buttons on the paper and send them along. Buttons are hard to come by here. I'm meaning the kind you would put on a man's shirt or jeans. Another thing I could really use is any kind of scraps you might have of trim for dresses. Bias tape, rick-rack, or bits of lace would come in handy for some of the women who are doing children's clothes. Don't buy any— just send bits and pieces, and don't send by airmail, it's too expensive.

We finally have some baby chickens. One of our hens hatched about 11, and Harold fixed her a pen that nothing can get into—a big wooden machinery box. They are doing fine. Now, he has one other hen setting, too, so it looks like we might have chickens to eat, eventually. The garden has been producing, too—many cucumbers, some cabbage, one corn stalk, parsley, sweet potatoes, which we use for greens now, and eventually we will be able to have potatoes from them. Also, eggplant is beginning to bear, also hot peppers. Our zucchini didn't make it. It must have been too wet, so Harold replanted it last week.

Another new PC boy dropped in on us. He will be stationed here, working on a low-cost housing project with the UN. He's just out of college, a big fellow, about Harold's height but weighs about 240. And has a big red beard. Actually, he looks something like Santa Claus. He says when he comes into a village in the country everyone disappears, and then peeks around a corner. Liberians are small people; in fact Harold is tall compared to most. And they are nearly all of slight build, seldom a fat one. When they see a fat person, they think the person is rich, that they've had plenty to eat. But when someone Harry's size comes along, they think the person is too strong, and might be dangerous. We introduced a Liberian fellow who works for the Chinese guys, to Harry, and later the fellow told us he was afraid to shake hands with him. Pearmines' houseboy, a 16-year-old school boy, said very seriously to Mary, "Teacher, what is wrong with Mr. Harry, he is so fat."

Harry's house isn't ready to be occupied so he will at least have to eat with us for a week or two, while he gets it organized. Kids like this pay for their food and provide their own towels and sheets, so it isn't too bad for the hosts. Everyone's income is the same here, PCs that is, so there's no question of who can afford more!

In my walks about the villages, I'm constantly shocked at the kinds of physical conditions I find. Some people come to the clinic but most never come. But when I come by, people start coming outside, bringing a sick person, or ask me to come into the house, or maybe I just spot someone that no one intended to bring to me. Some of the people are in such bad condition—huge running sores, hernias, swollen extremities, that sometimes I'm almost sick. Telling them they must go to the hospital is quite useless, too, because they won't go, just let the thing go on and on, until the person just dies. It's very hard to accept. Sometime I tell them they must come to the clinic the next day for medicine, but they never come. Many have "country medicine" rubbed on the part—on their faces, their body, etc., wherever the pain is. It looks like chalky mud. I haven't found out what else they put in it besides the mud.

Dear Mother and all,   **October 29, 1971, Gbedin**

It's a surprise to hear you mention fall, with the bright leaves and cool weather. We're just going into dry season, and the weather is hot. This is Liberian summer coming on, and school will soon be out, sometime in December. Mary and I were planning Thanksgiving today. Liberian Thanksgiving is November 5, so we decided to celebrate it as well as US. Turkey is out of the question, and chicken is hard to get, so we finally decided on shish-kebabs, made with wild meat—bush deer—and also goat meat, both of which we will marinate for a while. We'll use chunks of pineapple on the kebabs too. We've just had a young couple with two children stay with us for a week. He came to work with the Kennedy program, but decided not to stay.

I'm finally ready to open the well-child clinic. Since we are getting a new building, it takes a little more work, but slowly, I'm getting there. Perhaps you could send some pictures that I could use to make scrap books for kids, small kids that will be coming to the clinic. Also, some I'll be able to use to make posters for teaching. Also, some of the things I'd like to get hold of are the cutouts that the State Dairy Council used to give us for teaching.

We're at the Bermans' in Monrovia right now. Harold had to come down for a meeting at the PC office, helping to plan a training for another Ag group. They live on the beach in a beautiful home. They are delightful people and make us so welcome. He is deputy director here, and in 1972 will be director. He calls us his favorite volunteers. We will go back home Sunday.

Harold keeps busy with all his projects. He's still working on his car. It runs, but needs lots of new parts, tires, etc. He took it to the village a couple days ago to carry his tools and fix something. He had to come back for something and had the vehicle loaded with small kids—nine of them, some of whom had never been in a car before. One of the big kids had to hold a small one down or he would have jumped out, he was so afraid.

Harold really gets a kick out of the kids. Some of the little ones are afraid of white people, and run and cry when they see us, whenever we walk around the town. Some grab us by the legs and hang on or want to shake our hands.

Citrus season is coming on, and oranges, grapefruit, and tangerines are so plentiful, and so cheap. Oranges are two for 1 cent, grapefruit two or three for 5 cents. Pineapples are so sweet. Our papaya trees are loaded and we also have a guava bush and a passion fruit bush. I haven't tasted the latter, but they will soon be ripe. It's so nice to be surrounded with such nice things.

Some of the people never eat much fruit—feed the papaya to the pigs. One of the things I'm trying to do is to get the mothers to feed fruit to their children every day and help them to understand why. So many of the little kids have such a limited diet. One baby, about three months old, was brought to the clinic this week, sick. I learned that the mother went to the farm and left the baby with a small sister. The baby was fed by a bottle holding plantain and water. Plantain is a banana-like fruit, very starchy. I will make home visits to follow up what they do about getting the baby on milk, hopefully on "titty," as they call it.

Harold and Tommy Hoff, one of his assistants, working in the rice fields.

Dear Mother,   **November 8, 1971, Gbedin**

How the time slips by. I can't believe it's already November. This week, we have a family, a psychiatrist, Dr. Rigamer, and his wife and two small children. They're very enjoyable, and we try to show them life in the country, plus carrying on our usual activities. He's an MD as well, so he's been helping me in the clinic, seeing patients and advising, and going with me to villages to see some. Tomorrow is well-child clinic, so he will be examining children for me. I've really enjoyed having him, and it's been so helpful since there are so many for whom I don't know what to do—like what medicine or treatment to advise. He told me he would try to come back once a month—will be stationed in Monrovia.

Harold is keeping busy. It seems that everyone has to come and see Ol' Pa and get him to help them with something. Peace Corps is bringing in a group of about 20 new volunteers to work in Rural Public Works programs, and they asked Harold to help in the training program—put on training sessions for about three days, on trouble-shooting car care. They will all be driving government trucks, and most don't know how to keep them in good shape, like having the oil checked, etc. One of the Chinese fellows said yesterday, "I think Harold is Peace Corps chief for Nimba County." So many of them stop by and want him to check their cars or do something, or advise them how to do it.

The weather is growing hotter and drier. Rainy season has about ended, and it's really hot in the afternoon in our house. We are told that it will be much hotter. Also, there is less rain, which means the dust is pretty bad, when-ever you drive. Rainy season wasn't bad at all. I think we'll miss the rain, actually. Things look the same all the time though, giant trees, and bush, and tall grass. Fruit is ripening on the trees, and the Chinese keep us in vegetables. Right now, its eggplants, long, thin purple ones, string beans, and cucumbers that are about 12 inches long and one and a half inches in diameter.

Dear Vikki,   **November 11, 1971, Gbedin**

Thanks for your welcome letters. It's always nice to hear how everything is. We are fortunate that we get a fair number of letters from family and friends. Of course, I write a lot of letters. You know, I've written so often about all the new experiences we've been having. This week is no different.

The trial for Marcia's murderer started yesterday. I've been summoned as a witness. I'm outside on a bench under the trees, awaiting my turn. I'm dreading having to go through it, since I will have to describe the scene as I found her. It seems like every week or two, something occurs to bring everything back.

The court room itself, and the procedures, are something else. The judge and the lawyers wear black robes over their business suits. There is a jury of 12 men and women who were impaneled in about 15 minutes, after some were asked only where they lived—but only about whether their home was far enough away so they couldn't have talked with Robert. A few were excused.

The women all wore lappas, and some of the men wore country cloth robes. Everything is very informal, lots of emotional outbursts from the defense attorney, who has a reputation as a shyster, and one who can confuse witnesses. Even though Robert confessed and signed his confession, he now pleads not guilty. The defense lawyer told some PCVs that he will implicate John Chambers, saying he either goaded or paid Robert to kill Marcia. There are some people at Gbedin who believe this too. I don't.

All the proceedings are being recorded, by a typist, on a regular, manual typewriter. It's noisy and slow, since he transcribes every word, and the lawyers speak a few words and then wait. I've been waiting for three hours, and they are still examining the first witness, her houseboy.

We went to lunch at the home of a young PC couple who teach here. They have been here for three years. Their house is in a grove of trees in town here in Sanniquellie, where the trial is being held.

When we reached their house, there was much excitement—a Mamba snake had been spotted in one of the trees. Someone went to borrow a gun, and in the meantime, a boy shot a rock at it with a sling shot, and it slithered away. There were quite a bunch of school boys there, and everyone was looking for the snake. A Mamba is green and hard to see in the trees. Finally, after about a half an hour, someone yelled, "In da tree-o," and way up high, we could see it. Dave, the PCV, hit it with his first shot, but had to shoot it two more times to knock it out of the tree. It was six and a half feet long, a beautiful, velvety dark green shading to yellow-green at the tail. It had a chartreuse stomach. Its fangs were long. Dave told us it is the deadliest snake in West Africa, and there's no country snake medicine for its bite.

My well-baby clinic opened yesterday, and it was a smashing success, if numbers are any mark. We had at least 70 babies and kids less than five years. Today is supposed to be prenatal clinic, but since I was called away for the trial, people were sent home. I hate that because it's hard to get them to come in the first place. Will have to do a lot of follow up in the village, anyway, which I enjoy,

Yesterday was Beatrice's birthday so I baked a cake for her and put a candle on it. I don't think she has had one before.

Dry season has started. From now on, it will be so hot. It hasn't rained for five days. Mornings are pleasantly cool, kind of overcast, but around 2 PM until 5:30 PM our house is just too hot. Fortunately, we have a shower. It's necessary to water the garden mornings and evenings now.

Dear Mom and family,   **November 14, 1971, Gbedin**

Tomorrow, it will be exactly eight months since we left Philadelphia. In my last letter, I started to tell you about the trial. I had to be on the witness stand for parts of two days, a total of two to three hours. I had to tell exactly what I saw and did the day I found Marcia. I didn't think I'd be able to do it, to describe the awful scene, without breaking down. Fortunately, I was OK.

Hopefully, the trial will end this coming week. We don't know if Toe will get the death penalty, especially since there is a new president now, but most people say President Tolbert is a much harder man than the former President Tubman and expect him to sign the death warrant.

The courtroom conduct and the handling of the trial are much different than what we are used to. It's very informal. The prisoner sits in a raised, fenced-in cubicle on one side of the room. The witness sits in a similar box on the other side of the room. A soldier with a rifle sits near the prisoner, but at times, Toe sits in his "box" with no one responsible for guarding him. I fully expected him to leap out of the low window beside him the first day—no one was guarding him, and only a few people were in the court room. The lawyer for the prosecution is the assistant attorney general for Liberia, and very able.

I must tell you about our clinic. We were able to get the building that Marcia lived in for a clinic. She lived in a long single-wide trailer, with a building constructed around it. We will use the building, not the trailer, which was her bedroom. I can't stand to go in there. But the building part is OK. The carpenters have put rogue bars on the screened windows, put in a new sink, which Harold found in another building, patched holes in the screens, etc.

I hired a couple of school boys to scrub the place, and on Monday, we moved all the stuff from the old clinic, which was just an old shed. This one is newly painted inside, is roomy and in a better location. As soon as we can scrounge some planks, we'll have some more benches made. We'll also hire some school boys to go out and cut us some bamboo sticks and make us some benches for outside. With so many children it's so noisy, so having room outside for some will help.

I have to do most of this with my own money since we haven't collected any fees yet. Hopefully, we'll be able to charge 25 cents per child to register, which will give us some operating money.

Our first real day of business was last Tuesday, and we had close to 70 children. We gave lots of DPT vaccine, and will continue to try to inoculate all the kids, and later for smallpox. I've gotten a lot of powdered milk from CARE and also distribute it for the kids who are malnourished. It's hard to get the mothers to prepare it correctly, so some of the kids get diarrhea, and then the moms don't want to use it. The people just don't use clean water for their babies' bottles, if the mom doesn't have any milk, and bottles are washed poorly.

They feed their baby with their hands—force food and water down them—it's called "stuffing" the baby. They think if they stuff it full of water, even a tiny two-month-old one, the baby won't cry because it's hungry. It makes me sick to watch them. You'd think the baby will choke to death. I keep on telling them if they keep on doing it, and their baby gets sick, they can't come and cry on me for medicine. We'll see. It's hard to change old, old patterns of behavior.

At any rate, things are moving ahead. It's a lot of work, and my days are long. Well-baby clinic is on Tuesday, ante-natal clinic on Thursday. Each clinic needing a lot of records and reports, and home visits. On the other two days, I help in the general clinic, doing all the registrations and reports, sometime spending just the morning, but sometimes the afternoon, too.

Beatrice is still working with me. I'm hoping to teach her to do the health education part of the job and also do the clerk duties—records and reports—by the time I leave here. She has a sixth-grade education and was 22 this week. She has two little girls. She is expecting a baby in January. She is really a bright girl, learns quickly and wants to get some place.

Her husband is very pleased she is working with me, and wants her to stay here while I'm here, so she can learn something new. He's been transferred to another town and only comes home every three or four weeks. He came this week and brought us a rooster, which is considered a fine dash. I'm hoping I can eventually get her on the payroll of the Ag.

Department, which sponsors my clinic. Right now, I pay her $5 a week from my own PC allowance.

I was talking to Dr. Rigamer about acupuncture. He's an MD, as well as a psychiatrist. He said about a year ago he would have scoffed about it, but in the last year he's heard doctors who have gone to China to observe it report on its phenomenal results. And, even though he doesn't understand it, he believes it is effective for some things.

Lois [*Ruth's sister*] wrote about seeing some interesting African beads. When we take a trip through West Africa, we'll try to get a few more, since they are relatively inexpensive there, but more expensive here. Actually, Liberia has few art or native products. Many more come from Ghana, Nigeria, Mali, Niger, and Ivory Coast. There the carvings, weavings, leather work, etc., are much more artistic and fine.

Harold sends his love, too. We're both well and healthy, and Harold looks better than ever. We went to a PC party recently, a farewell for a fellow who is returning to the states. One of the young guys said, "Ruth, if I didn't know you were a grandmother, I might try to make time with you!" So, I guess I'm doing all right, too.

Dear Mother,   **November 21, 1971, Gbedin**

Another week gone by and eventful as ever. We had planned a full week here—my clinic business is keeping me hopping, and Harold's work too, is demanding. However, as usual, other things interfered. Tuesday, just as I was going out the door to hold well-child clinic, a man came with a subpoena for Harold and me to appear at the trial for the defense. I was really vexed, because there were 25 patients waiting for me, and getting people to come in the first place is no easy task here, plus we didn't want to be defense witnesses.

I had already been a witness for the prosecution the week before. Anyway, as you know, you can't ignore a subpoena or you're in contempt of the court, as in the US. So, we had to borrow the Chinese fellows' VW bus and go to Sanniquellie again.

Several people here were called, too, including all four of us who had been prosecution witnesses, as well as the project director, eight of us in all. We were sworn in, and for the next two and half days sat outside the court house, and waited to be called. The second day, we arrived at 9 AM, the appointed time, and learned after an hour that the defense lawyer and the judge were still suffering the effects of a hangover, from a drunken party the night before. We were told to come back at 2 PM, when the trial finally began. In the end, after two and a half days of waiting, we were told we wouldn't have to testify.

We are convinced they have the guilty man. A guilty verdict was announced on Friday, but it would be unfortunate if the man weren't guilty, since the trial was such a travesty of justice. The defense lawyer was so bad, just stupid and silly, and the prosecution had only circumstantial evidence. It seems that the NBI [*National Bureau of Investigation*], which investigated the murder, didn't secure finger prints, blood matching, or such essential things. They must have bungled since those things surely were available, from our acquaintance with the scene of the murder.

Tuesday, the sentence will be announced. Most people feel he will be hanged, since a convicted murderer of more than a year ago was hanged on Friday. Former President Tubman would never sign a death warrant, so for more than 24 years there has been no one executed for murder. Since there is now a new President, people expect it to be different. They say, "Murder too much. If some are executed, there will be less murder." Obi, the man who killed the Episcopal bishop last year, was hanged on a Friday. Many people went to Monrovia to watch it.

Yesterday, one man in Sanniquellie showed me a piece of the rope that was used to hang him. It was a piece about five inches long. He told me he would put it in a glass-covered case and hang it on his wall. People here in Gbedin say if Robert Toe is hanged in Sanniquellie, they will go to see it. I can't imagine it myself, but people are different here.

Well, enough about that gruesome subject. I spent three days in Sanniquellie at the end of the week, attending a workshop for health volunteers. It was long and boring, but I did get some useful information about operating a clinic.

It will be so good to get home this week, and get back on my usual work schedule. After getting people prepared to come once a month—a different group comes each month—it's hard to keep them coming, if you aren't there sometime. So many people are so used to coming only when their kids are sick, so they don't realize they should come when they are well, too, to get immunizations.

I'm supposed to teach something each time too, sometimes how to prepare and/or use the milk, how to prepare some of the native foods for kids, boiling water, nutrition for pregnancy, building toilets, and on and on. Very basic things using any kind of visual aids that will help get the message across. None can read or write the majority can't understand or speak English. Bea helps me to communicate. We still have a lot of work to do on the building, but things are coming along well. If things work out as planned, I'll be able to find a midwife by February or March, who will do most of the ante-natal work. Hopefully, by the time we leave, she, Daniel, the dresser at the clinic, and Bea, can do the whole thing. At least that is my goal right now. Only time will tell.

Right now, we are hearing that Peace Corps generally is having money problems—less Congressional support—so the future is pretty unpredictable. We plan to be here, though.

Harold, too, had to return to Sanniquellie after the trial, to assist with a training program for PC fellows, who will be doing road building and school and clinic construction. He is doing training in small groups, for car and truck maintenance so the guys can keep their vehicles from breaking down so much. He will go back for more sessions this week.

I'll go too, on Wednesday, and give the guys their gamma globulin injections (for hepatitis prevention), and rabies shots. There are 16 who need them. Fortunately, a car comes to get us, so we don't have the taxi hassle.

I forgot to mention that on the subpoena, Harold was listed as "Old Man Harry Jacobson"! When you speak to an older fellow here, out of respect you say, "Ol' Man, good morning," or some other appropriate greeting. The children all call me, Ma Ruth, or more likely, Ma Rufe, since Liberians have a hard time pronouncing the "th" sound.

Dry season is nearly upon us. Driving now has the hazard of blinding dust, like driving on the dirt roads around Brewster used to be. The dust is red, and no matter if you close the windows each time a car goes by, and you cover your head with a head-tie. You can't imagine the dust that is deposited. Our clothes are really red when we drive as far as Monrovia, and even less distance. Since it's so hot you can't stand to have the windows closed very much—you'd suffocate from the heat and humidity. Actually, I'm not bothered by the heat as much this year as I was in March and April when we arrived in country.

You know, Mother, the cartoons you send are quite beyond the people here. They just don't understand American humor. In fact, if you say "cartoon," they think you mean a carton, like a cardboard box. Liberians and the Lebanese storekeepers all call it a cartoon when you ask for a box. We say it too, now, so they will understand us. We will have things to unlearn when we get home, no doubt.

Dearest Mother and all,   November 29, 1971, Gbedin

I can hardly believe it is almost December. It will soon be nine months, since we came here. How time has flown by. It's also difficult to get the time of the year straight, since its winter season at home and hot season coming on here. It is also near the end of the school term. School kids will be out for "summer vacation"—from December 20 until sometime in March.

This week there are two holidays. One is for the President's birthday, and Wednesday for some early settler commemoration. There is no school or work on these days. It's been kind of nice to have a holiday from work, since we've been working very diligently.

Harold finished three days of classes for the new trainees, and I spent all one morning giving 16 new boys gamma globulin and rabies injections. On other days, my clinic duties keep me busy from 7:30 AM until 3 PM, and other interests go on from there. Harold always has a car or truck to regenerate after hours, as well.

I've been enjoying gathering seeds and trying to make necklaces. I've found a lot of Jobs tears. Little kids gather them and sell them to me for pennies. There are also rubber tree seeds, big brown oval ones, and lots of other seeds of various shapes, sizes, and colors. I've been combining them with locally made or purchased beads. I've been having fun with them—and will send some home.

Saturday we had an interesting, but strenuous day. Harold borrowed a Land Rover, and we left in the morning to make a visit to John's town in the country. This meant about a 30-mile drive over very bad, bumpy road, about one and a half hours, and then a five-mile hike on a trail through the bush. The walk took us an hour and 40 minutes and passed through or by eight villages before arriving in his village. At one point we waded through knee-high water, something we don't like to do because of the possibility of shistosomiasis, which is carried by a small snail. I'm wary of snakes and leeches, as well. The trail for a distance of about a half block is nearly always covered by water, and people just go through it.

All through the part of the country we traversed, the people were harvesting coffee and cocoa beans. All of their produce has to be carried by head loads to the motor road, where we parked our car. There the people sell their beans, etc., to Lebanese merchants, who pay them as little as they can. The people don't seem to realize if they are cheated, and if they do, there is little they can do about it, since there is no other way they can sell their coffee.

We also went by lots of grapefruit, orange, tangerine, and avocado trees. Much of the fruit was rotting on the ground. John said, "No man to buy it." And to get it to the market costs more than it is worth. The grape-

Pounding rice, to remove the hulls, outside John's mother's house.

fruit is huge and so sweet. We carried some home, but we too, could only carry so much.

When we reached John's village, people ran to greet us—some little kids ran and hid, however—and took us into the house, and from then on we were on display. It is Gio—pronounced "gee-o," with a hard G—country, and we couldn't understand a thing. Hardly any of them could speak or understand English.

People came in and sat down, greeted us by shaking hands, and then sat back down and looked at us. Little kids stood outside the window and watched. After a while, some of the people left, and soon others took their place. John's mother frequently came to me and took my hand, saying "E-zuo," meaning thank you. She told John to cook for us and then took a chicken out from under the box-like chair that Harold was sitting on!

The kitchen is always outside, a round thatch-covered hut, where cooking is done over a fire on the ground. They use either three stones on which to set their pots, or a metal three-legged frame, which is set over the fire. John cooked country rice and chicken soup, which they served at a table with a bowl for each of us, as well as a spoon for each of us. Usually, people eat from a common bowl, using their hands.

People kept coming and asking me to take care of a sick child—infected scalps, fevers, scabies, yaws, runny belly, infected eye. I had brought some first aid supplies and could take care of the worst things. One little boy, about two, had a puffy, runny eye. They told me he had gotten something in it the day before. I told them to boil some salt water, and I would wash his eye out. When they came with it, it was in a bucket, looking murky, with a dingy towel dangling in it. Finally, I got a clean bowl, strained the water through layers of gauze, cooled it off, and with Harold's help, poured it to wash out the eye. By the time we left in the afternoon, he could keep his eye open, so maybe it will be OK.

I told some of the people they needed to go to Karnple—a five-mile walk and a taxi ride—and get help at the clinic there. However, you know that 99 times out of 100, they won't do it, just go along with whatever happens.

When we left in the afternoon, the people gave us a chicken. They had tried to catch a guinea hen for us, but the birds are too elusive. We also left with two large bunches of plantain, some huge yams, a red squirrel skin, and could we have carried them, we would have taken a lot of guavas. They told us that the next time we plan to come to let them know, so they can prepare for us.

John's mother, her brother, and John's little sister "carried us part way," as they say here. It is a hospitable thing to do, walking about a mile with us and helping us across the water. They stride along the trail, single file, with anything they need to carry on their heads with their arms swinging free.

It was nearly dark when we got out to the road, and I was nearly exhausted, since we had to walk very fast before dark caught us. The trees overhang the trail so it gets dark very fast in the forest. It is really beautiful when walking in the bush. The foliage, the trees and bushes are so luxurious. Some trees are at least 10 feet in diameter, with huge leaves. Trees grow so tall here due to the abundant rainfall. It is like the redwoods, I guess, as far as height and size. Leaves similar to those in Hawaii are common—palm, bamboo, citrus fruits. There are some flowers, but not many.

Also there are dozens of butterflies, all brilliantly colored. We've been catching and mounting them, but without a net on such a hike, you're out of luck. We heard a lot of birds, but saw no wildlife. John said that the hunters keep the monkeys and other "meat" afraid, so they hide. Most wild animals are just called meat, not deer, squirrel, and so on.

The village we visited consisted of mud-stick huts, with palm thatch roofs. There is no grass in the town, just bare, packed earth, as is true in most villages, because of snake hazard. Grass invites snakes, and snake bites are too common.

There are coffee-drying areas all over the town. These are circular spaces enclosed by low wicker fences, which are about 12 inches high and look like big baskets. They are made by driving sticks into the ground and then weaving long strips of bamboo, or vines, in and out around the sticks. Apparently they stay there all the time. We saw them in each of the villages we passed through.

On the drive home we stopped to visit at the home of one of the Liberian Assistant Engineers that Harold works with. He had 100 acres, which he purchased years ago, and for which he has a deed. This isn't too common, since most land ownership is by tribe, a communal arrangement. He has 31 people living on his farm—all relatives of his wife. Also, he has a few of his own children, but there are plenty of kids belonging to others there. He raises coffee, cocoa, and citrus fruits. He has big turkeys too, something unusual around here. It was dark by the time we reached there, so we couldn't stay long. One day we will go in the daytime and walk around. Everything we see is so fascinating, so different from the things we know.

When we arrived, the man brought out a gourd of palm wine for us. They always take a drink first, pour out some on the ground, "for the old people," and then pass the gourd around for all to drink. When we left, they gave us a branch of bananas. There is no way you can refuse gifts like this without insulting people. They are so good to us, yet most have so little. By the time we had completed our long, bumpy ride home, it was dark, and we were ready to call it a day.

When we stopped in Sanniquellie that day, we learned from the county prosecutor that instead of sentencing Robert Toe, the judge, an absolutely incompetent man, decreed that a new trial must be held in February. He said unanswered statements regarding John Chambers's actions, brought out by the defense, were the reason. We are sick about the prospect of having to go through it all over again. The prosecutor said he was going to go to Monrovia this week to take it up with the attorney general, because he saw no basis for such an action. We will just have to wait and see.

Dear Mother,   **December 12, 1971, Gbedin**

It will be strange to spend Christmas here by ourselves. In fact, I can't get into the mood because there is nothing "Christmassy" here, no Christmas trees, just a very few rather odd decorations in store windows here. I think my only decorations will be some red candles with palm fronds and poinsettias, which grow wild all around. Won't have a tree—somehow a palm tree doesn't quite fit. I'll bake Christmas cookies, though, for treats for our visitors.

Yesterday, while walking around Monrovia, I slipped on a broken curb and injured my foot. Am on crutches now, awaiting x-rays tomorrow AM. The PC doctor thought I had broken a bone in my foot. I hope not since I can't take time to be laid up. We will be going back to Gbedin tomorrow afternoon. We have been here since Thursday for a meeting at the hospital, also visiting and shopping. We will be taking a new couple back with us for a few days. He's 71, and she is a bit younger. So you see you're never too old.

Dearest Vikki and Gill,   **December 15, 1971, Gbedin**

We're back in Gbedin, and I'm hobbling around on crutches. I hope my foot gets better soon. What a nuisance to be so slowed down. I'm listening to *Jesus Christ Super Star*. One of my friends in Monrovia loaned me the record. Mr. Tsi taped it for us, so we can enjoy it for a long time.

We've had guests again, an older couple—he's 71. They've been very enjoyable to have. She helped me at the clinic yesterday. It was almost more than she could stand; the sick babies bothered her a lot. Harold took them to Lamco today and to Sanniquellie. She bought me a lovely, carved ivory necklace. The chain is small, carved elephants, with a larger one as a pendant. I love ivory.

Dearest Mother,   **December 19, 1971, Gbedin**

Just a few days until Christmas, according to the calendar. However, to look outside or walk around, you'd never know it. It is sunny, hot and dusty, and green. Also, there are no Christmas decorations, except in a few stores, but not in our Lebanese store. People here get new clothes and do a lot of dancing, but that is about all for Christmas.

Yesterday, I made some chains from shiny paper, and hung them between the dining and living rooms. Lois sent us a package of Christmas things—bells, a Santa centerpiece, tablecloth, and napkins. It was fun to open it, and almost made me homesick but got me into the mood for Christmas. That is why I got at the chain making. This week, Bea and I will make some cookies. She would like to learn how, and I want to have some to treat people when they come in.

We will invite the Chinese guys for Christmas Eve for tea and cookies. On Christmas day, we will have dinner with the Pearmines, their folks, Harry, two PC couples from Sanniquellie, and our three houseboys—14 in all. Then we will all go to a soccer game here in Gbedin—two town teams—and probably go into the town in the evening to watch the dancing. (Mary and I are sharing the dinner.) So our Christmas will be quite different from one at home with the family. We will think of all of you together. I'm doing some sewing for Christmas—a floppy hat for Mary, shirts for Harold and John, and a lappa suit for myself.

Today, we took a drive to the Secretary of Agriculture's farm, which is about 25 miles away. One of our Chinese friends manages it for the secretary. They raise grapefruit and oranges and rubber. Harold does a lot of work for Secretary Philips, so he gave us about a gunny sack full of oranges and one of grapefruit. They are tree-ripened, and so sweet. Harold helped pick them. We eat many every day. I'm sure we get plenty of Vitamin C!

Dearest Mother and all,   **December 26, 1971, Gbedin**

By now, you've probably had a visit with most of the family. We have been thinking of you all enjoying yourselves with Christmas merrymaking. Ours has been a different Christmas, but enjoyable, none the less.

Right now, I'm sitting in the house, listening to Harold haggling with a "charlie," an itinerant trader, out on the piazza. He is trying to buy a string of amber beds from Mauritania. They are huge beads, about one and a half to two inches in diameter and an inch thick, strung on a heavy cord. They are quite valuable, but of course, Harold wants them for about a fourth of the asking price. This has been going on for more than an hour, which is the usual procedure. In between, they stop and talk about other things and then get back to their bargaining.

On Christmas eve, I made dinner for four Chinese men. I had told them they could bring their chopsticks, but they said they could use a fork. I made an American-style meal, with baked chicken and rice. Also Jell-O and cookies; one kind was called Chinese cookies. Mr. Chiang said, "I never did see any of these in China!"

Just about time for them to come, Harold had to leave to repair the generator which supplies our electricity. In the meantime, I had to work by candlelight. It took about two hours for Harold and his workers to get the generator working. So he finally came home, and we had a candlelight meal and enjoyable time. Our guests brought Harold a bottle of Scotch and me a canister of tea with a lovely Dragon design on it. The tea was a special green tea, with flower blossoms (jasmine) in it. They are such nice fellows.

Christmas day, we had planned the PC get-together with the Pearmine folks from Oregon. However, they brought word from Mary's folks that her father was dying, so she had to go on emergency leave yesterday. She will be in Oregon now for a few days.

We had bought a frozen goose in Lamco for Christmas dinner, so instead of having American guests, we invited two of Harold's mechanics, Harry Need, a new volunteer here in Gbedin, and the two houseboys. It was my first time roasting a goose. I stuffed it with a rice dressing. Also made apple pie (apples from a can), our first since leaving home.

As soon as we had eaten, we had to go to the school to watch a football game—soccer actually. Gbedin town challenged another town team. It's so much fun to watch them play. Almost anything goes, even spectators kicking the ball rather than letting it go between the goal posts. Afterward, the challenging team entertains the visitors with a dance and rice feed. They danced and drank cane juice until 3 AM. We didn't go to the dance, just walked around the town, and visited some of the people.

When they have a game between towns, the teams are made up of both boys and men who are the best players around. Many of the team members play barefoot. The whole town turns out. It is a real social occasion.

We are expecting Larry and his folks home this evening. With no way to communicate, except from someone driving by, we wait until things happen, which gives very little time to plan. Actually, it doesn't bother us—we're used to it now.

Just now, a "small boy" walked by carrying a large movie poster announcing a showing of a Julie Andrews movie, *Star*. It is shown in Harry Bar, the only local social center. Other than the mosquitoes, it's kind of fun because the people in the audience put on such a show. They yell and clap and groan, stand up and jump up and down. At times, you can't hear the movie because of the people. We're constantly amazed that so much actually goes on here. At home, it would no doubt be ignored, but here, anything is an occasion.

Our work is going on fine here. Harold is constantly plagued with lack of fuel and supplies, but otherwise, there is always something to do. We are waiting for January 3rd, when inauguration takes place. Many people expect things to start moving then. We would like to go to Monrovia for it, but getting there is such an ordeal. And I have to be back the next day for clinic, where things are going OK too. It is a constant job to get people to continue to get to the clinic when their children aren't sick. They are so used to coming only after the child has been sick for days. Bea and I have to go to the village all of the time to follow up with people. We've learned that a Ganta girl is just finishing midwife school at the Mission and wants to work here, so we're expecting her to come for an interview this week. Public Health people say they will hire her, so we will see.

Our cat is about ready to have kittens. Hope we can find homes for them. People around here eat cats, so maybe that is what will happen to them! School vacation has arrived. There is no school now until March sometime. So many kids come by and want work now. They are always looking for ways to earn money. We usually have two or three extra kids—pay them 5 cents to weed the garden or cut some grass. It's hard to find enough to keep them busy.

There is a PC couple here from Eugene; the wife has a lap loom, which cost $15 and was made by a friend of theirs. She makes interesting belts and such, up to three inches wide, but almost any length. I've been making beads, stringing them, rather. I bought some of the tar beads and collected seeds for the rest.

I'm sewing quite a bit—made Harold two Vai shirts for work. They are a loose-fitting pullover shirt with one button closing at the neck, made of wax-print cotton. I also made a Dashiki-style shirt for John for Christmas. This style is made of patterned Fanti cloth—a large design and border print. It is usually quite long, has loose sleeves and slips on. They are very popular here for men. Harold doesn't wear anything but Liberian style shirts, for work, church, parties, anytime. I think he's worn a *kwi* [*American*] shirt and tie only once since he's been here. I can make a shirt like this in about an hour, after cutting it out.

So many things we hear from the States indicate that the economy is in a bad way and doesn't seem to be picking up. Do you suppose that will continue until after the elections in 1972? Actually, things are pretty bad here, too, for Peace Corps—financial support is inadequate, and there is talk about sending lots of volunteers home by March. We just go from day to day, and do our work, waiting to hear what comes next.

Dear Sonja [Harold's niece] and Rob [her husband], December 28, 1971

What a wonderful surprise to receive your Christmas letter yesterday. Harold and I always get a special glow whenever we visit you. We received the same thrill when we read your letter. You're good for us! We have made so many new friends here, met so many fine people, and know that people are the same in any part of the world. One of the things that happened to us since we've been here is that our awareness of the color of a person's skin just isn't there anymore. I'm startled every once in a while when someone speaks of me as the white woman. I don't think I look any different than anyone else here. At first, I felt so conspicuous, but now I feel like I blend right in.

We spent Christmas here in Gbedin, Christmas Eve with our four Chinese neighbors, and Christmas Day with Liberian guests for dinner. We usually eat Liberian food, which is much more available, and of course, much less expensive. But on Christmas Day, I cooked kwi food—American food—roasted a goose (my first for that), made apple pie (apples from a can), candied sweet potatoes, and all. This is the first time in many years that we didn't go to church on Christmas. There just isn't one available, unless we make the two-day trip to Monrovia. And since we don't have a car, we can't make the 15 miles to the Methodist Mission, the nearest church.

We find the people such a strange mixture of faith in God, and still a great belief in the powers of bush witches and the country devils, which really control the towns. Most of the people's business actions and day-to-day treatment of each other do not reflect Christian principles or ethics. However, this is reflection of the culture.

We try to not judge actions on the basis of American standards, but really try to understand the culture we're in now.

*Peace Corps volunteers. Standing, front row from left: Mary Bennett,
Jeff Price, Ruth, Ed Jackam, Rich White. Back row, with cigarette,
Dale Veeneman. Kneeling, Norma Puterbaugh; in front left, Gerry
Puterbaugh. Sitting in chair, Chris Lyman. Seated in front of him, Gary
O'Neil. (Others unidentified.)*

1972

Dearest Mother,   **January 2, 1972, Gbedin**

This will just be a quick note to say Happy 1972 to all of you. Hope it
will be a wonderful year for you and for the world. Larry is just leaving
this morning for Monrovia for a week, so we decided to get some mail
ready for him to carry for us. Tomorrow is the inauguration, and Friday is
another holiday, so probably no mail pickup.

We've really enjoyed the senior Pearmines. We spent New Year's
Eve and day with them. Mary had to leave on Christmas day because her
father had a heart attack. He died on the 27th. She will probably come back
to Monrovia this weekend.

We've had a busy, enjoyable time during the holidays. One woman,
who comes to my clinic, the chief's head wife, delivered just before New
Year's. They named the baby for me; quite an honor, I thought. They said,
"You have goo', goo' way, (good, good)."

One small boy in the village, about 10 years old, had a very bad foot, from being tied up, or rather, fastened, at home, so he couldn't run away. His foot was put inside a small piece of a log, with nails driven through the wood to keep the foot inside. The foot was so injured, big sores on it, swollen to twice its size when I found him. All during the holidays, I've gone and dressed it and given him penicillin, and by yesterday he looked fine. He is epileptic, and they think it's better to confine him this way, than let him fall down someplace. I was practically in tears the first time I saw him and talked like anything to get them to stop what they were doing. But they won't. They will probably do the same thing another time. I will try to get some Dilantin for him.

Dearest Mother,   **January 7, 1972, Gbedin**

Our life goes along just fine. I was afraid that we would be homesick during the holidays, but there never was time for that. We always have a lot of company, and people were so good to us.

My foot got well pretty fast. I don't know what to give credit to. I used ice and crutches for a few days. Then, when I got up here to Gbedin, people told me about a man who can make country medicine for bones, so I decided to give it a try. I figured it wouldn't hurt, and even if it didn't do anything, it would help our relationship. So for three days, I plastered their goop on my foot and leg. It was a mixture of mud with some kind of plant mixed in it. Then one of our Chinese friends from another town came. He was said to be quite an expert with massage. He offered to work on my foot. By that time, my foot was feeling better, but was still swollen and sore. He massaged it very thoroughly, for at least an hour, using mashed up ginger root dipped in Scotch whiskey to rub it, too. Then they chopped up some leaves, which they called "fall on the ground and grow," but which I recognized as aloes, spread them on my foot, and wrapped it up. I left this on my foot a few hours and then went to bed. In the morning, my foot was no longer swollen or sore, and it's been fine ever since. We've been laughing about all of my cures, but anyway, it's OK, unless I step wrong.

This week Harold had a freak accident, which could have been bad, but fortunately, didn't do too much damage. He was test-driving a motor scooter after repairing it, hit some loose sand and lost control of it. He plowed into the sand head first, broke his glasses, knocked himself out, cut his face just below his eyebrow, and of course, skinned his face all up. He got some other cuts and bruises, but no broken bones. We had to take him to Ganta to the hospital to sew up his eyelid. Also, to have him checked over. He really looks awful, and feels full of aches. Tomorrow, they will remove the stitches, and by Monday he should be back to work.

You should have seen and heard the people when the accident happened. They always wail and cry loudly, when something bad happens. All the women were crying, and everyone ran to him, and soon, we had a huge crowd. They all trooped to the clinic, came inside, and watched and moaned. Later on, I think half the town came to the house to tell him, "Neh mi ya," which means, "never mind, ya," and is the way they express their sympathy. Even though they can't speak English, they say, "Neh my, ya, Ol Man," sit for a while, and then go. It's really heart-warming to have so many people tell you they are concerned about you

In fact, not only for Christmas but for New Year's, too, we have received so many gifts, such as rice, fruits, and vegetables, from people we've helped. One man came on New Year's Eve with his wife, carrying a pan of rice, a big pawpaw, and a bunch of plantain. He said, "When I came here, I was so sick, I thought I was going to die, and you helped me. This is to say thank you."

And I want to thank you, mom, for the thoughtful Christmas gifts. I've already been using the buttons and the hot pads are so nice. Bea was so pleased with her things, and asked me to tell you, "thank you." Her baby is due soon. She already has two darling little girls. The little one just loves Harold, and he adores her. She told Bea yesterday, she was going to marry Man, as she calls him, when she grows up. She will be two next week.

One woman at the clinic this week told me she wanted me to take her baby and raise it; this happens many times. She doesn't have any milk to nurse him, and he's only about six months old. She has been feeding him only mashed plantain mixed with water and brought him to me because he had diarrhea. I gave her CARE milk and have been working with her for a couple of months.

She can't seem to understand that a dirty bottle and sour food will make him sick and that plantain isn't enough for such a young baby. He's a darling baby, but way too thin. I told her I would come to her house and work with her to help her do it the right way and keep her supplied with milk. So many of the people say, "The milk make the baby's stomach run" (give it diarrhea), and can't realize it's due to a dirty bottle and contaminated water. It's a never-ending struggle, but I keep on trying.

At the last of December, the chief's wife had her seventh child, which she named for me—can't remember if I already mentioned that. The funny thing about naming a baby Ruth is Liberians have a hard time pronouncing the *th* sound; rather they pronounce it as *f.* So they say "Rufe." In fact some of the school boys write me letters, asking for work, etc., and write it as Rufe.

A new president was inaugurated here this week. Mrs. Nixon was a special guest in Liberia and was given quite a reception. The news from Ghana on VOA sounded like she had just as warm a welcome there. We didn't go to the inauguration, because the trip to Monrovia is just too long and strenuous.

Additionally, I had business with the Health Department, which couldn't be done during a National Holiday. This meant another trip a week later, which I just couldn't face. Harold and I will go down this coming week on Thursday and stay until Sunday or Monday.

Now that a new president is in office, after 28 years of one president, people are quite hopeful that the country will progress. It would be wonderful if some better roads and a communication system could be built. Of course, there are many more top priority things, too, so it will be interesting to see what the New Year will bring.

Dear Mother,   **January 17, 1972, Gbedin**

We're just on our way home after four days in Monrovia at the Berman's. I had to come to the city to pick up supplies for the clinic, since it's impossible to get the people to fill orders if you're not there. We did a lot of visiting and shopping, etc., and I never got down to writing letters. Harold had to see the PC doctor, too, about his accident and have a chest X-Ray. He found he has a broken rib, but isn't uncomfortable with an Ace bandage around it.

When we came down to Monrovia on Thursday, we were in a taxi full of Mandingoes, who are Muslims. They pray several times a day, so they stopped on the way, got out of the car, faced east, knelt, and went through their routine. There are lots of Mandingoes here, so it is a familiar sight to see groups of them praying. They also have strict dietary rules and never touch alcohol.

Now that we are going into dry season, we're seeing lots of different kinds of blooming trees. The coffee trees have beautifully fragrant white blossoms. When you walk in the bush, you can see many different flowering trees. The rubber tree leaves have turned color now, so the forest looks like fall at home. When we drive down a road lined with coffee trees, the fragrance is almost overwhelming.

Dear Mother,   **January 23, 1972, Gbedin**

It's getting close to a year now, since we left home. How fast the time has gone by. Now we are looking forward to a visit from Vikki and Gill. Hopefully, they will come around the middle of April, which should be a good time to visit here. Dry season is really not. The dust on the roads is bad and visibility is poor when you're driving. Lots of trees have begun to lose their leaves—they're brown and red. The rubber trees lose their leaves. The coffee trees are in bloom, oranges and grapefruit are being harvested, pineapple, too. It seems like the season is mixed up, but this is the pattern. It rains very little now. Two nights ago it rained very hard for a short time so the dust was settled on the roads, even puddles remained.

We have had guests all week, another couple from Los Angeles. He is 68 or 69, and she about 61. He's a mechanic. They were quite enjoyable, and liked to do lots of things, so we walked all over with them. We walked to two other bush towns, visited homes and farms. We cooked a lot of Liberian foods. They thought they had a fruitful "live in." They arrived in Liberia a week ago and are having training now. We are also expecting a new psychiatric nurse to stay for a few days and that should finish our live-ins for a while.

A lot of people are assigned to Monrovia and never get up-county if they aren't sent up when they first come. It's so much easier to stay in the city and have all the comforts of home, instead of having to cope with country living. Of course, you never really know the people, either, then. Living in the bush is not only physically more time consuming and demanding, it's also more demanding mentally and emotionally, since you're dealing with the people at a very basic level all of the time.

This week four children have died in Gbedin town, apparently from measles. Also, one here in the project. She was a darling little girl, four years old, who was brought to me the afternoon before by her big sister, who is around twelve years. She had a high fever, but I didn't think she was that sick, didn't know what was wrong with her, however. She died about 6:30 the next morning People wait so long before they bring their children for any medical care. People in the village started to wail and cry as soon as she died, carried on for about an hour. All day, people came to their house and sat with the family, which I did too. That night, many people sat all night with the family. They sang and beat drums until about 5:50 AM. Then they rested a while and went and buried the child. They never put a marker on the grave. Many people believe that the spirit doesn't die, but goes to live someplace else—in the same kind of body and looks just the same. Even people with some education believe this.

One father sent his small son about six years old to our house yesterday afternoon. He had told the boy to go see the "old Ma" for some medicine. His temp was 105, and he had walked the distance of several blocks to reach us. I gave him aspirin and an ice bag for his head and put him on the couch. Harold went and told the father his son was too sick to stay home. Maybe it was because the other children had just died, but anyway, he borrowed $5 from the storekeeper, and got a man to take him and his son to Ganta to the hospital. The fever had come down about 2 degrees by that time. I heard later that he had brought his son home again, and that he was better, but I haven't seen him yet. Some of the sick kids really scare me, and the families just wait to see what will happen.

I may have written before about a young boy named Paye, who has epilepsy, the one whom the family keeps restrained by putting his foot into a hole in a log. He's sitting here now, eating a grapefruit and playing with a balloon we gave him. Dr. Rigamet, the psychiatrist who stayed with us, gave me some Dilantin with Phenobarbital for him while I was in Monrovia last week.

Yesterday, we went to see the family to talk about him taking it every day. They are really country people, full of superstitions and bound by country ways and beliefs. The boy was lying on a mat outside the house, daubed with a chalky, country medicine, quite lethargic and not able to stand up. The *zo* (medicine man) had given the family, for a fee, some "medicine" to give Paye every day. He said the thing that is making him fall down is caused by a living thing in his stomach. So he must take the medicine every day, perhaps for months, until the living thing leaves him, by way of his mouth. But, they said, a person should not turn down an honest offer of help, so they want to try my medicine, too. I had told them it comes from a doctor who knows how to care for children, and who knows how to treat sickness in the head.

So then I had to tell them they should decide which medicine they would use. "The country medicine too strong, and my medicine too strong, and not safe to use at same time" I told them. "Not to say," I went on, "the country medicine not good, but the sickness not in Paye's stomach, but in his head, and my medicine for that." It's really touchy. I can't afford to offend the medicine man, but it is obvious that nothing the zo has done has helped the boy.

Of course, it is easy for them to rationalize why Paye has been *witched,* it's the moon, etc. The father said he would talk to the medicine man and see if he would release him from their "deal." I told them I would wait until they told me what they wanted me to do. If they want my medicine, they should let me know. Since Paye is here today, perhaps they have made a decision. He still has country medicine on his body—a black daub over his eyebrows and a chalky paste on the rest of his body. He said, when I asked him that his Pa had not given him any medicine today. The PH Mental Health Division will continue to furnish him with medicine, so we'll see.

Every week brings another situation to deal with that has so many different aspects to consider, that knowing what to do is very hard. I've been very fortunate; so far, the people trust me. One day, I was demonstrating to a woman and her friends, how to mix the powdered milk that CARE furnishes. I had told her I would come in the morning and show her. Well, most of the people in the town stayed home from the farm that day to watch. After showing them how to do it, I asked them to show me the spoon and the cup they would use, so I could get the proportions right. They didn't own a cup, only bowls, and large ones at that. I told them to come to my house for a jar and gave them a mayonnaise jar with cups marked on it with red nail polish. When they came, they brought me two large branches of bananas for a gift.

Beatrice had her baby last Monday, the 17th of January, a little girl they named Naomi. She had her at home, with her mother, a country midwife, helping. Her mother is the head midwife here. Everything is fine. Bea says she will be back to work on Tuesday, clinic day.

Harold is getting along fine, now. His rib was broken, but not painful anymore. His work has slowed up a lot because of no materials. The new president has been reorganizing the Cabinet, and we are in great hopes things will start to move in the Ag. Department. We're awaiting news about plans for Gbedin, since Harold's work will be involved.

Dear Vikki,   **January 31, 1972, Gbedin**

Yesterday, I spent an interesting morning learning how to make what the Chinese men called a Chinese dessert. Actually, it's more like a piroshky—a round of dough, with a ground meat, some chopped up green beans, and onion, plus some seasoning. The dough was folded over and tucked together in a unique way, and they were placed in a bamboo rack over steaming water for about 20 minutes. They are delicious. It took about two or three hours to make them, using 10 cups of flour and 10 cups of filling. They all did a part of it. What a riot to watch them, chopping greens, with the beans flying every which way, and wiping everything off onto the floor. They say, "Neh mine, neh mine." When the "pies" were cooked, one of them made egg drop soup—delicious. They served us the pies with soy sauce over them, soup, and Italian beer. We've had the best time with these guys.

One of my dearest friends died last night from a stroke. The family came for me about 4:30 AM, and I couldn't do anything but make arrangements to get her to the hospital. Tonight, we went to Gbedin town to her house where a wake will be held. A death here is so different from at home, because the people don't hide their feelings. They cry and wail, rock back and forth. It's quite a thing to be part of, but the people are so grateful to have friends come. I'll miss her. She was the "head wife," the old wife.

When we went into the country Saturday for a bush hike, we visited three different towns. In two of them, people asked if I was Harold's wife. They said a man like him usually had more than one wife and would leave the head wife home and take a younger one with him when he goes walking about.

Dearest Mother,   **February 13, 1972, Gbedin**

This week we're getting ready for a visit from the President. He's coming to Sanniquellie for about two days, and will stop here at the rice project on Wednesday. We're also expecting eight PC trainees for Wednesday and Thursday. Also the trial for Robert Toe is supposed to begin in Sanniquellie tomorrow. So this week sounds like a bummer, as the kids say, from the beginning. So far, we haven't been subpoenaed, so hopefully, we'll be able to avoid the trial.

It looks like we are going to be confronted with another decision, a very difficult one. The government has been undergoing a lot of reorganization since President Tolbert was inaugurated. A new agency was formed, and some of the Ag. Department people are heading it up. They are getting a lot of support from the President, budget, etc. It looks like Harold and I will be invited to work for them. Harold would have a responsible position having to do with maintenance of their equipment: road building, land clearing, and the like (as a PC volunteer, of course). I would be involved in planning and expediting health and education programs, clinics, and such. The major problem for us is we would have to leave Gbedin and go down to live in Monrovia. There is so much to be done here yet, that we don't see how we can go, and of course, we hate to leave our friends.

You can't possibly know the people in Monrovia like you can here in a small town. There is also the question, too, of how serious the government is about following through with continued support or if the money will be side-tracked into someone's pocket. We are just taking it a day at a time, right now, trying to find the right answer.

The little epileptic boy, Paye, has been coming each day for his Dilantin, and for 10 days now hasn't had a seizure. I'm still trying to heal up a burn on his leg from his last fall. He is really a little pest. I have to have him come morning and evening to take his tablets and then can't get rid of him very easily.

David's grandmother died Thursday. She was a very old lady. Harold and I went to Gbedin Town to say "neh my, ya" to the family the next morning. At first, we were told we couldn't go to the house because it was too late; the Women's Society had begun their rituals. However, soon an old lady came, took my hand, and said, "*Ko-lopeay*" (we will go), so I went with her to the Meniboon "quarter" of the town. She led me into a house where I had heard drumming sounds. I later learned they were using a turtle shell as a drum.

The body was lying in the middle of the small room, with a lappa covering it. The body was unclothed. About thirty women were sitting or kneeling around the room, encircling the body. They made room for me to sit on a low bench. At the woman's head there was a large pan of rice, some soup, and a bowl of palm oil. Soon, one of the women poured the soup and oil on the rice and started to pass it around. About this time I began to wonder what was proper for me to do. I never want to offend their practices and could easily do something wrong through ignorance. I think I've been very fortunate to have gained their trust and would hate to destroy it. None of the old country women "hear" any English, and I really stumble with Mano unless it's related to my clinic activities. A younger woman, whom I had not met before, came and sat down beside me. I could communicate with her well enough to say that I had come to tell them my heart was heavy for them, since the old woman had died. And that I didn't want to intrude on their services. They all told me thank you for thinking of them and indicated that I could stay if I wished. It's this kind of life I would miss, if we lived in the city.

None of the men are allowed, only the women who have been to bush-society school. The same is true for men, only men who have been in the men's Poro society school may take part in burial services for a man. They say the "devil" (their society spirit) has him, after he dies.

Did I tell you Beatrice had her baby? A little girl they named Naomi. She is a cute little thing. When she was born, the upper three-fourths of her ears were very black. Of course, she's pretty black, too, but Bea was quite disappointed over the black ears! They seem to be fading out and looking all the same shade now.

Our kittens were born the same day. They are growing like little weeds, and are so cute. All are spoken for, so we will soon be giving them away.

Leona [*Ruth's teaching colleague from Tacoma Vocational School*] sent me some nutrition teaching things. However, very little was useful here in Gbedin. If I were teaching in Monrovia in the nursing school, they would be fine, but here it is so much more basic. I'll pass some along when I go to Monrovia again. One thing that struck me as I looked over what she had sent was the totally different emphasis in America from here. All the nutrition pamphlets emphasized low calorie things, reduction diets, and weight control. Here, it's just the opposite. You seldom see anyone who is overweight. Getting enough calories is the problem, rather than keeping them down.

Tomorrow is Chinese Lunar New Year eve, Tuesday is New Year's Day. This is one of their three National Holidays, and probably their most important one. Our Chinese friends have been preparing for it all week, cooking all sorts of goodies. We've been invited for dinner with them tomorrow night, so we will have to fast all day to prepare for the feast! Today, I baked cinnamon rolls for them. It's hard to do anything for them, because they immediately send us something from their garden or something they've cooked. My meals are a strange combination of Chinese and Liberian cooking.

Just a bit ago I finished making sherbet from a fruit called soursop. This is green, prickly-looking, usually about the size and general shape of a medium zucchini. Inside, it has a white pulp and a lot of good-sized black seeds. I've learned to peel it and sieve it through a colander—the pulp is tough—mix it with sugar and a can of condensed milk, and then freeze it. It tastes something like strawberry sherbet, the closest thing we get to ice cream, which is $2 a quart in Monrovia. And there is no way we would get ice cream from Monrovia up here.

Dear Mother,   **February 19, 1972, Gbedin**

We just learned last eve that we won't have to leave here and work in Monrovia, and we're very pleased. We really like the country people and being part of their life. [*The government and Peace Corps officials had agreed that Harold should stay in Gbedin.*]

This week the President visited this county—held meetings in Sanniquellie for three days. People all along the route of his travels are supposed to turn out and decorate, etc. The farmers here gathered palm branches and young banana trees, which they stuck in the ground along the road. They also built a kind of arch from slender poles on each side of the road by the entrance of the project. This they decorated with thick moss and big poinsettia blossoms and purple bougainvillea.

People began to gather by the road about 9 AM, all dressed in their best, the farmers and all their wives, the project employees and wives and kids. They waited all day and when the sun was going down the motorcade began—sirens and flashing lights, NBI [*National Bureau of Investigation*], VWs and big government cars. When it was completely dark, the Presidents' car came by never even slowing down, going by in a cloud of dust. You couldn't even see the President. I suppose the people enjoyed having a day off from work. The next day most of the farmers went to Sanniquellie for a meeting with the President. They had a chance to discuss some of their problems with him—like the low price they get for their rice since Egyptian rice has been imported. Since we've been here the price of swamp rice has gone from $10.50 or $11 per 100 lbs. to less than $6. He told them he'd already stopped Egyptian rice from coming in. So we'll see.

We had a houseful again this week for two days—nine new volunteers who came to learn something about rice co-ops—two women and seven men mostly young fellows. We had to feed and house them—really kept us hopping. I hired an extra boy to help us and things went OK. In the meantime I had to keep my job going and also go to Sanniquellie for the beginning of the trial which we learned later was delayed because of the President's visit. Apparently it will begin this coming Monday but I'll wait to see if I'm summoned.

We had a party for John Chambers Friday eve since he is finally leaving Liberia. All the people here turned out—farmers, workers, some wives. There were speeches, dancing, lots of noise but generally a good time. We're not sorry to see him go since he's so hard to work with—a terrible temper and very self-centered. The party was given by the farmers and by the project employees.

A Liberian party is quite an experience—everyone gets in the spirit of the thing. They love to dance and talk loud. Often after so much palm wine there is some *palava*—an argument between several people at one time. I love to sit back and just watch. Once they decided to dance a quadrille. My partner was a one armed man, shorter than I. About three people were trying to give directions, all different, at the same time and there were two too many couples, anyway. I hadn't the faintest idea what was going on. When the record ended people kept on arguing about how it should be done—all this in Liberian English, which is entertaining in itself.

Monday, February 21, 1972. Yesterday we took John to Gbarnga to catch his ride to Monrovia. Harold still has a Land Rover he's repaired so we have some wheels temporarily.

After dropping him off we stayed in the town to visit some PC friends for lunch and then went to Cuttington College near there to see the African Art exhibit. This is an Episcopal college, a fairly good one, where they have a really fine collection of Liberian artifacts. So much of old Liberian art has been taken out of the county and very little has been published about it. A young American works for them on a Ford Foundation grant and he's spent the past year trying to assemble—making his own—slides of many of the things that are in private collections or still owned by old country people. He also has many masks and other artifacts in the museum. He took us into the storeroom and spent a lot of time showing and telling. We've seen a lot of things the "charlies" (traveling traders) bring but know so little about them and need to learn more. We've been quite cautious about buying many things because of the cost and also because we want authentic things. So far we've seen a few things we really like. It was a really enjoyable day—one of the few where there has been an opportunity to be leisurely when we visit. The ride was really bad—the road is like a washboard—about an 80-mile drive each way, there is loose gravel from recent grading and the dust is thick.

On the way home we stopped at Kpain at the orange and grapefruit farm run by one of the Chinese for the Sec. of Agriculture. They always give us a gunnysack of grapefruit and oranges. Harold keeps their trucks running in return. There are acres of fruit trees, just loaded with ripe fruit and some in bloom—beautiful white, waxy blossoms. The rubber trees along much of the motor road have new leaves now—shiny, light green ones. The trees have been losing their old leaves and almost simultaneously get new ones. It's quite beautiful to see the new leaves. Many more flowers are in bloom now in the bush, which makes a walk enjoyable. At the Cuttington College campus, they have large plumeria trees in bloom but with no leaves. I remembered how fragrant they were in Hawaii so was happy to see them here—picked up some of the blooms and have them in a bowl of water here on the table.

The longer we're here the more we are aware of the many, many differences in our culture and that of the people here. We learn about attitudes and practices that aren't obvious but seem to unfold continuously. Perhaps because we are interested in the people and never judge them, they are more open with us.

Dearest Mother,   **March 2, 1972, Gbedin**

This has been such a busy time that I have found it hard to sit down and write letters. Actually, we are in Monrovia again for four days. The Minister of Agriculture called all Ag volunteers in for a meeting. He had learned that some PCVs were being wooed by another department, namely, us and the Pearmines. He met with everyone to tell them all his plans about beefing up the work in his department. We were glad to hear we won't have to leave Gbedin for work in Monrovia.

The Independence Day celebration will be held in Nimba County, so the Gbedin Rice Project will be developed to be as a "showplace," as he calls it. Harold and Larry have some ambitious projects to carry out with the farmers, so it is going to be an interesting and apparently productive time, if the Minister supports it as he promised.

The trial is still going on. I had to testify one day last week. When I finished, they told me I could leave, and I haven't been back since. I can't bear to go through the same thing as last time. I had to look at the photographs of Marcia while I was on the stand. It was the first time I had seen them, and I had to identify her. It was horrible. Hopefully, the trial will be over this week. Then, if he is found guilty, no doubt he will be hanged in Sanniquellie. It will be like a holiday for the people, I'm sure.

Since writing to you last time, we have moved into a new house. When John C. left, the project director told us we could have his house, so we picked up our things last Saturday and moved. We now live next door to Larry and Mary in a nice big house. It has glass jalousie windows, three bedrooms, one really large one, a nice big kitchen, living room, store room, dining room, and a kind of basement area, all furnished with fairly decent furniture.

The house is set up on cement piers, off the ground. It also has a nice big yard and flowering trees. The house is so much cooler than our little house. We miss the view we had, since we were on a hill and could see the whole area, and our Chinese neighbors. But still, we're close by. This is a Dept. of Ag house, so no rent is charged us. Having guests will be so much less of a strain, with more room.

You asked about burying people. Usually, they have a carpenter make a "box," as they call it, for the body, which is only wrapped in a lappa before being put in the coffin. No, I didn't eat any of the rice the women passed around. I managed to depart before they gave any to me. I was afraid of doing something wrong during such a serious occasion, so didn't want to take a chance on it. People have been very good to me as far as accepting me, almost everywhere.

I finally got far enough along with Paye's family, that they let me take him to Monrovia with us yesterday and admit him on the psychiatric ward at JFK, for evaluation and regulation on the epilepsy medications.

Dear Mother,   **March 15, 1972 , Gbedin**

Today, it is a year since we left the US. It has been one of the most eventful years we have ever had. If the next year goes by as fast, we will be home before we're ready to leave here. We are settled into our new house—a really fine one for volunteers.

We have just come back from a week's holiday. We spent two days by taxi to reach Harper, on the coast, two days returning, and three days there. It is 320 miles one way and takes 12 hours at least, but usually longer. When we were coming home from Harper Sunday, the taxi driver was driving too fast, skidded on loose gravel on a curve, and lost control of the car. We whirled around two times in the road and skidded into the ditch, almost on the side of the car. Harold and I were sitting on the side that landed in the ditch, but thank heavens, no one was hurt. There were six passengers.

A truck with around 30 rubber workers came by after a while. They stopped and lifted our car, bodily—amidst much yelling and cheering—out of the ditch and set it up-right. They all had to shake our hands first and tell us, "Neh my, ya." There were a few dents in the car, but nothing more serious. Taxi drivers are pretty crazy.

Harper is an old town, the second largest in Liberia. It has many fine buildings built by President Tubman. Most of them have never been used because no money was ever granted to operate them, such as a library, a technical school, and a city hall. We enjoyed beach combing, sunning, and swimming. However, the beach was just as polluted as those at home with tar and oil from tankers. I found many pretty shells similar to those found in Hawaii, although not in the abundance as there.

Paye, my little epileptic friend, came home from the hospital today and has improved a lot. He hasn't had any seizures since I got him on the medications about five or six weeks ago. His burn is nearly healed, too. He looked so good—clean and with no sores on his face from falls. I'm sure by tomorrow evening he will be just as dirty as ever, but he's used to that. He hates to take baths. I'm hoping he can start school. The Doc says he should be there. Hard telling if the kids will let him without bugging him, and without him bugging them.

By the way, your valentine card came, also the St. Patrick one. Thanks. The boys had never seen a valentine before. Your bias tape and buttons have been coming in handy. I've learned that our mail was rogued in the truck that time. Several letters I had written home, all of my monthly reports for the MCH clinic. Those I must do over again

Harold and Larry leave early tomorrow AM for Monrovia, to meet with the Secretary of Agriculture. They are going to be in charge of constructing six to eight houses of mud-blocks here at the project. It is to be a "showpiece" for the July 26 Celebration. Also, they must get about 40 acres cleared and into rice before then. The Secretary has promised his support. Will have to wait and see.

Dearest Mother,   **March 19, 1972, Gbedin**

I have been wanting to write to you and tell you how much you mean to me. I guess I can show you what you mean to me by trying to be as much like you as I can. Harold said recently, "You're getting to be more like your mom every day!"

I hope and pray that your ribs are much improved by now. Broken ribs can be so painful for quite a while. Harold has had broken ribs twice since we've been here. Both times were due to a motorcycle accident. The second time, he and Chris were racing on the airstrip here, and he skidded on a turn. After that, I made him promise he'd not do any more racing, and so far he's refrained!

This past week was Ganta mission time. The seniors had a picnic and volleyball game with the faculty. I must say, I'm no great player! The next day, the Empirical Midwives had their graduation ceremony and reception. Then the next day, which was Sunday, the senior students graduated and had quite a ceremony. It is so interesting to attend such a thing here. The faculty and students all march in together, and things start rather sedately.

Then suddenly, some old lady will start to sing and clap hands, and soon lots of people are singing. Then the program goes along, speeches, etc., and then someone, an old country lady whose son is no doubt graduating, will get up and dance down the aisle, and go up and bring something to him. For a person to get through high school is quite a feat, especially for a girl, so to get through nursing school is a great accomplishment. There were four boys and one girl in this class. I have had all of the students at the mission now in one class or another either in the nutrition or the pediatric nursing classes, so it was fun to take part in the program.

Tonight we are going to celebrate my birthday at Lamco. The guys are taking me to dinner there. Three of the young fellows and Harold are taking me. These guys are so nice to us. They never treat us like "old fogies," just like any other friends.

Dear Vikki,   **March 19, 1972, Gbedin**

There is such a dearth of books for Liberian children to read and identify with. The few books they do have are American and, of course, are totally unrealistic for country children. I had hoped Ciam could read the book *Five Cent, Five Cent.* I wish I could write such things. They're so badly needed here.

Regarding PC financial problems, there were many anguished moments here in Liberia for the staff and some volunteers. A cut of 100 PCVs out of close to 400 was one alternative we heard of. Harold and I were sure we would be among the last to be cut, since our Liberian Department heads, especially Harold's, feel they need us.

Also, PC staff thinks we're tops, both because of our ability to adapt and maintain high morale, and because we've done a lot for PC Liberia. For instance, Harold's ability, and willingness to keep cars and trucks running at practically no cost, has made him their fair-haired boy. Two Land Rovers he put back together again saved them the price of new one, around $2,000, which it would have cost to have the work done in a private garage in Monrovia. He spent around $80 for the two.

American public opinion helped to persuade Congress to restore some of the funding for PC, although they will still be short. In a way, it isn't too bad, because it forces staff to re-examine their programs and pare away some of the waste that is unavoidable in a large government agency.

PC finally decided to make a 10 percent cut in volunteer and staff living allowances for the next three months, until the next fiscal year begins. This means Harold and I will take a $28 cut per month in our living allowance. It doesn't hurt us like it does some of the kids, because we know how to manage better than some.

We have just bought a Sony Tape recorder with reels. Harold wants to know if you will buy him an 1,800 foot one, and record some western songs on it from our records. He especially wants some Jim Reeves, who is very popular here. Please, not all Western on the 1,800 ft.—only some.

We'll put some other music on it here. (Harold says only "small" Western and some other type of music.)

We have another guest this week, Kerstin, a 20-year-old Swedish girl, who is visiting Liberia for six weeks. She wanted an up-country experience, so Norton asked us if we would keep her for a week. She arrived Thursday eve and will stay until Tuesday. Her home is in Malmo, Sweden. She is a rather big, blonde, attractive girl—pink and white skin. Likes to walk, and visit with people. She is quite a novelty here, being so blonde. Tomorrow, we will walk to the waterfall on the St. John River, about a three hour hike each way, through the bush. People say it is a beautiful walk, lots of butterflies, too.

Ali, our Lebanese storekeeper, has been very interested in Kerstin, so tonight he came over for a visit. He's about 25, a very sharp business man, lots of fun and very good to us. He took Mary and Larry to Lamco on Sunday, to see Woodstock. He couldn't believe what he saw. He liked the music, but had never seen anything like the picture.

Robert Toe will be hanged on April 7 in Sanniquellie. I will be glad when it's over. It's been so long and drawn out, with periodic reminders of the horrors of the whole thing. It is hard to imagine, but most people here will go and watch.

Dearest Mother,   **March 27, 1972, Gbedin**

While two little girls are doing my ironing, I'll try to get a letter written. Frankly, it would be much simpler to do the work myself, but we're constantly bothered with pleas for jobs, and actually, it's easier to have someone do it for me. The two girls are going to share the work. One, about 10, will do the flat things, for 10 cents a week. Another, about 14, will do other ironing for 25 cents a week. She will also do some other helping things. Her mother wants her to learn from a kwi person, how to do such things. The girls seem to be pretty unpredictable, so we will have to see how it goes.

This 10- year-old often comes carrying a two-year-old baby on her back. She minds the baby while the ma is at the farm. Girls learn to work while very young. Charles, the 10-year-old boy who cuts our grass, tells me he is making his own rice farm. (He cuts the grass with a grass whipper, something like a cutlass but curved instead of straight.) The man Charles stays with while he goes to school gave him a small plot of land—

perhaps 20 x 20 feet. He leveled it himself and now will plant rice plants in it, see that it is watered, mind the birds when the rice starts to head, and then harvest it. We are constantly astounded at the resourcefulness of the kids here. I'm sure if stories are true about the early days in the US, this same kind of thing was seen then, that is, kids earning their way at a very young age.

This week, I've been slowed down a lot by an infection in one toe. Last week, we went on a bush hike, and even though I wore tennis shoes, something *juked* me, pierced my shoe and into my toe. Consequently, I got a bad case of blood poisoning in one foot and a big "country sore" on the other shin. I've had to spend my time with hot soaks, and trips to the doctor at the mission for penicillin. Finally today it's improving. I must have gotten a really potent bug—haven't been able to do anything but sit. In a way, it was a boon. I have managed to sew by the hour—made a shirt

Ruth sewing with her treasured hand-operated machine. (Note rogue bars on the windows.)

for Harold, a jersey jump-suit for myself, a two-piece pant suit from tie-dyed damask, a blouse for myself, and a vest for John, plus some mending. Lately, my sewing has been mostly for other people, so it was nice to indulge myself for a change.

I give any cloth that is left over to Bea, who uses it to either make clothes for her little girls or to make quilts. She is always busy, sewing, making rice or cassava farm, or taking care of her garden.

I don't know if I told you yet, about the hike we took last Sunday. It was 10 miles round trip through the bush, with a good trail part of the way and an almost non-existent path part of the time. Our destination was a waterfall on the St. John River. It was a beautiful hike, huge trees, leaves of every kind, some orchids and lilies, and hundreds of butterflies.

Dear Vikki,   **March 27, 1972, Gbedin**

I think I told you last week about Kerstin, the Swedish girl who stayed with us for a week. She was a really cool girl. Everyone was entranced with her. For one thing, she was tall and sturdy, larger than Liberians, blonde, pink and white skin, and so friendly.

George, our Lebanese store man, was really smitten—gave her quite a rush. The night before she left, he thought we should have a farewell party for her and told me he would furnish everything, if I'd prepare it. So I made a list, and he kept sending things over. Mary helped, and we had a lot of fun. I made spaghetti with lots of mushrooms and meat. The Lebanese love garlic so I was lavish with it. Mary made garlic bread with lots of it. We made dip, antipasto and fresh pineapple upside down cake. He sent beer and wine and then later made Lebanese coffee, which is similar to Italian coffee, sweet and strong. It was quite an evening, had toasts and speeches.

The next day, when Kerstin was leaving, she kissed us all and told us to be sure to come and stay with them in Sweden. Who knows, we probably will. Her family breeds trotting horses, near Malmo.

It's 9:30 PM, and the lights have just gone out, so here we are with lamplight again. Actually, I like the dim lights, unless I have to be sewing or writing. Usually, I try to get things that have to be finished done by dark. It's easy to get out of the mood later.

Dearest Mother,   **April 1, 1972, Gbedin**

Paye, my little boy with epilepsy, is doing fine now. The family thinks he should come here and help me, and I can hardly drive him away. They have agreed he should start school, so next week we will try. I'll make his shirt and shorts—kids have to have standard uniforms—and will buy his copy book. So for this, he must come here every day and take care of the garbage and waste baskets, keep the bathroom sink clean, help in the garden, and keep his clothes clean. I hope that one of these days he will be responsible enough to take care of his medicine.

Bea and I went "walk about" last night in the village. The moon is "so-so" bright just now, a full moon making it almost light enough to read. I needed to follow up on people who had failed to come to the clinic for vaccinations, and in the daytime, they're at the farm and hard to find. We called on Paye's ma and pa who said "thank you" by giving me a chicken for my soup. So I continued on my visits, with a live chicken under my arm. This is considered about the best form of thank you. A chicken is considered a fine dash. Actually, they are very tough to eat, since they run around and hunt their own food, but they are pretty "dear" to buy and valuable to a Liberian.

We keep busy all the time, both on and off the job. Mary and I have decided we had better get used to not seeing our husbands for the next three to four months, since they are involved in so many projects.

Dearest Mother,   **April 9, 1972, Gbedin**

Last week, we went to a party given by one of the volunteers who came over with us. His mother, sister, and brother-law were visiting. He made palm butter soup with chicken, and rice, and the guests brought food, too. I made potato salad, my first in Liberia, since potatoes are imported from Europe and too expensive.

One of the Liberian friends that the host works with arranged the entertainment, which consisted of dancing to a record player and also country instruments. One of the Liberian farmers "danced with fire." He was dressed in khaki shorts. He held a short stick on which there was a kerosene soaked rag. It flamed for a long time, during which he danced and rolled the flame along his arms, legs, and abdomen. He lay on the ground and rolled over it and rolled the flame on himself, keeping time and executing very intricate steps. It was dark, with only some kerosene lanterns for light. It was really a fascinating thing to watch. There were no marks made on his body. People say he has "medicine" for it, so the fire won't burn him.

I'm not sure John's mother appreciated the performance, which was really unusual, and she has been so afraid of so many things. Using the outside latrine was almost more than she could bear. I must say, there are lots of things to get used to, in a year's time. I know I feel very different than when I first came here. I've never gotten used to the cockroaches, though, and they're harmless. But they are so big—two to three inches long, and they can fly. They always startle me. In the night, when I get up, I always shine the flashlight before stepping anyplace. They move so fast, it's very hard to kill them.

We see very few spiders, which is one thing I worried about. In the country houses, there are more spiders, but ours are just small. We do have lizards, though, up to ten inches long. Our cat always carries them into the house, and the small ones come in by themselves through the cracks. I don't mind them anymore.

I've really enjoyed your bias tape. So many of the kids who sew here can use it. Also, I make quite a few baby dresses, so it comes in handy for that. My little hand-operated sewing machine really gets a work out. During the past month, besides two shirts for Harold and the vest for John, I made a Vai shirt for Harry Need, a PC friend, three baby dresses, a shirt for a three-year-old boy. Also made a skirt and blouse for a school girl, who helps me in the house, and helped numerous girls sew their dresses and also cut out several.

I'm trying to teach them to cut their own since it is too time consuming for me. Besides, they should be able to do it, when I'm not here. The kids have to do some work for me before I'll sew for them, like iron, wash clothes, wash shelves, etc. All this plus the clinic keeps me hopping.

Dearest Vikki and Gill,   **April 9, 1972, Gbedin**

First of all, congratulations. We're thrilled about your big news and I'm sure would want to be there when you "born," as they say here. We'll be terribly disappointed if you're unable to come now, but of course wouldn't want you to do anything that might endanger you or the baby.

Here, if you're pregnant, they say you "got belly" or are a "belly woman." My prenatal clinic is called the "belly clinic" and there are lots of belly women here!

This week we cooked breadfruit for the first time—fried it something like parsnips. We bought one for 5 cents, and it's enough for two meals. Can't beat that for price, can you? Last evening we had baked fish with green onions and soy sauce, steamed rice, cabbage, avocado and green pepper salad, and papaya for dessert. Harold paid 50 cents for the fish, 1 cent each for the avocados, 25 cents for the cabbage. Everything else was given to us. The Chinese keep us in rice, insist on our taking it. We pick the pawpaws in the bush; the green peppers were dashed to us. This sounds like an American meal, doesn't it.

One of our friends has gone back to China for vacation and when he returns in one to two months he's bringing our camera—a Pentax Spotmatic 2, which was highly recommended. We're anxious to get it, since our little Instamatics are limited.

Incidentally, maybe you could send some more old sheer nighties and little half slips. The women love them—wear the nighties during the day with their lappas! Also the bras were very popular. I gave some to my friends and they were thrilled.

Dearest Mother,   **April 17, 1972, Gbedin**

Last evening we had what looked like a bad storm coming. The sky became very dark around 5 PM. The wind started to blow so hard that the trees were bending way over. Everything in the house started to fly around—pictures on the wall, magazines, table cloth flapping. Raindrops began flying in. It was very hard to get the shutters closed. Even with the shutters closed, the wind could come in the cracks. However, after about a half hour, things began to die down, and then the rain began. It rained most of the night. When there is no wind with the rain, it isn't nearly as hard on the house. Then the rain isn't driven in. There was also thunder and lightning for about two hours.

People here think if you have "medicine" for lightning, it won't hit your house. We have some that John's mother gave us. She had it in the corner of her bedroom. Harold wanted some to bring home for you to see. It's about six inches long, made of leather and other fibers, with cowry shells attached to it. It's quite ugly, but is supposed to have power. John says when a storm starts, people will cook rice for the medicine and set it in a pot by the thing and talk to the medicine.

People attribute a lot of power to many inanimate things, such as masks, which are used in many ceremonial activities, bush society, etc. The person who is wearing the mask becomes what he is portraying, in the minds of the people. Consequently, when the people see masks, many of them are frightened. We have one Mano mask that we can't hang on our wall—keep it in our bedroom—because the people don't like to see it. Bea says she feels like it is looking right at her, and it makes her shiver.

I don't think I told you about the flowers by our house. There are several shades of bougainvillea bushes all around the house, in bloom most of the time. There is a hibiscus hedge; they aren't nearly as beautiful as the ones in Hawaii. There are other flowering trees, tall ones such as acacia, plus some shrubs which have bright pink and red leaves. It is nice to be able to look out of the windows and see beautiful blossoms most of the time.

This house has been here for a long time and was usually for one of the administrators. None of the country people have flowers around their houses. In fact, they seldom try to beautify their homes with any decoration. Their yards are always swept clean, and no grass or shrubs grow around them, because of the danger of snakes lurking around. Most villages would fine the people if they failed to keep their yards clean. However, they could have some flowers around the edge of the yard, but I've never seen any. Sometimes, a person will pick a flower and wear it in their hair, but not often is this seen here, either.

Did I tell you that Mary had named her kitten Harold? (Our cat is its mother.) We are just starting a garden again. Harold and Larry have each rototilled a space and are laying out the rows. Our plantings are different from home. For example, we have collards, eggplant, leeks, and ginger root. Things like carrots and beets won't grow here. One of the farmers has been bringing us cucumbers, so today, I'm making pickles.

Dearest Mother,   **April 24, 1972, Gbedin**

I can't believe it's almost the end of the month. Lately, we've been in a state of suspended animation, waiting to learn if Vikki and Gil will be coming a week from now. We haven't had a letter since she wrote the first of the month, saying that she is pregnant and might not be able to come because of the immunizations that are required. Her doctor says she can't have the small pox vaccine and perhaps Liberia won't let anyone enter without one.

For some reason, we haven't received any mail all month, so we're sweating out her visit just now. In the meantime, I haven't been able to get serious about writing letters. Today is mail day, but we learned last week it is a national holiday, for the induction of the new vice president. There has been a holiday every week for the past six weeks. Last Wednesday, we learned at noon that it was a holiday—some special day in Sierra Leone— so everyone closed up as soon as they heard it.

You asked about Easter celebrations. Only the Christian people celebrate as we do, with church services and such. However, the schools have a week's holiday, and Good Friday is a national holiday as is Easter. Most of the people just enjoy the time off, but the farmers keep on working.

John's mother and stepfather came on Saturday to visit in Gbedin. This is the first time his mother has come to Gbedin since she was a child. They brought us three chickens—a rooster and two hens, penned in a small basket made from palm leaves and bamboo sticks, a 100 lb. bag of eddoes, and a huge branch of plantain, what the people call a "helluva" branch. It must have had at least 100 plantains on it. Plantains look like large, pointed bananas. All of these were carried by head load from his home to the motor road, about five miles, and then carried by taxi here. They wanted to tell us thank you for helping John. They had wanted to bring us 100 lb. of new country rice, which is really fine rice, but someone from here had told them we had plenty of rice here. John was vexed, because he really wanted us to have the rice.

Incidentally, Robert Toe has not been hanged yet. The case was taken to the Supreme Court, which has just been convened. We see him whenever we go to Sanniquellie. He is confined at the soldiers' barracks and is usually sitting in the yard, behind a stick fence. People say he has a chain on his foot.

Recently, Evelyn sent me a big bag of colored buttons, and some trimmings. It has been wonderful to have them, since most of the kids had to have new uniforms, and buttons aren't plentiful. These buttons were just the right color, so the kids were really tickled. They would look at the bag, and say, "Dammit," in an awed voice.

Harold's chicken flock has been increasing. He has some hens that hatched, plus the three new ones, plus three I've been dashed recently. We have a huge white American rooster that George, the Lebanese man, gave Harold, which Harold calls (the rooster), Gorgeous George. GG is afraid of his older, smaller country rooster though and has to stay around the edge of the yard.

We also have a nice big garden started. Mr. Tsi, one of our Chinese neighbors, helped Harold and Charles, our little "yard boy," plant it. He gave Harold starter plants of lettuce, eggplant, and cabbage and will fertilize it for him. Harold planted tomato seeds on Friday or Saturday, and they are up today, Monday. Things grow so fast here, must grow day and night.

Dearest Mother,   **May 1, 1972, Gbedin**

The months do go by, don't they? It is just about a year until we will be coming home. Some days when we are feeling discouraged, we wish it were sooner. Fortunately, we don't both get discouraged at the same time.

Looking forward to Vikki's visit has been a morale booster. She should be arriving in a week, although we still aren't certain because of the small pox vaccination. We are now receiving mail only every two weeks because of austerity in the PC budget. So planning with her about their visit has been a slow process at best.

I seem to keep so busy that it's hard to find time to read, for the first time in my life. Helping the girls to sew takes so much of my time, home visits, constant interruptions here at home, and overnight guests. Besides, I'm enjoying doing macramé and fiddling with seeds and beads. One of my friends, a "fini" country woman, came today and asked me to make her six-year-old son's school uniform shirt. I had made his shorts last week. The week prior to that, she had brought me a huge branch of bananas. I told her I would make the uniform, and then told her she could say thank you "not just in her mouth'" but by bringing some of her friends and dancing and singing for Vikki. She was really tickled about that and began dancing around the dining room right then, her little baby bouncing with her, tied to her back. It's such fun to watch.

She is an asthmatic, and I became acquainted with her when she had a bad attack, and I was able to help her. Since then, she stops in, often bringing me some small thing, eddoes, a pineapple, some rice. In turn, I occasionally take her something, like at July 26th, Christmas, New Year's.

Yesterday we took another good hike, practically straight up! There is a mountain behind us, about 1,000 feet high, separating Liberia from Guinea. Some people from a nearby village make a rice farm on the top of the mountain. We decided to climb to the top so we could see the surrounding country. It was a four-hour hike to go-come. Some parts of the trail were fairly easy to find, but often we had to hang on to saplings and roots to keep from falling or sliding backwards. Talk about getting out of breath. A school boy "carried" us or I'm sure we would have gotten lost. He was barefoot, of course.

There are so many interesting things to see, different kinds of foliage, although few flowers, and many odd growths. With a Liberian boy along, at least we knew what we could safely eat. Can you imagine, the people go up this hill, and others, every morning, to their farm, and home again at night, carrying all the needed items with them? Of course, the path they use daily is not so steep. We came home that way, but wanted to go up the other side of the mountain.

The next time we go to Monrovia, I'll try to buy some sturdy walking shoes. Tennis shoes just aren't enough protection from stickers and rocks, although I didn't hurt myself this time. We saw one big snake, but no animals. Because the farms are so far from their homes, the people have to go early and stay late. So it's hard to find any one at home during the day.

I had meant to mention that all the mountains, just like 99 percent of Liberia, are covered with bush and tall trees, except where the people have hacked out their rice and cassava farms.

Dear Vikki,   **May 6, 1972, Gbedin**

We've just received your letter telling us you can't come. In a way, we were prepared for the news, after they said you couldn't take certain shots. Needless to say, we're disappointed, but relieved too, in case something unforeseen might happen to you while you were travelling. We would love to have you at Christmas time, but will wait and see. After all, getting a new baby isn't like getting a new puppy.

As far as our plans are concerned, we hadn't really made any, with yours so up in the air. We had made arrangements to stay with people in Monrovia when you arrived, and also with some up-country friends. Peace Corps had promised us a car, and we made plans to carry you into the bush to John's home for an overnight stay. He will go next week and tell them not to prepare for you.

Anyway, if you come later, things can get going then. Lots of people here are looking for you. They say "Neh my, yah," when we tell them you can't come just now. Also, a couple of our charlie friends were looking forward to your visit—going to bring "fine, fine tings" for you to see and, hopefully, to buy!

Now that you aren't coming, we will take a few days off and go to Sierra Leone to the cloth market. It was one of the trips we wanted to take, with you. It is about a 250-mile trip to the northwestern tip of Liberia and then across the border to Sierra Leone. This is where so much of the fine wax print and tie-dye fabrics are made. The variety is fantastic, and the price is better, even though one pays a small duty. We want to get some cloth to send for Christmas. Besides, I really feel like I need a vacation.

How have you been feeling, Vikki? I've always felt that pregnancy is a very normal state, so a person should be able to carry on most activities, with slight modifications! Trying to figure out when people are expecting here (at the clinic) is a riot. First of all, they go by the country moon, not by the month. When the new moon is coming on, this is the beginning of the month for them, and it always occurs during the previous month. For instance, the May moon began about April16.

Then, of course, trying to get them to remember when they "last saw their time" is another problem. Was it before Christmas, after July 26, when they were brushing farm, scratching farm, and so on. The same is true for trying to learn when they "borned," so you can know the age of a child. I get a kick out of trying to figure it out.

Dear Mother,   **May 13, 1972, Monrovia**

Happy Mother's Day. Too bad, I always seem to be late for special days. We've been spending a few days in Monrovia, getting ready for a vacation in Ivory Coast. We have to have visas, exit and re-entry permits, foreign money and so on. So it all takes time. We'll leave next Friday.

Everything is fine here—busy as usual and feeling well. We're disappointed not to see the kids, but know it is all for the best. I hope all is well with you, and that you aren't working too hard.

Dearest Mother,   **May 14, 1972, Gbedin**

My card written yesterday, was so hurriedly done, I decided to write again today and take more time. We drove home from Monrovia yesterday. We left at 3 PM, and got home after 8. It is 190 miles of rough, hard driving, but fortunately, no rain.

I don't know if I've told you that Harold and Larry now have a Toyota pickup, at least until the end of July. It makes it much nicer to be able to go when we want to, instead of having to take taxies, which are really dangerous, since the drivers are so bad about speeding. The curvy roads, loose gravel, and ruts don't mix too well with speed. Harold can keep the truck repaired, and the DA provides the gas. Gas is around 60 cents a gallon, so we can't afford to buy much gas on our salaries!

I was going to tell you about an experience I had last week. About 8 PM, a fellow came to the house and said I was needed at the clinic. He said something had happened to Marie's baby. She is the daughter-in-law of the chief, about 20 years old, and one of my friends. Her baby was three weeks old. I took my flashlight and hurried off with him. As we came near the clinic, I could hear people crying real loud. I started to run.

When I reached the clinic, the father met me, and cried, "Ruth, the baby, the baby." It wasn't breathing. There was no heart beat. It was lying on a table, with people crowded around. I started mouth-to-mouth resuscitation, but it was no use, of course. With their color, you can't tell cyanosis. The baby was fine at noon when I had seen it, and Bea said it was fine at 7. Later, it had started to have breathing problems, and just stopped breathing.

One of the things people do here, which I'm trying every day to stop, is give new babies, and all young babies, water with their hands—lay it down across their lap, with the head lower than the body. The baby chokes, aspirates, always has a cough and bronchitis. I'm sure the mother, or her old ma, was trying to give the baby water this way and killed it.

Soon, everyone left except Bea, Daniel the dresser, and myself, with the baby. No one seemed to know what to do, so finally, I picked up the baby and said, "I will carry it to the chief's quarter." So they agreed. Soon, it began to rain in torrents, so we had to run or get drenched.

At the chief's house several men were sitting on the porch, but the women were all in the house crying. They laid the baby on a small table and then just sat there, with only a kerosene lantern for light. They said they had to bury the baby that night, that a baby that young couldn't sleep in the town all night. The rain finally stopped about midnight. Then they went and dug the grave and buried the baby.

The baby's father, Henry, said to me, "I won't cry for this baby anymore. He came to try me, and now, he's gone back." They say the baby went back, when it dies. This seems to be a common idea. Life just goes on, as though it never happened. It was a very traumatic experience for me. I couldn't sleep after I finally got home.

This all happened on the same day we got word from Vikki that she couldn't come to see us, because the doctor was afraid the malaria medicine would be bad for her baby. I must say, I can't feel too bad about their not coming, when I see so many babies die here.

We're all set to go on Friday AM to Ivory Coast. We got our visas and the other necessary papers already. Larry will drive us to the border, which is about 30 to 40 miles north and east of here. We will get a taxi at the border and drive to Man (pronounced "mon"), a kind of resort area which is about a day's drive from the border. Neither of us wants to spend a lot of time traveling, just want to go and "sit down" someplace and relax. Bea and Daniel will take care of things for me.

Dearest Mother,   **May 21, 1972, Ivory Coast**

The drive from Gbedin to the Ivory Coast border was about the worst we have experienced, so far as road conditions are concerned. It is about a fifty-mile trip, but turned out to be a three-hour ordeal in our Toyota pickup. Larry drove, since he wanted to stop in the town of Karmple on the way back to talk to the paramount chief about co-ops, and this gave him a reason to justify the gas. Harold "rode shot gun," and several times he had to get out, cross a log bridge that was in a terrible state of repair (all the cross planks were gone and only four to five planks were stretched across). Then Harold had to guide Larry as he approached and drove across the bridge.

One time a big Mercedes transport truck just barely made it across, the truck crew guiding and directing the driver. Then driver and crew all came back to the bridge, and, with Harold, gestured and generally confused Larry as he crept across. (There was a stream under the bridge.) How Larry got back alone we don't know yet.

The road from Sanniquellie to the border was a succession of wash outs, gullies down the center of the road, deep puddles, and steep up and down and around curves. I was holding on as though I was on a roller coaster. We arrived at the border, however, without mishap, where Larry turned around and left us. We crossed the river on a raft made of logs lashed together. It was about four by twelve in size. The driver pulled it by means of a cable stretched from shore to shore. The river is only about 100 feet wide at that place. Any goods that are transported between Ivory Coast and Liberia here are trucked in the big trucks, rafted across, and reloaded in waiting vehicles on the other side of the river. Cattle are just driven across from Ivory Coast, driven down the road to Karmple where they are loaded and hauled to Monrovia for butchering.

Just on the other side of the river there is a customs check—very routine, and where you wait for a taxi. This too, proved to be different. It was just a shack with a few benches outside. People had already begun to collect and by 11 AM, after waiting two hours, about 40 more people were waiting, still no taxi.

We had become acquainted with a Jamaican man who had become a Liberian citizen. He was a cattle buyer and butcher in Monrovia. He spoke excellent English and had traveled extensively in West Africa. It was our good luck that he was there, since getting away from the border wasn't easy, and he really helped. When a money bus finally came, it was loaded, a pickup with a covered top, packed to the gills. Before the passengers even started to get out, the new passengers began to scramble in, suitcases, bundles and all. Some of the passengers had to crawl out through the sides, no way through the ends. What a riot, yelling, laughing, and hubbub. We just stood and watched, didn't know what to do.

A second pickup came, the same thing occurred, only this time we stuck with our new-found friend, who was going to dicker for the front seat. He jumped in one side, a woman jumped in the other side. The back was full immediately, easily seventeen people scrunched in, bag and baggage, with much on top too. However, this taxi had come as a charter, and the law in Ivory Coast is that if a bus is chartered to go-come, he can't take passengers back from that point. What a hassle, more screaming and hollering and gesturing and running around, chatter, chatter in French, of course.

After about a half-hour, the driver persuaded the people to get out of the vehicle. Fortunately for us, Mr. Wilson knew the driver well, and told us to just take it easy, we'll get a ride. Finally, the driver was allowed to go, Harold and I got in the front seat, Wilson and his assistant in the back. Actually, not being able to take the other passengers was no penalty, because there were many villages along the road and, before long, our truck was loaded.

The scenery was just about like it is in Liberia—a narrow dirt road through the tall bush, with small villages every mile or so. It was only about a 30-minute drive to Danane, the small town where we had to have our passports checked. Unfortunately, it was then about 12:30, and here, as in Liberia, everything closes from 12 to 2:30. We walked around and found a place to buy a soft drink, no water at all. You just can't take a chance on drinking water in most West African countries.

It was another long wait at the police station, where they checked our passports, and did the necessary paper work, and finally, we could go find transportation for Man. A bus was just about ready to go, actually a pickup again. We got the last two seats in the back and by 4:30 took off for Man. What a dusty, rough trip. I held a small boy, about four years, on my lap most of the way. He fell asleep and would have bounced off the seat if I hadn't held him. Two or three times we had to stop at customs checks, and each time there was someone whose papers weren't in order, so we had to wait interminably. All this time, since 6 AM, we hadn't had anything to drink except a bottle of orange soda, and two boiled eggs to eat.

Finally, about 6:30 we arrived in Man, which was about 50 miles from home. We found our hotel, checked in, had showers and kind of revived. The hotel is rather nice. It is located on a hill overlooking the city, has a section called the *complement,* which is only half price, which is where we are staying. It has a bathroom with shower and sink (toilet down the hall), a comfortable bed with mosquito netting, and costs us 1359 francs a day ($5) With the devaluation of the dollar, the franc is not worth as much now, unfortunately for us. We can't drink the water here, either, unless we put four iodine tablets in it.

This is a French-speaking country, and my high school French is pretty hazy. However, I have a French dictionary, and so far we're getting along OK. I'll have to tell you about the dinner we had last night. We were both starved, as you can imagine, with no food all day, and exhausted too. Dinner hour begins at 8 PM. We decided to order the "meal of the house," for 1000 francs each. It started with a vegetable puree soup and French bread, then a plate of cold meat—chicken, ham, roast beef, salami, and other sliced meat, with olives, pickles, and potato salad. Then they came with a green salad with endive, and then they brought a tray of cheeses—many kinds of French cheeses. Later they brought fruit. The last was espresso coffee, very strong. We just made it back to our room where we fell into bed and just died for about 12 hours.

Today, we spent at the market, until noon. It must cover at least two city blocks, some outside, some under a roof, with everything imaginable for sale. We want to buy country cloth, a hand-woven cotton material, woven in strips about four inches wide, sewn into lappa sizes. It is much less expensive here than in Liberia, so during the week we will do some serious shopping.

The hotel has a swimming pool, miniature golf, lawn bowling, and tennis. We spent most of the afternoon at the swimming pool, lying in the sun and swimming. We expect to be really lazy while we are here. We are both very tired, and feel we need a real rest, away from the constant interruptions at home.

It is so strange to be in a country where a foreign language is spoken almost exclusively. You don't understand them, and they don't understand you, which leads to a strange sense of isolation. When we first landed in Liberia, it was somewhat the same, even though English is the official national language. Since the bulk of the people speak Liberian English, that is nearly unintelligible until you get the hang of it. Additionally, the people don't understand you unless you speak it. Now, I have to watch myself so I don't use it when I don't have to.

Ivory Coast appears to be a more prosperous country than Liberia. For one thing, it appears that there is less large scale "money eating" in the government. The roads are better; in fact, all the villages can be reached by motor car, while in Liberia, I believe, more cannot be than can be reached by car. There are more hard-surfaced roads.

Here in Man, the housing looks to be of better quality. For one thing, Ivory Coast was formerly a French colony, and while the Europeans exploited these colonies, they also made improvements that benefited the country. People say this is evident in the former British colonies as well. Ghana is an example.

The people dress differently than in Liberia. For instance in Monrovia, most men wear Western-style trousers and suits, often a Liberian-style, colorful shirt, short sleeved, open neck. Many women there wear kwi clothes. Here, the men dress in loose-fitting gowns that come below the knee. Actually, they are just a long lappa, folded in half, a neck opening cut in and the sides only sewn at the bottom. They wear trousers to match, tight at the bottom and loose and gathered at the top, or else, just trousers made from a lappa, folded in half, sewn along the sides except for a place at the bottom for the legs and feet to slip through, and gathered at the top.

Everything here is very colorful, lots of wax prints, and tie dye, etc., fabrics. The women wear the usual lappa, over-blouse, and head tie. Often their garments are very nice with design stitching along the edges, made with a sewing machine that is similar to the Necchi.

Actually, there is so much to see wherever you go, that it is fascinating any time. And to have someone tell you about it isn't nearly as interesting as seeing it yourself. It's difficult to do justice to it for someone else. However, this may give you a little glimpse of life here. We keep saying how much you would enjoy seeing West Africa.

Dearest Mother,   **May 31, 1972, Gbedin**

This will be a short letter. Harold is going to Monrovia, so I'll have a chance to mail it sooner than expected. He has to go to the dentist, and the only two dentists in the country are either in Lamco or Monrovia. He will stay overnight and come back the next AM. There are always errands to do there when either one of us goes to the city, so it always takes longer than one plans.

We got back from Ivory Coast on the weekend. It was a long trip. One taxi (pick-up) we rode in from the border to Sanniquellie, which is about 35-40 miles, broke down four times. The trip, the 35-mile part, took us six hours. It wasn't really so bad, everyone was good natured. Harold had to finally fix the taxi.

Rainy season has begun early this year. Each day, around 4 PM, it starts to pour; lightning and wind come. Sometimes at night it rains too, so the ground is pretty soggy to walk about. A few hours after the rain has stopped, the mud is dried up and it is fine until the next downpour.

Things are going OK with my work. I think I'll finally be successful in getting the services of a trained midwife one day a week, the day I hold the baby and child clinic. I'm hoping by working closely with her, Bea will be able to learn enough to be able to handle things when I leave.

I'm also slowly getting more supplies. Last week, I finally got a sphygmomanometer (to take blood pressures) and a stethoscope, after requesting one for five months. It is very discouraging to try to get supplies, things one is promised, and one waits and waits, and never gets an answer. It is the same in the Ag Dept.

Today, a cassava snake was killed, here in the field. It was about three feet long, but nearly five inches thick. It was a strange looking thing, light tan with brown designs on it. Harold is getting the skin. It is one of the really deadly ones, but very slow moving.

I made passion fruit jelly today. I experimented with it, since I don't have a recipe. I put some lime juice and sugar in it, and it turned out just fine.

Dearest Mother,   **June 4, 1972, Gbedin**

An interesting situation has come up. One of our friends and his wife (he works for US Geological Survey and has been here two years) are looking for a baby to take home. They have a small son and want to adopt a part Chinese child.

You know, there are a lot of Chinese men here, working as rice and agriculture specialists, for the government. Some have been here for several years, so there are a fair number of part Chinese babies, darling little things of whom the families are very proud. One thing that some Liberian parents do is force their young daughters to "be loving to," as they call it, the Chinese or Americans, or people with money so the man will give the parents money. There are three Chinese babies here at Gbedin. The Forces (the geological fellow) want a year-old girl. One of the school girls, Annie Dolo, has a baby girl a year old, born in January. We were asked to talk to Annie and her parents, to see if they want to let the people adopt her baby.

People give their children away here so often, if they think the child will have a better life. Half the school kids here at Gbedin are living with someone else, usually so they can go to school, or if the family can't afford to take care of them. Or maybe, only one of the couple is the parent, while the other lives elsewhere. Lots of people (men) have "outside" children living in the home, children they've had with someone else. The father in Liberia has the claim of the child. Even though it may be living with the mother, he can take it at any time.

The Chinese father of Annie's baby is back in Liberia, but living in a town at least fifty miles away from here. He does support the child. He will have to be consulted and could be the one to say no. Larry and I talked with Annie and her grandmother and told them they should tell us today. So far, we haven't seen them. We only put it before them and didn't discuss the pros and cons at all. We certainly don't want to influence them. Seeing how girls fare in this country, and how so many babies have such a hard time, I'm hoping they decide to give the baby away. I think eventually, Annie will be forced to, anyway. So, we will wait and see.

Harold and I talk so often about how much you'd enjoy it here, even if the weather is so warm and humid. Now we have a wild idea so decided to write and see what you think about coming to visit us. You're going to be celebrating your 80th birthday this fall, a kind of special time. Anyway, see what you think of the idea and let us know.

Dearest Mother,   **June 11, 1972, Gbedin**

Another week gone by. There is always so much to do that I never seem to have enough time. Lately, I've been besieged by girls who want to sew, so my afternoons are a madhouse. With two or three girls, all beginners, their little sisters or the babies they're minding, plus a friend or two, there is never a dull moment. These are girls who have probably never used a sewing machine, and don't know the first thing about cutting out their clothes. And remember, this is a hand-operated machine! They never want to quit until their dress is finished. Finally, Harold laid down

Ruth making biscuits in her little kitchen.

the law—they have to be out of the house by 5 o'clock. I don't let them come on Sundays. One thing I'm trying to get them to learn to do is to sew simple things by themselves, and then they'll be able to earn some money by sewing children's or baby clothes. There are few ready-made things for sale, and what there is are too dear, so everyone has to have their children's clothes made by a tailor. Some of the tailors do very poor work, so I'm sure some of the girls can do better than that. The girls do small things for me, like clean vegetables and do my hand washing, such things. But remember, most of them have to be shown how to do any new task, since it's not something they do in their homes, except washing. One day, I sent one girl into the bathroom to wash the sink. You should have seen the room when I checked. The sink was clean, but there was water everywhere.

Yesterday, we drove to Sanniquellie to the market. Saturday is the big day there. It is always a fascinating experience. There are people everywhere with their produce spread out on a mat or displayed on the ground. Noise, bright colors, strange sights and smells. We take a couple of rice bags [hand-woven, country-style, carry-all bags] along and stock up for the week on meat (tough cow meat), fish, or maybe if we're lucky some deer meat. You can buy other kinds, like monkey and snails, but we "can't able," as they say here. Also, we get vegetables and fruits. Yesterday I bought a small pineapple for 2 cents! Also got ground peas (peanuts), brought them home, washed them, salted them, and put them in the oven for about two hours on very low heat. They are just like the roasted peanuts you get at home. They cost us 20 cents for about a pint of shelled nuts. We can pound them up in a mortar and make peanut butter. And at the market there is always a lot of cloth for sale, also beads, mats, baskets, gourds, etc.

Harold says to tell you he still loves you and misses you. He also said to tell you his projects are coming along fine. The mud-block house is almost up, and the roof should go on this week. The farmers made the blocks for the house from mud and a little cement, using a hand-operated ram (press). They had to make about 5,000 of them, then sun-dry them for a few days. The land clearing is coming along well, too. The 40 acres will soon be ready for planting. The ditches are being dug by the farmers, by hand, and then they can plant the rice. Everything goes so much slower than you can imagine, for lots of crazy reasons.

Dearest Mother,   **June 13, 1972, Gbedin**

One thing that is different in Liberia from the US, at least in the northwest, is that everything is the same here, from one end of the country to the other. It's all just "so, so" [almost competely] bush—palm trees, tall leaf trees, and all kinds of bushy bush, very monotonous. In one season or the other, it is always the same. During dry season some of the leaf trees do change color, so there is a little contrast. When I flew from here to Monrovia, I was amazed to see absolutely the same scenery all the way.

There are so many fascinating things to see and hear and experience here, I wish I had the ability and determination to record some of them. Some of the stories people tell me about their life in the country towns, and stories the old people have told them would interest other people, I'm sure. Nearly every day I hear something new from Bea that gives me more understanding of the people. Or else, maybe I'll never understand them. I'm more aware than ever, that you can't judge things from your own standards and values.

This whole experience in Gbedin, trying to get people to move from country farm, with one crop a year, to growing paddy rice with harvests three times a year, using fertilizer and machines, demonstrates it vividly. There is no explanation for the way some of them do some of the time. There are about two farmers, out of close to 100, who really operate with good practices consistently. Of course, I have to remember that in the past ten years here, the government hasn't been consistent or dependable in the support and assistance they promised the farmers. We are seeing that now in the things they've asked us to do here, and how the support really comes. But we do enjoy the people, regardless. Last week Bea and I went walking to Gbedin Town, which was so typical of many of our days here.

I read an interesting book about Liberia, *Journey Without Maps*, by Graham Greene, a British author, about a trip he took about 30 years ago. It was published in 1936. The author took a walking trip across Liberia, and even though written so long ago, the picture he paints is surprisingly similar to the interior today. I think you would enjoy it, since he is a good writer, as well. He describes the trip to the waterfall, for example, where we hiked.

Dearest Mother,   **June 25, 1972, Gbedin**

How the weeks fly by. Tomorrow, Larry and Mary leave for Monrovia, to pick up Mary's mother at the airport. She will stay a month with them, and then go home when they do.

We have another house guest, a young man from Wyoming, who is visiting friends in Monrovia. They wanted him to have a visit up-country, and asked us to have him. We've gained quite a reputation as a place to come to get a great up-country experience! We should be so successful! Anyway, he's a nice kid, but a vegetarian, the second one we've had here.

So many of the kids we came over with have already gone home. Most became discouraged because their jobs weren't what they expected, or the support needed wasn't there, or for other personal reasons. Some just couldn't seem to adjust to being alone in a village with only country people.

People who have been here before, when Peace Corps first came, say it was very unusual for volunteers to terminate early, at that time. I would hate to give up before I had fulfilled my obligation. I think 50 percent of our group has gone home. Another couple, the one our age, will likely leave when the school term ends the last of August.

We are thinking we will go home next year by way of Taiwan and Japan. Our Chinese friends here say they will welcome us with open arms, and really show us their country. So if things work out OK, we expect to do that. We live frugally here, so we can save enough to be able to see some more of the world before we come back home.

We think our experience here, learning the culture and relating with the people, is greatly enhanced by adopting as much of their ways as we can. Of course, if we really lived like they do, we'd likely be sick, malnourished, and uncomfortable as well.

I've just gotten a new job, on top of my others, although I expect to cut out a lot of the sewing instruction. Beginning July 10th, I will teach nutrition at the School of Nursing at Ganta Methodist Mission. There are two missionary nurses who teach there, but one is going home for four months. While she is gone, I'll start with nutrition, and probably do Diet Therapy when that is finished. Vera [Hughlett], the other nurse, said, "Of course, if you want to teach other subjects, any are available."

I won't tell the PC health person (an American) since she wouldn't approve. She approves of little that I do, actually. You may remember I had to go over her head to the PC director and the director of Public Health to even begin working here at Gbedin. So it is understandable that she would be hypercritical of me. Ganta Mission will send a car for me and bring me home. Also told me I could have the hours and days I wanted. I will go Monday, Wednesday, and Friday afternoons. I'm looking forward to teaching again.

Dearest Mother,   July 9, 1972, Gbedin

Here it is a rainy Sunday. It has been really pouring since 7 AM, four hours ago. There seems to be much more rain this year than last rainy season. It does interfere with the projects that have to be completed. When the weather was OK, there was no fuel. Finally, the fuel arrived, and now it's too wet for the Cats to work.

Harold gets directions from someone in the Ministry of Agriculture, and before he can carry them out, someone else countermands it and says something else is supposed to happen. He's in a quandary half the time and is getting quite disgusted. Anyway, July will soon be over, and we will take stock. I don't know if I mentioned that a private company from Israel is now responsible for all the land clearing and development, which puts a different slant on Harold's role. Right now, he's in charge of the project for them and has to do it until the big celebration. However, Harold says he won't work for a private company, that his responsibility is to the government. So we will see.

It looks like I will have to stop writing for a while to do some repair work. One of the workers got in a fight with another worker here—some kind of "woman business." He fell down, or was knocked down, and landed against a bench and cut his face wide open just below his eye. No one goes to Ganta for stitches, so I usually manage to get it together with a "butterfly" bandage, and so far have had good luck. They all think "Mah" can fix them.

Did I ever tell you that John Chambers is back in Liberia? He took a job in another part of Liberia, for a private company, as head mechanic. We haven't seen him, but one of our friends ran into him in Monrovia. We're hoping our paths won't cross again. He caused us a lot of grief. He always swore he wouldn't set foot in Liberia again, but was back in Liberia within two months.

We also learned yesterday that the Supreme Court has completed their session, and apparently has made a ruling in the Robert Toe case. The County Prosecutor told Harold yesterday that he would let him know what the action is to be. We see Robert whenever we go to Sanniquellie, because he's still in custody at the soldier's barracks, right beside the road as we enter the town. He is inside a stick fence, has a little hut there with two or three other prisoners.

The National Public Health service is sending a smallpox vaccination team to Nimba County this month, so I must get all the villages around here notified and ready to respond when the team comes here. Usually, you have to make the people think that the President has ordered everyone to be vaccinated, or else, in order to get them to come and bring their kids. There is a great deal of traffic from Guinea here, and since there is no vaccination program there, the Liberian Health Department is trying to get the people who live near the Guinea entry points, vaccinated. We are only a few yards from the St. John River, which separates the two countries. In fact, we have lots of children at the clinic who come from Guinea. They are Mano, but live on the other side.

Tomorrow, my first class at Ganta begins, so today I expect to be busy preparing lessons. Hopefully, it will enable me to cut down the sewing with the kids, which really wears me out.

Dear Vikki,   **July 16, 1972, Gbedin**

We do a lot of talking about what we will do in a year or two. We can't quite see settling down in Tacoma again, or having me all caught up in the career rat race again. We could stay here in PC, providing there would be challenging jobs for us. Right now, I can't see staying if the government doesn't support things better. Harold could stay and work for a private company or even for the government if he wanted to, but there would be a lot of details to agree upon. The next few months will tell us a lot, I'm sure, and help us to make some decisions.

We were able to listen to some of the Democratic Convention on VOA—to McGovern's acceptance speech, for one thing. What do you think his chances for election are? I suppose it's impossible to defeat a president who has been in only one term. Incumbents always seem to have an advantage.

When the vice president was elected here in January, after Tolbert was inaugurated, there was only one person to vote for. Later, the newspapers told about the fine note of confidence he received.

Yesterday we had another soccer game here and also a volley ball game. I wish you could see the football, as they call it here. Some of the kids play in bare feet and kick the ball with no problem. After the game is over (our school lost both games, 2 to 0 for the soccer) the host school has to provide entertainment, which means they have to cook for the visitors and have a dance. The girls did the cooking, cooked two bags of rice (100 lb. bags) and potato greens soup with fish. They also provided cane juice, palm wine, and beer. Remember, this is a grade school! They always have a great time, noisy as all get out, as the evening wears on.

Today, we got a new diesel light plant. Our old one was quite bad. Now we should have electricity from 7 AM until 10 at night, that is, providing the fuel is supplied.

I wish you could see the little model house they have built—one of the efforts for the "26" celebration. The mason here is a real craftsman, and is one of the few people we've met here who is really consistent in doing good work. He has done a beautiful job of building the house, laying the blocks that the farmers made. He then plastered both the inside and the outside with a cement mixture. The carpenters have made doors and window frames, and shutters. The shutters, doors and window casings are made of solid mahogany, one-inch thick for the shutters.

Now they are supposed to paint it, which I hate because it's such beautiful wood. But that is what the Agriculture Dept. says they must do. The house has a living room, two bedrooms, and a piazza—kind of like a living room, but without a door. People call our living room our piazza. The kitchen will be outside, a separate building out the back door. Also will be a separate bath house and toilet. No one takes a bath inside.

They are supposed to build several other houses, apparently have some private financing for them. But they really need someone to push the work, such as Harold and Larry have done, in order to get the things done. UN building specialists are supposed to help in some way, too.

Mary and Larry will be leaving in about two weeks for a six-week vacation. I will miss them while they're gone. We live next door and do a lot of visiting back and forth. No other Caucasians live here. However, we do have other friends, Liberian and Chinese, so we're not lonely.

Soon the big 26th Celebration will be here. They say the President will make a brief visit here to see the model house and the new farm areas. I hope he doesn't disappoint the people. They have worked very hard to get things ready, much of the time without the promised government support. For example, Harold and Larry promoted the oil palm venture because the government (the DA) said they would give the seedling trees if the people would prepare the land and also because the income from the trees would be quite an addition for the co-op members. The farmers hand-slashed about 20 acres, and the bulldozers cleared another 20 acres. Then the farmers had to cut sticks in the bush to mark each hole. Each *ku* (work group) had to dig 300 holes each (two feet by two feet and two feet deep), and then were paid 1½ cents a hole for the other 1,500. Then this week, a DA official called up on the radio and said the trees were already two weeks late and asked who would pay for the trees. The first time any money has been discussed.

Finally, yesterday, they got the money business straightened out, and apparently, the trees are on the way. They have to be planted by the 26th for the President to see! The trees should begin to bear in about three years, and actually should be a good cash crop for the farmers. But since rice is what they know, and why they came here to Gbedin from their home villages, it's hard to get them interested in this work.

I've been helping John get his speech ready for after the football and volleyball games tomorrow. He's Vice President of the school and is supposed to make a speech, along with some other kids, before the post-game festivities, a rice and soup feed for the visiting team. He had written his speech, but wanted me to give him a big word to impress the audience. These people are the greatest speechmakers. They love to talk, and sometimes everyone and his brother has to give his bit. You should attend a PTA meeting here sometime! I gave him "victorious," and "overcome." He was quite elated over the additions.

Today, I took Mary's mother for a walk to Gbedin town. It is a 20-minute walk down the railroad track. I wanted to visit some babies there, and she wanted to see a village. The weather is overcast now in the morning, so we left about 8:30 and returned around 11. She was so warm and sweaty, but I was just right. It made me realize how I've become acclimated to this warm, moist atmosphere. I remember how uncomfortable I was last year by the time I'd taken a walk.

Dearest Mother,   **July 16, 1972, Gbedin**

We have been collecting butterflies. We have one that is six and a half inches across. Sometimes when we go into the bush, we see dozens, a whole flock of one kind flying together and also many different kinds. We've never had our butterfly net with us on hikes, but Harold said he'll make one with a collapsible handle so we can carry it easier.

When we're walking in the bush, many times there may be a path, but things are so overgrown that they meet in front of us. You have to be able to push brush and vines aside or sometimes slash them with a cutlass. One of the fellows always has a cutlass, so we have a trail cut out for us.

I wish you could see how the kids go through the bush. They're barefoot, wearing just a pair of shorts, and they never get juked—punctured or scratched. They shinny up the trees and slide back down the trunks, or swing down on branches, and seem to never get hurt. I'm always afraid they will fall out of a palm tree, but I guess after climbing trees like that since they were practically babies, they're pretty sure of themselves. I always come home with a lot of scratches and have learned to wear heavy stockings and long trousers.

My class at Ganta is going well. I've never had it so easy—a class I've taught many times before and that I like, a class of only eight students. Teaching here is so different from what I was used to. Students all learn by rote memory, and if you attempt to use a different method, they become confused. I'm trying to follow the course materials and methods the other teachers use. The nurse I'm replacing will be back in four months, and then I'll be through. One thing that is convenient for me is that they send a car for me, and take me home again. This gives me a chance to do some shopping at Ganta without the hassle of trying to find a ride. It's a distance of 12 miles, but waiting for a taxi to come by can make the trip long.

You were mentioning the 4th of July fireworks. Here, you're likely to hear them around New Year's. Independence Day in Liberia is more likely just to mean a day off from work, a time for people to visit, and give gifts. We're expecting to be asked over and over, "Where my 26th?" Harold is going to get a bunch of pennies for the kids.

Last year, I made a bunch of biscuits for when people came. I don't know yet what I'll do this year. We're expecting to be flooded with guests, since the President will be here and in Nimba County all the "big people" will be present part of the time. Daniel Goe, the Peace Corps deputy director, a Liberian, will stay with us. He's one of our special friends, so we're glad he will be here. But we expect to have a lot of Peace Corps volunteers from other parts of the country, as well. We have two beds in John's room and two spare Peace Corps beds in our store room, plus a couch in the living room, so can put up plenty. Besides, lots of times the kids just sleep on the floor.

When we have so many extra people staying, we often get an extra schoolboy to help. There are always boys who want to earn some money, so for 50 cents or so they will come and help wash dishes, cook, and do other odd jobs.

It takes so much longer here to prepare meals and clean up afterward. First of all, most things are made from scratch, after you've gone to gather them. Then to wash dishes, you must heat water to wash them, and they must be scalded to be safe. And many things, you have to teach the boys first how to do them.

One day, I told Charles to go to the kitchen and get me a couple of bananas. He went to the kitchen and looked all over for a cup of bananas. Later, he told me he had gone to John for help in figuring out what I meant. We all had a good laugh about it. We have to be very careful in giving instructions because what we think is plain English is incomprehensible to most of the people we deal with. We mean one thing, and they hear something entirely different.

I will probably meet Sheila Kanarr [a *daughter of Ruth's mother's friend*], since the health volunteers have arrived and will be having some of their training in Sanniquellie. I hope she will be able to get along in the PC health program. It is an awfully bad one. I think half of the girls who came last July have left or transferred to other programs. And half of the group that came the year before terminated early. Reasons were poor support from the Department of Health and no communication with the Liberian or American who was in charge. My difficulty in getting started in the first place is an example of their non-cooperation. Enough of that for now.

Today, we went out into the bush looking for palm nuts, so we could cook palm butter soup. John and Harry, Pearmines' houseboy, and I went. We walked a long way, on a trail, through bush that was higher than our heads. Much of it was on a hillside, so we were always going up or down. Finally, we located a "head" of palm nuts, a large cluster—maybe 5 or 10 lbs.—then one has to get up into the palm tree to cut it off.

Today, John went up two trees, each about 15 feet high. The base of a palm tree is dry and stickery, all the branches have sharp, heavy thorns along each side. He had to have a way to get up into the crown of the tree without tearing himself to pieces. First, with his cutlass, he cut a stick, what we might call a sapling, about 20 feet long, which he leaned up against the crown of the tree and shinnied up. He was wearing only shorts and no shoes and carried his cutlass between his chin and shoulder. One time, the cutlass fell, so he lowered a vine (country rope), and Harold tied the cutlass to that and up it went. It was a simple matter to whack out the big bunch of palm nuts and let them fall to the ground. To get back down, he chopped the stickers off a palm branch and slid down. The boys carried the big palm nut branches home on their heads.

There are so many ants in the bush. You have to take great care that you aren't in the midst of a bunch before you know it. Ants can really bite. Harold always gets a bunch up his trouser legs or inside his shirt.

I've been doing some more decorating in our house. So many of the fabrics are so pretty, so bright and gay. So we've hung several on our walls instead of pictures, in our bedroom, hall, and living room. On one wall, we hung an indigo and kola nut tie-dye lappa and hung two large masks on it. It looks great. As I mentioned before, we have this in our bedroom because some of the Mano people are very afraid of the masks.

I also made covers for the seat and back cushions on our couch, and two armchairs. I used bright lappas, but it seems to fit here. Tomorrow, I'll finish the couch covers. The long strip that I sent you, the red, blue, yellow, and black, is what I used. It's called Java wax print. It's quite colorfast, from $1.50 to $2.50 for a two-yard lappa, and is 48 inches wide. I made work shirts for Harold out of such cloth, pull over, V-neck, no buttons. I can make one in about an hour. He won't wear any of the shirts he brought with him. These are so comfortable for him to work in. I think he's worn a necktie once—for Marcia's funeral.

Our kittens are gradually leaving us. We now have only two left. One will go after the 26th, and we will keep one—Mary's kitten, named Harold—until she comes back. Of course, by then we will no doubt have another batch. People speak for them way before they are born, always looking for rat-catchers.

Dearest Mother,   **July 27, 1972, Gbedin**

Well, here it is a day after the big celebration, and we're still alive. Of course, the celebrations in Sanniquellie will continue for the rest of the week. We spent all day there yesterday. The weather has been perfect for the celebration, no rain, and therefore, no mud, which is awful if you're trying to get dressed up.

Everyone was in their very best clothes. It was so colorful and fascinating, everything from hot pants to tribal dress, the latter predominating. There were tribal dancers, parades, long devils (on stilts), and short devils. The Guinea President arrived with all sorts of security and pomp, and you should have seen all the Mandingoes, who are mostly Guinean. All were in long, white robes and dresses. They are beautiful people anyway. They marched, danced, and sang, hundreds of them.

President Tolbert and his party made one tour through the town, waving at the people. Ordinarily, Sanniquellie is a grubby-looking town, dirt streets and squalid houses. For the 26th everyone had to whitewash or paint their houses and stores. The main street was paved, streetlights put in, a new school auditorium built, a new city administration building put up, and 20 out-houses scattered about the town—never have had any out-houses before.

It's amazing what they can budget for when they want to. The President made stops in different towns on the way to Sanniquellie. At each stop, he handed out $100 bills to the school administrator, chief, what have you, depending on the project he viewed. Here, for example, he gave the farmers $300 for their co-op.

Harold standing next to the Minister of Agriculture; President Tolbert in the hat.

The President and his wife visited Gbedin on Tuesday and spent about an hour here. He was quite impressed with the projects. The Minister of Agriculture, too, expressed satisfaction with what had been done, so Harold and Larry, who were responsible for things being done, were quite pleased.

All the things they said they would do were finished and look great. There are 60 acres of new oil palms planted, which was mostly handwork, even to the land clearing. There are about 40 new rice acres, most of it planted or at least being cultivated, and the water supply job is completed, with new piping and three faucets in the town. Now people won't have to carry water to their homes.

The little model house looks really fine, painted, screened, and complete. The walls of the model house were painted by the light of kerosene lanterns the night before the President visited. We were all introduced to the President, shook his hand, Harold drove one of the Land Rovers in the procession to show him around the project. Larry gave a short speech about the house building, so Peace Corps got a good "shake."

In fact, the house building was successful enough that now the UNDP [*United Nations Development Programme*] has long-range plans for house development. They said about 1,000 acres of new rice land will be opened up and new families brought in. Apparently, the UN has given funds for construction of 25 new houses in Gbedin. The Minister told Harold and Larry they are to be completed in the next year. So it looks like the fellows will be busy again after all.

PS. Sheila Kanarr stopped to see me. Her car had a flat tire right here, so she found some children to take her to me. She sounds happy to be here and looks like she can take it. She will visit again.

Dear Vikki,   **July 27, 1972, Gbedin**

Today is the day after our big 26th celebration, after all the exciting goings on, it's nice to just sit down alone. We've had four guests for most of the week, people sleeping in the living room as well as in the bedrooms, and coming and going at all hours. There were plenty of parties, too, so now I'm not doing anything.

The people will all leave today, and maybe, we'll be lucky to not have any company for a week or two. Actually, we like having visitors, since we're so alone here, but sometimes it does get wearing. Some of them (Peace Corps volunteers) bring their own sheets and towels, which is great, when all the washing has to be done on the wash board. One week, John had to do eight extra sheets.

Did I tell you I had written to Mom about her coming for a visit? She would like to come but doesn't know about the money. I told her I'd write to the brothers and sisters, and ask them if they would like to give her an 80th birthday present.

Dearest Mother,   July 31, 1972, Gbedin

We just received your letter written July 20th, and I must sit right down and answer it. Both of us are feeling just a bit homesick about now. Perhaps it's a letdown after the big build up. Also, Larry and Mary left Thursday for six weeks in Oregon, and we are thinking about how nice it must be in the Northwest. We're the only volunteers in Gbedin now.

When I read your letter, it made me feel bad about you worrying about us here. Actually, we're very safe. It's just different kinds of hazards, and heaven knows there are plenty in the United States, just different from here. Also, we live very comfortably here, but much more frugally than at home, and that doesn't hurt us a bit. We can't go to a restaurant instead of cooking at home, can't run to the corner drug store at the last minute, can't get, and couldn't afford it if we could, prepackaged and ready-made things.

Our house is very comfortable and spacious. I'm writing this at the rustic desk in the bedroom. The room is at least twelve by fifteen, has windows with screens and shutters, very secure. Some of our floors are covered with tile, others are bare boards and some still have paint on them! We have running cold water, flush toilet, which is quite a luxury here, a tub with a hand-held shower. Of course, we run a constant war with cockroaches and ants, and never quite win.

We have a big yard, edged with hibiscus bushes and several kinds of flowering trees. Our furniture is quite comfortable, some made from rattan, and some of local mahogany made by the local carpenter. I've made covers for all the furniture, which are colorful and attractive.

Yesterday, Harold and I took a hike around the rice fields and into the edge of the bush. While Harold took his cutlass as usual, I totally forgot about the possibility of seeing any snakes. Other wild things keep out of sight, except for an occasional "possum," as they call it here, or a squirrel. I always take a flashlight if I go to take something off the clothesline at night, or go visiting, just to look at varmints. However, I've never seen any yet.

We're working quite hard, long hours. But of course, I did at home too. And I imagine that if there are frustrations here, there were comparable ones at home, too. I will admit that at home, I was more able to take direct action. Here, so much is out of our hands, and we have to let what will happen, just happen, and in its own time.

In a way, the teaching at Ganta is an extra load; it is a pleasant and personally satisfying experience. The people needed someone who could teach, who knew the subject, and wanted me, and make it possible for me to get there. On the other hand, my work with the Peace Corps health program has been accomplished in the face of the actual objections by the Peace Corps program director, and consequent niggardly support. Add to this the lack of budget and qualified Liberian public health staff, and you have a combination that's frustrating to buck. But frequently I tell myself if it were otherwise, there wouldn't be any need for volunteers in Liberia! I think we'll make it for another few months.

Regarding Robert Toe, he is still confined in the jail in Sanniquellie. We don't hear anything about him. The Supreme Court has finished their deliberations, and apparently concurred with the first sentence. However, we think now the President won't sign his death warrant for an interesting reason: soon after he took office, he had them hang a convicted murderer, a Ghanaian, who was immensely popular. Then he sentenced three more murderers to hang, one of whom was his own relative, I think a nephew. Soon after, President Tolbert's daughter, about 30 years of age, took sick and died very suddenly. Now there is talk that she was "witched" because he had his relative hanged, and people are saying that he won't hang any-one else. There is always a lot of talk about everything, never supported by facts, so this may just be rumor.

Harold is having some dental work done so we're taking a much needed break from the bush and going to Monrovia Wednesday and will return on Sunday. I expect to go to the beach, get a haircut, and do some shopping and some visiting. We have had so much company, so now we'll go to the city and let them host us for a change. After a few days in the city, we're ready to come back home. Harold has the use of the truck while Larry is away, so we have our own transportation.

Harold hasn't had a haircut for four or five months. His hair is quite curly. He says "I don't have enough on top, so I have to have some on the sides." The Peace Corps kids call him a "middle-aged hippie." They say when they meet up with him, "Here comes that damn old hippie" They are really fond of him, think he can do anything. He's taught a lot of them car care during their training programs. Believe it or not, my hair is shorter than his. We really laugh when we think about how he used to bug Judith about getting Ciam's hair cut when he was a little guy.

Now it is Thursday already. We are in Monrovia, and Harold is on the way to the dentist. This time, I haven't any business to take care of, other than picking up some medicines, so I can relax for a bit. It is pouring rain. They said that yesterday it rained 3.2 inches. Things have been so damp, more so than last year. I took an orlon dress from the closet yesterday, one I hadn't worn for a long time, and found it full of mildew, black spots all over it. Most washed out. It is a constant struggle to keep mildew from taking over; leather shoes and belts and such are especially bad.

Yesterday's activities, before we left for the city, will give you an idea of working here. I had planned to walk around and give measles vaccine to some of the little kids we missed in our mass effort. It had rained all night and was still raining at 8 AM, but I figured if I was going to get anything done, I'd just have to take off. I put on jeans and tennis shoes and took an umbrella and my bag of supplies. Everything was a soggy, muddy mess, but not a bit cold. Bea and I started off, visited quite a few houses, gave some vaccine, talked to others about their various problems with their kids, such as feeding, diarrhea, etc. I was wet and muddy all the way to my knees, but not uncomfortable at all. I couldn't help but think about how I'd have felt if I had to get around like this at home.

Finally, it was getting late, and I had to prepare for the trip to Ganta to teach. Harold had one of his men take his truck and pick me up and take me to "old camp"—a part of the project that is about a two-mile walk from our house. I usually walk there. I finished the vaccine bottle, which has to be finished within eight hours or it's no good, so has to be used or just wasted. It's too hard to come by to consider that. When I arrived home, I put my feet under the water faucet outside, washed off the mud on my shoes, and they looked as good as new!

After lunch, the driver came to take me to Ganta, and I taught the class. Harold picked me up after and off we went to Monrovia, which was a four and a half to five-hour trip, through continuous rain. The road was a mess of mud, bumps, and ruts.

We're glad we don't live in Monrovia. In many ways, it's like living in any large city, just a bit less convenient. For instance, none of our friends have hot water. It's only the really fine houses that have such luxuries. But in Monrovia, it costs much more to live than it does in the interior. There is more to spend your money on, and of course, people dress much more stylishly. At home, we always wear casual clothing, sandals and tennis shoes, no nylons, ever. Also, in the city, rogues are very busy. Nearly everyone we know has been rogued, even though most have iron grills over windows, extra locks, etc.

So many people have lost radios, tape recorders, and such things, besides clothes and luggage. Nothing like this has happened in Gbedin, in more than a year. However, we always have John sleep in our house whenever we are gone.

I'm at the P.O. just now, waiting for Customs to open. They close from 12 to 2, as does most everything here. I expect this could be the box of buttons from Carol, or perhaps a box Vikki mailed when she learned she would not be coming until later.

Dear Vikki,   **August 9, 1972, Gbedin**

Things go up and down here. We are still awaiting some moves on the part of the Agriculture Department. They want us to stay here in Gbedin, which we'll do until the end of our term. Another department, a really gung-ho new Ministry, has invited us to work for them, but we told them we have to fulfill our obligation to the D of A first.

There is a real power struggle between the two departments, and we think we would be sent home if we even tried to change departments.

We just spent four days in Monrovia, so Harold could go to the dentist. He's getting his denture replaced (Peace Corps is paying). We enjoy getting away for a few days, but are always glad to get back home.

Harold has the truck now, until Larry gets back, so at least we can get around easier. He manages to scrounge gas tickets from people he does work for, so we have enough gas to get around without paying. Gas is sixty cents a gallon, so you can see why it's important.

My teaching at Ganta is going along fine. It's actually more like teaching practical nursing as far as the level is concerned. They are all high school graduates, but the quality of education here is not comparable to the average US high school. Plus, they use US textbooks in the nursing school, and so much is unfamiliar to the Liberian kids. I am enjoying it and am taking it slowly. It's a nice break from the clinic.

You should see our flock of chickens. Harold always has two or three setting and more hatching. There must be at least fifty of various sizes. I was dashed two more roosters for the 26th, too!

Dearest Mother,   **August 16, 1972, Gbedin**

In a few days it will be Harold's birthday. It will be a different birthday, with no family to share it with. I plan to bake some cakes and invite some of the fellows he works with to come for cake and coffee. This is something Liberian people never make—a cake, and especially one with frosting. I haven't made a cake before except one box cake someone brought us when they stayed with us. I hope I can be successful. Our little gas stove works fine but burns things easily in the oven.

Did I ever tell you that most people here eat with their hands, from one big bowl? The women cook an absolutely huge amount of rice, like maybe a five-gallon bucket-full each day. They put some kind of soup on it, made of greens, fish, and palm oil, with plenty of hot peppers, and sometimes meat instead of fish. Some of the more "civilized" ones use a spoon, but usually eat from the common bowl.

We've never eaten in a Liberian home yet, so haven't had to face it yet. Sometimes, they do serve kwi people from a separate dish and with a spoon. But it depends on how deep in the bush you are, I think. Some of the villages are so far in the bush they've never had a white person visit there. We expect to make some trips to some villages like that, but of course will go with someone from the area. People usually welcome you, call the whole village out, have speeches and offer you the best of what they have.

Our life goes on as busy as ever. So many times, I think of how much you could do here. So many kids and people come here and ask for help, mending clothes, remodeling shirts to a smaller size, sewing school uniforms, washing out eyes, dressing infected wounds, and so on. Harold is busy so much of the time fixing radios, refrigerators, rice threshers, sewing machines, cars. They come to him and say, "Ol' Man, you mu' help me with my radio," for instance. He always says, "I'm not much of a radio man, but I'll take a look at it." And usually, he can fix it. We really laugh at it a lot.

There are a lot of UNICEF hand-operated sewing machines, for the Home Ec. programs. They have been here a long time, and have sat around in storage a lot, and hardly one is operable. When PC learned Harold could probably fix sewing machines, they began to bring him sewing machines. So far, he's worked on a half dozen, and still has a half dozen sitting in the corners of our living room. With so much furniture to make and shelves to build, he's been very busy.

Actually, our house is quite nice, even if it started as such a shack. With the woven mats on the floors, and bright lappas at the windows, and wicker chairs, it's rather attractive. Did I tell you about the stools and table Harold made out of salt meat barrels? He cut them in half and turned them upside-down. I made cushions for them, and we use them on the porch. He took an old board, planed it off and nailed it on the bottom of another half-barrel, and it made a coffee table. They are rustic but fine.

We finally received a notice that *Newsweek* will start coming in August. Thanks so much. I know we will enjoy reading it. You asked before about something to send for Christmas. One thing we would both enjoy is music tapes. People can record from their own music if they want to, and it only costs about 50 cents to mail them. We're sorry we didn't bring any with us, since our radio doesn't give us good music programs—too much noise.

This morning while we were eating breakfast, we were commenting that to look out our dining room window, you could think you were at our old place at Weyerhaeuser. The trees in the distance look about the same as far as color, height, and so on. And right now, it feels about the same weather-wise. In fact, it's kind of overcast, at times now, but always warm enough.

Last week, I finally had to wear a sweater and my jeans to keep warm. Then later in the day it warms up and gets almost too warm to do much walking around outside. I do walk around a lot though, to visit in the village. That is what they call using "one cent taxi."

Both of us think it would be so nice if we could get along without a car when we get home again, but know our life there is totally different. We never ride in a car here, unless we're going to the town ten miles away. Those that are one to three miles away, we just visit on foot. And of course, we only go to Ganta or Sanniquellie to shop, or sometimes to visit Peace Corps friends. We have so many visitors that we never get lonely.

This week, we and the other PCs here, the project director, and the British engineer were invited to a dinner party by the four Chinese men. They served us the most lavish and delicious meal, about a dozen different dishes they had prepared themselves. I even made a new dress for the occasion from the enclosed piece of material, which is a wax-print made in Sierra Leone. It is a long sheath, like my Hawaiian muumuu.

This week we had the funniest experience. We had gone for a walk to another village. When we returned, we were met by the chief and a woman, who farms here, a loud-mouth type who loves palava. She said, "A man came to my farm and hurt me." She held out her thumb which was all bloody. It seems that the man wanted her to marry him. She is a widow, and he's been living with her and working on her farm for about two years. She told him "no," and some kind of argument began; she hit him in the mouth and then he grabbed her hand and bit her thumb.

By the time we reached our house, a crowd, including the man in the case who was much smaller than the woman, had gathered. He had a loose tooth from the fracas. By the time I had them patched up, there had been a lot of talking and laughter by the spectators. I had a hard time to keep from laughing too.

The next day, the project manager "carried" the man to the county seat, and had him put in jail. Actually, I think he wasn't as much in the wrong as she was. When you are in jail in this country, you don't eat unless the family brings food for you. The woman said she would take food for him while he was in jail. What a strange way to live.

Dear Vikki,   **August 20, 1972, Gbedin**

Today was Harold's [57th] birthday, actually tomorrow, but we celebrated it today. Yesterday, John's mother, stepfather, young sister, and a 17-year-old girl, friend of the family, arrived to visit John. He was just about to leave to visit them in the country when they arrived. We had looked forward to a weekend by ourselves, and instead ended up with four houseguests, none of whom speak English. They are Gio, a neighboring tribe. So this meant reorganizing dinner, making beds, and so on. They are nice people, but it's difficult having people you can't communicate with. John's ma is so interested in everything, so whenever I'm doing anything in the kitchen, she is right there to watch, to help stir, etc.

I had invited some people for birthday cake, so after giving everyone breakfast I made two cakes and Lazy-Daisy frosting (a coconut and brown sugar, boiled frosting). We had to crack the coconut and grate it and squeeze limes for the limeade. Everything is made from scratch. My small oven bakes only one layer at a time, and help from three women who have never been in such a kitchen before made for an interesting time. Also, had a few sick people, as usual.

I wish you could see your dad on this day, with his long, curly hair, orange tie-dye bell-bottoms, and dashiki style shirt, and thongs. For some reason, he isn't out of place. No one gives him a second look.

I made him a pair of shorts and found him a palm wine gourd for his birthday, so his birthday gifts were anything but run-of-the-mill. The palm wine gourd is grown on a gourd tree. It's a round fruit and, when dry, makes an excellent container. A gourd should hold around a gallon of palm wine, which costs 25 cents.

Palm wine is the natural juice of a bamboo palm tree. It ferments as the day goes by, becoming more alcoholic as time goes on. Just about everyone has a palm wine tree, which yields two buckets a day, morning and evening. People can really drink palm wine!

Besides John's family, we also had the seven Chinese fellows, some Liberian fellows that Harold works with, and various school kids and farmers. John's family brought Harold a young goat, a little black and white thing that Harold says we'll raise for a while. Incidentally, our house is set on cement piers, about six feet off the ground, so there is room for the goat as well as all the chickens under there. You can hardly tell us from hillbillies! Harold just told me he has named his little goat Herman. It's a funny little, short-legged thing.

This is the first time we have had really country people stay overnight with us, and it is different. Everything is new to them. They are afraid to use the toilet, prefer to take a bucket-bath outside, and are curious and interested in everything we do.

While I was making the cakes, the three women were right beside me, wanted to stir and see everything. None of them spoke a word of English. They are Gio, and all I can say in Gio is hello and good bye. They are afraid to try many of our foods.

One of the Chinese fellows, who is fairly new here, gave Harold a small gift, and enclosed a card on which he had written, "Greeting Birthday Happy." We really have some hilarious conversations. One of them asked me if I wanted some "rootis" for our salad. I said, "Oh, radish! Please." So what does he bring me? Lettuce! Of course, it was lettuce he was trying to say, not radish.

Today, John's mother and step-dad spent a lot of time showing me how to make country thread —how to spin, fluff the cotton, the whole process—in between the comings and goings. Right now, I have a basket about the size of a big water bucket full of cotton balls. (One old woman told me she would bring me some country thread, so I said, "Fine." Then when she came, it was only cotton balls!) The cotton comes from very tall trees. There are many small black seeds in it, so you have to first get them out, before you can begin to fluff the cotton, preparatory to spinning.

One thing we learn here is that people have lots of time on their hands, but they seldom sit idly doing nothing. So no matter how long it takes to do something, there is no way to compute the cost as far as labor is concerned.

Nearly everyone here knows how to make country thread, men and women alike, so I figure by leaving my basket by the door in the dining room, I'll eventually get it all done by people who come to visit and who are so intrigued by us wanting to learn such things. They just have to try it, too, and show me how.

Harold and Mark, who replaced Larry while he is home, leave for Monrovia tomorrow for about four days. This is the first time I've stayed alone, because Mary and I usually get together if the men are away.

Harold has to attend a Home Economics volunteer workshop to teach the girls how to care for their sewing machines. I can't get away because of my M-W-F teaching schedule and my T-Th clinic schedule.

Barbara and Bruce Weir, the PC couple who we usually stay with when we come to the city, may come back with Harold, for a couple of days. They hate going up-country, so I don't really expect them. They came up one time, nearly a year ago, and haven't left Monrovia since. Anyway, I'll prepare for them. If they don't come, no doubt, someone else will soon!

Dearest Mother,   **August 20, 1972, Gbedin**

Today we celebrated Harold's birthday, since he has to be away tomorrow. What an interesting day it was, and I am exhausted.

We had a constant stream of visitors. When everyone had left, I started to fry chicken and make spaghetti. John's family left to visit his father's brother, who is a farmer here. We finally sat down to eat about 7 PM, and before we had finished, John's family returned, and we learned they hadn't been offered food by the farmer. This meant starting to cook rice, since people here don't really like spaghetti. So now, they are eating rice and spaghetti sauce, and John is cleaning up the kitchen. And I finally have a chance to sit down and relax.

This past week was an especially good week for me. I finally secured a midwife to work with me every Thursday at our antenatal clinic. She is a young woman who just completed a one-year midwifery course at Phebe Hospital. Phebe is a Lutheran Mission Hospital at Gbarnga, which is farther down the road toward Monrovia. They have midwife, practical nurse, and registered nurse programs. The midwives have to take a National Certifying Exam. She will stay with us on Wednesday nights, in order to be here on time for the antenatal clinic on Thursday morning, since taxis are so unpredictable.

Today is her first overnight visit. She is Gio, so can talk with the people easily. We have mostly Mano and Gio people living here, and if you can't speak one dialect, you can usually "hear" (understand) the other. It is certainly a relief to have her here, because I've really felt out of my depth with the antenatal examining. Several women had complications that I couldn't have detected, let alone treated. She will do the class for the "belly women," as well, examine them, and instruct the patients. Hopefully, we will have a full-time midwife by the time I leave.

On that same day, the mother-child health supervisor from Monrovia paid us a visit, and things were going so beautifully, our records were shipshape, our teaching aids admirable, and all in all, it was one of my better times. I must say, such experiences aren't too frequent, which makes them all the more important.

People say that Lamco, the iron mine people, are putting on a public rail-bus. And people can go from here to Buchanan, on the coast, and then take a taxi on a paved road from there to Monrovia. The fare is said to be $12 round-trip, and $4 for the taxi. This is double the taxi fare from here, so I don't think we will do it often. Right now, Lamco operates a rail-bus for their employees, and it is possible to get a free pass. We have heard there is a lot of hassle to do it, but it looks like that is going to end when they go public.

Dearest Mother,   **August 30, 1972, Gbedin**

The Pearmines have decided to extend for another year and should have gone home in May. However, because of the July 26th push, they agreed to stay here until after the President came. As far as we are concerned, we have at least eight months left and maybe ten. Our termination date is still up in the air. You can leave a month early or a month later.

You asked about cancer here. I don't know what the cancer rate here is—never hear of people dying of what sounds like cancer. Of course, many people are sick in the bush, and a doctor never sees them, so no way of knowing what the cause of death is.

Yesterday a man brought an old woman, maybe his mother, to the clinic. There was "country medicine," a kind of whitish clay mixed with leaves, rubbed on her forehead. Her complaint was severe headache. Her pulse was pounding, and her blood pressure was 240. I tried to urge him to take her to the hospital, but it wasn't likely he would do that. Daniel, the dresser, my colleague in the clinic, gave her aspirin.

We aren't supplied with anything for heart conditions. Fox glove grows here. The people use the leaves in their soup, when they want it to be slippery, to eat with fufu or gaypa (made from cassava), so it will slide down easily. I wish I knew more about making a digitalis infusion from it. Since the people believe more in country medicine, they might as well try this! Surprisingly, none of the zo people I've met use it for heart trouble.

The Liberian Board of Nurse Examiners is celebrating their 30th anniversary in September, having an all-day program, luncheon, and so on. They've asked me to be one of the speakers, to talk about State Board testing. It will be held in Monrovia at Kennedy Hospital. After so much of that sort of thing at home, this is the first time for anything like that here.

Sunday. We drove to Monrovia yesterday. Harold will go to the dentist and then go to the university farm to teach some home economic volunteers about maintenance of their sewing machines. I will see the Peace Corps doctor for a routine check, and get my immunizations up to date. Every three months we need some kind of shot.

On the way to town, we stopped at Cuttington College, at Suakoko, which is about half way to Monrovia, to visit the Daniels. They are the older couple who stayed with us last Christmas, both in their 70s. He is in charge of maintenance at the college, and she is the librarian. We really enjoy them. He is so much like Harold, can fix anything, and she is a lot of fun. We had pumpkin pie and homemade ice cream with them.

When we reached the city we found there was a John Wayne movie showing, so we all went to see it. The movie house is quite luxurious, prices the same, but there is a place in front, called the pit, lower than the main floor, and about 10 rows close to the screen. Admission there is 50

cents. It wasn't too bad, and watching the spectators gives more entertainment than the movie. Liberians love fighting movies, although they
are not violent people themselves. The more shooting and fighting, the
better they like it. They jump up, and shout and laugh loudly. What fun it
is to see them if too many people are in front!

Tomorrow is our anniversary—the 31st, can you imagine? When
we arrived at the Weirs', they said we would have to stay until Tuesday,
because they had planned a party for us for tonight. That should be enjoyable, so now we are staying an extra day. I should be in Gbedin tomorrow
for baby clinic, but left Bea in charge just in case something happened. On
these roads, you can never be sure of any schedule, anyway.

I will add this quick note, along with my letter. I will be coming to
Washington, DC, in a few days for some minor surgery. Yesterday, when I
checked in with the Peace Corps doctor, he decided I must have a biopsy of
a small lump in one breast—have had it since May. The Pathology capability here is nil, so I have to go to either Europe or the United States for this.
I will be in the George Washington University Medical School Hospital in
DC. However, I have to stay in the States for two weeks, in order to take
advantage of the excursion fare.

[*Ruth and Harold spent three weeks in Washington, DC, and upstate New
York visiting her brother Richard. The lump was benign.*]

Dearest Mother,   **October 11, 1972, Gbedin**

Yesterday, there were so many people at the baby clinic. Very few came
while I was away, according to Daniel. Tomorrow is "belly" day, so perhaps we will have a good attendance. I usually have to do a lot of home
visiting in order to get new people to come. No one wants to say they are
pregnant, at first.

Yesterday, we were invited to have dinner with the Chinese fellows for
a special holiday, some kind of Independence celebration. As usual, the
food was delicious, and many different dishes. We've invited them to eat
with us Saturday eve, since Mr. Chiang is leaving for Taiwan on Monday.
Actually, three of them are our special friends, but seven live here now so
we decided to have them all. We're going to make a complete American
meal this time. We will serve fried chicken, mashed potatoes, pumpkin
pie, and so on. Both John and Charles will help me, so I should manage

OK. You know, our stove is so small, our pots and pans and dishes are very minimum so it takes some ingenuity to do a meal with a lot different foods. Anyway, we will try.

I think rainy season is about over. The weather is very hot and humid. I'm wet with perspiration all the time. One advantage though is that my skin is never dry here. I never have to use hand lotion or skin cream.

Ruth supervising the arrival of an injured patient.

Dear Vikki and Gill,   **October 15, 1972, Gbedin**

We're back in the thick of things again here. In fact, the day I arrived in Gbedin, I had to go in the evening to see a woman whose incision had burst open from infection.

Harold found, too, that everything had come to a standstill while he was away, so he had to get people moving again. Most of the men haven't been paid since July so they aren't too interested in working until they see some money. This happens so much, and makes you wonder if you aren't wasting your time completely, when the government runs things this way. Most of the officials, all actually, do very well financially, but never have any funds for this level here. Everything seems to be diverted to private interests.

Dearest Mother,   October 16, 1972, Gbedin

My class is keeping me hopping, with more preparation this time, and of course, I was behind schedule by the time I got started, the same with the clinic. Things pile up, especially the daily records, which I take care of. Also, we've had at least one house guest staying ever since we got back—Peace Corps guys that stayed in our house while we were gone. They're just like our kids, but it always means extra work and cooking, etc., especially with big boys. I've had to have Charles, our little yard boy, help in the house, in order to get things done.

Saturday, we had seven Chinese guys and Steve Thain, a volunteer from Spokane, here for dinner. Two of the fellows are leaving for Taiwan today, so we wanted to entertain them. We did fried chicken, pumpkin pie, and so on, a real American meal for a change. With both John and Charles helping, we managed to do all the necessary preparations. Harold penned up some chickens the night before. In the morning, John let one get loose, so he and Charles had to chase it for a half hour before they could proceed with the fried chicken. It was a little different from getting a plastic-wrapped chicken at the supermarket! The same with the pie. I had to have the boys walk into the village and find someone who had a pumpkin vine, before we could make pies.

Mr. Sim Pocin, one of our Chinese neighbors, just came by with 100 pounds of oranges from the Agriculture Minister's farm at Kpain, which is many miles from here. Can you imagine one hundred pounds of oranges and one hundred pounds of grapefruit, at one time? We give gobs away.

Dearest Mother,   October 18, 1972, Gbedin

We have really been having a rain storm, since about 4 AM, a steady torrential down pour. It's now 10:30 in the morning. Everything is just running with water. With all the rain, and the temperature around 70 degrees, it's actually too chilly for comfort. And we thought rainy season was about over. Actually, it's been quite hot, so I'm kind of glad for the rain.

I have been swamped, with too many things to do. Both of us are going to be glad when the time is over. It is so obvious that two years isn't nearly long enough to get anything done of a lasting nature, unless the government is willing to continue to put some effort there. And with this bunch of people running things, like in most so-called developing countries, what is personally, or politically, expedient is what gets done. Consequently, the only thing that really counts is what is happening with the people at the time and most of those relationships are what makes things worthwhile, and enjoyable. We will miss the people and a lot of the friends we have here. It will be hard to say goodbye to John and Charles and, especially, to Bea.

Did I tell you that our cat "borned" again? There are four kittens, all of them spoken for already. As soon as people hear you have kittens, they come and ask for them. We could even sell them for a dollar or two! Charles found a kitten about a month old yesterday, and carried it to Frisky, the mama. She took it so we'll keep it until its old enough for him to take home.

Mr. Chiang left for home yesterday. We will miss him, but expect to visit him in Taiwan on the way home. I have certainly learned a lot about Chinese cooking from him.

Dear Vikki,   **October 22, 1971, Gbedin**

Harold is really frustrated about his job here. The Ag Department doesn't follow through with the necessary support to do the work they expect him to do. Its good we only have six months left to go, because things have really deteriorated, making it hard to keep morale up.

I'm very busy, what with my class at the mission hospital, the clinic work, and the visiting I have to do. It's doubtful whether the Health Dept. will continue their support after I'm gone, but I'll work on that too. Right now, I'm trying to get all the kids under five immunized for measles and get a smallpox team to come and vaccinate everyone next month.

Dearest Mother,   **October 23, 1972, Gbedin**

Happy Birthday, Mother dear. It would be so nice to say that in person! I'm sorry to be late with a birthday present—didn't realize November 1st was so near.

Lately, the little kids have been coming to play "doll babies." I've just kept the boxes of dolls here, and when the women come to sew or to get medicine or just to visit, their little ones play with the dolls, little boys, too.

Today, one of my ladies delivered twins—boys. She already has four children. These little ones were born in her home, a little mud-stick house on a mat on the floor. Three old women, country midwives, delivered the babies. They learned their skills from old women in their villages long ago. Their practices are so mixed up with things from their tribal society that have no benefit for the delivery and could so often be harmful. The mother, Norn, seemed to have gotten along all right, even though the babies were pretty good sized.

I went over to her house as soon as I heard they were born. In a small, dim room about 8 or 10 feet square, I found about 12 to 15 village women squatting or seated on the floor, all happy about the event. Norn was sitting on a woven mat, leaning against the wall, with the babies wrapped in lappas, on a mat nearby. The babies have no clothes.

No one prepares for a baby, since so many of them die so soon. They say if they prepare for a baby, it will surely die. But money is all right, "Money can't spoil," one of my pregnant friends told me. I came home and made two little sacques (baby gowns) and went back with them. It will really be a hardship to care for two babies; even one is a lot of work for the women, when they have to do so much outside work and have absolutely no conveniences. But people are always happy about a new baby.

One of the women had a bottle of cane juice, which they all had been nipping on, and offered me a drink. I can't bear the smell, let alone the taste of cane juice. When I declined, they didn't mind. It is a very potent beverage. It may seem odd to you, but I don't feel strange in such a group. It seems quite natural to be sitting there on the floor with them. They seem to be glad to have me, even though our ability to converse is pretty limited. When I bock-bocked, someone said, "Who is it?," and another said, "It kwi-plu," meaning "white woman." When I'm sitting among them visiting, I don't feel like I look any different than they do, even though they are a different color and are dressed only in a lappa from the waist down. I'll really miss the people when I leave here.

One of my friends here has been sick. She is a beautiful young girl, about twenty-six years of age. She became ill about a month ago, and was in Ganta Hospital—trouble with her stomach, crying a lot. The doctors said she was psychotic and should be taken to Monrovia to the psychiatric hospital.

However, her husband, who has some education, and her friends say it's African sickness caused by "witching." "She dreamed something," they say, "and won't tell all, so the sickness catch her." They say she will only be well if country medicine is used. They say only certain people, "sign cutters," can make the medicine. She has some kind of country medicine—it looks like mud and chalk, smeared on her body, dirty strings tied around both wrists.

So far, there is no improvement. She just lies in bed crying, she won't eat and is vomiting frequently. She looks like a ghost of herself. Today, her husband is taking her to Suakoko, about a two-hour drive from here, to his people where he says they will treat her, and she will be well in three days.

She said to me this morning, "Give my husband my picture when I die." Her husband says, "She knows something and won't talk it." She cries and says, "I don't know anything." She says she can't move her arms and hands and, of course, is too weak to walk. I won't be surprised to hear that she is dead in a short time. However, the psychological effect of their medicine is just as helpful as kwi medicine.

Dear Vikki,   **November 3, 1972, Gbedin**

No news from you yet. It's really difficult to wait, being so far away. We've had plenty of babies here lately. The new twin boys are getting along fine. Both were over six pounds.

Their names are Konah (first one) and Yonge (the second one), which is what Mano twin boys are always named. Later, they may get a bush school name, and no doubt when they go to school, they will take a school name. Talk about confusing. Some adults use their school name first, then their society (bush school) name as a middle name, and then some kind of family name. For instance, the county health doctor's name is William Sei Boayue. Only his close family will always call him Sei.

I have two little girls playing here just now, with the "doll babies" that Mom sent. It reminds me of when the little neighbor girls came to play with your dolls after you went away to school. We enjoy having the little girls and boys who come to play, but sometimes have to finally send them home, because they would stay all night if we let them. Sometimes, we just get tired of all the people, there are so many of them all the time. And I get tired of people asking for things, all the time, unless they are willing to do something for me in return. We don't think giving free hand-outs is what we came here for. Most of the people are fine and often come back with something for me, maybe bananas, plantains, or pineapple.

Even though Harold's work here has changed, he is still too busy. Since most of his helpers have been fired, everything falls on him. He's cutting out a lot of the work that was done for other government agencies, since the Liberian mechanics should be doing it, rather than him. He hopes this might help convince the DA that they really have to put some people back here.

One of Harold's best mechanics and friend, whom he's trying to get back on the payroll, comes every day and helps him, in hopes that he'll finally get his job back. Harold has sent messages and talked to the big people in Monrovia about him. The trouble is, the big people in the city have little idea what life is like in the interior, and they appear to like it that way. Oh, well. So much for that.

Now that the weather is better, we are planning some trips and hikes. We have both decided that we will just take some time off when we feel like it, and see some more of Liberia, and also take some trips into the bush. That is one of my favorite activities. It's always different, even though sometimes very rugged, that is part of the fascination. There is a huge lake in the extreme southwestern end of the country, near the coast, which is a nice vacation area. You can rent a house from someone and be quite comfortable, and even swim there. We may go there near the end of the year. We will also go to Foya, in the northwestern part, near the Sierra Leone border. This is where you can find fine hand-woven country cloth and tie dye materials.

This week, two young girls, about 10 and 12, stole some money from one of the little shops, I think around $2. They divided and spent the money. When they were caught, they were first taken to the chief, where he had them beaten with switches. Then they were put to work in the village, cleaning grass and sod, with short hoes. Some big boy was put behind each girl to see that they worked that day. The next punishment was to work for the person who owned the shop, on his rice farm, when he returns from the country. However, the next day, the two girls stole a hen from one of the farmers, cooked it, and ate it. I don't know what they will do to the girls now. People here say, "If you steal a chicken, you will always steal." Taking someone's chicken is a really bad thing to do. Neither of these girls were in real need, that is, no more than anyone else.

Our little goat is growing. He is really noisy, and the best place to keep him, according to Harold, is right outside our bedroom window! About daylight, every morning he starts to talk, and until Charles comes around 6 o'clock to feed him some cassava leaves, he doesn't quiet down. I finally got tired of it and told John to turn him loose, because he knows our place. However, he heads right for the neighbor's garden, so it's back to the tether again! Yesterday, Harold and Larry castrated him, with the expectation he will grow bigger.

We also have untold numbers of chickens—so does Larry. Harold estimated that between the two of them they must have at least sixty chickens. Some have just hatched, but some can really crow, very early in the morning. Many of them sleep under the house. George, our big white, Leghorn rooster, flaps his wings noisily, and starts crowing around 4:30 AM. Then a rooster in the village answers him. Then he crows, and on and on.

Last Thursday was Liberian Thanksgiving. We and the Pearmines, and Chris Lyman, a new volunteer here, cooked an American-style dinner for the Chinese fellows. We stuffed and roasted four chickens, made pies and rolls, and Jell-O. For celery in the stuffing, we used palm cabbage (known as hearts of palm), which we cut in the bush. It's very good.

We will probably take another year in Peace Corps, but likely in another country, which will give us a chance to see another African country. Our friends, the Berman's, are in Botswana, where he is the country director now. He wants us to come there. From what we have heard from people who have been there recently, the government is serious about developing the country, which is not true here.

Dearest Mother,   **November 5, 1972, Gbedin**

Time has just slipped away from me. I've had a hard time catching up, with so many things piling up while we were gone. I've also found it difficult to get with it again. I guess I'm getting lonesome for everyone at home, discouraged about the impossibility of accomplishing much here, thinking of Vikki and wishing I could be with her, and so on. Anyway, I've gotten behind with letter writing. I will do much better from now on.

My class at Ganta will finish in three weeks, when the students go on vacation. The other teacher will be back from home leave after Christmas, so I won't have to help out any more. It's been a nice change for me, but a lot of extra work, when it was the first time I'd done the class. Of course, with such a few students, it wasn't all that hard.

We brought a belt back for John, supposedly from you. Was he tickled! He's a good boy, such a child in many ways, but also, very grown-up in many others. He works very hard for us—washing, scrubbing, and cooking. It would be a much harder life for him though, if he were working in the rice fields and getting one meal a day to get along. We take care of furnishing his clothes, food, dental care, etc., as well as school expenses. Now we're trying to get him situated in a Mission school when we leave, so we can take care of his school expenses to try to get him through high school, at least.

We've been helping another boy who is in the eighth grade, taking care of his tuition, uniforms, and books. In return, he brings us "country things," so we aren't just giving him a handout.

Larry is getting a new Land Rover, so he and Harold are going to pick it up. Besides, Harold has to go to the dentist again. I thought I would go with them just to get a change of scenery, but they're going by taxi, and that is not for me. Besides, I can hardly afford to miss my class. It will be finished in two more weeks, and then we can take a longer weekend, and go to Foya to the cloth market.

Dear Vikki,   **November 12, 1972, Gbedin**

So you have a new son! We are happy to get the news of your new baby, and to know that all is well. Dale Gillis sent the cable, which arrived Tuesday eve. Harold was in Monrovia, so got the news, and the next AM called me on the radio. So by Wednesday we had the news in Gbedin. Mary and the rest of the kids called me Granny all day and that evening we all got together and drank a toast to Baird [*their new grandson*]. If you were here and people were congratulating you, they would say, "Thank you, ya."

We have a young couple staying with us this week, new volunteers from Los Angeles. He's a teacher, and she is a home economics teacher, with a major in sewing. She has been helping me with my sewing girls and really enjoying it. They are on their "live-in" for cross-cultural experiences. They told us that in Monrovia, they were told that coming to Gbedin was a choice spot! Anyway, we are enjoying them. They are interested in everything and game for trying anything new.

I had hoped that Harold would write to you while he was in Monrovia, after receiving the cable, but you know him and letter writing. I guess he didn't even think of it. I'm sorry it's so long until you hear from us, and know we got the message. Chris came over and said, "Trick or Treat," but really came to invite us over for cider and doughnuts that he and Mary made—the doughnuts, that is. He's always making cookies and cakes. He's a nice kid, comes from a Catholic family of nine, seven of them boys. One sister is a nun. He's an accountant from Washington, DC. He will stay here to replace Larry.

Dry season is here now. It is really warm these days, and doesn't rain much.

Dearest Mother,   **November 13, 1972, Gbedin**

Another week gone by and all kinds of things happening. Paye had a seizure, the first one since February or March. He fell into the fire and burned his leg and his hand very badly. I'm just sick about it, especially since his family is using country medicine to treat it, and he's really sick. I'm sure in a day or two he will have serious infection, and it will be months before he heals.

Harold and Larry got back from Monrovia with a new truck, a Land Rover for Larry. We will all enjoy it, since it will make getting places much easier. We may even get to go to Lamco to go swimming. They have a lovely big pool there.

The news just arrived that the President is coming by tomorrow, so everyone is hurrying around cutting palm branches to decorate, cutting grass, and cleaning up the place.

Dear Vikki,   **November 1972, Gbedin**

My class is finally over, now just have to correct finals and figure grades. I enjoyed the contacts there, but can't say I'm sorry to be finished. It meant three afternoons away, and with all my other chores, just kept me too busy. The sewing classes come in bunches, and just lately I've been swamped.

Rainy season has ended, and we now only have an occasional shower. Some of the leaves have already begun to turn red. None of the trees are ever bare, because new leaves come continuously. It is so interesting to look at the hillsides in the distance with the varied colors during dry season. Otherwise, it's an uninterrupted green, sometimes quite boring, mile after mile. When you fly over, the only break is a tiny village, and they, too, all look alike, reddish brown tin roofs or tan thatch roofs, all shaped the same.

Dearest Vikki and Gill,   **November 27, 1972, Gbedin**

It's hard to believe it's nearly Christmas. With dry season here—hot muggy weather and little rain—it just doesn't put one in mind of the holiday season we're used to.

Right now, there is a self-help project going on, to build three additional rooms on the school, so we can have seventh, eighth, and ninth grades here next year. This is a joint Peace Corps and government project, with money for the project from CARE. If the school is finished, and if they send teachers, John will be able to go here next year, instead of to Sanniquellie, which will mean quite a saving of money since he can stay with us as long as we are here.

Charles is working for Chris now, so we can have John's younger brother as our second boy. He's just from the country, about 10, has never gone to school, and speaks only small English. John wants us to keep his money so he will have it when school starts, and thus will be able to start school.

It's quite a lesson in patience and sensitivity to take a youngster who has always lived in a little mud hut, with dirt floors, sleeping on a mat on the floor, eating from a common bowl with his hands, one pair of shorts and a shirt, no shoes, into a kwi house, to learn how to take care of things like dishes, unfamiliar foods, ironing, and on and on. We have a lot of laughs. You don't give him a wastebasket and tell him to empty it. You say, "Take the basket outside, waste the paper in the drum, wash the basket with water, fini clean. Bring the basket in the house, and put it there. You hear?" or words to that effect, all in Liberian English.

Dearest Mother and all,   **November 28, 1971, Gbedin**

My nutrition class is about finished at Ganta. I'm glad it's over, but it was enjoyable. They want me to teach it again next term—will arrange the schedule so it can be taught first semester, beginning in February, so I'll have time to finish it. I'll wait and see after Christmas.

Tomorrow is Chris's birthday, so Mary and I are making a birthday cake and dinner for him. He's just moving into his house, so I'm making a cookbook for him.

Incidentally, I have a bicycle now, provided by PC, at Harold's insistence, so both John and I are enjoying it. The people look quite surprised to see me wheeling by.

We have two more guys for "live ins." They are new volunteers who will be teaching. This always makes extra work, although we receive per diem for them, so can hire an extra boy to help. Today Larry, Chris, and I took them for a hike up the mountain behind our house.

We got a young kid to take us, along with four of his friends, all barefoot. It's a very steep climb, all through the high bush, but today the kids couldn't find their way down. It was a different route than going up, since we wanted to visit a second farm. We came down one ridge, clear to the bottom. There was high bush all around, so we couldn't see where we were really going. We found we were in the wrong place, went up again, a steep climb, went down again, etc., etc.

It took us five hours to finally get down to the road—should have taken us three. Then we were way up the road from Gbedin, which meant a long walk home. We were exhausted and hot but none the worse for our adventure.

Did I tell you Paye is in the hospital? He had a seizure and fell into the fire. He burnt himself again. The family agreed, after a week, for me to take him to the hospital in Ganta. He's coming along OK and should be able to come home in about a week. He has a cast on one leg to prevent contracture.

Dearest Mother,   **December 3, 1971, Gbedin**

I can't believe it is the Christmas season—no decorations, no baking, songs, and such. I haven't heard one Christmas carol. We plan to go to Monrovia around the 13th or 14th, when I can get Christmas letters mailed. So maybe we will be quite late with our Christmas greetings. I wrote to Sheila Kanarr, inviting her for Christmas. (We're going to barbecue Billy Goat.)

One of our mutual friends stopped by today and told us Sheila was happier now. She has a more interesting job at Kennedy Hospital, teaching in a kindergarten program. Interestingly enough, most of the girls in the group that Sheila came with are unhappy with their situations. You may remember I mentioned previously some of the problems with the health program. They have set up meetings with the PC director, PC doctor, and the health program director and asked all the health volunteers to attend. That is the reason I'm going down on the 14th. I don't expect much to come of it, but will go and add my voice, too.

Paye is back from the hospital with the burn partially healed. They had it in a cast for a while to prevent deformity. Keeping it clean now will be a chore, the way he runs around and gets into trouble. I may have told you we have two guys staying with us for three weeks, new teachers getting used to the country. This week we are taking them to a village, for three days or so. This is pretty strenuous for new volunteers, but they seem game for anything. Living in a village like the Liberians takes some fortitude—no screens, different diets, none of the usual conveniences.

Right now, I'm making papaya, orange, and ginger marmalade. It's very tasty and inexpensive to make—just the cost of the sugar and the gas to cook it, since the fruit is free.

I have about eight small kids here, half of them playing with their doll babies and the rest looking at picture books. A couple of the girls are only about three feet tall and are carrying babies on their backs. The babies weigh at least 20 pounds. The girls mind the babies every day while their mothers work in the rice fields.

It's easy to see why girls get sway-backed, their little bones are still forming, and they always carry more than they should. Sometimes little girls as young as five are toting babies as old as one and a half years of age, and it isn't as though the babies can't walk. They are just used to being on someone's back. Lots of times, little girls are carrying dolls or sticks on their backs if they don't have a baby to carry. Incidentally, the boys enjoy the dolls you sent. They are all intrigued with the fact that the clothes can come off and the dolls can open and shut their eyes and move their heads, arms, and legs.

Dearest Vikki,   **December 4, 1972, Gbedin**

Before I forget, I'll answer some of the things you referred to in your last letter. Norton Berman is associate director here. We met him in Philadelphia when we were leaving for Liberia. He was lined up to become director here, but the then director elected to extend, which left Norton hanging. After about a year here, he was given the post of director in Botswana. We had become good friends before he left, stayed with them whenever we went to Monrovia. When he left, he said he wanted us to come, too. He needs mechanics there; nothing definite for me.

Harold has feelings about staying here. He wants to do more, if the Minister will support him. At least three other areas here want us, too;

Cuttington College for maintenance, and teaching in their nursing program for me; ADP, another government agency, headed by a person who seems to be getting things done. The Peace Corps doctor wants me at Kennedy Hospital, any job I'd like.

We really like Liberia and aren't in all that much of a hurry to leave. But things have to be laid out for us before we'll accept anything. On the 13th or 14th we're going to Monrovia to talk with the various people, with the intention of making a final decision. And Norton thinks we're 99 percent committed to Botswana. Anyway, we will keep you informed. If we do extend for another year, we'll be coming home around May 1st. If we don't extend, we'll do some travelling for a month or two, depending on our friends. We want to come via Taiwan, Japan, and Hawaii.

Now about the goat, Harold decided to call him Herman, but John calls him Billy Goat, all the time. For Christmas, one of our friends is going to barbecue him for all of us.

I actually don't like the idea of a pet goat, too much. He makes an awfully lot of noise, always outside our bedroom window! Frisky, the cat, comes on the porch outside our window every morning and yowls. As to the rooster, he was given to us by the Lebanese store keeper, whose name is really Ali. George called the rooster Douglas, which he pronounced "dooglas," but we got into the habit of calling him George (never to Ali, though). Anyway, our George is a giant white rooster with a really red, "rose" comb, quite handsome.

We are now down to one kitten and should get rid of it this week. Then I suppose, in about two months will have some more. There is never a problem in getting rid of kittens.

We have heard that the National Exam grades will be here by next week, so the kids should have them soon. School grades count three times, and National Exam grades once. I'm sure John will be OK. Apparently, after this year, the sixth grade will not be required to take the exams, only grades nine and twelve. A young couple that stayed with us last month liked John a lot and told him he could come and work for them and go to school where they live, after we leave. The young man teaches at Cuttington College. The only problem for John is that it is in a Kpelle tribal area, and while John can speak Kpelle, he's really afraid of the Kpelle "devil." We haven't discussed it much yet—want to first wait to see what we are going to do next.

Did I tell you that when Mr. Chiang went home, we gave him the money so he could buy us a camera in Hong Kong? He will send it back with one of his friends who is coming here in January.

Incidentally, we are planning to travel for about a month. We'll leave in January and go to Mali, perhaps to Ghana and Upper Volta. When we go to Monrovia next week, we will talk to a travel agent to get some ideas about when and how. Lots of our friends are going to Europe on a charter. One of the iron mines has a round trip for about $230. But we don't like the cold that much! We'll save Europe for a different time of year.

PS. Some people killed a boa constrictor here last week. It was 17½ feet long and as big around as my thigh! They caught it in a fish net.

Dearest Mother,   **December 26, 1972, Gbedin**

We thought of all of you yesterday, and missed you so much. Families and Christmas just seem to go together. Actually, we had quite a nice day, beginning with Christmas Eve with Chris, Mary and Larry, and Harold and I at their house. Mary had made a Christmas tree of palm branches. We put the tinsel on that you had sent, made decorations out of the Christmas cards. We used the napkins and tablecloth you sent for dinner the next day. I also had the fat Santa that Lois sent last year, on the table. One of our friends came back from Monrovia and brought us all a lot of mail, but we were all kind of low-down, thinking of our people at home.

Today, Chris and Sarah Nichols from Sanniquellie, and another guy, Bob Artel, all Peace Corps teachers, came. Chris built a barbecue pit. Harold had dug the pit and Chris put some cement blocks on the sides and laid a grill on it. Harold had already butchered Billy Goat, and Chris marinated the meat in a zesty barbecue sauce. They grilled it for about three hours. It was cut into chunks, which didn't remind you that you were eating your friend!

After the goat was cooked, the guys decided the coals were too good to waste, so they ran around and caught three chickens. They dressed them, tossed them in the barbecue sauce, and cooked them.

We all did some of the food preparations. Mr. Wo gave me a watermelon, which we hollowed out and made fruit salad in. The salad was made from fresh pineapple, oranges, watermelon, papaya, bananas, and freshly grated coconut. We had paid 5 cents for the coconut, 7 cents for the pineapple, and all the rest of the fruit was free, mostly dashed to us.

We brought our chairs outside by the pit, under a tree, and ate our dinner. Earlier, we had presents. I made orange marmalade and cookies for my gift, also a little patchwork quilt for Mary from scraps of Fanti cloth. Chris made the cutest little cradle for Mary and Larry. He also made a beautiful coffee table for us, made from a slab of mahogany—a cross-section of a tree, more than three feet across and two inches thick. Harold has to varnish it. It was quite a surprise. So we had a quite enjoyable, if different, Christmas. I made cookies for some of our Liberian friends, and the Chinese fellows, which we walked around the village and delivered and visited. Christmas Eve people came to the house too, to give us our "Christmas." The gifts included two live chickens, a branch of bananas, and several bunches of eddoes. We can't use them all, so will have to give some away later.

Harold, Larry, and Chris are building a chicken yard. We all have so many chickens running around that it's impossible to have a garden. It should be finished soon, and then the boys can get busy and dig a garden spot. John is away for two weeks visiting his mother in the country. His young brother, about twelve, I think, is helping me. He speaks very little English, and besides, he has come just recently from the bush village, so knows very little about living in a house like this. I can't just say, "Wash the sink." Instead, I have to say, in very few words, each step. "You mu' open the pump (faucet), put some watah there (in the sink). Put small Vano (soap powder) there. You mu' take the cloth, etc., etc. It's really a riot sometimes.

Harold doesn't have the patience for this kind of directing, but I get a kick out of it. Maybe it's because I spend so much time explaining to people in the clinic.

Thanks so much for the gifts. Harold wore the pedometer and learned that he had walked ten miles that day just working around here.

Dear Judith,   **December 26, 1972, Gbedin**

We were really lonesome for you yesterday, even though we had a nice time with our young friends. There were ten of us—seven men. Our chickens, live ones, wandered around while we were eating, picking up scraps. It seemed almost like life in the Ozarks, but pretty typical here. People sit on mats while they are eating, either in or out of the house. Sometimes it's hard to keep the chickens from pecking at your food.

On Friday afternoon, Harold had a party for the fellows he works with. We have one social center here, a bar where people gather to visit, play checkers, and even sometimes drink beer or Fanta. The man who owns it is the electrician here. He is a Bassa man named Harry, and Harold's good friend. Harold told Harry to get a couple cases of beer, and after work they all went to Harry Bar [*that was its name; no apostrophe*]. They sent for Mary and me, Harry's wife and a couple of women who were visiting there. Usually, only men come to such parties. Harry had a record player, and some people danced. It was just Hi-Life music, which the people love and can they dance! It doesn't matter if one has a partner. The Liberians love to make speeches, usually quite lengthy ones that don't say very much but are very amusing. The more they drink, the windier they become!

We bought another mask this week from a Mandingo Charlie who lives in the next town. We've looked at so many masks since we've come here, dozens in fact, that Charlies have brought around. We are always looking for authentic, possibly older, used ones. Of course, we don't know enough about artifacts to begin with. This is a Mano mask and appears to be the real thing.

We talked to the man three different times in one day. He would name a price, and finally Harold would give him an offer; they would talk more, he couldn't accept it, and off he'd go, a couple times to Larry's. Larry was interested but wouldn't pay what the Charlie wanted. The man was really wanting to sell it. We thought he was jammed for money. Finally, Harold agreed to pay $25 for it. (He had asked $60 to begin with). We think it is worth much more, in comparison to others we've seen. We have another Mano mask and a Gio one, both of which are worth much more than the small amount we paid for them, according to some of the charlies who have offered to buy them from us to take to Monrovia and sell.

Dearest Mother,   **December 31, 1972, Foya**

We're spending the New Year's weekend here in Foya, which is in the northwest corner of Liberia. It is about 220 miles one way, and was a really nice trip since there wasn't too much traffic and not too much dust. We left Gbedin Friday evening, and have been having a fantastic time. We'll return Tuesday.

I wrote before about the Israeli company, Agrimeco, that had taken over a lot of the work that Harold had been doing. When they first came, the company manager, Mr. Bensvee, stayed with us in Gbedin and consulted a lot with Harold on who to hire, such as mechanics, Cat operators, tractor drivers, etc., also on machinery they were taking over. Harold had trained some of the men. Anyway, the hirees have proven to be good workers. Consequently, the manager can't do enough for Harold. He invited us to Foya, where they are located and clearing land.

So far, they have cleared 2,000 acres and are starting on 2,000 more. Then they will plow it and prepare it for planting rice first, and the next time in coffee, cocoa, and oil palms. He wanted Harold to look over the place (I'm sure he would like to hire him) and look at some of the machinery.

Friday, he sent a brand new Land Rover with a driver who drove us the 220 miles here, gave us the key to his guest house, which is stocked with food and drinks, and provided a cook and a night watchman. He put the car and driver at our disposal and then will drive us back to Gbedin on Tuesday. The house is very fine, set on a hill at the edge of town, with a view of the entire area. This is a different tribal area, so we don't understand some of the people. However, Liberian English gets us by a lot of the time. Besides, our driver is a native of this area and speaks Mandingo, as well, so we have no problem communicating.

Yesterday morning we got up early and were taken on a tour of the area by one of the employees. We saw paddy rice at every stage of growth, saw newly cleared land, watched the bull dozers operating. They don't have to blast or cut trees down, just push them over—huge trees, too. The palms have surprisingly shallow roots. A lot of the land is short bush and elephant grass, which is about as high as a person or less.

While the Cats are operating, people are all about looking for small animals, which they call meat. They flush out small deer, groundhog (not like Eastern Washington groundhog), possum, squirrel, mice. Then the people run and catch them. It's hilarious to watch. Later, they divide it among all the people. Some days they catch as many as 20 animals. Yesterday when we arrived, they had built a small fire, burnt the hair off, and cut up the animals and were in the process of wrapping the meat in palm leaves to carry home. There must have been eight or ten to divide. Everyone was happy since meat is scarce in the market, and dear besides.

Later, our driver took us to another town to meet the paramount chief. This chief has a large area in his chiefdom and about five clan chiefs under him. He was holding court in a roofed pavilion that had low walls all around it, all occupied by people who were there to have matters judged by the chief. Some were just there to listen. The old chief and two or three assistants sat at the far end of the rectangular court. Our driver knew him well and took us in to introduce us.

We were given seats next to him and sat and visited for a few minutes. The chief is an unlettered man and is said to be a wise and fair chief. He is known throughout Liberia because of his good ways. He has an assistant who is called an Honorable and who is educated. We also ran into one of our Chinese friends who used to be in Gbedin, so we stopped and visited with him too. He gave us four big watermelons.

Saturday is market day in Foya. I wish you could see such a sight. It is an open-air market, made up of hundreds of individuals who are making market, selling an untold variety of things, food, clothing, many kinds of cheap dime-store things.

The people mostly spread their goods out on woven mats on the ground in little piles. Peanuts in 1 cent piles, peppers in 5 cent rounds, bananas and oranges in groupings of four or five, whatever is offered for 5 cents or 10 cents. Peanut butter, which is made from ground peas, is beaten in a mortar and molded into little balls and piled on a table. Cloth is folded and laid out in stacks on the ground or hung on strings. Bread is stacked in the open on tables. You buy a long thin loaf, for 5 or 10 cents and carry it off with no wrapping. If you buy a fish, it's wrapped in newspaper with the head and tail hanging out.

This particular market occupies about three acres, with all the individual markets so close together you can hardly move around. You can buy a needle for 10 cents, two aspirin for 5 cents, a cigarette for 5 cents. Everything is available "one, one," rather than in lots. I love to wander around and see what is happening.

While I was there yesterday, I ran into a Gbedin girl who worked for me while she went to Gbedin School. This term she has been going to school in Sanniquellie so we didn't see her often. I learned that her foster father works here for Agrimeco and is himself a Gbedin man. In fact, he is the one who toured us around the area. His wife and I were acquainted; last year her baby was quite sick, and I took care of it in Gbedin. I took her and the baby to Ganta and helped her—paid her registration fee—and tried to follow up when she carried the baby home. She has been here in

Foya for most of the past year and was so glad to see me and thank me for my help.

Harold's good friend, Daniel Suah, the mechanic he trained and recommended for this job, was overjoyed to see us here, too. These people all live in the same general area here. So last evening Daniel, Mary the school girl, Yah the woman, and her baby, and also the other wife and her child, all came to visit. Daniel brought Harold some beer, and Yah presented me with a wax-print lappa. I immediately put it on, which really pleased them.

I forgot to mention that earlier we had gone with the driver to see another area that is being cleared. We arrived in the driver's "born town," a tiny village built on a hill with the houses quite close together, and the road meandering all around in the town. Again, the chief was holding court in a similar but smaller building. A few men were seated around him, and all the walls were occupied by spectators or participants. On

A typical Liberian market scene. This market is in Borkeza.

the floor in front of him was a small object encrusted with cowry shells embedded in a black, sticky substance, called medicine. When a person testifies, he first swears on this medicine, and if he is lying, this medicine "will catch him," so we were told. I don't know in what way, but they say it will indicate if you're testifying falsely.

We were introduced and given seats and sat and visited again. The chief sent someone out and soon three fellows wearing Sam Brown belts

and different caps, returned carrying a white chicken, which was presented to us, along with a speech. It was quite a day. We gave our friends three
of our watermelons and, today, ate the chicken with rice. Mary and Yah
ate with us. Around eleven we will go to church with them.

Today was another interesting day. We started out this morning for
Koindu, across the border in Sierra Leone, where their Sunday markets
are well known, especially for cloth. Mary and Yah and another Gbedin
boy named Moses, Harold and I, and the driver, all went. As usual, we had
picked up a few more before we reached Koindu.

As always, Liberian roads were awful, but Sierra Leone's were worse.
This was a one-lane track, up and down a rutted, twisting route through
coffee trees and tall elephant grass. Whenever you cross a border, you
have to stop at police check points, customs, and immigration gates, this
time a total of seven between Foya and Koindu.

This market is much larger than the Foya market. It is well known for
its volume of tie-dye and wax print (batik) fabrics for sale. There is also a
lot of country cloth, a hand-woven material made from hand-spun thread
of country cotton, as well as commercially made thread. It is woven in
strips about four inches wide, which is then sewn together to make
garments. Fortunately, our driver spoke Mandingo, as well as his native
tribal dialect, so he did the bargaining for us. I had been saving money for
this market, so was able to buy four satin lappas, really gorgeous tie-dye,
four damask tie-dye, and one country cloth bundle. It took a lot of looking
and a lot of bargaining, all of which were interesting.

When we wanted to eat lunch, Kamara, the driver, took us to his
sister's combination store and restaurant. She is a Leonian citizen, a huge,
fat woman, dressed in a beautifully stitched green satin dress. We went
into her piazza, a long narrow room behind her store. It was lined with
arm chairs on either side of the room with a low table in the center. She
had many photographs of herself, her husband and family, the President,
and other dignitaries, hanging high up on the walls, tilted so you could see
them easily. They brought us meat in a peppery, oily sauce, and big loaves
of bread. There were four soup bowls of cow meat, and the six of us ate
together from them, dipping our bread in the sauce and picking out the
meat with our fingers. The house was very clean, the linoleum floor was
shining. The bowls of meat were 20 cents each, and the bread, about 10
inches long, were 5 cents each.

Wherever we've gone these past two days, we've been introduced to another of our driver's brothers and now his sister. Of course, many times when people say brother, father, mother, sister, they really aren't their "born" brother, etc. It might be their cousin, or just a good friend. For instance, yesterday someone asked Yah, when they met us on the street, looking at me, "Is this your Ma?" She replied, "Yes."

Today when I asked Kamara about his brothers, he said 29 were born to his father, who had five wives. And you know, if there are 29 children living, there had been many more, since so many children don't live.

Tomorrow, we will take a drive, maybe 25 miles from here, to visit the Walageisi iron mine. It is a new mine, opened in 1972, in Liberia where it joins Guinea and Sierra Leone. Apparently it is a fabulously rich iron deposit and will be operated by a Japanese company. We have never visited the Lamco mine, as close as it is, so decided we should try to see this one while we are here.

Tuesday, Harold will ride as far as Gbarnga and then take a taxi home. I'll go on to Monrovia with Kamara and make reservations for our trip to Cameroon, which will be January 2nd. This sounds like a lot of playing, but it's the first real vacation we've had. The other two trips used holiday time instead of vacation time.

Today while we were in Koindu, Kamara met a friend who told him he had seen Kamara's son (nine years old) in a Lebanese store there. Apparently the boy ran away from home about six months ago because he didn't want to go to school. The boy had gone to a taxi stand and met one of Kamara's friends and told him Kamara wanted the man to carry him to Foya, which the man did. The boy then went to Koindu on his own, about ten miles away, where he's been staying with a Lebanese merchant and his family. Kamara took him in the car with us when we left and is going to take him to his family in a town near here. He told the boy he has to attend school. These glimpses of life are so fascinating to us, and every day brings more.

Taxi stand in Gbarnga, with people loading their goods.

1973

Dear Mother,   **January 4, 1973, Gbedin**

We're back home now. Before we left Foya on Monday, we visited the Walageisi iron mine, about 30 miles from Foya. Actually, the mining hasn't begun yet. The development of the area, drilling for core samples, all kinds of geological surveys have been going on for about three years. It is a very rich iron deposit. We spent quite a while visiting with the manager, a young naturalized Liberian man whose parents became citizens when he was eleven. He invited us to stay the night, but we told him we would come again.

Harold and I left there early on Tuesday morning and had a nice ride to Gbarnga. The road was pretty good, and not too much traffic, and therefore, not too much dust. The dusty roads make driving particularly hazardous, and I'm always relieved if it's rained recently or if the traffic is scarce. The President has a farm in Lofa County, so the roads are kept in fairly good shape. They are graded regularly, since he goes to the farm to stay quite often.

When we reached Gbarnga, Harold left us (the driver and me), and took a money bus, which is a pickup with seats in the back and a covered canopy on which all manner of goods are piled high. He had to get back to Gbedin for work. The driver and I went on to Monrovia so I could make the final plans for our anticipated trip. The next day, I took a taxi home. I always thank God when I reach home alive.

We plan to leave on the 21st of this month for Cameroon. We hope to be gone about a month. So far, we've taken very little time off and need to get away. Harold works ten to twelve hours a day, and seldom has a whole Saturday or Sunday off. So, unless we leave, there is no rest.

We decided, because of the high price of airfare, to fly only one way. We will meet a friend, a former Cameroon volunteer, in Douala, Cameroon. She will have made lots of contacts for us, so we will have places to stay that won't be too expensive. Then we will come back by state transport (big buses) and taxis, coming all the way along the coast, through Nigeria, Dahomey, Togo, Ghana, to Abidgan, Ivory Coast, where we will take a plane to Monrovia. Getting from Ivory Coast to Liberia by taxi is a real headache.

I hope nothing interferes with our plans, since both Harold and I are very involved just now with lots of various activities. Harold, for example, is responsible for getting more land cleared, about 40 acres, for rice farming. Agrimeco [*an Israeli company*] has sent a Cat, and he must oversee the entire thing, keeping the fellows working in the planned area and, in the meantime, keep the shop running.

We had our first attack of driver ants this week. Have you ever read anything about them? They are small black ants, generally, although some, called "soldiers," are about three-fourths inch long. They have fierce pincers on their rear ends, and have the capability of attacking and consuming large animals. The night before we came home, they invaded our and Pearmines' yards, under our houses where the chickens sleep in a kind of carport. Larry and Mary heard the chickens about 4 AM, and came out and found three small chickens dying from the ants on their bodies and other chickens suffering. They picked ants off like crazy. It's particularly hard because the ants get on your feet and legs and start to pinch.

The night I came back from Monrovia, the ants came again. Our yard was black with them, and we could hear the chickens crying. So we all went out, our guests too, with flashlights, Aladdin and kerosene lamps, and DDT, and tried to fight the ants off, moving chickens as well. The next afternoon, John, Jon Jon, Harold, and I went out with the rake and cutlass and kerosene and really hunted and tried to concentrate on their trails. They always seem to go on a specific trail, sometimes an inch or more wide and solid black with ants. Harold says that tonight they seem to be gone. If there is any kind of meat, like a dead animal or a fatty substance, they are attracted right away. I'd sure hate to get them in our house!

January 6, Twelfth Night. The ants seem to have left us, thank goodness. There is always some kind of insect to cope with here. We're always working to keep little brown ants out of our kitchen and cockroaches of all sizes out of the house. There are always mosquitoes and some little black flies that bite your legs and make you itch like crazy. We got some insect powder for the house, use insect repellent and a mosquito net over our bed, then use Caladryl or some such when we do get bit. I seem to be less susceptible to mosquitoes now than when we came. You get used to things; it's part of life. It doesn't get me down, anyway.

Dear Vikki and Gill,   **January 1973, Gbedin**

I was just checking my letter box and realized the last letter I had from you was dated December 9th. Peace Corps has been so awful about bringing us our mail. They came two or three days after Christmas, and that is the last time. Fortunately, we can send ours through Lamco. We are all composing letters of protest to Peace Corps Monrovia, but I'm sure it won't make any difference. Anyway, all of us here in Gbedin are feeling quite depressed at the lack of news from home. Maybe tomorrow!

We are all involved in our vacation preparations. We will leave here on Thursday for Monrovia, and take off on Sunday. I hope there won't be any visa hitches. The travel agency is taking care of them for us. We'll need six, since we are coming back by land, and have to check into each country at their border, even if we just want to drive through. When we went to Koindu, in Sierra Leone, we were stopped eight times, three in Liberia and four in Sierra Leone, police check, immigration, customs, etc., etc. I think the smaller the country, the more importance they put on such hassles.

Harold is working so hard these days and always something to do on the weekends. Yesterday and today he's been working on the wiring system of a car that belongs to one of his Liberian friends. He has also been responsible for another sizable land clearing project. Harold has not only to see that the work goes on, but also has to lay it out, such as diverting a big creek, building up a road above the paddy area, placing *bunds* correctly. [*Bunds are narrow, raised earthen dividers between the rice plots.*]

Regarding our future plans: we will come back here for another year in Peace Corps, rather than go to Botswana. We've had several job offers and are weighing each. If the agriculture minister comes through with Harold's requests, it will be in Gbedin. Otherwise in Gbarnga at Cuttington College or in Monrovia for another agency, called ADP. When we return from our vacation we will know, because Harold has told the minister that is his deadline. The minister says he won't let Harold go, so Harold says, "OK show me."

Dear Mother,   January 20, 1973, Monrovia

We have all the necessary visas, exit and reentry permits from immigration, bought our tickets, and exchanged some money for Cameroon money. Now we have a whole day to relax here in Monrovia before taking off tomorrow morning. It's the first time I've ever been ready ahead of time to go anyplace. We're staying with some friends who live on the beach and have been enjoying the sound of the waves.

Tonight, we will have dinner with Jordan Holtam, the man we originally came to work with here. He's no longer with Peace Corps, but now is with ADP, another government agency. ADP is interested in getting Harold to come to work with them, as a Peace Corps volunteer. They are a community development agency, involved in road building, clinics and schools. So tonight we will talk possibilities with him.

The weather is really funny now. No rain for weeks, cold at night, hot later in the day. The roads are very dusty. This is the time of the year that a wind, called a Harmitan, an annual phenomenon, blows over the Sahara in this direction, bringing a lot of fine sand. Everything looks hazy, like there is smoke in the air. It is very hard to breathe, especially up-country.

Both Harold and I feel like we're coming down with chest colds after the trip down here.

The trip took ages because our brakes failed—the brake line broke. Harold had to use "Rube Goldberg" methods in order to have any brakes for two-thirds of the way. It took about seven hours instead of the usual four and a half to five. The Harmitan wind is worse this year. Even small planes are grounded some of the time, because of low visibility.

Dear Mother,   January 25, 1973, Buea, Cameroon

We've just been having an argument about whether it's Thursday or Friday. It's so hard to keep track of the date when we are traveling, and especially when there isn't a daily calendar around. Things have been going very smoothly. Our flight here to Cameroon was very nice, with two stops: in Ivory Coast and in Lome, Togo, that made it possible for us to see some of the countryside. In Ivory Coast we saw hundreds of acres of oil palms.

In Douala, Cameroon, the people speak French—in fact, the Western part of Cameroon is French speaking. However, our plans were to mostly stay in East Cameroon, which is all English speaking. We took a taxi, which is the only form of transport, to Victoria, a town on the coast, where we found a place to stay in a Presbyterian (Swiss) Mission, by the beach. They gave us their guest house for $1.60 a night, and we could cook there, too.

We stayed two days, and then came here to Buea, which is about an hour's drive from Victoria. There are about six Peace Corps volunteers here, working in agriculture programs. We are staying with two boys and a girl. They are really nice kids. One was working at home on some reports, so he gave us his Suzuki today to get around town. We saw a really awful movie last night at USIS [*United States Information Service*]. Today they all got together and cooked a spaghetti dinner. It was a nice evening and visit.

Tomorrow we will start north so we can visit an area that is the center of artisans work—brass, carving, weaving. Two of the kids we met tonight live up that way, and said we could stay in their house even though they aren't going to be there. I think we have such room arrangements made for the rest of the time we will be in Cameroon, either with volunteers, or in missions. Otherwise, you spend all your money on hotels, which aren't so great. We always take our own sheets and towels, and of course, buy some food for the people. Everyone has been so friendly, it has been very easy to travel. The roads haven't been as bad as in Liberia, so even the taxi trips haven't been too strenuous. Also, so far we haven't had to go through any customs and border checks. Always a hassle.

When you are in a lot of major towns, it's easy to forget you're in Africa, because things appear to be quite modern. There are new buildings, people in Western dress, and foods can even be the same. We usually seek out the native stores and eating houses, and try to visit with native people, rather than with Europeans and Americans. This way we can learn more about the country. Actually, in most towns, you can find Americans and stay with them and never meet a real African, if you want to.

Dear Mother,   **January 31, 1973, Cameroon**

The time has been going by so fast in the past week that we have hardly sat down long enough to write anything. Every two days we've been on the road, and other times have been visiting or sightseeing. Traveling here is similar to Liberia—crowded taxis and up-country, narrow, dusty, crooked roads. Actually it isn't too bad, if one is expecting it to be like this. We have been fortunate to find Peace Corps volunteers who offer us a bed, or find inexpensive guest houses at missions.

This country seems to be more advanced as far as agriculture is concerned. We've seen miles and miles of coffee trees, bananas, and rubber trees. They have tea plantations and rice paddies. Wherever we go, the people have been so nice and friendly, both Cameroons and volunteers. It's been a good chance to try different food—sometimes there is little choice!

One day we visited a town that has a street called Rue des Artisans where there are many brass workers, wood carvers, furniture makers. It was fascinating to watch them work. The brass workers use the "lost wax" method and fire the pieces in a little furnace that is kept burning by air forced in as they beat on a sort of skin-covered drum, quite a rhythmic beat. We bargained with some of the people and bought a few small pieces of brass. Since we have to carry everything in our packs, we could only buy small things. The markets are so interesting. There are so many hand-crafted things as well as all manner of food stuff, really weird things. Each town and village has market day once a week; other days there is only a little to buy.

It is really strange being where you are the only white people. In Liberia, there are usually others, at least Lebanese. Here, in town after town, we walk around and only see black people. We've seen so many hand-crafted things that aren't done in Liberia, like lovely baskets, weaving, and clay pots. I've bought several baskets—one was 10 francs (2½ cents). Carrying them in a taxi is a problem sometimes. Most people we meet are surprised we will travel this way. They say, "You must have a lot of stamina." It's really the better way to see the people, rather than flying in and out and only seeing large cities.

Today, we will go to a small village where a lot of fish farming is being developed. The local big man, called the *fon*, has a large farm there and a palace that we can visit. This is an English-speaking area, which is easier for us. For a few days we were in the French sector and found it a bit frustrating to communicate. I can understand some French so we aren't lost but can't really pronounce it correctly.

Dearest Kids,   **February 7, 1973, Lagos, Nigeria**

We had a fine two weeks in Cameroon. Wanted to stay longer but would have had to renew our visas which was too time consuming and costly. Fortunately, we met a lot of nice Peace Corps kids who put us up half the time, and the other times we found good accommodations at missions that were within our budgets.

We're in Lagos now, on a rooftop by the ocean, at an Anglican church mission guest house. It's by far the most costly place we've stayed but apparently this city is one of the four most expensive places to live in the world—according to a recent *Time* magazine article. We'll stay until tomorrow and have a good rest. We entered Nigeria Sunday and arrived in Lagos last eve, after a 300-mile, seven and a half hour trip from eastern Nigeria. These were two really hard days of travel—getting across the border was a lengthy hassle. Nine stops—customs, immigration, gendarmes, police in both countries.

Nigeria is a huge country. The government seems to be very nationalistic. We don't feel quite as comfortable as we did in Cameroon. Apparently the Biafran war and the new government are too recent for them to feel easy. There is also a lot of smuggling across borders so the checks going across borders are very thorough and numerous. For example, when we left Cameroon we had to make four stops, customs, immigration, police, gendarmes. Entering Nigeria, we were stopped five times and had our luggage checked two times. It all takes time but we just stay loose and get along. Fortunately, both of these places are English-speaking, as in Ghana.

The weather, now in dry season, is hot and muggy. The eastern section was the Biafrin area and shows the effects of the war, which ended three years ago. The cities are huge, teeming with people and there is a water shortage in most of the places we went through. We stayed in one government rest house and one hotel, both pretty awful—no water in the shower or toilet. Couldn't even brush our teeth in the one place since the only water was dirty! Most places all we could drink was coke or beer—talk about getting dehydrated! We've ridden in just about every kind of vehicle—packed pick-up trucks, packed mammy wagons, which are huge truck-like buses, loaded on top with cargo and with close to a hundred people inside sitting and standing, Ford station wagons, Peugeot cars—all with at least two too many passengers.

From here on the going should be a bit easier. Roads are supposed to be better and in some cases they even have big comfy buses. The only hang up will be the borders. Keeping up with the different money systems keeps us on our toes—francs, pounds and shillings, nairas and kobas, cedis and pesawas. The money changed here January 1st, so we have two systems to keep up with.

Dearest Mother,   **February 13, 1973, Accra, Ghana**

Since we left Lagos, Nigeria, last Thursday, the traveling has been much easier. The roads are wide and well surfaced, and the taxis are not packed so full. We drove along the coast nearly all the way—a beautiful drive. The beaches are dotted with thatch huts and coconut palms and dugout fishing boats. The constant breeze keeps things cooler. From Cotonou, Dahorney all the way to Lome, Togo, there are continuous coconut plantations along the road. We stayed a day in Cotonou and then went on to Lome, where we stayed three days. Both are French-speaking countries but in Togo there are some who speak English since it is next to Ghana where English is spoken. We're determined to learn to converse in French before we visit such countries again.

Ghana is an interesting place—there is so much development here, many industries, even Kaiser Aluminum. There is military rule since last February, and the government is trying hard to get the country on its own. No foreign goods can be imported if there are any Ghanaian made ones—so there is a lot of security at the borders to eliminate smuggling. They have their own money system, cedis and pesawas, and you aren't allowed to carry any money out of the country. There is a thriving currency black market just across the borders where you can buy many more cedis per $1 than you get from the banks. While it is all illegal, it's right out in the open. As soon as you get out of a taxi you're accosted from all sides with "Do you want to change money?" We try to get our money to come out even so we don't have to worry about changing to another currency as we go to another country.

There is much beautiful cloth here. Two kinds that are distinctively Ghanaian are Kente cloth, a hand-woven colorful cloth done in four-inch strips and then sewn together, and Adinkra cloth, which is hand stamped using a black dye of some kind and a stamp carved from dried gourds. It's done in long strips about 20 inches wide and then sewn together with colorful thread, the thread making a band about one and a half to two inches wide. It's sold in large pieces about the size of a king-sized bed. Both of these have been done in this way for years and many of the designs were at one time reserved only for the rulers.

Dear Vikki and Gill,   **February 13, 1973, Accra, Ghana**

Our travels will soon be over. We will get back to Monrovia in about seven days. We have been in Accra for two days.

We were in a minor taxi accident in Lome. Our driver went into an intersection too fast, and hit a motorcycle. There are hundreds of cycles, and everyone drives like they're crazy. The cycle driver flipped over the hood of the car, and landed on his feet, didn't seem to be hurt but his cycle was damaged. Our driver got out, and there was a lot of palava. Finally, we got out of the car and walked away while all of the excitement was going on. We found out we were close to our destination anyway. We decided we were well out of it.

We enjoyed Lome. It is right on the Atlantic, and the beach is nice. It is an expensive city to stay in, though, as is Lagos. Now, we are staying in Accra for four days. It, too, is right on the Atlantic and is a thriving city. Ghana is really going places. Things are very inexpensive here for tourists, mainly because of their money system. The borders are checked very closely to prevent illegal importing of goods. Our taxi was stopped about 10 times in a 140-mile trip, and about half the time, our vehicle was searched in some way. Harold said he saw the driver give the officers money more than once, which seems to be the rule rather than the exception.

I went wild over the beads in the markets, both in Lome and in Accra. These beads are about one and half inches long—tubular, with lots of colors. I can buy a long string for one cedi, which on the black market rate is 50 cents. In Monrovia, they are sold for $4 and more a string. They are known as slave beads, used during the slave days for trading.

Dearest Mother,   **February 20, 1973, Half Assini, Ghana**

Just now I'm sitting in a government "rest house," a fine structure on the Atlantic Ocean at the west end of Ghana. The ocean is about 100 feet away, and I've just come from a nice swim.

Harold is out helping some fishermen haul in their net—if they don't catch anything, we won't have any dinner! They set a long net with a rope at each end—take it out with a hand-hewn canoe sometimes thirty or more feet long and about four inches high. After the net has been out about three hours, two teams of men and boys start to haul on the ropes. It takes a couple of hours to pull it in. Sometimes there is a ton of fish in the net. Usually there are about 20 men and boys on each rope. They are Fante fishermen. They fish here in Ghana, Ivory Coast, and Liberia. They're excellent swimmers, too.

We've spent about five days on the coast here in Ghana, and it has been fascinating. Starting in 1482, a series of forts and castles were built all along what they called the gold coast—mostly the full length of Ghana—by the Portuguese, Dutch, English, and I think, Danish, to protect their interests here in gold, ivory, slaves, etc. Many of the castles have been restored and are being used by the government and some as rest houses, operated by the government. We stayed in a castle, built in the 1600s for one night. It was a delightful experience.

The next day we moved to another town, Dixcoree, but found the fort not as nice—dirty and poor facilities for toilets, bath, and cooking. To add to the problem, the castles are situated in very small towns, fishing villages actually, and there are no stores or restaurants. On top of this, Ghana restricts imports so there is a real shortage of food—you can't find canned goods at all. I've looked for two days for toothpaste, and they just don't stock it.

Fortunately, we've found bananas and pineapple, fried plantain, ground nuts, and bread. Harold has been satisfied eating in a native chop house where they serve fufu and fish soup. This is a rather gluey glob of mashed plantain, something like eating unbaked bread dough. But I can't quite manage it especially when you have to either eat with your hands or with the one spoon the chop house owns! Rice is very scarce, and the only time you can get it is in the morning. It's served with beans on it.

Actually since we've been in Ghana, we have existed on the bare minimum because food is really quite scarce. If we find the fish tonight, we'll take it to the home of a couple of Peace Corps volunteers here in town, and they will cook it. (This fine house, well furnished and spacious, even has a cook, but there's no cooking gas, no electricity until next month, and no running water!)

We've been so fortunate to find nice places to stay. The castles are inexpensive—about $2 a night; this guest house is 1 cedi 50, which is about $1.10 a night. It is really for government officials, but we met a person a few days ago in another town who introduced us to the district supervisor who is responsible for guest houses. He put us up in that town for 50 cents and made arrangements for us to stay here for two nights.

Tomorrow we'll cross the border about five miles from here, go on to Abidjan, Ivory Coast, and hope to catch a plane for home the next day (Thursday). We've had a fabulous time, uncomfortable and difficult some of the time, but well worth it. But we're looking forward to getting home.

Sunday when we reached one small town called Axim, on the coast, we couldn't find any place to eat—hadn't had anything but fruit for breakfast. The same girl who helped us find the room told us she'd prepare something for us if we wanted to get something. We went to the market with her where she bought fish and rice and vegetables. Later she sent a feast to the rest house for us. She is the head teacher at a primary school here. She introduced me the next day to her friend as her new mama and gave me her picture. I gave her one of my dresses. People have been so wonderful to us.

In fact that day when we were leaving there, one of her friends was walking to the lorry station with us—the only transportation is in big trucks fitted out with seats. She said, "I think you could ride in the mail van, let me see." So she hunted up the driver who was persuaded to give us a ride to this town—a 60-mile trip which lasted about four hours. The road was rough but also he had to drop off two bags of mail in all the little towns, so we had a real sightseeing trip. It was a bright red Land Rover.

Monday. We're now waiting at the wharf on the Ghana border for the ferry to take us across the mouth of the river to the Ivory Coast border. This point is about seven miles from the town we were staying in. Our trip out was a riot. We boarded a decrepit lorry in the town—there were six-inch planks laid across the bed of the truck for seats. It was soon obvious that there were no brakes—the car boys ran alongside and stuffed a coconut in front of a wheel to help them stop; no starter—it had to be pushed; no key—they crossed and uncrossed some wires instead. As soon as we'd get up to 25 miles an hour, they'd undo the wires and let the car coast to cool off the motor which was soon something like a house on fire. Whenever we'd stop, one small boy would fill a bucket from a reserve can in back of the truck and go to pour it into the radiator.

I think we were lucky to get here because ever since, about one and a half hours, the truck has been laid up here with people working on it. It's gradually filling up with people, plantains, and fish, so probably it will get under way again.

I mentioned that Harold was out with the fisherman yesterday. He stayed and helped them haul in their nets—about a three-hour job. The net owner dashed him a big fish—a tuna. Many of the fish were quite small but all are sold right away. We took our fish to the home of two Peace Corps boys who had invited us for dinner. They deep fried it, and it was really delicious—French-fried onions too. Later we walked home in the moonlight along the beach—what a beautiful scene, coconut palms silhouetted against the sky, the waves so silvery on the beach.

It looks like we'll be here quite a while. The launch we're to go in won't start—it's diesel-powered, and parts of the engine are lying out on the deck being worked on by about four people. This boat is about 30 feet long, quite deep, with a zinc roof. The seats are just benches stretched across. It should be a nice ride if we ever get started! We're sitting here eating coconut, waiting patiently. Most of the people here raise coconut, press the oil from it and sell it to a soap company.

Later. The launch never started. After about three hours of tinkering, another one arrived. We transferred people, chickens, plantain, luggage, etc., and took off across the bay—about a 30-minute ride. It was a long day, what with the stops at customs—three times inspecting our bags—arranging for taxis two times, and finally arrived in Abidjan at the airport about 6:30 PM.

We traveled about 100 miles in Ivory Coast, and the entire time we passed by fields of pineapple, bananas, coffee trees, or oil palms. They must raise an amazing amount of pineapple. Trucks passed by loaded with beautiful big ones. One time Harold held out his hand as we went by a truck, and one of the boys who was riding in the back tossed one to him—unfortunately it didn't quite reach him.

Dearest Mother and all,   **February 28, 1973, Gbedin**

We came back from our vacation on Saturday evening and for the next two days it was like old home week—everyone had to come greet us and welcome us back—some of my clinic patients brought their babies for me to see, some of our friends brought us things like eddoes and plantains. It's kind of a standing joke here the way I always have plantain to share. I receive so many branches of it, and we just can't eat all of it. So if any of the volunteers here need any, they know where to go!

It's really nice to be back; we flew from Abidjan to Monrovia—after nearly five weeks of taxis, lorries, pickups, rafts, buses. Harold said he couldn't bear to ride from Abidjan to Gbedin, another 800 to 900 miles with really poor roads.

We'd saved enough travelers checks for the air tickets but hadn't counted on Nixon's dollar devaluation. We just barely made it home, had about $4 left when we hit Monrovia! It was hard to cash the checks in Ivory Coast, and they'd hardly take more than $100 to exchange, plus 10 percent less, what a mess. I was ready to take a taxi but Harold wouldn't budge, and we finally made it.

It appears that the minister of agriculture is going to come through with all of Harold's requests and that we will remain here in Gbedin. They've told him they are providing him with a new Land Rover soon, more employees for Gbedin, and such, which he had told them he had to have if he was to do the work they requested. We both feel another year to work with the people might get much more done than we can see now.

Mary is expecting her baby any day. She's all ready for it, made some clothes, has her desk fitted out with the bath basin and all the needs. I will go with her to the hospital if I'm around. She misses her mother so I'm glad enough to substitute. When the baby is six weeks old, they will leave.

She and Larry just drove up, returning from the doctor where they learned that the baby is in breech position, so it's a little worrisome for them. Have to see what their doctor decides to do—maybe send her to Monrovia.

Dearest Mother,   **March 8, 1973, Monrovia**

It's so sunny and hot here. We have had a couple of rains which saved the rice crops for now. It's still very dusty but there should be more rain soon. Our cat, Polly, had four babies last Sunday. One is a calico. They are all spoken for already. She is in a cage on our back porch that was built for the monkey—quite snug and comfy for her but she continues to try to carry them inside into our store room.

Harold and I are in Monrovia again trying to get our trip home lined up and getting supplies for Harold's job. He has the back of the truck loaded down with tanks of gas, a tank of oxygen, etc. It makes a better ride home on the bumpy roads with more weight in back.

Tonight we'll go back half way and stay with some friends at Phebe Hospital, a Lutheran mission at Suakoko, and go the rest of the way in the AM. It will be less strenuous, and we enjoy the people.

We just picked up some mail and learned that you broke your ribs. Here the people would all come and tell you "Neh my, ya!" (never mind, ya!), a standard comment if you're ill or hurt or if someone dies. In fact the people are offended if other people don't come and tell them "Neh my, ya."

My classes are nearly finished, a couple more weeks and then I can spend more time at home clearing out all our expendable items, packing, etc. I've been helping one of the school girls (whom I taught to sew) make uniforms for school kids for sale. She makes about 75 cents on each piece, which will go a long way toward her school expenses. But it is a real hassle with so much going on in the house, plus her five-month-old baby to care for.

Dearest Mother,   **March 14, 1973, Gbedin**

Mary's baby was finally born on Sunday afternoon. Although it was a breech, it came just fine. I had to spend a lot of time with her the past two weeks. She kept thinking her labor was beginning, and they were worried about how she would do, so kept wanting me there. We went to Ganta one weekend and stayed about three days but it was just false labor, I guess. Then we came home and waited until the next weekend when it actually started. (She had a nice boy.) The same night we had to take her to the hospital, Bruce and Barbara Weir came from Monrovia to spend a few days with us and John left us to go to school in Sanniquellie, so it was a *busy* time. We'd promised to take them to the waterfall, which means a two to three hour hike each way, so Harold and the kids and Chris went with them. Packed a lunch and had a nice but very strenuous trip.

Harold, Larry, and Chris finally finished the chicken pen so our garden now has a chance to grow. It's nice not having the rooster sleeping under our house and crowing and flapping his wings at 4:30 AM. But it's also very nice having some tender chicken!

The weather has been very hot and so dry. The dust is something awful. And when you only have screens and not glass, the dust can really come in. The Harmitan winds are particularly bad this year. Things are hazy most of the time, almost as though there were a brush fire somewhere. By the time you've ridden for 50 miles, you're really red with dust. It's cool at night, though. Everyone is looking for rainy season to begin since there's been so little rain and dry season is lasting longer than usual. One of the wells at the Ganta Mission went dry. In fact at the hospital when Mary delivered, there was hardly any water available. Some of the rice paddies are "catching hard time," as they say here, because of the water shortage.

Sunday evening we're going to Monrovia for a few days. Peace Corps has asked me to help with a training program for the next health volunteers so I'm going down to meet with the staff about it and see if it's something I can and want to do. While there, we'll make our reservations since it's Memorial weekend when we'll be traveling, and we don't want any hang ups. I'm getting very anxious to see all of you—hard to keep my mind on every-day work!

Sunday is the graduation exercise at the Ganta Mission School of Nursing. I'm to be in the faculty procession so got out my uniform for the first time in Liberia (I wear a blue one to the clinic). Must dig down in the trunk and see if I can find my cap! Starting the first of April, I'll teach nutrition again—only go one day a week and do a three-hour class: one hour in the AM and two after lunch, rather than one hour three days a week. This will be much easier for me because it always took most of the afternoon whenever I went—getting together with the driver before and after, allowing time for car trouble, and so on. I'll finish nutrition just before we leave and then do diet therapy when I return.

The little girls, big ones too, really enjoy the dolls. At first they were afraid of the little cloth ones you made, something they've never seen.

And when they have features and bodies that aren't just like a real human, they don't know what to make of them. It's the same way with cartoons and comic strips. They don't understand—many adults, even—that these are only drawings and no living person really looks like that.

We've just bought a beautiful piece of carved ivory that we must store someplace since we don't want to keep it here. It was carved by the ivory carver in Sanniquellie who is really excellent, and it is pretty valuable. We paid a lot for it, saved from our living allowance, and it will probably be the only piece of ivory we buy. It's about ten inches high with a mahogany base and top and the whole thing depicts a palver hut. The ivory part shows people in various kinds of activities. It's the hollow end of a tusk.

The day Mary came home from the hospital, or rather that evening, a lot of the farmers came to congratulate them. Chris and Harold and I barbecued some of our chicken—we'd just finished eating when the men came, bringing two huge gourds of palm wine, one held about two and a half gallons. There was a lot of toasting and passing the cup around—there are usually only three or four cups, and you must drink yours and pass it back to be refilled for the next person. There were speeches—whenever they get together they all make speeches, and when Harold and I are there, they always tell about us because Harold is their "old man," and he's the mechanic. Then he has to get up and respond. Someone brought music so there was dancing—only the men; the women don't usually come to such a thing. Two people brought chickens.

They stayed so long and were so noisy that I finally took Mary and the baby to our house and put them to bed. Larry finally got them to go around 1 AM. They had planned to stay and make merry all night since that's the way they do for their own people. They're really fascinated with this little white baby—gave it a Mano name right away. They call it Saye, for the first born son, and farmer since Larry is a farmer. Some call it Saye Gbedin. The chief called him Saye Miapeh, meaning "one who knows his own head" since he was so slow in getting around to being born. The names always are interesting to me, since many have a special meaning to the country people.

Dearest Mother,   **March 31, 1973, Gbedin**

It's Sunday afternoon and I'm in my usual Sunday activity, letter writing. The kids have gone back to Sanniquellie, where they go to school, and the house is quiet for a change. They come on Friday night and stay until Sunday PM. Do the washing, sweeping, mopping, bake bread, cook dinner at least once, and by Sunday night we look quite neat for a few days!

John is a good worker, but I always have to keep an eye on things to make sure everything is done. You know kids, it's easy to play. We pay $4 a month rent for him and $2.50 a week for food plus tuition, uniforms, and school supplies, taxi fare, and such; it all adds up so I don't mind seeing that he earns it. Something for nothing isn't good for people anywhere.

You asked about paramount chief. He's the top chief in an area, elected by the people in the various clans that are in his district. The superintendent of the county can dismiss him if he doesn't behave, but some in Liberia have been in power for a long time.

You mentioned reading about Lassa fever. There were some cases here in Liberia about two years ago for the first time, up in the Zorzor area, thought to have been brought in from Guinea. The tragic thing about it was that one of the people who died from it was Esther Bacon, a very dedicated nurse midwife from the Lutheran mission there. She had spent over 30 years there, delivering babies in the bush, walking miles and miles, teaching midwifery, a tireless worker. In fact, it is said if she hadn't been so insistent on overworking, she may have been able to recover. The people who contracted Lassa fever [*a severe viral illness*] died very suddenly with high, high fevers. All Peace Corps were recalled from there until the danger was over. Specialists from the CDC in Atlanta were flown here, because no one knew what it was, let alone how to treat it.

Dearest Mother,   **April 1, 1973, Gbedin**

Did I tell you I was planning a healthy baby contest? It's going to be May 14, which is a holiday here. I'm going around to the Lebanese merchants asking for prizes to be donated. We'll have judges from another area. I've never done anything like that but think it might stimulate people to take better care of their babies. I'm starting this week to teach at Ganta again so the next two months will be busy. Oh yes, working on the new training program for health volunteers is an "extra," time-consuming task. But since the program has been so bad before (most of the girls leave it for another one or leave for home), I decided I might be able to influence it a bit for the better so am willing to take some time with the planning process.

Rainy season seems to be starting. We've had a really nice rain about every three days lately—cools us off, and makes it much more comfortable, especially for sleeping. There are fewer mosquitoes if the wind blows a bit.

While I was writing this, two fellows stopped in to stay the night, a Peace Corps fellow and his Liberian counterpart, from down by Harper on their way to an Agriculture Department meeting near Foya, a two-day trip. This happens so much and you just take them in since there's no place to stay up-country. Charles was here so I enlisted his help to make dinner, chicken greens and "pig" meat soup with rice. This is a wild green. Paye had brought me two bunches earlier; luckily I had some pork in the freezing part of the refrigerator. Charles is eleven; he used to work for us but we "gave" him to Chris when he needed a houseboy. Now we could use him again with John gone to school, but Chris is happy with him.

Dearest Vikki and Gill,   **April 2, 1973, Gbedin**

Lately, with Mary and Larry "coming to go," there have been lots of parties, dinners, etc., with different friends coming to say goodbye. We've had a couple of barbecues (chicken), and Saturday some people came and made cheese fondue. It was really good. We made a fondue cooker from a big powdered milk can, a tea can, and a Planters Peanut can. Had a good little alcohol burner, using cotton and rubbing alcohol. Amazing how you can improvise and manage with little.

Thursday evening Mary's doctor from the mission and his wife are coming, and Harold has to barbecue chicken again (we have dozens between us). He's Liberian and she's an American Negro. Friday evening, the farmers are having a big farewell party for them. They will no doubt have plenty of palm wine, cane juice, speeches, music, dancing, presentation of gifts and it will go on most of the night.

I don't know how the people do it. They drink horrible amounts of palm wine and cane juice, which is lethal in large quantities, cane juice that is, and they dance on and on, and the noise is horrendous. It's really fun to be there though, outside in the moonlight. I use plenty of repellant for the mosquitoes, and drink plenty of coffee before we go so I can stay awake! Harold was supposed to go to Voinjaina, in Lofa County, Thursday and Friday for Agriculture Department meetings but he sent word that things were too pressing in Gbedin to get away this week!

Wednesday I started teaching at Ganta nursing school—will spend Wednesday there each week until we come home. It's extra work but I enjoy the contact with professional people—it's kind of a nice contrast to my village activities.

Thursday Martha Quewon, the Liberian midwife from Ganta mission, came as usual to help with my clinic. She stayed the evening before, hoping to have me help with some sewing. However we had a *big* party put on by the farmers as a farewell for Larry and Mary. We had lots of dancing, etc., as I had mentioned. I got up and danced, too, and the people were so happy. The women came and danced around me, and the men played music (on shovel handles!) and danced me all the way home, about three city blocks! When we arrived on our steps, they made speeches, and there was more dancing, what an evening. Because we are older, they honor us so much; it's quite touching.

We have a Peace Corps guest from Cameroon, a fellow we met when we were on our vacation there. We persuaded the Monrovia staff to bring him here on his way home to talk about fish farming. Cameroon has quite a program there, and it looked like a natural for Liberia. The people need protein, and they really like fish. He and Harold have been biking around looking at the area so we'll see what the future brings. Our friendly staff member sent him up to us for a couple of days so tomorrow Harold will carry him to Monrovia and take care of some business at the same time. I'll have to find someone to stay with me. Mary and I usually stay together but they left today and I don't like to stay by myself here.

Dearest Mother and all,   **April 10, 1973, Gbedin**

Last night I had a really funny experience. Harold left yesterday for Monrovia for three days, and since Larry and Mary left, my usual sleeping companions were gone. Rather than stay with Chris I asked Charles, the 11-year-old, to stay with me. (I'm really kind of nervous about staying by myself)

About 4:30 AM I got up to go to the bathroom. I, used my flashlight since we don't have electricity after 9 PM. After I got to the bed again, I thought I heard something pattering around in the living room but since I'm always hearing noises when I'm alone, I decided I was imagining things. Heard it some more. "Maybe it's a rat in the attic," I think. Tried to lie down and sleep, but here it was pattering down the hall past my room into Charles's, and back again into the living room. "It must be a huge rat."

Quaking, I reached outside my mosquito net and found the flashlight on the floor, aimed it at the door, and waited while the animal wandered around in the living room. Sure enough it started back and reached the light, and here came a pangolin, a kind of anteater, about the size of a big cat—must have been eighteen inches long from nose to tail. It kept on walking right into my bedroom, behind the door, into the closet, out again, beside my bed, and I started to yell for Charles. Liberian kids sleep so soundly, I didn't think I'd ever arouse him, but after about six increasingly loud shouts, he woke up, and I told him what was in the room and that the cutlass was in my room, too. Here he came, stumbling in half asleep.

By that time the animal was under my bed. I knew it wouldn't hurt me but it was pretty creepy; maybe it would try to get in my bed! When Charles saw it, he was elated and said "This is good, oh, good meat." It kept right on tripping along into a store room beyond our room and climbed into a cardboard box, and Charles started to hit it with a cutlass. This animal is called a handbag because at the slightest fright it will curl itself into a ball with its tail curled around like a handle. It's armor plated with heavy scales like an armadillo. Charles carried the box out into the living room with the thing in the bottom, all curled up. He closed the lid up, and we went back to bed, but soon I heard the thing stirring again. Called Charles, who got up and put the breadboard and a big watermelon on top of it! By this time I was in no mood to go to sleep—it was 5 AM—so I got up and worked on some lesson plans for my class.

When Charles got up, he carried it to his home where the people immediately killed it and made soup. Charles said "The soup sweet, oh." Some people told me today that the people say if you walk in the bush and walk in some of the pangolins "poo-poo," it will follow you home. I don't think Harold and I have walked into any of his poo-poo lately! But what is a mystery is how the thing got into our house, since it would have had to come in the door since there aren't any holes for it to come in. Harold will probably be sorry I gave it away since he's been wanting to taste pangolin. The people were really happy to get it because meat is scarce here, and the people eat anything. Actually a person could keep it for a pet, which we don't need, but I'll admit I felt sick at having it killed. Today Charles said it seemed like a dream.

Later. When Harold came home, he discovered a broken window screen and decided the animal had climbed up the wall from the porch, got stuck in the window louvers, and pushed on through the screen. They can climb trees easily looking for ants and have a very hard nose. So our mystery is solved, and I was right—Harold's first comment was, "Why didn't you keep it for me. I've been wanting to eat some pangolin."

Today we went to church in the Lutheran church in Monrovia. Came down yesterday to say goodbye to Larry and Mary. Since this is Palm Sunday, the church was decorated with palm branches. What a difference from the potted palms we see in our churches at home. This church is near the beach where there are many, many coconut palms. Over and around the entry way were palm branches braided to form an arch, with hibiscus, plumeria, and red stephanotis blossoms entwined. On the floor in the aisle from the door to the altar were palm branches laid down like mats. On the end of each pew a palm branch was tied, using a palm frond for rope. Tall branches, maybe ten feet long, were standing against the walls on either side of the church. On the altar branches were laid, again generously entwined with the same blossoms. The children were all given small crosses made of two strips of a palm frond.

Somehow the naturalness of the casually decorated church was (to me) much more in keeping with Palm Sunday than the more formal expression I've been used to at home with the rented plants. Of course, I realize you can't go out there and pick a bunch of palm branches!

Our flowering trees are beginning to bloom again; soon they will be huge masses of color. Some of the trees are very tall and spreading, and the blossoms completely hide the leaves, brilliant yellows, oranges, vermilions. The plumeria, which is called frangipani here, grow very tall, and the waxy blossoms are in big clusters. In the bush, the lilies have started to bloom as well, tall white ones similar to Easter lilies. We don't have a lot of variety of flowers but what there are, are in huge numbers. Hibiscus and bougainvillea bloom all the time and in large quantities. Just now poinsettias are in bloom too, big bushes. People call them Christmas leaf.

Dearest Mother,   **April 22, 1973, Gbedin**

Here we are by our Aladdin lamp after a quiet Easter Sunday. We can always hear the crickets and other night life, after the generator goes off at around 9:30 PM.

We went to church in Ganta today at the Methodist Mission. We have a car temporarily so have a chance to go. The minister is Liberian and really preaches *loud*. Another one interprets in Mano so it makes the service long. They have a Mano choir with native drums and a gourd filled with seeds (that one old woman shakes with wonderful rhythm). Along with the kind of chant-like singing, it is quite effective and would fit well with the folk masses at home. I spent the afternoon correcting test papers and homework and preparing another test for next time. Teaching for three hours on Wednesdays is easier on me and, I think, better for the students, giving us time in class to do some work together.

Last eve a couple of kids brought Harold three bamboo worms—a kind of grub-like white fat worm that lives in the palm wine tree, about three inches long. Today he fried them in butter and ate them. He said they were quite tasty but couldn't describe the taste. I had to keep my feelings to myself so I wouldn't spoil his enjoyment of them! The people here really like them. Actually they aren't much different from snails, I suppose. There are big land snails here, some of the shells are six inches long, and the snails huge. You can buy them for about 25 cents for eight in the market. They don't taste like much to me, but Harold likes to try everything and likes the snails.

Next Saturday we're going to a Liberian wedding. The people are Americo-Liberians and probably kind of kwi—live like Europeans or Americans, in some ways. I think it will be a church ceremony and then a big party at the home of one of them. There will be rice and soup a-plenty, plus all kinds of things to drink. They told us to plan to stay all night, which I'm sure we will do since it's a 40-mile trip on the usual kind of road. It's sure to be interesting.

A rogue came in our house while we were in Monrovia last weekend. Must have known we were gone and walked in quite bravely, through a window. However Harry, the Pearmines' houseboy, was sleeping here, and he scared him out. Harry was scared too and jumped out his bedroom window, shouting "rogue," and soon there were lots of people here, but the person disappeared. There's so much thieving.

Dearest Mother,   **April 28, 1973, Gbedin**

Here I am with another quick note. Harold just walked in saying he has to hurry to Monrovia immediately and pick up a vehicle. It looks like the ministry is going to come through with some of his requests, and of course, it's got to be right now! I'll stay here since there are so many, many things to be done before we leave for the States. One thing the new Land Rover means is that he will have to be able to go to other areas to trouble shoot. The reason for the hurry just now is an all-week trip to Foya for some repair work. I'll get Charles to stay with me. He likes it, and it make me feel safer.

I'm doing a lot of sewing—actually helping the girls to do their sewing—so I'm usually running around in a circle! We went to Lamco to the big wedding Saturday. It was a lot of fun. More about that when I'm not so rushed. Came home about 12:30 midnight and met some people on our steps with a little boy who'd been circumcised in the AM by a country man, the usual way here, and he'd begun to bleed. Nothing to do but take him to Ganta Hospital where we found the doctor on duty treating a man with a snake bite. It was late when we finally got home to bed.

Dearest Mother,   **May 13, 1973, Zleh Town**

We're having a visit with some Liberian friends in Zleh Town, a small town and government rice project about half-way to Harper, which is on the coast. Harold had some work to do on a truck and the light plant here, and since we'd been invited many times to stay with Hubern and Mary Edwards, we decided to combine business and pleasure. We left Thursday noon as soon as my clinic was over, loaded the truck with a young couple and their belongings, who were moving down this way, chickens etc., and arrived by 6 PM. It is a very dusty ride this time of the year, and you're always covered with red dust in a short time but we're kind of used to that now. You can always take a bath when you get to your destination. We'll go back Sunday.

This is such an interesting place and people to visit. Hubern's parents were American Negroes. He came here when he was nine (in 1930). His father was an MD, and they became Liberian citizens. He has a legal wife and grown family in Monrovia but lives here with a country wife, a charming woman, and their five children, all under eight years old. He's built the house and all the furniture, using piasava palm for most of the furniture, doors, window frames, ceilings, and bathroom washstand and toilet stool. It's very picturesque. Mahogany is the other wood he used. There are lots of photographs on the walls, all framed with piasava and mahogany frames. In fact all the furniture was made by him, and with no power tools. Outside is a big palava hut, palm thatched, which is their outdoor living area. It has a hammock and chairs and a table and floor mats. It is such a nice cool place to sit or rest. The dining chairs are covered with deer skin; there are many deer in the area.

He is the project director here, a college grad and quite a world traveler. Mary is a charming energetic woman, a trained midwife and now for the past three years a rice farmer as well as president of the farmers' co-op here. She has been planting cocoa trees, has a garden and chickens, and does all the sewing for the family. They have four school boys who live here and are sent to school and fed, and in turn do lot of work in the rice field and at home—keep the house clean, wash dishes, help with the cooking, etc. Each has an assigned task, and Mary keeps track of it all and works hard herself.

Outside around the house are many flowering trees, hibiscus, bougainvillea, yellow bills, and others I don't know. It's been such a pleasant restful time, which I could use but can't help but think of all the work I have to do at home before we get ready to leave for home. The food here has been strictly Liberian—some tea in the AM and then one rice meal in the afternoon. However, we have Chinese friends here, and they've invited us for lavish dinners two times!

Dearest Vikki and Gill,   **May 18, 1973, Gbedin**

One more week and a half, and we'll be on our way! Since Harold got his truck less than a month ago, the DA has given him a lot of extra projects to take care of. And I'm trying to squeeze my class sessions into less time so I can finish this week, catch up with kids who need immunizations and don't get to the clinic, do some last minute sewing, and on and on. Lots of fun.

We're all packed although we keep finding someone else who wants us to carry something for them and then have to redo the bags. With our 44-pound weight limit each, we're kind of handicapped. However a young Liberian fellow is taking the same plane, so he can travel with us and he will check some of our extra pounds through. He'll be going to school in NYC.

We came to Monrovia yesterday to have physical check-ups before leaving and will take off tomorrow AM for home. Today we visited with a young couple who have been here two years. He's a mining engineer graduate and wants to work in Australian mines. He bought an old Toyota truck, rebuilt it, built a canopy for it in the back with a bed inside and all their gear, and today they took off for East Africa. Plan to take two to four months to get there, then sell their truck and fly to Australia and try to get a job. I think it would be fun to go that way rather than the way we traveled since taxis and lodging are such a hassle unless you have lots of money. They didn't want to go until Harold could give his final OK on the truck!

[*Ruth and Harold spent two months in the US visiting family and friends before returning to Liberia for a third year in the Peace Corps. Judith's nine-year-old son, Ciam, came back with them for the experience of living in Africa.*]

Dearest Mother and all,   **July 24, 1973, Gbedin**

It's a week today since we arrived back in Gbedin, and it seems like much longer. We were busy almost at once and haven't stopped since. It was 10:30 PM when we finally reached here. We had expectations of sleeping in, in the AM but someone sent word that there was a clinic full of kids and moms waiting for me, so away I went. It's been quite hard to get acclimated again—can't get caught up with my sleep so have been taking a rest in the afternoon every day.

Ciam is doing well here, despite everyone's curiosity and interest. He is the first little white boy to stay here, and most people have never seen a white boy, at least to actually touch. They all have to shake his hand. He's pretty much at ease with most of them, even when they laugh at him, which is pretty often, when he talks to them. They say he's a fine boy and want their children to look like him, "strong in the body." He's learned to greet people in the dialect, and already I hear him talking Liberian English with the kids.

We found our house in pretty good shape, only much in need of cleaning, since the dust is so bad here. Nellie Doe and James, her husband, stayed in our house when we were in the US. He is a rice extension worker here, about twenty-nine years old and a high school graduate. Nellie is younger than he, probably not more than an eighth or ninth grade education, attractive and energetic; she sews with me a lot. She and James aren't Mano so unless the people can speak some English, they don't have any more ability than we do in communicating with them. Nellie is lonesome for Monrovia, and James wants to get a better job so I expect they won't be in Gbedin too many months. I gave her some of the things you gave me when I got back here and she said she wanted to write and thank you. James tells us all kinds of stories about tribal life in the bush; we hope to get some of them on tape soon.

The cockroaches really had a heyday during our absence, so I've been on a raiding party every night. I have annihilated dozens, and should be about finished with them for the present. Surprisingly, nothing seems to be missing from the place. That is, nothing but chickens. Apparently a bush cat of some sort came several times and killed a lot of chickens. Only about 14 remain, and worst of all, most of our good setting hens were taken. Chris had some hunters watch the place but they couldn't catch anything. We'll have to get busy and set some more hens so we can build up our flock; it's such a mainstay of our diet.

We had to take a taxi in from Robertsfield when we arrived, since our friends the Alcocks couldn't get a car to come for us. It cost us $10. We stayed overnight with the Alcocks. Chris came down in his land rover, and after getting Ciam's gamma globulin and rabies shots and buying some groceries, we took off for Gbedin. I was pleased to learn when I arrived in Ganta that my diet therapy class wouldn't begin until the latter part of August, which really gives me a breather.

Harold has been busy all week too—catching up with different projects. Tomorrow he'll leave at 5 AM for Monrovia to pick up supplies such as oxygen and vehicle parts. Also the Alcock's stove, which is in better condition than ours. (They're leaving at the end of this month.)

While I was away, several of my ladies had their babies, so Tuesday everyone came with their new ones. Each one was so pleased to show the baby off and have me check them. I was happy to give each of them a little gown, or sacque, that Vikki had given me. I've made several home visits already, checking on new offspring.

Friday eve a fellow came and asked me to come and see his baby (two years old). She had a 106 degree fever and was having convulsions, apparently from malaria. I gave her cool sponges and aspirin and chloroquim but the next day she was just as sick. I went about three or four times to give her cool baths and medicine. Finally in the late afternoon, they agreed to take her to the hospital. Harold had to drive them since his is the only car here. She is still in the hospital but apparently will be OK. Most of the time the people won't agree to go to the doctor, even though the baby looks like it's going to die.

Thursday is Liberian Independence day (July 26), which will be emphasized in another county, as we did here in Nimba last year. After our recent travels we're in no mood for another long trip. So Chris decided to have a combined welcome home and anti-26th party here. We'll have hot dogs, baked beans, potato salad, etc. He says about 25 PCVs will be here from the surrounding area. Should be fun.

Dearest Mother and all,   **August 6, 1973, Gbedin**

Things are going along as usual here. Harold keeps busy with a variety of things. Tomorrow he will make an all-day trip to another county to see about some repairs on a rice project there. It doesn't sound like I'll get the new help I had requested at the clinic, at least the doctor didn't sound encouraging. Maybe in February he says. So I will cut down my work there except for my two clinics and start to do more teaching in the nursing school. This week I'll start teaching public health and later in the month start with diet therapy. One of the problems, though, is that people continue to come to the house begging for treatment and I feel very mean when I don't treat them. However I feel that as long as I will keep on doing it, the public health people will not begin to do their part.

Ciam just came in from the shop. He likes to go there and "help" Harold. His arms were all dirty; he said he was under the car connecting a cable. It's nice for both of them to do things together. Ciam isn't ready to start school so we are going to wait until he is. He's been a little slow about getting out and playing with the kids, so we're just letting him "do his own thing." There is a lot to get used to and adding school, and such a different one, to everything else, seems to be rushing things. Right now he's still a nine-day wonder to everyone so maybe when that's over, he will want to go. Actually he's doing very well, and everyone enjoys him. Chris has a houseguest now, a new PCV, who can do card tricks. Ciam is fascinated with his magic and vows he too will be a magician when he grows up.

Saturday eve we went to another wedding, this one in Sanniquellie at the Catholic Church. The ceremony was very informal; in fact the priest didn't seem to be very well versed in wedding ceremonies. The church was full and as usual half the people were talking during the entire time so if you were halfway back you couldn't hear what was going on. The groom was a former PCV who has been working in Liberia for some time and the bride a Liberian girl from Sanniquellie.

Ciam and friends at a party.

The party, held in the Town Hall, was really great and so different from home. There was a "country" dancing devil, dressed in a mask, raffia skirt and entirely shrouded in a cloth costume that covered him, hands and all. He had several music makers assisting him who rattled things and banged on pieces of metal. Periodically someone would give him money, and they'd take off again. There was also a fellow who played some kind of guitar made of a gourd and thin strips of bamboo strung with strings. They were about two and a half feet in length, and he held one in each hand and strummed them simultaneously. There was a band from Monrovia, too, which started to play later. They were quite good.

They served rice and several different kinds of soup, beer, soft drinks, and other kinds of liquor. It was a noisy, fun party, lots of our friends were there as well. Ciam drank four bottles of coke and ate three pieces of wedding cake and danced and danced. The windows were lined with onlookers, children and adults, and there were two soldiers with guns on their shoulders patrolling the place and keeping uninvited guests out, also two or three uniformed policemen. We had two houseguests afterward, since Sanniquellie was overflowing with Monrovia guests. There were lots of beautiful costumes, both on men and women, which I enjoy looking at. You can wear just about anything and be OK.

Dearest Mother,   **August 12, 1973, Gbedin**

Harold and Chris are making another trip to Monrovia early tomorrow AM so I'm sitting up with the Aladdin lamp again to get some letters done. By the time we read stories and do the other bedtime things with Ciam, it's nearly time for the lights to go out. Tonight I was doing some more complicated cooking, and we kept having people stop in so it was 8:30 before we finished eating. I made deep-fried barracuda, collard greens cooked with onions, fried salt pork and allspice, and hot biscuits.

The rain is really something. It rained about four times today. In between, we got some washing dry—in and out of the house with it two or three times. When it rains so hard, it comes inside in several places. Windows don't close tightly, and it leaks around them or through shutters. However, with our kind of house, it doesn't really matter too much. Things are very moldy; our shoes mold in the closets in two or three days.

With the new class I'm teaching, there is a lot of preparation. The text is new to me, and I've never taught public health to the extent they require in an RN school. It's a nice contrast to the rest of my work though, even though it pushes me a bit.

Last week someone gave us a monkey. The last thing I need. But Harold and Ciam were tickled with her until she wanted to bite and refused to go into her cage. Harold decided she was too old to train, and they (he and Ciam) should have a baby so he took her back, Ciam and the monkey riding together in the back of the truck very happily all the way to Ganta. Now the Lebanese man is looking for a baby for us so I'm afraid we'll be finding a monkey on our doorstep soon. Harold wanted one, and now he can say it's for Ciam.

Dearest Vikki and Gill,   **August 13, 1973, Gbedin**

I go to Ganta Mission two times a week—teach from 1:30 to 5:30 each day, two class sessions each day. I take a taxi there, and they drive me home in the evening. Ciam went with me Friday to swim in a small pool they have there and then Harold brought him home as he drove home from Kpain where he was doing some work for the Minister of Agriculture's farm.

I went with him the afternoon before just to get away from the constant demands here—sat in the shade and worked on my lessons. Two Chinese fellows there are in charge of the operation—citrus fruits, vegetables, and paddy rice. Harold keeps their power tillers and threshers, trucks and diesel power plant and pumps working. As a result when he goes there, they are lavish with their produce—bags of oranges and grapefruit, etc. Right now there are no citrus fruits ripe; it will be another month because dry season was so severe. But they do have vegetables, so we brought back half a gunny sack of Japanese eggplant, beautiful big sweet peppers, and green beans.

They cooked lunch for us, and they always treat Harold to a drink of Scotch. Ciam had a great time climbing a big tree with some small boys there, swinging from a big bouncy branch and going hand over hand along it. He got kind of sun burned but by the AM, it was faded out and looking more like a tan.

I have another young girl, Oreta, helping me in the house along with Annie [*a school girl who helps around the house*]. She does the washing and ironing and a few other odd jobs. She has a baby named Yah Ruth, which she brings every day and puts in the little infa-seat that Mary left for me. When she fusses, Oreta puts her on her back and keeps on working. Actually she is a pretty good baby and does better having a chance to be alone instead of being constantly carried around. But when she starts to cry, Oreta picks her up and nurses her. She's a real "country" girl, never went to school, and is probably about eighteen. She lived with a mission family when she was younger so learned to wash and iron well. Some days when we want to eat Liberian chop, she cooks for us.

I've just finished reading *Captains and the Kings,* by Taylor Caldwell. It was quite interesting but kind of depressing too—too much of it is true. Ciam and I are reading book one of the *Lord of the Rings* trilogy, and Harold and Ciam are reading *Zoo in my Luggage,* by Durrell. It is particularly interesting to us because it takes place in an area of West Cameroon where we spent several days and is very descriptive of what we experienced, too. Since Ciam is here, I find much of my time used up—always something to do with him, and is he a chatter box.

Today I've helped Oreta to sew on her dress, visited with the midwife, Martha, who comes from Ganta, and visited with Daniel, the dresser, and Oreta's mother, all these arrived at different times but stayed for a long chat about belly clinic business.

Dearest Mother,   **August 17, 1973, Gbedin**

Maybe today I can take a more leisurely time to write. My lesson is prepared, and I have two hours before I have to leave for Ganta. There is quite a lot of preparation for this particular class. New tests have to be prepared, something that always takes quite a while. I usually spend all morning of the day I'm teaching getting ready for the class.

I just finished a batch of sour plum jam. These are small yellow plums, very tart, about the size of a banty egg, with a large oval seed inside; nearly two-thirds of the plum is seed. I cook the plums in water, then put them in the mortar and beat them to free the seeds and get the peelings off. Then I put the pulp in a pot with an equal amount of sugar and cook it down. Today I put some cinnamon and allspice in. It looks something like apple butter. Several of my Liberian friends have learned to make it since I started to. Usually the fruit just falls on the ground and rots.

Harold's birthday is next week is so Chris and I are planning a surprise birthday party for him. We'll have the boys cook lots of palm butter and rice. There will probably be a dozen and a half people here and it takes a lot to fill up young guys, especially ones who've been doing their own cooking.

Tuesday afternoon I must take a taxi to Monrovia to go to the dentist. When I return, I'll bring a couple gallons of paint and some paint brushes and we'll have a painting party. Chris and his new roommate, Dale, and Jerry and Norma from Ganta will come. We'll make pizza, and everyone will paint our living, dining, kitchen and bathroom.

The house was painted about four years ago, and it looks so dingy and dirty. The more you scrub, the worse it looks because the paint is coming off. Harold thinks this is going to be his birthday party so may-be we'll fool him, since the real one will be the next night, and I'll be satisfied to have the house looking better.

Later. I got a ride to Monrovia with a PCV yesterday and stayed with a young couple who have an eight-month-old baby boy. She's Vicki, too. I babysat for them so they could go to the show.

Today when I saw the dentist, he didn't think there was anything serious. However he took an x-ray, and since the water supply has failed, couldn't develop it. Can you imagine? He'll let me know by mail if I should come back.

I also had time for a haircut, some shopping, and now its noon. So after a quick bite to eat, I'll take a taxi to Waterside to the up-country taxi stand and start to haggle for a taxi. If I'm lucky I'll be able to get home before its dark. These roads are nothing to be stranded on at night and dark comes by 7 PM.

Dearest Judith, Ed [her husband], and Mom,   **August 27, 1973**

Does it seem like two months since you said goodbye to all of us? It doesn't for us even though we miss you a lot. When we first came, Ciam said he

Ruth and Ciam (lower right) walking with a friend in Monrovia's Waterside Market.

would go home with Vikki. Now he's saying he will stay as long as we do! He's also saying he will start school at the beginning of September, so we will see.

We're not having any problems. He spends part of every day with Harold at the shop, helping with some jobs. Now Dale is working there, too. He and Ciam have a mutual admiration society and have good times together.

This past weekend we had a lot of fun. You know Harold's birthday was last Tuesday, the day I had to go to the dentist. The boys went to Lamco, so here were Harold and Ciam, all alone on his birthday. He was feeling kind of forgotten and took a dim view of a "painting" birthday party, although it was a lot of fun.

Unknown to him, the boys and I planned a party for him on Saturday. A young couple who had visited us last year, Gail and Geoff Thompson from Cuttington College, arrived Friday (a holiday). Norma and Jerry from Ganta came Friday, and Martha Quewon, the Liberian midwife who works with me. We had three gallons of paint, rollers, brushes, and case of beer and all painted and visited. Annie and Martha, the school girls who help me here, and Ciam all helped paint. Gail said, "I don't even like to paint but wouldn't have missed it."

Then Norma and I made fondue, and Chris and Jerry made pizza. They all stayed all night, and Harold thought that was his birthday party. The next day John Cooper came from school and started making palm butter with chicken and cow meat and rice. People started to drop in, and Harold still didn't realize it was planned but wondered why so many people decided to come that day. Finally after we'd eaten, the boys went over to Chris's and got a birthday cake he had baked, and when everyone sang Happy Birthday, Harold finally got it. We went through two cakes, five pumpkin pies I had made, three loaves of banana bread John had made, plus popcorn, ground nuts, beer, etc. Everyone had healthy appetites. Some of the people stayed that night and took off Sunday AM. We had been invited to dinner at the mission with the nurses I work with. Vera baked a cake for Harold like a little truck, iced with blue frosting, the color of his truck. Ciam was fascinated with it. He got to go swimming, too, while I went to a graduation ceremony there.

Dearest Vikki and Gill,   **August 27, 1973, Gbedin**

Well our big weekend is over and our house looks pretty good, surprisingly since it was kind of crowded, and there was plenty of beer drinking.

You should hear Ciam chattering in Liberian English—like he's always done it. He's doing just fine. Every day he goes to the shop with Harold and Dale, helps them some, goes out to the rice farm and helps Annie "drive birds"—throws clods of dirt at flocks of rice birds, using a woven sling. Right now the water is pretty full since it's been raining pretty heavily every day so he's wearing his rubber boots when he goes to the rice paddy.

One day last week the Chinese fellows invited him for lunch. He ate with chop sticks, all of them offering him tidbits. They like him and like to do things for him. Listening to their conversation is humorous because their English is atrocious, part Liberian English with Chinese accents. Ciam gets along though since he's really doing well with Liberian English and they can understand him. So can our Liberian friends.

Dearest Mother,   **September 3, 1973, Gbedin**

We just realized that today is Labor Day at home. Ciam says he will start school now, since it's when he would at home. He is really a character. Yesterday we were planning to take a walk into the bush to visit a small village and reach to the St. John River, taking Chris and Dale and a couple of the Liberian fellows we work with. Ciam said he was going to make a camera to take along. So he got up early, found a little cardboard box, scotch tape, paper, and string, and concocted a little "camera," complete with a telescopic lens. He hung it around his neck and "took pictures" the whole time we were walking, just as serious as anything. We were visiting at home, and he "snapped" a picture of Nellie, one of my Liberian friends, and she said "I want to see my picture." He said, "OK, I'll go print it," and trotted off to his room and made a picture of her, just like a snapshot.

Just now I'm sitting in the crowded waiting room at Ganta Hospital with Galayi, a Gio woman from Gbedin who has a large goiter. I want the surgeon to look at her and advise the family so Harold brought us down. It's pouring rain, has been for hours but, of course, isn't cold. I just wear plastic sandals so it doesn't matter if my feet get wet.

There is so much rain it's quite muddy when you go hiking. But things are so beautiful, with green leaves, mammoth trees and vines, ferns, some blossoms, never many but always unique, butterflies and unusual insects, but never any animals.

When we came back, I baked pumpkin pies again for us and the boys, and benne (sesame) seed cookies. They are really good.

This has been a hectic week, what with two more afternoons in Ganta for class, very busy clinics, and company for meals. Also, I've been visiting towns and villages at night to talk to them about the baby and belly clinics—trying to get them to bring well babies; to get the pregnant women to come early in their pregnancy; to get them to call me when they are delivering early enough to prevent problems with delivery; and to get the midwives to attend class regularly. This means visiting at least five towns since our people come from that many. It also means evening visits since so many people are at the farms in the day time. When we go, we go to the chief and talk with him, he sends the town crier into the village to "holler the news," as they say, and then we sit down to wait for people to straggle in. There are always flocks of children crowding around, giggling, and staring, especially since Ciam was with us. Finally the men and women arrive where we are gathered under a big grass palava hut that belongs to the chief. Our light was two coal oil lanterns sitting on the ground. People bring their own stools and chairs, and the small kids squat on the floor.

I did the speech making, Daniel interpreted, then the chief, the head midwife, and various other people made speeches, often saying the same thing as the people before. But at all the meetings, the people agreed that they want the maternal child health clinics to continue, they will do as we ask, the midwives will come to class, etc.

Getting them to do all these things is the hard part, takes constant visits and reminders. Two women lost their babies, after prolonged labor, since I've come back, and I decided if that is the way they want to do, I won't continue with the belly clinic, and that is why I called the meetings.

Actually though, the midwives have been coming to refresher class— nine of them were here on Thursday, including the main woman. Thursday about midnight the people called me to go to a woman who was delivering, and I was so grateful to see the head midwife washing her hands in a basin of water, as I'd been showing them.

Today, Saturday, we're going to take about a two-hundred-mile trip to the President's farm in another county. One of our Chinese friends is in charge of the rice farm there and we're going to spend the day with him.

Dear Vikki and Gill,   **September 13, 1973, Gbedin**

My household help is only in the morning, and they usually get me sorted out—wash dishes, sweep, and do the washing and ironing. But by the end of the day, I'm pooped and in need of bailing out again. I'm doing all the cooking this semester, and that is quite time consuming—one has to pick over the rice, fan it, wash it several times and "rock it," to make sure all the small, small rocks are out, before beginning to cook it. If I'm doing a Chinese or Indian dinner, by the time we get the garlic, ginger, onions, green pepper plus any other vegetable, cleaned and peeled and diced, the meat chopped—in between the innumerable interruptions—an hour or more has passed, and probably by this time it's getting dark, and I'm creeping around trying to see what I'm doing by candle light.

I've been making pumpkin pies—never really appreciated them as much as now, when food is rather scarce. Someone gave me a huge squash, which they call pumpkin; after one meal of baked pumpkin, I cooked the rest, and it made about nine or ten pies. We were having lots of company around that time, around Harold's birthday, so they disappeared pretty fast. Ciam really enjoyed them, and of course the boys next door like any kind of dessert.

Just now cooking and kitchen work is somewhat complicated by three small chickens living by the refrigerator in a box, but often out of it and following me around. The mother hen hatched thirteen babies several days ago and left three un-hatched eggs. Harold thought they had been laid by an interloper so decided to try keeping them warm in the house for a few days. After about three days in a plastic container behind our kerosene refrigerator, one started to hatch. I could hear it peeping inside the shell! The flame on the refrigerator is near the floor and makes a dim light and quite a bit of warmth. Anyway that one hatched in the evening, the next day (yesterday) one more hatched, and today number three came out. The hen will refuse them and probably kill them, so we will try to take care of them here. Whenever they get out of their box, they come after us and love to settle down on our laps. Right now they're really cute little fluffy brown and black balls.

Harold is recovering from his first bout of malaria—came down with it Monday and has been in bed for the past four days. By now he's over the worst of it and is just feeling weak. His main symptom was a severe headache that nothing would shake for two full days. Surprisingly he didn't have any fever, which fooled me at first.

Thanks so much for the sweet card for our anniversary. Do you know until your card arrived we had forgotten our anniversary? What a laugh.

Ciam has been going to school for two weeks and so far is doing OK. This school has been going since March so starting this late in the term isn't too easy, especially since the methods and subjects are so different. It doesn't seem to be too traumatic; he's made some friends and seems to be enjoying it. It's a good thing he's not going to get an education in "book" since it's a pretty haphazard situation. Every day some teacher is absent so they don't have that subject. Fridays are mostly for work around the school; there are at least fifty kids in his room in three grades; and none of the teachers have had more than twelve years of school and one year of teacher's training.

I've just finished reading *The Comedians,* by Grahame Greene, and Harold, *The Captains and the Kings,* by Taylor Caldwell. I think he will start the Ken Kesey book we brought back with us.

Dearest Mother,   **September 21, 1973, Gbedin**

Every day seems to get more confused than the day before. My added time at Ganta has really put pressure on me, especially since I don't have good help here at home. Fortunately, John will be finished with school the first week of December and will be here with us again. I didn't realize what a great help he was until he left.

Three baby chicks are living in our house, and running around. They are a week old now, and are really cute. Fortunately, little chicks make little messes, and our wooden floors are a mess most of the time anyway, with all the dirt and dust around. Ciam is really enjoying them. Harold says he will make a pen in the garage soon. Actually, they're a lot easier to have around than a monkey or some of the other pets Harold and Ciam talk about.

Martha, the midwife who helps me in the clinic on Thursdays, and I have started to teach classes for country midwives. We have eight enrolled, all older women who have delivered hundreds of babies. We will try to give them a week of experience in the Mission hospital. They come and observe at our ante-natal clinic, and then we have about an hour class. They really have some stories to tell about their experiences, some of which are stories they have been told, and that you know can't be true. They are more like myths and supernatural activities.

We have just come back from an evening at Henry and Marie Zowolo's new house. You may remember the little house Harold and Larry helped build for last July 26. Harry, who runs the rice mill for the farmers, just moved his family into it, and they asked us to come and eat palm butter and rice with them. He's a fine Liberian fellow, about 25, and his wife, also. She works with me at the clinic. She is the girl who lost her baby (stillborn) right after I got back last year, and her new three-week-old baby died suddenly one night. When we went to eat with them, we took them some plates and spoons, and Chris and Dale took them two chairs. It's a cute house. He has built a mud-stick shed outside the back door for the kitchen and bathroom. The toilet is built farther away and is always separate. They served us a big pot of rice, palm butter with chicken, potato greens and fish soup, and palm wine.

Dearest Mother and all,   **September 29, 1973, Monrovia**

I'm in Monrovia for two days with the five senior nursing students. Brought them for their Public Health field trip—a strenuous time with all the walking and standing and listening. Our VW bus broke down, the generator "spoiled," so we all have to go back today by taxi. I stayed with a young Peace Corps couple who came to Liberia just before we did, Vicki and Tim Nighschwander. They have a little baby boy, Aaron, who will be one year on Christmas Day. I babysat for them last night so they could have an evening out, and the baby slept the whole time.

We finally had an experience we hoped to avoid last week. A rogue entered our house while we slept—took the glass louvers from a window, bent the screen and crawled in. What is really upsetting is that he came into our bedroom and took our watches and my ring, my billfold, and Harold's trousers containing his billfold, and we never heard a thing. It was a rainy night so it was quite noisy and that, no doubt, obscured any sounds. He only got about $10 from us plus a bunch of gas tickets.

Then he took a butcher knife from the kitchen and went to Chris's house, cut a screen and opened his door and went to Dales' room, took his trousers, and was in the process of emptying the pockets in the dining room when Chris woke up, and the person fled. Chris came and called us, and we looked around outside (it was 2 AM) and could see nothing.

The next day we found that a young fellow who had been arrested for stealing rice here some months ago was now wanted in another area for theft, and when we learned he was staying in Gbedin that week we had him taken to the police where he was kept for two days and then taken to Suakako for the other incident. The police came to investigate but we have very little expectations of seeing any of our things again. Investigative ability isn't an attribute that is found often here, plus it's easy to dash someone and be free. Needless to say, we are being more careful, putting the radio and tape recorder away at night, locking the door to the hallway, getting rogue bars for the windows. I really felt bad about losing my ring.

Harold has had a hard time getting over his bout with malaria and thinks it's about time to leave Liberia, what with the events of the past month!

Dearest Judith and Ed,   **September 30, 1973, Gbedin**

We're having a Sunday without guests for a change, other than Liberian school boys here to study and sit around, so it looks like I might have a little leisure time.

Thursday I took five senior nurses to Monrovia for a public health field trip and came back last night in time to go to a party at Jerry and Norma Puterbaugh's at the Mission. They are Peace Corps volunteers teaching in the mission school. There is a small swimming pool there, which used to be the water reservoir. It is spring fed and usually quite cold. Harold took Ciam in the afternoon, and he had a great time swimming. One of the girls there was a competitive swimmer before joining Peace Corps so she helped Ciam swim.

Ciam is getting along fine at school, does his homework when he's supposed to. Sometimes some of the kids come here to study with him. Chris's housemate, Dale, is a vegetarian, so this is another common bond Ciam has with him. He's really a nice sensitive fellow, a CO [*conscientious objector*], aeronautical engineer, and a very good mechanic, working with Harold. Harold is enjoying working with him since they complement each other. Dale thinks he's really lucky to be able to work with Harold, and Dale and Chris get along fine.

I had them over for dinner tonight for eggplant casserole, stuffed zucchini squash with tomatoes and cheese, and potato pancakes. In the midst of my preparations someone came to get me to see a woman who was in labor. So I dropped everything and left Chris with the potato pancake job while I went out to the farm. It was dark by this time so Harold took me in the truck, and then I had to walk down a winding trail to the palm thatch hut where she was with all her friends. The only light was from two or three little kerosene lanterns and a small fire in the center of the hut. There were about fifteen women seated around the inside of the low thatched building, all wearing only a lappa, some with head ties. [*The letter ends abruptly, probably so Ruth could get it into the mail.*]

Dearest Vikki and Gill,   **October 1, 1973, Gbedin**

It was exciting to read your last letter and learn that you would be coming in less than a month!

We have a baby kitten now, a little yellow and white female, Ciam named her Polynesia. We've had tough luck with pets since he's been here so I hope nothing happens to her. Our baby chickens all met untimely deaths. One ate a pin with a big head, one ate too much sand and stopped up his gizzard, and one got caught in the screen door when a visitor went out. They were fun to have but we should have kept them confined. They were so tiny and followed us around all the time and were easily injured. When I would be getting dinner, standing by the counter chopping vegetables and such, they would come and roost on my feet. They really liked people and were fun to hold.

Today a volunteer came to have his truck fixed and left his new pet deer in our house until he was ready to go. It was about eighteen inches high and weighed about five pounds, dark brown with white spots and stripes. It didn't seem to be afraid of people. I gave him a baby bottle to feed it.

Dearest Mother and family,   **October 7, 1973, Gbedin**

Ciam has been attending school for five weeks now and getting along all right, although I know it's a strain, too. He's certainly adjusted well to the language and is even learning some Mano. Right now I think he's planning to come home with Vikki and Gil when they visit. Lately he's been a bit lonesome for his mother and Ed.

Today two of the Peace Corps guys are helping him to build an airplane—kind of a big kite to hold when he's riding his bike. I don't know if it will work but at least they are having a good time trying.

The longer I'm here the more I realize that a non-African would have to be here for years and years before they really understand what is going on and the best way to deal with things. Here is an example.

During one of my midwife classes, one of the ladies (who is a Christian but is also a troublemaker) told the other midwives they must call her when a person was in labor so she could help, too. She told a "parable" to illustrate her point, saying, "The place where you laughing now, someday you will cry." This angered the head midwives, who are zo women, members of the women's secret tribal society.

There was much palava in the class, which was the day I had to be in Monrovia with my nursing students. Martha, my assistant, thought they had finally settled it. Norn apologized for her parable, and everyone left. Later they apparently continued to discuss Norn's parable in the town, which they interpreted as putting a bad spell on them, hexing or witching them and the pregnant women.

So they carried the complaint to the town chief, a weak and crafty man, whose answer was to fine Norn a bag of rice, five chickens, two bottles of palm oil, and some money; in a way, this was asking her to make a sacrifice so the spell would be made harmless.

All this occurred while I was in Monrovia. In addition, the daughter-in-law of the head midwife went into labor a few days later and after she was in labor all night, Harold had to take her to the hospital where she was for two more hours before delivering a 10½ pound baby. The people were convinced that Norn's words were the cause of her difficulty, causing something to "catch" the baby so it couldn't come out. Actually she wasn't fully dilated until she was in the hospital for a while.

I was very angry with the women for carrying class matters and "women business" to the chief and irked at the chief for not coming to me to see what was going on before making a judgment and, of course, at Norn for using the class to make palava.

I told them all that unless the fine was withdrawn, and unless the women would discontinue taking matters that concern the midwife class to the chief, I would discontinue my classes, close the belly clinic, discontinue my assistance to the belly women in the town, and also the assistance of the Ganta midwife. So far the past few days, the matter seems to have cooled down. Needless to say, Norn also has instructions to listen and not try to instruct the other women.

So many things have a supernatural explanation and trying to explain things on a scientific basis, in simple terms, and expecting people to believe them, is pretty much a waste of time. If a baby develops a staph skin infection a few days after a really dirty delivery, it's caused by the mother having eaten bitter ball (a form of eggplant) when she was pregnant. Most of the people, even well-educated ones, believe in the power of witchcraft, they believe a person can put a spell on another one just by uttering a few words. And of course, there is a lot of conflict between the people who are "God mouths" (Christians) and those who are into the tribal societies. When I write something like this episode and it only takes two or three pages, it is misleading as to its significance here. Many hours of talk were involved, emotionally as well as physically exhausting, many people are involved whenever there is such a discussion because so many people "talk it," too. It is educational, I'll admit.

Dearest Vikki and Gill,   **October 23, 1973, Gbedin**

My clinics are still going strong—baby clinic Tuesday and belly clinic Thursday. Plus I'm teaching, with Martha the midwife, a class every Thursday AM for the country midwives here, nine of them. They come for the clinic and then we have about an hour class.

When the course is finished in about a month, we will have some kind of ceremony for them and present them with a government certificate and a bag with supplies such as cord ties, towels, etc., furnished by a Scandinavian group. Each Thursday after lunch, I teach a health class for the school girls. So there's always something to do. Sunday Harold and I and Ciam, too, finally finished the painting, did the kitchen and the bathroom. I really slapped the paint on but at least it looks bright and clean.

Dearest Mother and all,   **October 23, 1973, Gbedin**

This week and next week our old midwives are spending at the hospital in Ganta for some practical experience. Yesterday Harold took three of them and me to Ganta. What a riot, getting them all ready, their bundles and themselves in the car and started off. Bags of rice, bunches of vegetables, bundles of personal belongings.

Right now most of the young children and babies are wearing a key hung on a string around their necks. The people are saying that "the *jin-i* (a spirit of some sort, sometimes called Mami Watah) baby don't got any key. So when she see baby that don't got key, she will take the baby, and the baby will die." They laugh when they tell me this but say, "That what the people say," and make sure that their baby wears a key. This will probably last for a while, and then all of a sudden you'll notice that no one is wearing a key again.

Dearest Judith,   **October 24, 1973, Gbedin**

Here it is nearly time for Vikki to come. How nice it would be if you were here too! Since they tried two times already, I won't be sure they will come until I see them!

Ciam has decided to stay until later, although when Vikki leaves he may feel differently. Don't feel that you're imposing on us to have him here. Of course, there is more work involved with an extra person any time but that's no problem. We're all enjoying each other, he's doing OK in school, and making friends and learning Liberian English like he's been here a year. The people like him and so do the Peace Corps volunteers, and he gets along fine with them. My going to Ganta two times a week and coming home late makes it a bit of a strain but that ends next week, and I won't take a late class again. They're already making plans to have me start teaching in March again, but I'm not thinking of it right now.

Today is Unification Day, a national holiday, and at all schools the kids "drill," that is, march like military groups. They love it. Today will be Ciam's first try at it so we'll see how it goes. He has so much energy. School only goes half a day, so he's home by 1:00 PM each day. Then there are many things to do, like shooting at bird nests with his sling shot. Rice birds are a real nuisance for the farmers. He plays football, really soccer, builds camps, does his homework, and reads. By 8 o'clock at night he's ready to fall into bed. The heat is very tiring, so we're all ready for bed early. (He now has a little green and orange parrot, given to him by a Lebanese friend in Ganta. What a zoo this is.)

Harold is working very hard, as ever. He is finally going to get started on his big water project. Our water comes from a stream up on the hill above our house and the pipes are always breaking down. So he's found a big tank for storage. He'll drag it up with the bulldozer, get better pipes and install them. It sounds easy, but the way you have to do things here, nothing is easy.

Dearest Mother,   **November 9, 1973, Monrovia**

Today Vikki will arrive. I was too excited to sleep, so have been up since 5:00 AM writing letters. We have been staying with Tim and Vicki Nighschwander and their 10-month-old baby. She is in home economics and has done a lot of tie dye and wax print work. Now she has inspired me to try to do some of it. I have a book that describes how to, very clearly, all kinds of designs, so when our Vikki goes home, I hope to begin. My class is over now, except for correcting the finals and getting the grades done, so I should have some free time.

Dear Mother,   **November 27, 1973, Gbedin**

We are sorry to say goodbye today to our kids. It has been so nice to have them here. Our friends have enjoyed them a lot, too. Everyone was so good to them while they were here.

Our house was full of people whenever we've been home, all coming to see our "strangers" and bringing gifts for them. We didn't get to take them to all the places we wanted to. There just wasn't enough time, especially with the warm, dusty driving conditions.

Celebrating at Harry Bar. From right, clockwise, Chris Lyman, Harry's wife Mary, Harry, Ruth, Dale Veeneman, Harold, and their daughter Vikki.

Last week, we took the kids to a small town to visit some friends, where we stayed for three days. It's a Liberian family, and their life style is different from ours—no luxuries—but adequate. It gave them a chance to experience a different kind of life, even though it wasn't as comfortable as at home. The people are very nice.

Now that they will be gone, I'm expecting to have quite a bit of time for my own activities, since the classes are done for three months. And letter writing will have top priority.

Ciam's school will soon be over, just final tests and closing exercises. It has been a strain in some ways, but a good way to get to know the kids. He's no longer an oddity among them, and gets along just fine. Coming into the fourth grade hasn't been so bad either. He picked things up with no problems. One thing that took some getting used to was the way the teachers speak. Their English isn't so easy to understand, but he speaks the same way now!

Our plans now are to leave May 1st, take a few weeks to get home, via North Africa, and on through the Orient—Taiwan, Japan, and Hawaii. Of course, plans are so daily, many things can happen in the meantime.

Dear Vikki and Gill,   **December 4, 1973, Gbedin**

Your visit seems just like a dream already. It came and went so fast. Every minute was enjoyable to us. I hope so much it was to you, too, even though sometimes it might have been somewhat uncomfortable for you. There were so many more things to show you, but not enough time or energy.

Ciam took some of his exams. He had to pay 50 cents to take one late, and has a couple more next Monday. Closing exercises will be next Wednesday, and then we can be a bit more free. I want to take him to Gbapa to Jeff's, so he can dig for diamonds before Jeff leaves and also take him swimming at Lamco.

John is home from school now, came last evening. So he and Ciam will be doing some things together. Harold took the truck to Sanniquellie today, and hauled all the kids' household goods back to Gbedin—John, Martha, and Harry.

Today, I got busy with my butterflies, and made one collage. It was a figure of a woman with a baby on her back, and carrying a head load. It turned out quite well, so I think I'll do some more. I took your advice and started small. This figure is about eight inches high. I also cut out a pantsuit from the green, orange, and white wax print, which I had used as a tablecloth while you were here. There was enough material left to make a skirt, too. I also cut out things for Luapu, two blouses for her and a dress for Yah Sunday.

Dearest Mother,   **December 5, 1973, Gbapa**

Ciam and I are sitting in a little open piazza of a zinc-roofed house in Gbapa, a small town in upper Nimba County, near Lamco. This is a diamond digging area. Many hundreds of people dig all through the hills here. Jeff, a Peace Corps volunteer, is getting ready to go home after three years. He's been very nice to Ciam and invited him to come and try his luck at diamond digging before he left for home. I'm sure the adventure will be its own compensation, since his chance of finding a diamond is pretty remote.

This is a very picturesque town. This house is on a hill above the town, and spread out below us is a mass of red zinc roofs, all clustered close together. Here and there are palm and banana trees, and some pawpaw trees, scattered among the houses. The only transportation on the one street winding through the town is an occasional taxi, in clouds of dust, scattering children and chickens. This is a cozy house, only shutters, no glass, with an outside kitchen with a raised hearth. There is an outside toilet and a bathing fence made of bamboo poles.

One of Jeff's students took us to his father's diggings, and showed us all the steps in the process of finding diamonds. We watched the people going through all steps of searching for diamonds, and what hard work it is. Then the school boy who took us sifted sand that had been prepared for the jigging process. (This means putting the sand in a small screen sifter and jiggling it in the water. The black rocks and the diamonds, being heavier, sink to the bottom. Then it's tipped over on a flat mud surface, and the man looks for any diamonds.)

Believe it or not, a small diamond was there! We jigged a few more sifters full but didn't see any more diamonds. Later, when we got back to Jeff's house and all sat down to eat lunch, the school boy made a little speech and presented the diamond to Ciam. Was he excited! The boy could have sold it in Gbapa to the diamond broker for about $3. We were told that the price doubles about three to five times before it reaches the customer in a ring or setting of some sort.

Now, we are sitting on the side of the road with a flat tire. Our tire tools won't work, so Chris had to hitchhike back to Lamco, which is about ten miles from here, and find someone to come help us. Too bad Harold isn't here, because he can always manage. Two Liberian friends and Ciam are with me. There is never any shade along the road, and the dust from the passing cars is something else. We've found a tree to sit under, and Ciam and I always find something to do in such cases.

Harold built a nice cage for our parrot so now our bird is in the house. The cage is of chicken wire, like a tube about three feet high, and can stand on the floor on newspaper. In the center is branch from a tree with several twigs for the bird to perch on. He is small and green with an orange breast and bright yellow feathers under his wings, quite pretty. Ciam thinks he's going to teach him to talk, but I don't know how that will go.

Dear Mother,   **December 22, 1973, Gbedin**

Another Christmas in Liberia. I can't believe it's the third one away from home. If all goes well, it will be the last one. Can you believe we'll be leaving here in less than four months? The time is going very fast.

The past week was very hectic. You remember, I have been having classes for the local midwives. Anyway, they have finished their course now, and we plan a closing ceremony. It sounds simple, doesn't it? Nothing is simple here. It has to be discussed endlessly, everyone must be involved, even people who have nothing to do with it offer their opinions. You can't imagine the palava. And when you think you have it settled, you discover someone is vexed about something, and you have to start all over.

Also, there are certain ways the country people do things, and of course, these must be observed, such as ideas about the preparation of food. The ladies decided they wanted to serve a meal, not just have tea and cookies.

So we arranged for the school, detailed our boys to get palm branches and flowers and decorate the building. We got a group of school girls to cook (rice, goat soup, goat gravy, goat and potato greens soup). All of this was done outside the school, in big iron pots, over an open fire. (Wood had to be gathered first.) The goat was killed just before they started cooking, and just about every bit of it went into the soup, the head, intestines, everything. They cooked about fifty pounds of rice, so you can see how many people came. We had to collect dishes and spoons. We had invited people from the hospital in Ganta, and told them it would start at 2 PM, but it started finally at about 4:45 PM. Actually, nothing ever starts on time in Liberia, and I should have known it wouldn't really start at 2. Then we had "all kind" of speeches. There were several chiefs here and government and hospital people.

It was a very fine program. I got a lot of thanks and praise for my work, which was gratifying, since I wonder frequently what in the world I'm knocking myself out for!

The doctor couldn't come because he'd been in Monrovia on business, and the women had a goat and one hundred pounds of rice they wanted to give him. This is a customary way to say "thank you" here, with something like that. So what to do now. I asked him to come during the week so the ladies could do their thing, and decided to cook for the ladies and him. This time, I got the kids that work for me and Chris—two boys and a girl—to cook palm butter and rice. We got a bunch of palm wine and had another shorter and smaller program for the doctor on Wednesday afternoon.

In between these two big undertakings, I had been helping Nellie, one of my friends here, to make two bridesmaid dresses, long formals, and a long dress for herself. She and I spent one afternoon doing some more tie-dye again. This is a real job, but lots of fun.

There was also the clinic to take care of, had some of the mission people here for lunch on Wednesday, and took them around the project. Oh yes, in between, one of my ladies was delivering, and I had to run back and forth to her house until the baby came. I hope things will slow down soon so I can do some of my own things for a while, sewing, for example, which I've been saving for when I had free time.

I'm so glad the classes came to a finish, not just because of the time they take, but because getting the people to stay with something week after week isn't easy. It is the first time these women have ever attended a class. The Swedish midwife at Ganta made up nice bags for each one, with everything needed for a normal delivery. I made up certificates for them, although later we will have official government certificates for them.

Ciam is enjoying being out of school. He has lots of time to go to the shop with Harold and Dale, to go out in the bush with John, to play with the kids, and do lots of other things. He is so full of energy, you can't slow him down. He will probably leave here about March 1.

The weather has now changed. It is very dry, no rain in a month, hot and dusty, but at night, the temperature goes down to about 56 degrees, which is really cold. We all wear sweaters in the morning, and Ciam puts on his zipper jacket to go out to feed the chickens and goat. I think this will last until March.

Dear Vikki and Gill,   **December 24, 1973, Gbedin**

Since Chris is going to Lamco this morning for some last minute things for our dinner tomorrow (he can't imagine Christmas without fruitcake!), I will dash off another letter. It has suddenly turned warm again, although John says it will be cold again soon. Ciam and John will go this AM for palm branches so we can concoct some sort of tree. We have so many homemade decorations collected in the past three years that our tree should look quite dressed up.

Yesterday I finally began to feel like Christmas, when I was packing cookie boxes. It made me think of the times we used to bake cookies and share them at Christmas time. I baked seven kinds, and packed boxes for Mr. Chiang, Harry and Annie, Tommy Hoff, Elizabeth, and Chris and Dale. I'll try to send some to Ming Ho at Gamu. Mr. Chiang brought us a bottle of Scotch and a big watermelon. Yesterday, Elizabeth sent us our "Christmas"—a big bowl of rice and a bowl of fine palm butter. Friday evening, Harold and the fellows in the mechanic shop had their party at Harry Bar. Annie cooked goat soup (our little goat) and rice. We had James's record player, and everyone was dancing, especially the little kids. Even Bea's little two- year-old, Baby Sister, was dancing.

Dear Uncle Emil and Wilda,   **December 30, 1973, Gbedin**

Our past three years have been interesting and, generally, quite good, but taken piece by piece, there are parts I wouldn't want to see again. We wouldn't trade our experiences, but now are looking forward to coming home for a while. It has been a wonderful experience to meet so many people from so many different countries and cultures. Of all the different ones, it's only the French we have met in West Africa who are at all anti-American, and it's really not that as much as they seem to believe that it is only the French that matter, their foods, ways, language, etc., are much better than others. Of course, too, it may be because the French who live and work in the former French colonies, such as Ivory Coast, are quite separate from the native people. They live a very fine life, many levels above the people they work with and supposedly serve. They are mostly civil servants, and while most of them have had years of English language study in schools in France, they refuse to speak one word of English. It's no doubt a good thing for me, since it has made me polish up what little French I remember from high school!

Ciam and I made a Christmas tree from palm branches. We leaned it up against the wall and hung a wild collection of decorations on it: some felt mobiles Mary sent last year and stars that Mom had made. Then we had a box of decorated Easter eggs that Mom sent for Easter that arrived in June or July and were saved for the tree. It was quite a sight and lots of fun to do. With a little boy in the house, I find myself doing things I didn't bother with before. The native people here have never heard of or seen a Christmas tree before, and unless they are Christians, and very few are, Christmas is only a time for new clothes and dancing.

Ciam and I and the two Peace Corps guys next door have been enjoying playing Scrabble together. Surprisingly, Ciam does as well as any of us. In fact, today he won me, as he says, by almost thirty points. The Liberian kids enjoy the game, too, and will sit and ponder and look up words in the dictionary for two or three hours at a time. We've encouraged John Cooper, the boy who works for us, to play it as an aid to vocabulary.

I want to thank you for your generous gift. About the time your letter arrived, we were preparing for the midwife students' completion ceremony. There were six midwives and three helpers. It was quite an occasion and, to the people here, quite an accomplishment, since we are awarding an official government certificate to each of them. A Swedish midwife at Ganta Mission had access to nice bags for them for their supplies. Your $10 went toward helping to fit them out with things like cord ties, razor blades, plastic sheet, hand brushes, basins, and such.

Thanks so much, dear people. When we get home, I'll show you the picture we took of all of them holding their new bags with a copy book in which they are to have someone record the delivery date, etc. Then they are to take their notebooks, from time to time, to someone who will fill out the birth registration form. This can be done by anyone who can write, and will be forwarded to the county health officer, so it can be recorded in Monrovia. Right now, I do this, but I'll leave the forms with someone here, and maybe it will be done. The ladies are very serious about their work, so I think they will try.

Most of the people here have no idea of their exact age, or that of their children. The husband keeps track, if anyone does. I talked with the director of Vital Statistics in Monrovia. He told me of the difficulties of getting statistical information and said the Peace Corps volunteers are the main ones doing birth registrations.

Ruth visiting one of the mothers in the village.

1974

Dear Judith and Ed,   **January 4, 1974, Gbedin**

Christmas was quite different, but for the first time, we had a Christmas tree. Having a little boy in the house made it more fun. On Christmas morning he sat under the tree and opened his little presents, and played with them, just as in other Christmases in days long ago. We will take our funny little tree down on Twelfth Night, and then divide the decorations among some of our friends. They will hang them in their rooms to decorate them a bit.

Ciam has been going to the shop with Harold every morning, except on Tuesday, when he goes to the clinic with me to help with the baby clinic. He weighs kids, passes out numbers, serves CARE food, and runs errands. The women really enjoy him. At the shop, he helps "small," goes for tools for Harold, takes things apart, pounds on things, getting familiar with all kinds of tools and machinery. I think Ciam's experience with Harold is priceless. Ciam says, "You have to get your hands dirty and learn to smell gasoline, if you're going to learn to be a mechanic!"

So many of our good friends are gone now, so things are quite different. I guess we've stayed too long, when we see so many of our friends "coming to finish" before we do.

We just had a letter from Mary Pearmine in which she asked about our interest in a place in Oregon, and whether you were coming too, and if they should be looking. I do hope we can find what we are looking for there. Actually, our plans for the future are pretty slim, I'm afraid. Harold is worrying about what he will do when we get home, but I can't get too concerned, because things always seem to work out for the best, in ways you can't anticipate.

If we were smart and cautious, we'd come right home and not spend any money on travel, in case we are out of work for a while. But we both feel we can't miss this opportunity to see more of the world, while we're already half way home, regardless of whether we use some of our "readjustment" money. We see it as a necessary expense!

Dear Vikki and Gill,   **January 4, 1974, Gbedin**

Ciam and John are trying to catch crayfish—like big shrimp, very tasty. Harold made them a trap of chicken wire, something on the order of a crab pot. They tie it down in the stream by the dam, put cassava and palm nuts in it, and check it each day. Last week, they only caught a total of eight, so Harold kept redesigning the trap, and they experimented with bait. This morning, they brought home eight. Maybe now, their luck will be better, and we can have a shrimp feed.

Adama was here yesterday. Her child, Abou, was with her but not feeling too good since he had drunk kerosene a couple weeks ago and was still feeling the effects of that. This happens a lot, since everyone uses kerosene and buys it in beer or Fanta bottles. I'm sure no one takes much care in where they put the stuff. She gave me a pair of beads and Harold a little tobacco mortar. Sometimes she calls Harold "Mr. Ruth"!

George Wayzani had a New Year's Eve party for the Lebanese in Ganta, and Chris, Harold and I were invited, too. They had all kinds of beautiful food, lots of liquid refreshments, including arak, fireworks, decorations, Lebanese music, and dancing. It was a really fun party. We stayed until after midnight, and then planned to stop at Gbedin to dance, but by the time we got there, everyone had gone across the river to Guinea to dance. George's wife is only 17, a beautiful, poised girl. Unfortunately, she only speaks English "one-one" [*"just a few words"*]. She was a charming hostess that evening. She does speak French, coming from Senegal, so I try with French, and she likes to help me.

Dear Mom,   January 7, 1974, Gbedin

At last count, I've written 44 letters since December 10th, have used up all my stamps and air sheets, and have three pieces of rather messy paper left. We've been without gas for a week, so can't even get to Lamco to stock up unless we want to fight the taxi situation. There are lots of things to do here, though, so we never get bored.

I've been doing a lot of sewing, or rather, helping other people sew. I did make a pants suit for Christmas and now am making hats. One for Ciam and one for Harold, plus two for a friend who gave me the pattern and the cloth. I didn't know how much work it would be when I told him I'd do it. The hat is made from tie-dye material, has four pockets on the crown, each with a button-down flap. The brim has button holes on two sides and can also button up onto the crown. (It's really an Australian bush hat design.) His was made in Gambia and is very good looking. I have two more to make, and think I'll charge $5 if anyone wants me to make one!

Ciam's having a good time, but will be ready to go anytime. Christmas was fun with him here. I couldn't help but think how different his Christmas was here—only three presents, plus his new suit, and he was perfectly happy.

I have to tell you of an experience we had yesterday. Harold and I went for a walk around the project. A man came for me, saying a woman was sick, in the town. I went with him, and Harold went on home. I found the woman, who was older then I, lying by the fire in her house. She had shallow, noisy, respirations, and a fast pulse, and appeared very sick. The old man said he wanted to take her to her home village so they could make country medicine. I said she is too sick, no country medicine for this kind of sickness. She had to go to the hospital right away. He agreed and asked if we could help with the car, since a taxi trip on Sunday is nil and very hard to get anytime.

I went to get Harold and Chris, and they had to get gas and do something to the truck, so maybe 30 to 40 minutes passed. We finally reached the house, where a crowd of people had gathered, helping to get her ready. I waited in the truck. Then they helped her to walk, rather than carry her to the truck. Her husband and brother were in the back of the truck as we drove away. We had gone about a block, when I said, "Harold, stop the truck. I think she is dying." I called to the men in the back, "The woman coming to die." Then, oh my, the husband started to wail, call her name, jerked at her and beat on the car. He was just beside himself.

Obviously now, there was no need to drive to Ganta, a 30-minute drive, so we turned around and beat it back to Gbedin, the man completely out of control. Before we arrived at their house, a crowd had again gathered since everyone in town knew what had happened, by the way her husband was carrying on. I could hardly hold her up, or keep her from sliding all over. Everyone crowded around the car, screaming and crying.

Finally, Harold told the people that we had to get the woman out of the car because I couldn't move. So three men and I carried her inside where they laid her beside the fire again. As different women came in and looked at her, they would cry and wail, kneel beside her, call her name. It was pretty unnerving.

Finally, I told them to move her into her bedroom, where we covered her with a lappa, but people were still outside crying. Her husband was so pitiful. Soon, the old man of the project, named Moses, who is always looked to for leadership, asked Harold if he would take some of the family and himself to her home village to tell her people. The village was about five miles beyond Ganta. Harold and a few men took off and went through somewhat the same thing when they announced her death to her people.

On his return, he carried some of her people back with him to a town between Ganta and Gbedin called Dingama, where she was to be buried. They wrapped her body in a lappa, placed it in the back of the truck, and tied palm branches on the radiator (the usual practice when carrying a body). Then a bunch of people climbed into the back of the truck, including the music makers, who beat on shovel handles (the metal parts) all the way, which was about a 25- or 30-minute trip. Harold said they had all been drinking cane juice before he came, and continued to drink cane juice on the trip. Chris took a load too, in his Land Rover.

After the fellows discharged their passengers and the body, they came back home, but the people stayed there and held a wake all night. I'm sure they did plenty of drinking, making music, and dancing.

Harold and Chris had to go back today about 4 PM to bring everyone back again The two music men beat on their shovels all the time, accompanying the singing. The old man is a really fine fellow, a good farmer, and well thought of, which accounts somewhat for the turn-out. However, such an occasion as a death means quite a lot of excitement for the town, even though the people do grieve, too. They get all of their grief out of their system with such carrying on, really quite a good idea. If a baby dies, though, the people don't want the mother to cry. They think if she cries, the spirit of the dead baby will come back and take her next child.

Harold said when he was loading the truck, they put in about 200 pounds of rice, two baskets of chickens (two or three chickens in each), some palm oil, and her belongings. They always have to cook for the people who are there and, depending upon how important the person was who died, may have to cook for three to four days, probably kill a pig and a goat. As poor as people are, they always can find the money for the death responsibilities.

It was quite a day. It must have been 5 or 6 PM before Harold got through running around, and it was emotionally wearing for him, too. John and Ciam were home, but when they heard the wailing, they came to see what was happening, so Ciam had a chance to observe a slice of life in Liberia. Harold said at home he'd never be able to take such things, but here, there doesn't seem to be much choice, and he just had to take it. He also said, "Everyone at Dingama had to come and shake his hand and say thank you."

Dear Vikki and Gill,   **January 9, 1974, Gbedin**

Your Christmas package with the puppets came this morning. They're really darling. Ciam is already planning to put on a puppet show for us! (This part of the letter paper was torn/eaten by Ciam's monkey.)

Yesterday morning I was called for a delivery. The husband came for me and said the women said they needed me. It was for one of my clinic clients. I got Chris to take me, since it is about an hour's walk, and I feared there were problems. The husbands are never told anything by the midwives. When I got there, I was directed to the bush behind the house; fortunately, it was daylight. By the time I arrived on the scene, the baby had just been born, beside the fire in a little clearing, a nine and a half pound boy. There were many women there, later I counted 16.

It was gratifying to see that the midwife had used her equipment properly, and everything was just fine. They handed me the baby immediately, and started to dance and sing. After we got baby and mother cleaned up and everything tidied up, they buried the placenta, got the baby and the mother dressed, amidst dancing and singing, and we all walked into town.

After getting the new mother and baby settled in their hut, and the ritual hollering to announce the arrival of the new baby, the people, especially the women, began to dance in a circle, going round and around, singing and having a great time. I danced with them for a while and then had to leave to get the clinic ready for well baby day. It was only 9 AM by this time, still cloudy and cool, so the walk home was leisurely and enjoyable, on a winding trail through tall cane, which was way over my head. I'm always so relieved when there are no problems, since I don't know if I could cope with complications.

Dearest Mother,   **January 13, 1974, Monrovia**

We've just come in from our usual Sunday walk around the project. In the mornings, it's quite cool now, so it's a good time to go "walk about." With the new land, about 40 acres, just getting under cultivation, it's kind of fun to see it at least once a week, to watch its progress.

The 40 acres have been divided among six good farmers, which just about doubled the amount of acres each one has. They are doing such hard work digging ditches around the fields for waste water to run off. Then they will be ready for their fields to be flooded, power tilled, and then leveled. They will then be ready to plant. If they keep on as they are going, we will see their rice harvested before we leave.

Ciam and John, and three other boys went into the bush this past week and found where a family of giant rats, that is, pouched rats, live. They built a fire and made the smoke go inside their hole. When the animals staggered out, the boys captured three, the mother and two young ones. Ciam came in proudly bearing the big one, which must have weighed three to four pounds. It was about two feet long, including its tail. John skinned it, cooked potato greens soup with the rat, of course. We all had to eat some. Actually, tasted OK, but my imagination is too active for a lot of things. This is a vegetarian animal.

The way the people prepare such meat, any small animal, is to burn off the hair, clean out the viscera, and cut the whole thing up and cook it in their soup. The burnt flavor isn't too appetizing to me.

Ciam is enjoying playing with the puppets. You know, things like that frighten the kids here. They are too much like the masks, which people associate with the secret societies' power. In fact, the little dolls you made that have the little plastic eyes that move really terrified some of the children. They would scream and run away when someone held the doll up. The children were OK with the dolls that had only button eyes.

Sometime, kids dress up in large old clothes, put on a mask, like a Santa Claus, or any false face. They sing and dance, with a troupe of other little kids who make music, as a means of begging for money. Such a child is called *beggah*, and comes to our house on holidays, and is so hilariously funny, we all have a great laugh and lots of fun. When he isn't in his costume, he's a very shy little boy.

Dear Vikki and Gill,   **January 13, 1974, Gbedin**

Harold went to the hospital last month because he was having stomach palava and other complaints. Can you believe, after three years he didn't have one intestinal parasite. He's feeling better now. I think it's just his wanting to be home, you and Gill leaving, job frustration, etc. For some reason, it doesn't seem to affect me that way. I'm just frustrated and irritable!

Lately, things have been really hard to live with, due to frustrations with my work at the clinic, working with Daniel, seeing people doing things I've tried to eliminate for three years. I tell myself I can't expect things to be different just like that, but when it involves people I expect to have more sense, I really get upset. Too bad it's so hard to get around, maybe I'd be away as much as possible and not be aware of so much. But the roads are so dusty and bumpy now, gas allowance has been cut way down, and taxi fares have been almost doubled, that is, when you can get a taxi to and from Gbedin.

Well, I'd better cheer up! As Harold reminds me, it's only three more months!

Dearest Mother,   **January 20, 1974, Gbedin**

We've just returned from an interesting trip into the bush, so I'll try to describe some of our experiences for you.

We had promised Ciam a bush hike to a village, and since John's people had invited us to their town, we decided to combine these two things. We could have stayed overnight, but I have a bad cold, and the weather is very cold at night, so it didn't seem wise to sleep there. Country houses are pretty primitive! However, we will go back one more time with John, in April, and spend the night so they can entertain us as they'd like to do, with dancing and music.

This morning we got up at 5:30 so we could get an early start. We left at 6:30, with our canteens and a chicken, and some other gifts, such as soap, and medicine, very high priority items in a village. It is a 30-mile trip, and we were able to make it in one and a half hours, our best time yet. The motor road is really something, areas of washouts, with deep ditches in the middle of the road, then a "washboard" area, then very rocky. The road is never worked on. Harold says they may grade it once during wet season. And of course, now it's so dry that the dust is terrible.

We parked our truck by the roadside, and took off into the bush before 8:30. John was all dressed up in his best clothes, since he was going to his "born town," and had to "bluff" a bit, with a small gunny sack of our gifts on his head. Ciam carried the canteen and his Frisbee he planned to give to the kids. Harold carried the white chicken, which is considered a very fine gift, and his camera. I brought up the rear with a rice bag containing some medicine, a few small gifts, and the usual odds and ends in one's travel bag.

It was quite cold when we started out, maybe 60 degrees, and in the deep bush no way for the sun to warm us, but no one wanted to wear sweaters and have to carry them on the return trip. We walked through many coffee and cocoa groves. A tremendous amount is grown in this area, and head-loaded out to the market, much to Ivory Coast, where the price is better and the distance not too far.

We passed through several small villages and found coffee and cocoa beans drying on the ground, being hulled by beating it in big mortars, some being harvested. The berries are harvested something like huckleberries at home. Woven mats are put under the trees with the corners tucked together to make erect sides, then people beat on the branches and let the berries fall on the mat. We only saw women doing this kind of work.

In most of the villages we walked through, people quickly gathered around us. In many instances, people knew John and had come to shake his hand, stare at us, shake our hands, make comments about us, and ask questions. We gathered quite a following as we passed through the towns. There is a lot of fruit growing wild here, much that is not used by the people. We saw grapefruit, oranges, tangerines, limes, bananas, plantains, pineapple, breadfruit, papaya, and avocado, much just rotting on the ground. We carried about 20 big grapefruit and a dozen big avocados home in our gunny sack on our return trip. John climbed the trees and tossed the fruit down to Harold. On our trip in, we all sat down on the ground and each ate a big grapefruit, so sweet, you can't imagine, with the juice running down our arms like water.

It was about a five-mile trip, but quite easy since it was a good, level trail, although the grass and other foliage grows tall on either side, right to the edge of the trail, which is only wide enough for one person to pass at a time. When you meet someone on the path, one has to step aside. The trees are hundreds of feet high, with such wide spreading branches that often you cannot see the sky. We didn't waste any time, because it was so cold, and we wanted to spend as much time in John's town as possible.

When we emerged from the bush to the edge of the town and someone saw us, we were immediately surrounded, mostly by people who knew John. Everyone must shake your hand, make exclamations of surprise and amazement and satisfaction. Ciam was quite a novelty. I don't think a kwi boy had ever visited there. We gathered quite a following as we passed through the town. John's mother and stepfather greeted us so warmly and, right away, wanted us to spend the night.

This is a fairly large town, named Gienple, maybe one hundred houses, most with thatched roofs, and constructed from mud and sticks (poles). Most people are trying to improve the town, "It's Higher Heights time," they say (the present president's motto) and are building mud-block houses with corrugated zinc roofs. A lot of the houses are round, quite small, thatched roofed, with a fire area in the center. The ceilings are made with bamboo, laid in a lattice-like design, several layers thick, and thus furnishing an attic storage area for rice and for treasures that people aren't supposed to see, such as masks and other secret society things. You can't imagine the layers of smoke and grease on the ceilings above the fire area; there is no chimney in these houses. Most people have a round hut for their kitchen, where they do most of their cooking. In the one small round house we went into, however, three people live and sleep there, on mats laid on three sides of the fire.

John's mother, with whom I can't communicate at all since she speaks only Gio, her tribal dialect, immediately started two little girls beating rice in the mortar. His father brought a hen into the house and showed us what they would cook for our soup, the usual country way. John had to help with the preparation of the chicken, and he fixed it as we do here. Otherwise, they would have put the whole chicken in the pot—head, feet, intestines, never waste anything.

He gave the viscera to the two little girls who were helping. They were no older than Ciam, wearing only a little lappa around their hips and upper legs. I wish you could have seen them prepare their soup. They scrubbed the feet, picked some of the feathers from the head, used a feather to split the intestines and get the contents out. They put all into a small amount of water and swished it around a bit, then put it into a small iron pot, added water, salt, hot pepper, and set it beside the fire, where it soon cooked.

They shared it with a few other kids, eating, juice and all, with their hands, making a lot of slurps and smacks. There was a dog nosing around all the time the food preparations were going on, but you can imagine, that dog got very little of the chicken. The people here break the bones and eat the marrow, eat the ends of the bones—one bone lasts a long time.

I forgot to mention that the food preparation took place outside, under a tangerine tree, where the people placed chairs for us to sit. After the rice is beaten, in the mortar, it is tossed on a wicker fanner (tray) so that the chaff will fly out, leaving clean grains of rice. In any town, there are always chickens scratching about and are always there when rice is fanned to enjoy the gleanings. Country chickens are quite pretty, many colors and such varied feather combinations.

After the food was prepared, we were served, along with John's father. We were each served with our own dish and spoon. Most people eat from a common bowl, using their right hand. The children always wait. Then, when you are finished, you must leave something in your plate and pass it to one of the children. Actually, the soup was very good, just chicken, a little palm oil, salt, and chicken bouillon cubes, called "Maggi" cubes. She beat fresh hot peppers into a paste, and if you wanted them you could add them. Peppers would be in the soup if it were for just Liberians. Lately, Harold hasn't been able to eat hot pepper, but I love it.

By this time, it was mid-afternoon, and we had planned to leave by three or so, in order to reach our car before dark. We had given John's parents our small gifts earlier, and were preparing to leave, when some old men came into the house and sat down. Then John's ma came in with a cloth wrapped bundle. John's father, Sonjah, stood up and started to talk, thanking us for coming and for helping their son. Then he gave Harold a chief's robe. The robe was made of country-woven cloth. To me he gave a lappa of blue and white striped country cloth, made from the local cotton (trees), spun, dyed with local dye and woven by hand. I was also given two little "G-strings" made of country cloth, worn by the women and girls when they are in the bush (secret) society. We were also given a few pounds of rice, five stalks of sugar cane for Ciam, and some dried corn. When we were walking out, as we passed through one village where a friend of John's lives, they said ,"Wait small." They then ran and got a chicken from a little palm branch cage and gave it to John for us.

It was hard to say goodbye to the people, knowing we would not see them again. These people have come to us in Gbedin three or four times. Each time, they stay with us, and we cook for them and send them back with gifts that are worth very little, but to them are very useful—like empty jugs, soap, or some of our clothes.

The trip out was wearing. By that time I was running a fever and feeling light-headed, and Ciam was tired, but as they say here, "What to do." We all had to carry more this time, especially after we stopped and sent John up the grapefruit tree! The people—a dozen or more—"carried" us part way, walked about a mile with us and helped to carry our loads. People rarely let you leave their house without accompanying you at least part of the way, sometimes all the way to your door, and then they often come in and sit for a few minutes before returning to their home. It was dark by the time we got home, and I wasted no time in getting into bed, that is, after washing all the travel dirt off, layers and layers.

You know, many days, our work situation is so unpleasant and frustrating, and disappointing, and we say, "What are we doing here; why don't we go home now?" Then we have experiences like yesterday in Gienple, John's town, and the people are so warm and generous, and we know we've made so many friends, and we know it's worthwhile. It will be hard to leave here. Harold says we will get up and leave about 5 AM before people are awake, so we won't have to say any last minute good-byes.

This afternoon, I'm babysitting a four-month-old baby while her mother, a young school-girl friend, goes fishing. She [*the mother*] leaves her little sister, about nine years old, to mind the baby for me while she is gone. Little girls learn pretty young, how to mind the babies. The baby is sleeping on the couch. Three other little girls just came in to visit. One is two years old, another is five, and the other is about eight. They come in, play with the dolls, sit and stare at us, then go. Mamie, the two year old, just went to sleep, so they will all probably be here for a while. This happens a lot. Some of Ciam's classmates, girls about 12 to 14, come to see him, sit and look at him, hardly talking, unless they are spoken to, then say, "I'm going now," and off they go.

January 22. I'm sitting in the car, waiting for Harold to return. We are about a mile from home, and the car died, so he went off on foot to get the truck to tow us home. We are on the way home from the hospital where we took a woman who had delivered earlier today and then had a prolapsed uterus.

After I'd seen her in the village and told them they must carry her to the hospital for treatment, the midwives told the husband they had country medicine for it, and then it would go back inside. After about an hour's palava, she decided she would go to the hospital for treatment. Lo and behold, when we got to the emergency room, she refused treatment. The doctor told her if she refused she would have a serious infection and probably die, or at least, lose her uterus.

It took another hour and half of more palava, before she agreed and then about ten minutes to take care of her problem! So here it is, 5 PM, and I started dealing with her at 12:30. Anyway, she should be OK now, after about a day in the hospital.

Since I started this letter, the husband of one of my friends, Annie Dunbar, died after a four month illness, which people attributed to her having "made witch" on him, but which hospital people say was cancer. Tonight they will hold a wake at their house. She wants me to come, so I guess we must. Harold says he's had about all the life and death experiences he can take so will be glad when we're gone from here.

I've been sewing a suit for Ciam to wear home, since it will no doubt be cold, and his Liberian clothes won't do. We went shopping in Ganta at the market last Thursday and found cloth a lot like corduroy, which looks fine as a suit. One of our friends came yesterday with a tailor and had Ciam measured for a "Higher Heights" suit to carry home. This is a French-style suit, with a short sleeved jacket.

Dear Vikki and Gill,   **January 30, 1974, Gbedin**

To avoid any possible hitch in getting a message to Judith in time, I'm writing to you, too. Here is the information regarding Ciam's departure. We were able just today to get it confirmed. He's leaving here with a young guy who will take him to New York and get him on the Seattle flight.

He will be on his own from New York and will have finished with customs and immigration, etc. He is bringing his parrot along, which may take some time in New York with the Department of Agriculture, but I think Red Jones, the Peace Corps volunteer with whom he is traveling, will do whatever is necessary. I kind of hate to send him off alone but know he will get along OK. And the stewardesses are really good with kids, plus people respond favorably to Ciam.

Dear Mother,   **February 11, 1974, Monrovia**

I hate to think of the actual process of leaving Gbedin, if Ciam's departure is any indication. People were so sad to say goodbye to him, and he was so sad, too. Lots of tears. People say to me, "We will cry too much when you go."

We have a guest right now, a new volunteer, who arrived in Gbedin Friday, for a "live in" in the bush. He is 77 years old and very spry and strong. He will be helping to construct clinics, schools, and roads. We had to leave him in the hands of our school kid helpers and Chris and Dale until we get back to Gbedin. Today they were to take him hiking to the waterfall on the St. John River, about a two and a half to three hour hike, one way. He's apparently quite a hiker and was looking forward to it. They will carry a picnic lunch and canteens of water. This was such a hectic week, getting Ciam ready, having just started again to teach, having a guest, all kinds of visitors, never any peace and quiet!

I didn't tell you about one of my last hair-raising belly-patient experiences. A young girl was having her first baby, in her mother's little hut. I was called about 6 AM, and when I checked her, things seemed OK. The midwives were there, with the correct equipment, and were all set up properly, so I went home to cook breakfast.

At 8 AM, the ma came and wanted me to hurry there. She is Gio, which I can't understand. When I reached the house, which was just a short walk, I discovered the baby's head trying to be born, but the girl was much too small. There was no way to continue without an episiotomy being done.

I thought I would die. Everyone (many women) was excited, jabbering, jumping up and down, looking at me to solve the problem. No time to get her to the hospital, and on these roads, I could just see her lacerating into the rectum.

Finally, I could just pray. I opened the cord-tie packet, took out a new razor blade and the cord dressing, said, "Ma, we mu' cut," and did the episiotomy. The baby came out almost at once. The girl was crying, "No, Ma Ruth, no." I had no Novocaine, no way to suture her, and no way to get the people to carry her to the hospital for repair. I gave her phisohex and told her she had to take warm sitz baths too, and gave her bacterial ointment to use on the cut, which by now looked HUGE.

Anyway, she got along beautifully, apparently followed my directions, and is now nearly healed. It is now two weeks tomorrow since the big event. When I got home, I really fell apart. I will really be glad to trade this kind of situation and responsibility for something less traumatic! The Lord had certainly been looking after me.

Dearest Mother,   **February 15, 1974, Gbedin**

Happy Valentine's Day. Maybe, when we're home we will miss all this hub-bub, but right now I think it will be nice to have more privacy. There is hardly a time between 6 AM and dark when there isn't someone in our house. Of course with Ciam gone, it may be different, since he had friends here, too.

Since I have many things to do between now and May 1, it will be good to have more free time. On Monday, Harold, Chris, and I will go to Lamco and have a tie-dying lesson. I have four more hats to sew, as well as a pair of knit slacks, a culotte-skirt for our trip, and three or four dresses for one of my Mandingo friends. Also, a course (60-hour) to rewrite for the mission, lots of weekend trips to take to visit friends, plus our regular jobs! Right now, I'm teaching at Ganta two days a week and having clinic activities two days a week.

Harold is feeling fine now. The doctor decided his stomach problems were the result of too much aspirin, which he was taking for muscle spasms he was having in his shoulder. As soon as he got the shoulder problem cured with different medicine, he seemed much improved.

The weather is fantastically dry, much more so than last year. We can now see daylight through many wide cracks in our floor, and there is a constant layer of dust on everything, no matter how often you wipe it off. The water is drying up, and many of the rice paddies will be ruined. Some of the people have prepared their fields—two to five acres—have seedlings ready to set out and now no water. Some have rice just beginning to head, which will be lost. Since this is their only source of income, it's very serious.

When we first came, rice was $5 for a 100-pound bag, and now it's $18 for a bag here at the mill. If you're the one selling the rice, that's OK, but for the bulk of the people who buy rice, it's tragic, and people say it will go higher. And no rain is expected for another two months! We've seen no change in the people's wages during this time.

We are trying to dispose of most of our belongings, so when the time comes to leave nothing will hold us up. It looks like one of Harold's colleagues at the shop will take nearly everything, so that helps. We are hoping to net about $200 from our sale for use on our trip.

Have you heard of the World Medical Mission? Recently two groups came here, the first one, 150 doctors and nurses for three weeks. The second group was smaller, for two weeks. It is a wonderful thing. The people pay their own way to come, are housed on whatever mission station they are sent to, and work the entire time they are here.

In the first group, 12 people were sent to Ganta. There were surgeons, such as orthopedic, chest, eye specialists, anesthesiologists, dentists, etc. You can't imagine the work they did while they were here. One day, the eye surgeon did 14 enucleations [*removal of the eye*] and cataract operations, at no cost to the patients. They also brought special eye glasses, and artificial eyes. Apparently, World Medical Mission sends groups like this all over the world, but this is the first group that has been sent to Liberia.

I had a chance to visit with one of them when I took the patient with the prolapsed uterus to the hospital. In between trying to convince her to take the treatment, I had time to do a lot of visiting. Did I tell you her husband brought me a chicken to say thank you, and yesterday, the parents of the girl whose birth I had to assist, came with a chicken.

I wish I had kept a record of the chickens I've received in thanks. I'm sure it's over two dozen. Ciam received one the day before he left, so we cooked it for him. The people say, "Here your soup," and then make some kind of speech.

Dear Mother,   **February 25, 1974, Gbedin**

Since we have only eight weeks here until we leave, our weekends are pretty laid out, and this always makes the time pass so fast. We expect to do a lot of visiting each weekend. This past one we spent with a young couple at Gbarnga—about a two-hour drive each way—on a college campus. They're such an enjoyable couple, and we always have a good time together. We stayed Saturday and Sunday.

Next weekend, we'll go to Karmple, toward Ivory Coast, an hour and half each way (bad road). One of our volunteer friends has invited us to stay there. In another week or two, we'll go to Foya, up near the Sierra Leone border, about an eight-hour trip, and we'll stay from Friday until Monday. There is a government guest house there, which the Agricultural Minister has told Harold he can use. So this is the way it's going, and during the week it's a madhouse to get things caught up and our jobs done.

It's been quite an experience working here at Ganta Hospital, and very good for me, I'm sure. It's amazing how little you can manage with. When you go into the children's ward, which is one room, you can always find mothers lying on mats under the cribs. They stay all the time with their children, and most moms have at least one other member of the family with them all the time. People are all over outside the ward, cooking and eating and sleeping, until the sick family member goes home.

There is no hot water in the hospital, it all has to be heated on a hot plate if it's needed. This is a good hospital, compared to the government hospital.

Dear Vikki and Gill,   **February 25, 1974, Gbedin**

Martha and her baby Vicki are staying with us now. Her parents decided she didn't have to go to school any more. "Girls who born are *fini* with school," they said, so they told her she should move to John's uncle's house and let him care for her. (Her father had just sold $400 of rice, can you imagine.)

We hate to have a girl who is in the eighth grade, and who really wants to go to school—she wants to be a midwife—have to stop her education. So we took her in and will try to get her settled in Sanniquellie, since there's no eighth grade in Gbedin. Her school fees aren't much, but room and board is too much for us, since we are already keeping John there.

Anyway, she has gone to Sanniquellie today trying to get a free room with a friend, and then we'll try to send enough money for her food each month. It's so hard for girls to get an education. Too bad we're not staying here longer. Annie is still with me. She will work during the week when John is gone. He'll come home on weekends to do the washing and mopping.

Dear Vikki and Gill,   **March 10, 1974, Gbedin**

Martha will be leaving for Sanniquellie tomorrow. She's been with us about two weeks, and has been sewing like mad. I bought uniform cloth, and she's been making shirts and blouses and skirts and shorts and has been selling them. She makes about 75 cents on each piece, which is a good profit here. I just take the price of the cloth. She should make enough to take care of her food for this term. If we can get one of the sewing machines fixed up for her, she will have a continuing income. Her baby is growing, can sit up now.

Dearest Mother and all,   **March 27, 1974, Gbedin**

Can you believe the month of March is nearly gone? Only one more month in Gbedin. My class finished today except for the final so that will give me more time to get things sorted out and wound up at home.

Last weekend we went to John's town—five-mile hike in the bush— and stayed overnight there. We had the school teachers' room but no mattress on the wooden bed and no pillow. Talk about hard! Also had to keep the shutters to the one window closed because of the mosquitoes and also fear of intruders—none of the country people keep windows open at night.

Then about 4 AM, a new baby was born, and the people started to celebrate. You never heard such a racket, dancing, singing, yelling, beating on various kinds of drums—one is taller than I am, a hollowed-out log with animal skin over the end and short legs on the other. The drummer stands on a tripod made of sticks and beats with short drum sticks. You can hear the drum for miles away, which is one way other villages are notified of trouble in the town. The celebrating went on the rest of the morning and was still going when we left about 2 PM. Everyone was drinking cane juice and palm wine, and a lot were really drunk. I don't see how they could keep going and don't know how the new mother could stand it with such a din just outside her little palm-thatched round hut.

John's people cooked for us—gave us three chickens, which were used in the soup, and then when we left after speeches as usual, they gave us a young goat. When we were on the trail, we were accompanied by about ten small boys—who were responsible for the goat—the school teacher, and John's mother, father and uncle! We were also carrying rice, benne seed, limes, and grapefruit. It was hard to say goodbye, when you know you won't meet again.

I had made a lappa suit for John's ma and a shirt for his father and a dress for his little sister, plus soap, etc., for gifts.

We took bucket baths inside a bamboo bath fence and used the bushes for a toilet. Such is life in the bush.

Dearest Vikki,   **March 30, 1974, Easter Sunday, Gbedin**

This week has been something. On Wednesday Dave Hunter, from DC, came to Sanniquellie so there was a dinner party for him, which we all went to. Thursday he came here for lunch, along with the Peace Corps director, a couple of other officials, and Joseph Campbell, our project director. The kids cooked cassava green soup and rice. That night we were invited to the Chinese men's for dinner, along with Chris and Dale. You know, their meals have at least a dozen dishes, each delicious, and all kinds of liquid refreshments.

Then Saturday (yesterday) Chris gave what he called a "good riddance" party for us, and all kinds of Peace Corps volunteers arrived, and many stayed all night. Harold killed the goat and seven chickens, and the Peace Corps volunteers did all the rest. They barbecued the meat and made salads; the boys made palm butter and rice; they made guacamole and Lebanese bread; and every other person brought a case of beer! Harry Edwards and Henry Zawqalo came, too, and there must have been two dozen (plus our kids) Peace Corps volunteers. You should have seen the food disappear!

Later we all went to the volleyball field and all played volleyball. About that time, Harold brought a couple of gallons of palm wine. After the game ended—by this time it was too dark to play—the whole crowd, including lots of the spectators, went to Harry Bar for more beer and dancing. Quite a party. All the guys danced me around; they were so nice to us, have been all the time we've been here. As usual, the little kids were there, too, dancing in one corner of the room.

We bedded people down on the floor in both houses, and this morning, I baked a bunch of biscuits for everyone. Since one of the guys brought two big goat legs yesterday, which we didn't use, Harold and Chris are preparing to barbecue them. John baked biscuits, and one of the guys, a vegetarian is making a big batch of baked ziti, something like lasagna, so it looks like there will be another feast today.

Monday evening, the farmers are having something for us, don't really know what. Then Thursday we have planned a trip to Foyah, finally. Tommy Hoff will go with us and we'll come back on Monday, which leaves less than a week here. The midwives are making a party for me on the last Friday afternoon. Daniel Freeman told me they've bought a "big billygoat" for $20 for the party. I hope we survive all the festivities!

Harold is trying hard to finish his water project before we leave, so hard when you can't get everything you need together at the same time. He keeps on trying.

This week I must sew Paye's uniform and rewrite the public health course for Loretta. Did I tell you Paye has been going to school? He's in ABC class and is the president. I can't believe he's been in class for nearly six weeks and apparently not causing a lot of humbug.

A typical village seen from the air.

THE MISSION YEARS

Dear Vikki and Gill,   **April 3, 1974, Gbedin**

We've decided to return to Liberia! About a month ago, Harold was offered the job of maintenance engineer at Phebe Hospital, the Lutheran Mission Hospital at Suakoko. We were interested, but had to wait to learn what the Mission Board had to say about it, which we just learned today.

They need him right now, but we have to finish at Gbedin—the Agriculture Minister refused to let Harold go, even a month early. So at the end of this month, we will terminate with Peace Corps and move to Phebe, where Harold will be employed for two to three months to take up the slack right now and to get a feel for the job. If he wants to stay, we will come home for two to three months, leave in July, and return for two years.

For Harold, it's so good for him to be working at something he feels is really worthwhile, for people who think he's great. At home he thinks he'd be working at some job just to have money for us to live, and at his age, maybe even have difficulty getting into an interesting field.

We would be provided a fine, furnished, roomy house at the mission on the hospital grounds, utilities, necessary transportation, medical care, travel to and from home, plus a good salary for Harold, around $9,000 a year, which is quite adequate in Liberia, with a chance to save quite a bit.

[*As with many missionary wives, Ruth wasn't hired or sworn in as a missionary, as Harold was, but was expected to find work to do and not just be idle.*] At home, I know it wouldn't be anything, considering the cost of living.

The hospital is about 100 beds, air-conditioning, good water supply (no more boiling needed). There is an education building for both registered nurses and LPNs, surgical techs and midwives. They have big maintenance shops, many homes for staff, a hostel for missionary kids, a plane and pilot to serve the Lutheran Mission bush stations, and an outreach preventive health program, which I am interested in. There is also a paddy rice project, just started.

Harold would be responsible for seeing that everything runs and gets done, even to building houses as needed. There is quite a maintenance staff to do the actual work. It's a big job, but one I'm sure he can handle, and they feel he can do well.

So my dears, I hope this doesn't come as too much of a shock. I do feel bad about missing so much of you three, and Judith and her family, and especially Mom. However, we feel that all of you want us to do what we feel is best for us, and we don't feel ready to come home and fit into the family—brothers and sisters on both sides—and routines there.

Baby Yah Ruth drank kerosene a couple nights ago and was pretty sick when we left Gbedin.

Dear Mother,   **April 21, 1974, Foya**

We plan to leave Monrovia and go directly to New York City to the Lutheran Board of Missions office, to get Harold's job details completed. Then we'll go on the same day to Washington, DC, for one or two days. We have to see people in the Peace Corp office there. Then we'll be on our way to the West Coast, to Vikki's probably first. As soon as we reach the States, we will call you. We are so excited about coming home—can hardly wait to see you and everyone.

We are having a short holiday just now. Thursday morning we left Gbedin for Foya, a 250-mile trip to the northwestern part of Liberia. You may remember, I wrote to you about the area on New Year's about a year ago. One of Harold's friends from the job, Thomas, came too.

We all stayed in the Ministry of Agriculture's guest house. It is quite nice, comfortable beds, clean linens, and a house boy to wash dishes, etc.

They do have huge cockroaches, though, the biggest I've ever seen. One was three inches long! Harold brought bug spray, as usual, which usually takes care of things like that.

We have several friends in Foya, former colleagues of Harold's, so it was fun to go back there. There are also a half dozen volunteers, so between all our friends, we were quite well taken care of for dinners.

Today, we left Foya and drove as far as the Walageisi mine area. It's about 17 miles off the main road, where a new iron mine is being developed. One of Harold's friends from Gbedin has a saw mill behind the mine site, and he had invited us to visit, for a long time now. We've just finished a chicken and rice dinner and soon will go "walk about" with his wife. It's quite a beautiful area, high forest, high mountains around almost solid iron, a very peaceful setting. There are lots of palm trees, bamboo trees, vines, typical bush, and also many tall timber trees, such as mahogany, whismore [*the Liberian name for niangon, a hardwood*], teak, and so on. These trees go straight up for one to two hundred feet before they have a branch.

Richard Dunbar, the mill owner, has a nice two-bedroom house here, electricity, good mountain water, and an efficient sawmill set-up. He says he must pay 40 percent of his gross for taxes to the government. Then you hear the government "big people" telling the populace they must help develop the country, operate their own businesses, etc. Pretty hard to sort out.

Anyway, we're enjoying a chance to see more of the country, if only for a few days. We will start home tomorrow, stop for lunch at the Lutheran Mission in Zorzor with some friends. Then it's on to Phebe for Harold to have another look around and get home by evening.

[*Ruth and Harold spent the next three months in the States visiting family and friends.*]

Dearest Vikki and all,   **August 9, 1974, Phebe Station**

We reached here on Saturday, after a three and a half hour ride on a muddy, slippery road, in a heavy rainfall all the way. We drove a VW bus fitted up as an ambulance, so had transportation all the way.

We were warmly welcomed. Arches made of palm branches were put up before each of the two driveways into our yard. They were bedecked with hibiscus blossoms. Dishes and kitchen utensils, linens, even a dozen eggs and a pineapple in the fridge, and a torch lily in a bowl on the table greeted us in the house. None of our own things have arrived yet.

We were given lunch by one family, invited to dinner by the chief doctor, a Liberian, and his wife, Puerto Rican, and dinner on Sunday by an American missionary family. He teaches in the campus school. Harold was immediately besieged by all kinds of urgent requests, among them air conditioning that doesn't work in the hospital, and an itemized list of maintenance needs for the next year, in one week! He will be very busy, so many things to be responsible for, including a crew of about fifty.

I've started to spend time with the Liberian nurse in charge of the outreach program. It's very similar to what I have been doing, but in different locations every day and also with more people. The hospital is hiring a Liberian counterpart to work with me, so perhaps I can work myself out of a job! This is my primary aim, since Liberians should handle their own business as soon as they can. Kirsten, the girl who started the program, was a new Cuttington graduate and did an outstanding job. The new nurse is one of my former students from Ganta. She just graduated in March.

Yesterday, I went to my first clinic, in a small town about 30 minutes away. We set up our equipment in a little palava hut, where patients were registered, diagnosed, treated, vaccinated, and given health talks. They pay 35 cents per child. We also had prenatal patients. Among the patients were one with cholera, a very ill child, one who was aborting, and one with TB. These were referred to the hospital, but we learned later that the child was taken into the bush instead.

It's been fun catching up with some of our old friends. Chris and Bruce Gaylord came one day and visited, and this weekend, Chris and Dale will stay overnight. Chris is on the way home, leaving Thursday. Jeff and Gail Thompson came to visit, too. It will be nice living near enough to see them often. Of course, in Monrovia, we saw lots of old friends too. Everyone was happy to see us back.

Dearest Mother and all,   **September 27, 1974, Lamco**

Time has flown by, and we have been swamped with work and all kinds of visitors, meetings, problems, etc. Both have a full schedule and are exhausted and ready for bed early. We leave the house at 7 AM and sometimes don't get back until 6 PM, or so. Right now, we're at Lamco mine for a weekend of rest—although Harold came yesterday for machine shop business. We've had a young Peace Corps couple as guests this week. He's a psychiatrist and she an RN, both will work in Monrovia. So we decided to bring them here to see more of up-country and for ourselves to get away from the constant pressures at Phebe.

The Lutheran church has a guest house here for mission and church workers which we are staying in. It is a completely furnished, two-bed-room house, so we're quite comfortable. Today we will go to the market, a usual Saturday activity and always interesting to new volunteers, go to the swimming pool, and tonight, go out to dinner, all a pleasant change.

There is a good vocational high school near here for boys, which we want to look at for John for next year (run by Anglican Church broth-ers). So we will go there sometime today too. We are going to try to send Martha to a Lutheran mission high school next year, so are working on that too. Kids have to pass an entrance exam to get in.

Dearest Mother,   **October 4, 1974, Monrovia**

While Harold is off taking care of business, I will get a letter ready to mail before we leave Monrovia. We came yesterday AM for all kinds of supplies—medicine, parts for motors and cars, groceries, and so on. It's always a hassle finding what you're looking for and taking care of any kind of paper work. You can't imagine the inefficiency in most of the busi-ness houses and government offices. I guess I shouldn't be writing such things; could get me in trouble!

Harold's shopping for a motor bike, a 90 Honda, for use at the mission. He has so much running around to do over the whole mission station, and so often the vehicles are needed elsewhere, so this will save lots of energy. Our house is a ten-minute walk from his office and the hos-pital, and he is back and forth and around and constantly in a hurry.

Kirsten, the Liberian girl who was in charge of the community health outreach program, finally left for Minnesota for two years' study, so I'm now officially director of the program. [*Kirsten had received a grant to study in the States.*]

There is much to do, a staff of eight plus two new Peace Corps vol-unteers, and the entire county to cover. The first thing we're going to do is take a couple of days off and sit down together and make some plans for the year. So far the planning has been for a week at a time, and I can't manage that way. We're in the midst of a measles vaccination campaign, too. Measles epidemics occur beginning in December or January so we're working against time just now. It takes six weeks to gain immunity. (Measles is one of the leading causes of death among young kids in West Africa.)

Yesterday three young RNs arrived from California to work for Phebe for six to nine months as volunteers. An organization called Vespers, a Lutheran group, recruited them and helped pay their way over, and Phebe will provide housing but no pay or money to live on. They've all been working in hospitals in Oakland, California, and are eager to work with my program, so I'm kind of excited about all the possibilities. There is another nurse who has been at Zorzor hospital working with their outreach program for the past one and a half years. She has done some outstanding things there, especially developing teaching methods and aids that are effective for illiterate people. I've spent some time with her and expect to continue to do so, in order to utilize some of her ideas. Fortunately, I can go by plane in thirty minutes, rather than spending three to four hours on the road and arriving too exhausted to do anything.

We've just received word that the ship carrying our things has arrived in port so maybe by the end of next week we will get them in Phebe. They have to get through customs and then get transported up country, so there is still hope! I'm really anxious for my sewing machine to be here.

Dearest Mother and all,   October 6, 1974, Phebe

I'm finally in charge officially of the Public Health program so we are taking a day or two off just to try to assess where the program is and where we should be going in the next few months. I don't know how this will work since two-thirds of my staff are pretty uneducated and have never participated in any such activity.

Today Harold went for a short airplane ride, his first here in Liberia. The pilot had to fly a patient home; he'd come in for suturing earlier, after sending a radio message here. Harold has been wanting to go for a ride but either never had time or there was no seat in the plane. This one can take three to four passengers and can take off and land on very short fields.

I will fly with him to Zorzor again next week, so much nicer than driving. Everyone says we will have coal-tar road to Gbarnga by July 26, 1975.

I'll be surprised if it actually happens that fast since it hasn't been completely surveyed yet. Parts of the road are indescribably bad. Harold and I went to Monrovia Thursday and Friday for business for Phebe. It is 114 miles, 80 of which are coal-tar. The trip took three hours each way.

Dearest Mother,   **October 19, 1974, Phebe**

All is well here, but we are very, very busy. Harold has had so many problems to cope with and works until late every evening and even on weekends. I'm trying to reorganize the community health department, retrain the staff, develop procedures, and such, so never seem to finish.

I just spent two days at Zorzor Hospital with a nurse who has a fine outreach program and was very generous with her ideas and materials. It will be a big help to me.

I flew up and back, a half hour trip each way which is so interesting. You fly over miles of trees, tall, fully leafed, no ground showing through at all but occasionally a glint of water through the leaves. Then you come to an area where there are lots of palm trees and among them are upland rice farms—the brush is cut down by hand (with cutlass), planted, and scratched in by hand. There is always a palm-thatched hut or two, where the people spend the day, out of the sun or rain. The farms cover acres and acres way out in the bush; you will fly over a town among the trees—up to 100 houses, some at least an eight-hour walk to a motor road. Also a few houses may be clustered together way out in the bush. The pilot says he sees elephants every once in a while. I always watch closely but so far haven't seen any.

Martha is here this weekend. She took the entrance exam for the Lutheran Training Institute, a school near Zorzor junior and senior high. It costs about $400 a year (room, board, tuition, and books) but is a good school and should prepare her for nursing, which she wants to try for.

Our things finally arrived Friday so we've had a good time getting things unpacked and stowed away. Everything arrived without mishap, even bone china cups.

Dearest Mother and all,   **October 26, 1974, Phebe**

Hopefully this will reach you in time to say happy birthday. Sending a letter now doesn't take so long since it goes from here to Monrovia by plane, and the plane goes several times a week.

There is a new group of Peace Corps volunteers, and I'm helping with their training along with my job. Yesterday Agnes, the Liberian lady (third grade education), who teaches health on our outreach team, went with me to Gbarnga, where we each took a group and showed them how to cook baby food from rice, greens, beans, benne (sesame) seeds, etc. They had to pound the rice in the mortar until it is fine like flour and make gruel from it. Beat the beans and benne seeds, etc., to either mix with the rice or make other food. They worked hard but had fun.

The main thing we try to teach the village women is to start to feed their babies by four to five months, along with nursing them, and to prepare body-building foods that the baby can digest rather than giving them plain cooked rice with only palm oil on it. You have to do it over and over. Agnes is very effective since she speaks eight or nine dialects, communicates so well with the people, and has been given a good foundation in basic health concepts.

Thursday one of the practical nurses on our team and I went by air, a twenty-minute trip, to a town in the bush that has a nice little airstrip. We took measles vaccine and vaccinated all the kids from six months to six years. The town has about 50 houses and is only accessible by air or by an all-day walk. Having the plane is wonderful for being able to reach places like this that can never have decent health care because they are so isolated. We will start to bring our under-fives and prenatal clinic there once a month so we can continue immunization for other communicable diseases and try to improve their health practices with our educational program. That is a long process since people don't change the way they live very easily. Most of the complaints are fevers and diarrhea, both of which are related to malnutrition. So there is a lot of work to do!

The people were very cooperative. We held a meeting with them about returning, always very interesting with many people having to talk. Later one man had his wife cook rice and soup for us (potato greens, fish, dried meat, pepper, and palm oil). One lady brought me a tiny basket about the size of a cup which she had made, containing what they call country bread. This is rice that has been parched, and then beaten in a mortar until it is about the size of bulgur wheat. Tastes a bit like popcorn, although it's still raw rice!

Something new happened to me there. While we were working, giving the injections, I got a lot of bites on the backs of my legs, thighs. Great welts appeared, itched like mad, and by the time I was back at Phebe, all the area was red and swollen. Yesterday Agnes looked at it and said it was bed bug bites! They apparently were hidden in the wicker chair I sat on and were too happy to find some new blood! I think they will be on me, the bites I mean, for days, itching too much. Next time I think I'll just take a little wooden stool, rather than a fine chair, which is always brought for a "stranger."

This town is at the edge of a river, the St. Paul, and many people in the town go across to make rice farms. They use a long dug-out canoe and a small paddle, and even though the river is fairly swift, they push off upstream and by the time they are across have drifted down stream maybe a half a block where there is another landing. There are either crocodiles or alligators in the river, and one man in the town is an alligator hunter and fisherman. He has a long net which he stretches far out into the river for fish every day.

Harold is fine but busy with multitudes of problems. Every day brings a new one. Prices have gone up so drastically here in Liberia, so many employees are becoming dissatisfied with their wages, which have not been raised for a long time, if ever. Since this is a mission-supported church, the budget is always too low, so Harold is really in a bind when workers want more money. Actually even government workers have not had raises, and prices have been allowed to go up more than double in many cases. A bag of rice is over $20, and most people feed a big family. Agnes feeds 14, mostly nieces, nephews, and grandchildren; a bag of rice lasts three weeks in her family, and they cook once a day!

Dearest Mother,   **October 29, 1974, Phebe**

We are finally getting our house fixed up the way we'd like it; with our own things here, it's a little more homey. We bought two hammocks made from palm thatch rope and have them hanging in our big screened piazza, also some wicker chairs and end tables. Now we will paint the floor (it's cement), and things should be nicer. There are leafy trees all around our house so when you're on the piazza, it's like you're in the woods, shady and cool.

Our life is much easier here with so many conveniences and comforts. Our Peace Corps friends kid us about our house, which is pretty nice. We do have lots of unexpected overnight guests.

Last week a new volunteer, Bridget Hagerty, very Irish, stayed with us. She's 71, an RN and midwife, very energetic. Has worked in Malaysia and Indonesia, in fact was a prisoner in Singapore for three and a half years when Pearl Harbor fell. Quite an interesting lady.

Right now I'm helping with the Peace Corps training program for new health volunteers, about 22 people. It's taking lots of time and energy so I'll be glad when it's over, middle of next week for most of it. They've been going out on mobile clinic visits with us, with vaccination teams, home visits, etc., learning about setting up and operating an outreach program.

Do you still have your old LPN magazines? If so we could use them for our LPN and midwife student library. I'm working with a committee to set one up, and we could use nursing magazines suitable for LPN level.

Dearest Mother and all,   **November 16, 1975, Lamco**

The leaves are already beginning to fall from some of the trees. Rubber trees lose their leaves after turning red and brown. It is so noticeable because there are so many rubber farms wherever you go. Liberia is pretty hilly, not high but up and down, and when you are high enough to look over an expanse of land, it looks like fall in the northwest. Lots of brilliant red trees in among the green.

We've spent the weekend at Lamco mine again. Harold has electric motor repair work done here at the vocational training center, so we could combine business with pleasure. It's so good to get completely away from Phebe—the only way to avoid constant requests for help, etc., night and day, for Harold. We know a lot of people all the way up the road—100 miles—and also here, so it's nice to have a chance to visit.

Yesterday I was at the open air produce market and met an old friend from Gbedin, the head midwife with whom I worked so much. Her name is Ma Naabah; she doesn't speak any English but I was able to converse in Mano enough so we could find out where we both were staying, what we were doing, how she is feeling, etc. Later we went to her daughter's house, where she's staying for two to three months, and took her a lappa "for her something." They wanted to cook for us but we had other plans plus there are about eight little kids in the house, and I couldn't stay and eat the food the kids needed.

But she said we must come today because she would look for something for me. You can't refuse without offending people. It's just their generous way. It was a really happy time. All the market ladies around were so pleased to see us happy together and clapped every time I'd say something in their dialect. Laughed too since my accent is pretty bad!

We will start back today and stop in Sanniquellie and have lunch with John and Martha. School will be finished soon, so John will go to the country and work on his mother's sugar cane farm, and Martha will come to Phebe and stay with us and help me at the hospital, and we'll help her with some extra studies to make sure she will be ready for a better school next term.

Dear Rich, Evelyn, and boys,   **November 17, 1974, Phebe**

Harold and I just returned from a weekend trip to Lamco mine area. It's a Swedish enclave since the iron mine there is operated by the Swedes. You can hardly realize you're in Liberia with so many white, blond people around. There is a large Liberian community too, but management is predominantly Swedish.

It's a very modern mine production, and they ship lots of ore, very high grade ore, by rail to the ocean, 200 miles away, and then load it on ships. We live 100 miles from there and go about once a month. Harold has electrical motor work done there at the vocational training center. We went Friday afternoon, went out to dinner and a movie; to the market on Saturday, visited several friends, and left this morning.

The road is so dusty just now, rainy season is nearly finished and the roads are like the ones in Eastern Washington between Brewster and Grandpa's ranch. The traffic is quite heavy at times, and visibility is almost nil. The dust is red, and my hair is usually the same color. It's impossible to keep windows up because of the heat.

People keep saying the road will be paved by July 26 (Independence Day), but it doesn't seem likely. Surveyors have been on the road ever since we came from home leave, pounding stakes in at the edge of the road, peering through their transits. This was done another time a couple of years ago, and nothing came of it, although the surveyors (they're from Australia) say the money has been allocated. It would be a blessing to have coal-tar roads.

I send a VW bus out five days a week with a mobile clinic team, and a Land Rover jeep about three days a week with vaccination people. The hardest part of the job is keeping the vehicles in running order, with the kind of roads we travel on. It takes close to an hour to go 20 to 30 miles, and some of our clinic towns are 40 to 50 miles away so you can see how much time we spend just traveling.

We take a nurse or health assistant to examine and prescribe, one to dispense medicine and vaccinate, a native woman to do the health teaching, and a fellow with about a sixth grade education to register and weigh the kids and also to drive the bus. We hold under-fives and prenatal clinics and give instructions regarding family spacing. Actually we're involved with many related things—send out a vaccination team, also, into the bush, publish a newsletter monthly, do in-service education for the fellows in the county health posts, supervise seven Peace Corps volunteers and some nursing students, and so on. Life is never dull but sometimes it's good to get away for a day or two, like up to Lamco.

Harold has just bought a 90 Honda for himself. He got it duty free since it's just mainly for his travel around the mission. It's a big place, and he's on the go a good deal of the time, and so often his truck has to be used for other business. I'm sure he didn't need much excuse to buy it; he's always enjoyed riding one, and I can ride on the back.

Some of the clinics we go to can only be reached by footpath or by air, and some are one- or two-days walk, so we go in the plane, a 20- to 30-minute flight. The Lutheran church has a four-passenger plane with STOL [*short take-off and landing*] capability, and every Thursday they take two to three of our team (depending on the size of the strip) into one of these isolated towns. It's really enjoyable to fly as low as we do over the jungle.

Two weeks ago (I wasn't there), they saw five elephants so the pilot circled round and round so they could take pictures. I'm always watching but haven't seen any yet. Looking down on the rain forest is like looking down on densely packed broccoli and parsley! It always amazes me to see a town in the midst of such a distant place, sometimes over 100 houses. Of course, it wasn't long ago that there were not any roads at all, so I guess a town just grew almost anywhere. Nowadays, you expect to see them along the motor road.

Dearest Mother and all,   **November 20, 1974, Sankpillai**

We are sitting here in this town, Sankpillai, which is way up in the northeastern corner of Bong County—about a one and a half hour drive,

44 miles from Phebe. The town is at the end of the road, very near the Guinea border. We came today to bring new freezing tins for the vaccines that our team is carrying in the bush. The driver, two Peace Corps guys, and I arrived about 12 and sat down to wait in the town for the three vaccination people. One came to meet us, but we're still awaiting the other two who stopped in another town to vaccinate. It's close to four so we'll get home late, but we have to wait for the ice box.

But it's been an interesting, entertaining day so we haven't minded the wait. The town has over 100 houses, most of them with thatched roofs, whitewashed, and some decorated with designs painted with thin brown or gray clay. Many of the windows are covered with woven mats, and ceilings are covered this way, too. It looks like a more prosperous town; the people have coffee and cocoa farms nearby and also have rice farms.

The health assistant who operates the clinic met us and immediately took us to his house for food—rice and a soup made with some kind of meat (I didn't ask what it was) and beans, kind of like a gravy. It tasted all right and not too hot. Many people came in and stood and watched us eat and talked about us. Surprisingly, quite a few of the people speak some kind of English.

One fellow who appears to have some education has been our escort all the time and is so funny—partly from cane juice, I'm afraid. He told us he could read Kpelle book, and this is how it came about. When he was a boy he fell asleep for three days, and the people were "coming to bury him" when he woke up. And when he was conscious again, he could read the Kpelle language. (It is written in a phonetic alphabet.) He wanted to demonstrate this gift so we agreed. He went and got a well-worn Kpelle language book and proceeded to read us a biblical story—"let who is without sin cast the first stone," of course with a Liberian twist. He had one of our fellows interpret for him. Several people came in and listened, too, very attentively, although I'm sure they've all heard him read the same story many times. He took us to see his parents' graves—they are behind his house and have a thatched-roofed hut, without walls, built over them.

Next day. We got home late yesterday—had to stop and visit a clinic on the way to set up a meeting for the county health workers. One is held each month in a different site around the county. We also stopped in a town where the blacksmith who makes the little brass figures lives.

It's really interesting to see how they work. Their blacksmith shop is a large, thatched-roofed, circular building with no walls—just posts around the edge. There is a small fire pit and anvil and a bellows that a small boy beats like a drum. They all sit cross legged, bare foot, and beat everything out by hand. Amazing what nice work can be done this way.

We have a Swiss guest just now, a diesel mechanic who is working on our power plant. Tomorrow evening Betsy and Bob Cummings (he's the psychiatrist who was here before) will come for the weekend, and next weekend one of our Gbedin friends will come with her baby—never a dull moment here!

Dearest Mother and all,   **December 1, 1974, Phebe**

This has been another busy week, but we have a holiday tomorrow and had one on Friday so it's given us a breather. We spent Thursday eve (Thanksgiving) with friends in Lamco for turkey dinner and brought a friend from Gbedin back with us for the weekend. She has a darling three-month-old girl. She just left this morning. It's kind of nice to be alone since we do have a *lot* of visitors, many for overnight.

I have a man who does the housework and does some cooking but goes home around two in the afternoon. So guests make quite a bit of work for me. Martha will be spending vacation with us (two months) so she will be a big help. She will also help with my outreach clinic. We've been taking care of her school and living expenses for the past year and want to help her get through high school. (She starts ninth grade in March.)

The weather has been so comfortable since we returned, and now dry season is here and the nights will be cooler. The leaves on many types of trees turn red and fall from some so the bush looks quite different this season. There are many poinsettias; one by our house is as tall as the roof peak, and it has become fiery red in the past month. There are so many beautiful trees and bushes although not nearly as many flowering ones as in Hawaii.

Did I tell you I'd finished sewing curtains for the living room, a dark blue and white African print, also made cushions for porch chairs and hammocks from tie-dye cloth, so we're looking much more homey.

There is a tennis court, just packed dirt, next to our house so we are talking about trying to learn to play tennis. Harold has been playing horseshoes for relaxation in the evening but I don't do anything but come home and cook dinner and keep on working on material for my department. So we'll see how ambitious I am!

Dearest Mother and all,   December 13, 1974, Phebe

While we are in Monrovia, we'll get some letters off. It's 6 AM, and everyone is sleeping so I have a nice quiet time. We are staying with Betsy and Bob Cumming for a couple of days while we take care of business. They live on the beach, so the roar of the surf is a constant sound, makes me think I'm back at Westport or Copalis, except for the weather, which is always quite warm and humid in Monrovia.

We went to a "swearing in" ceremony and party for the new Peace Corps volunteers whom I had helped train, so we combined that with business for the mission. Today we'll go back. I'm trying to do Christmas shopping too, not easy here since things are very hard to find, and prices are ridiculous, especially on anything that is imported. I don't know how people here manage with such low incomes. They receive as low as $40 per month, some get $60 to $70, and a pair of men's shoes costs $30.

It really doesn't seem like Christmas. It's school vacation now and along with the warm weather and no holiday decorations, I have to keep reminding myself that Christmas will soon be here. We are going to have a brunch for the people who stay at Phebe over Christmas, and all of us will have a potluck Christmas dinner together. Some of the people haven't been away from home at Christmas before and are feeling quite homesick, especially some of the single people. So two other women and I decided we'd have a kind of progressive Christmas day for that reason.

Dearest Mother,   December 27, 1974, Phebe

It hardly seems that Christmas can be over already. A lot of people had artificial Christmas trees and lights and the usual home decorations but I can't quite get used to that here. We had a palm branch standing in a corner—palm branches are long, this one reached from floor to ceiling—decorated with your pretty baubles.

On Christmas Eve we went to a candlelight service at the chapel. It was quite lovely with many white candles lit, green leaves, similar to evergreen, bright red poinsettia blossoms, which grow profusely here and, actually, are trees, and red hibiscus all around the alter and along the sides of the chapel.

The next morning we were awakened early by carolers who walked along carrying candles as they sang. Then we went to church for a sharing service, in which everyone who wished, spoke, read from the Bible, sang or asked the group to sing a special song. When we finished, everyone came to our house for coffee and sweet rolls and stayed and visited together. There were over 30, including kids.

About the time these people left, Geoff Thompson, a Peace Corps volunteer from Cuttington whom we've known for a couple of years, came with three new guys who have only been in Liberia three weeks. Geoff's wife Gail is home in Los Angeles with a broken ankle, and we knew he and the new Peace Corps volunteers would be lonesome so invited them for dinner. I made mashed potatoes, fried chicken, frozen peas, etc., just like home (we usually eat rice and soup!). Martha had arrived the day before so she was here, too.

Well, anyway, we all had more than enough to eat. Then later people started to drop in, there are several young nurses here on a short-term basis whom we've enjoyed, and they stayed for a while. When they left, toward evening, we walked about to visit people and ended up at Dr. Minge's, where they were having an open house with coffee and Christmas cookies. (There are some really nice people here; of course, some we don't find quite as compatible but in general there are no problems.) So it was a full and friendly day, which we both enjoyed, but we could get a bit sentimental when we read Christmas messages from home, easy to get lumps in throats and a few tears in the corners of our eyes.

I've been indescribably busy with a dozen things and found it hard to do anything for Christmas. One of the things that has taken a lot of work was starting to write and mimeograph a monthly public health newsletter. We've done two issues now, and people are quite happy with it, although from state-side standards, there's much to be desired. My days of having a secretary and duplicating department, etc., really spoiled me— so many things I've never done. But I've learned to run the mimeo and ditto machine, cut stencils. I can't type, though, more's the pity. Now with the new Peace Corps nurse and health educators who will work with us, I'll turn the production of the newsletter over to them and only do an overall review of the material, a big load off me.

Another big project was writing a report of this program (it's a year old) and preparing the new budget estimates. The report is meant to go to Ministry of Health people, mission people in New York, donors to our program, hospital board, and such types.

The day before Christmas, Dr. Gwenigale, the hospital administrator, brought me a letter from the Ministry of Health saying Bong County was one of three counties selected for a special "expansion of immunization" program, supported by WHO, and needed a proposed plan from us quick, quick. So here we go again!

Fortunately, there is a new missionary coming in early January to work with me in outreach. He has an MS in public health, and when I suggested to Dr. Gwenigale that he be put in charge of the new immunization program, he agreed. So all I have to do just now is plan it enough to satisfy the ministry and then just help orient the new fellow, maybe.

In between I try to get some sewing done, made a robe for Harold for Christmas, some dresses for baby Vicki, a tiny Liberian shirt for Dr. G's new baby boy, and a caftan for myself for Christmas. I'm also trying to make curtains for two of the bedrooms, but now that Martha is here, she can sew the curtains. Martha will stay with us until school starts, March 1. She'll help me at home and with mobile clinics and do her school sewing. It's fun having her; she's a very pleasant girl, 18 years old, and will start ninth grade. Kids start school so late and then have three years before first grade, so you can see why so many are this age and just starting high school.

The only high schools that are good are the mission schools. Government schools have a long way to go before the schooling kids get there can be considered adequate. And if you want to go on to school, you can't make it coming out of a government school. So we will try to keep her there through high school, and John at Carrol High, the Catholic boy's school. It is in upper Nimba County, near Lamco. Both of the children have developed into very responsible, dependable kids and really apply themselves to study. They work like troopers when they are with us, which we've encouraged, since we see so many youngsters who expect their parents or some benefactor to pay their way, and then when vacation comes they come around and bluff (act the big man).

*Harold with Poliakah, Ruth with Maria, who lived with them for a
while, Martha, and John.*

1975

Dearest Vikki and Gill,   **January 1, 1975, Phebe**

Today is a nice quiet day. We had people in for dinner last evening, and
went out visiting later for a New Year celebration. Later today, we will
take a drive over behind Cuttington College where some big land clearing is being done for the July 26th celebration. They are putting in a new
road way back in the bush, for about 12 miles. At one spot, they went up
over the top of a mountain, actually just a big hill, compared to Northwest
mountains, but steep and high.

There is a tiny village on the top, where the view is fantastic. You are
above the tree tops and the valley below, and you can see for miles all
around. We want to go to take some pictures, because when the land is
cleared, the bush will be gone. We'll take the Alameda nurses with us. So
many of the people here (volunteers and missionaries) just never get out
into the villages but are always anxious to go.

There are so many people coming and going here that it's hard to keep track of all of them. Lots of short-term people who come without pay but receive their transportation and housing. I also have a Peace Corps RN working with me, especially in in-service education for the health assistants who run the 33 health posts in the county. She is also going to take over my monthly newsletter. We've published two so far. We try to aim it at people who have limited education, like less than high school.

Dearest Mother,   **January 1, 1975, Gbedin**

I'm going to start off the New Year by writing to you and resolve to be more regular about writing. It looks as though I'll be a bit less busy, so I'm looking forward to some free time for writing and sewing.

Martha is with us now until school starts so she will be a help here as well as in the public health program. She is going to do her school sewing and some for me and for Poliakah, who will be living with us and starting first grade. Martha will sew curtains for two bedrooms from lappas, and a couple of bedspreads for a set of bunk beds in one of the rooms.

Harold constructed lamps for me—three for the living room and two for our bedroom, and another for a guest room. They are made from baskets with fixtures attached. They're very inexpensive, since the baskets cost less than a dollar. They cast a nice light and are attractive. There are some ugly chairs on our piazza with ratty-looking seats, so I made covers using patchwork from my sewing scraps, and now they are much less ugly. My sewing machine is a godsend.

Yesterday, a new nurse-anesthetist arrived for a six month stay, to replace Carmen Gwenigale, who just had a baby. She is retired from the army and is much older than I. She was sent by World Brotherhood Exchange, who pays for travel for the short term volunteer workers. She is provided her room here, but must pay for her food. A farmer is being sent for Zorzor, to take over the rice project. He's sponsored by the same group. Then in two weeks a public health man and his wife, an RN, are coming to work with me. They are sent by the mission for two to three years. Hopefully he will be satisfactory. I can use some help.

Dear Vikki and Gill,   **January 5, 1975, Phebe**

This has been a nice weekend, nothing that I had to do, just time for myself. Stephanie and Greg arrived just before dinner on Friday evening on their way to Monrovia. They are getting ready to leave Liberia, starting with Cameroon. They stayed overnight, and left about noon the next day. She had borrowed a shirt pattern and couldn't seem to do the sleeves, so we worked on it. Then I cut a dress from one she was wearing, and sewed it. I used the design stitching disc to trim the neck and armholes. It's from green and pink tie-dye. The back is low. Today, I sewed a short dress from Fanti cloth, and again trimmed it with the design disc stitching, so there is no handwork.

We had also invited a doctor and his wife for dinner. He is Gio, has been studying and working in Italy for 14 years. He will be assigned to Grand Gedeh County as county health officer. The doctor's wife is Italian, blonde, doesn't speak any English. We cooked Joloff rice, with beef, chicken, and shrimp, for them.

You can't imagine the amount of company we have for meals. Of course, most of the time we are pretty casual, so it's fairly easy. Friday eve I'm cooking Chinese food for some friends here. They have four young children. I'll try to do shrimp, fish, pork, and chicken, some greens and chicken broth. We will use the wok for the first time.

We now have a part-time dog. Some people moved away and left their dog. Harold is trying to persuade him to come and live with us and be our watchdog. He is quite independent, comes and eats, comes inside for a while, sits down outside, and then takes off. Harold thinks he will be good rogue insurance.

A rogue came into our house about a month ago. Removed the window louvers on the back porch one night, but couldn't find anything to take except small change from my purse. We lock the door into the hall, the empty bedroom door, our bedroom, and the storage closet, every night. Then I forgot to put my purse away!

There are always people coming and going here. It's amazing the people who come to Liberia. Tonight, an American medical student, a pretty girl, arrived for a month's experience. Next week, a man and his wife are coming to work with me. He has an MS in public health. Hope he's got his head on straight! We do get some strange people! Oh, yes. An Indian MD is coming for a year assignment. Housing all these people is a real problem. Harold and his crew are responsible for keeping the houses in good (ha ha) repair, so he is frequently tearing his hair due to lack of materials or money to do the work. And things deteriorate so fast in this country.

Martha is busy sewing these days, trying to get things ready for school. She will start vacation school this week in Gbarnga for five weeks, and try to get a little math review.

Dearest Mother,   **January 12, 1975, Phebe**

We have not had rain for weeks now. The leaves have fallen from many of the trees, and the grass looks pretty brown. When we walk in our yard it's quite noisy with the dry, crackly leaves. There's a family of little chickens that visit quite often, and they scratch in the grass and leaves and sound like a big person walking past.

Today we took a drive—74 miles round trip—which took four hours. We were delivering an ice box to a clinic so Harold drove the bus so he could set up the box and get it started. It's just a small kerosene ice box for vaccines. The road is off the main route way back in the bush so we took a young woman medical student with us. She's come to spend 10 weeks here and hasn't seen any of the country yet.

When we were going by one town, we came upon a place where the men tried to divert us into the town rather than by passing it. However Harold continued on, and then we discovered why they didn't want us to pass that way. They were constructing the fence that guards the "devil bush," which is where the boys go to bush school They had four large posts about eight feet tall driven into the ground about two to three feet apart. On the ground in front and near the road was a lot of freshly made raffia, stripped from palm branches, which would be used to weave the fence, apparently around these posts. I've seen such a fence before but never just being made. When we came back we made sure we went through the town and didn't take a chance on being stopped and sent back. Bush society is very secret, and a person can get in serious trouble if they defy or ignore the rules.

Yesterday I had to go to a town in another part of the county for our monthly health meeting. It also was 75 miles round trip but in just the opposite direction, up near the Guinea border. We took our VW bus and the Cuttington bus and Dr. Gwenigale's car, making about 35 people plus others who reached there other ways. These are the health assistants and other public health people in the county. The people entertained us well, even had their music makers. The instruments are hand-carved and the music is a combination of singing and blowing or beating on the drum.

The town people built a beautiful palm-thatch shelter for us, made benches by driving sticks into the ground and laying sticks on top and tying them together with rattan. It was really fine. They cooked rice, huge pans of it, palm butter and meat, pepper soup with pig meat and palm cabbage, all very hot. Also served palm wine and Fanta. Everyone who attends pays a dollar to help with the food. The 20-passenger bus we rented from Cuttington used four gallons of oil. Was I glad to get back, afraid all the time I'd be stranded in the bush with 20 people to worry about.

Dearest Vikki,   **January 12, 1975, Phebe**

It's getting late, after a busy weekend, but I want to write a few lines anyway. Yesterday I spent all day in a little town in the bush. It was close to 40 miles away, up near the Guinea border, for a public health meeting. It was a long day. Harold wanted to start the kerosene fridge for the man, and take him some vaccines. We also took a female medical student. We drove 75 miles round trip.

One of the health volunteers will work there in the clinic, so she went with us, and we carried her belongings in the bus, too. It was an enjoyable trip but very wearing. You know what the roads are like. It's very dusty and hot if you have to close the windows very much.

There are so many people coming and going you wouldn't believe it. Yesterday, three eye doctors and a surgical nurse arrived for a two-week stay. They are with the Christian Medical Society, whose members go to a foreign country for two to three weeks on their vacation. They pay their own way, except that the hospital furnishes room and board. They will do lots of eye surgeries. An anesthetist is here for six weeks and will work while Carmen is on maternity leave. A young seminary student is here for nine months doing his internship. Every month we seem to get someone for a short-term stay.

Dearest Mother,   **January 20, 1975, Phebe**

We took last weekend off and went to Lamco, mostly to get away, but Harold had to get parts for my outreach bus, mostly brakes, which he can buy in Lamco. It was a nice break, but the dust is so bad on the roads that it's not too pleasant to drive. It's about a four-hour drive, 100 miles from Phebe.

You can't imagine what happened to us on the way. We left about noon Friday, hoping to reach there before businesses closed. We were in a VW bus, which we rent from the hospital for 10 cents a mile. Just outside of Gbarnga, 12 miles from home, the motor started to roar, and soon Harold said, "I think the motor fell out." He got out and looked, and sure enough, the motor had indeed fallen out and was resting in the dirt!

It happened near the home of a Lebanese family we know, who arrived soon after. With their help, we pushed the car off the road and into their driveway. We left Martha in the vehicle to watch our things, and Claudia, the new medical student, and I went to the Lebanese people's house, about a half mile away, to wait. Harold caught a ride back to Phebe. There he got a pickup and a mechanic, came back, and with a jack and pole, they hoisted the motor up, tied it with a rope secured around the bumper, and Harold drove it back to Phebe! We four then transferred our things into the pickup and took off again. It was then 4 PM.

We dropped Martha off at her family in Gbedin and finally reached Lamco, where we all took showers to remove about five pounds of dirt from each of us. By the time we went out to eat, it was nearly midnight. Nearly everything, like stores, closes by five or six, so there is no way to buy anything to cook if you arrive after hours.

Today, when we came back, we stopped to pick up Martha. Her father had brought a gourd of palm wine, so we all had to sit down in their piazza and drink some. They gave Martha a big pan of rice when we left. Of course, there were many others who came to visit us—many of Ciam's old friends and they all asked about him. We also visited Bea. Her three little girls have grown so much. They all had birthdays this month, so I bought them each a little pair of panties.

Then we took off, but saw people we knew as we drove through Gbedin town, so again and again, we had to stop and see all the new babies and old friends. They kept saying, "Ma, why you can't come back to us?" One of Harold's mechanic friends lives in this town, so we went to his house, where again they had palm wine, this time in a water bucket, full too!

The house was soon jammed with people, many of whom had been my patients in the clinic and many who gave me credit for their babies being alive. It was a very nostalgic time and lots of fun. For Claudia, it was quite an experience, since she wouldn't have a chance to visit in anyone's home in this way around Phebe. She has been here two weeks, and will stay eight more, soon to graduate from medical school in Pennsylvania. We finally reached home about 5:50—had left Lamco at 10:30.

Before I had finished preparing dinner, a taxi pulled up into our yard, and Adama stepped out. She is a friend from Ganta, a Mandingo lady who sells cloth and jewelry. So then, we had to prepare dinner for her and her little three-year-old boy, Abou.

She and Abou will stay a few days. She wants to "rest a while," and not have any children for a while. So I'll take her to the clinic, and have Gertrude, our family planning midwife, give her a loop [*intrauterine contraceptive device*], if she can.

We certainly have our bad days and get pretty frustrated and discouraged, but it is only temporary. We feel we are where God wants us to be, and that he has a plan, even though we don't know what it is all the time.

Dearest Mother,   **January 26, 1975, Phebe**

This is budget meeting time, and we have just learned that our support will be way under what is needed. So there are many things to ponder, how to manage, what to cut, etc. It's especially hard for Harold who has the biggest responsibility, trying to keep things operating and running.

One good thing was permission to renovate an old building that is currently being used as a kitchen (for patients' families to cook for themselves) and turn it into an outreach office and classroom. (We will have to build a palava hut for the cooking business first.)

My outreach people, around 15, have been working out of a tiny office in the hospital. Packing up medicine and vaccines, doing visual aids work, record keeping, etc. It's mass confusion most of the time. Dr. Gwenigale finally decided I could have the kitchen (I asked for it two or three months ago), and Harold estimates we can renovate it, make work tables and shelves, put up mud block walls, etc., for under $500, including the work. We have some gift money already ($235), so we're ready to go as soon as he can get some supplies—cement and planks. I usually work at home, have staff meetings, etc., because there's no room elsewhere, and the office is sweltering since it's an inside room with no windows or ventilation.

Yesterday we had an interesting trip. We took a group of senior nursing students from Monrovia, who are in public health affiliation with me, on a bush walk to a waterfall about 10 miles from here. Harold drove the bus and took seven females. The falls are a series of rocky ledges, the first one quite high, and during rainy season all are covered with torrents of water but just now there is much less. It was cool and shady, quite a lovely spot for a picnic.

These students are Liberian girls but have always lived in Monrovia so this was quite an adventure for them. Most haven't been in a village since they were small children. In fact, I've met quite a few people who have gone to school in Monrovia or lived on a mission near there and know very little about their own country in the interior. I've seen much more of the bush than they have!

Dearest Mother,   **February 2, 1975, Phebe**

Here it is, another new week, and we've been here six months already. My work keeps me so busy that the days aren't long enough, and the evenings are busy, too, because we have so many meal guests. When strangers come, they are rotated around, and we seem to get more than our share. People say they are going to put up a hotel sign for us!

Also, now we have our children with us for this month, John and Martha, getting them ready for school, which starts March 1. Also Poliakah, John's small sister, will live with us and attend school here. She is about eight, and she has never gone to school. It will be different having a little girl with us again. I had her checked at the hospital when she came, and found she had both hookworm and malaria, both of which are being treated now. For hookworm, one can take one dose of medicine in the morning, and this should get rid of the infestation. Malaria is treated with chloroquin for three days. Actually, she didn't seem sick, just kind of listless.

Last week I visited a town in the outreach bus, to meet with the health assistant there. When I arrived, he met me with a woman and her three-day-old baby boy who had a cleft palate and hare lip. He wanted me to take her to Phebe because she couldn't feed the baby, and besides, the people in the town thought the baby was an ape, and it was caused by some kind of "witching business." In earlier times, and no doubt to some extent now in the bush, such a child was never "brought from behind the house," which is the term used for the birthing area. The infant would have been killed, maybe by smothering, and it would be said that the baby was born dead, that it wasn't even a human being (a person) yet, buried, and forgotten.

At Phebe, they will operate on it as soon as possible. It weighs only five pounds, and has to be bigger first, and try to get the mother to maintain her milk supply until the baby can suck. Otherwise it will starve, since powdered milk is too expensive, or die from diarrhea because of dirty nursing bottles. For a mother not to have milk is a death warrant for a baby.

Dearest Mother,   **February 12, 1975, Phebe**

I'll dash off a quick note to send with a friend who is going to Monrovia tomorrow morning. I was getting ready to go myself to take John to get school clothes, etc., and then learned I have to be here on Friday for a budget hearing. I'll try to go on Sunday instead. After getting home at 6 PM, I had to borrow a car and drive to Gbarnga and look up a taxi driver who had been hired to come in the morning to pick us up and tell him, no way. This is a 40-minute trip, but there is no telephone system.

A person has to make the drive or send a message, and that never works because you can't depend that the person will actually carry the message. And most of the time, the message has to be verbal, because the people can't read or write!

The baby with the harelip has been here for two weeks, being fed with a Breck feeder and a spoon, and we were able to make arrangements for a visiting plastic surgeon to repair the baby this Friday at Ganta, at no cost. Dr. Getty, the Methodist Mission surgeon, came yesterday to pick up the baby and the ma and carry them to Ganta. We found that she had run away.

The nurses said the ma said she didn't want the baby, even before it was born, and said someone had witched her, "made witch," they say, and the baby came looking like some kind of animal. It's hard to say where she went, perhaps to the town where we found her, but more likely back to her own town, no doubt deep in the bush.

I expect the baby will die, since it won't be fed anything but rice water and will probably aspirate some of that and choke to death. It could even be deliberately killed or taken into the forest and left to die. The longer I'm here, the more I realize the force of tribal ways and that so many of our western ways are only on the surface and just not believed in.

We had an interesting experience Saturday at a town down the road about 20 miles, called Gbartala. It was our usual monthly health meeting, which was scheduled for 10 AM at the schoolhouse. However, when we arrived, we found a huge crowd of people assembled to elect a new clan chief. The election officials were seated on the piazza. In front of them were two men who were seated on chairs. They were the candidates. One was the incumbent. (The President had decreed that every four years chiefs had to be re-voted upon.)

Apparently, this clan chief was not well liked, because all but eight men were lined up behind the other candidate. Even the incumbent's wives were behind the other man. People were beating drums and dancing and having an enjoyable time. We had listed the ex-chief on our program for remarks, but had to make a quick revision after the election!

Dearest Vikki,   **February 12, 1975, Phebe**

I've become involved with proposal writing lately. Phebe has always been besieged with money problems, but it is more acute this year, primarily because of the ridiculous raise in all costs. Anyway, we're trying to get some money to build some low-cost nurses' quarters. They can't get nurses to come or stay and live in the bush unless there is a place for them to live. We are also trying for a new outreach bus and a hospital bus. Workers live in Gbarnga, and there is no public transportation. As usual, there is a deadline for these proposals.

Darlene, the girl next door, gave Poliakah a teddy bear, the first toy Poliakah has ever had. Tonight she showed me the "baby" was sleeping, all wrapped up on her bed. She seems like a very adaptable little girl. It will be nice when she makes some friends. None of the little girls, who are daughters of missionaries here, have come to play with her or invited her to come and play with them. They go to a different school than Poliakah will be going to. Actually, I don't know if the mothers would even encourage it. Sometimes, people can be a bit clannish.

Which reminds me, clans are the important thing here. The political divisions here are county, district, chiefdom, and clan. For instance, in this county, there are four districts, I don't know how many chiefdoms, maybe four, each with a paramount chief, and many clans. And the people in a clan do stick together. This has been election week. The President has decreed that there must be elections every four years for chiefs. We are in the midst of this now, and everything stops for campaigning and election business, since people are really into it. We have had to cancel our vaccination trips, because people have no time for it until voting is ended.

I wish you could smell the nosegay I have here on the table. It is a gardenia with a sprig of jasmine, both so fragrant and so beautiful, with waxy white blossoms and shiny green leaves.

Dearest Mother,   **February 25, 1975, Phebe**

Our life seems to grow more difficult week by week—too much to do and too few resources. Poor Harold, he has so many problems and solutions aren't easy. And there are so few people who work for him who know their jobs or care about their jobs enough.

This hospital is in a rural area, and Gbarnga, where a lot of the nurses and other workers live, is eight miles away. Harold has to arrange for their transportation—three shifts—and other trips for supplies and to carry nursing students back and forth from Cuttington College. His one bus is old and out of commission every time he turns around. I have two vehicles for my programs and one, the Land Rover, has a cracked block, and the bus has a dead battery! It's ridiculous, the ends Harold has to go to, to keep things running. It's like robbing Peter to pay Paul. Yet I manage to keep a public health program going.

Sunday we were notified of a possible yellow fever outbreak between the Guinea and Liberia border, so we had to gear up and start on a vaccination drive in that area, dropping plans already made for bush vaccination trips. (Gene flies our team every Thursday into the bush to hold clinics, a different town each week for four times, then repeats them. In two of the towns, they sleep over, because there are so many people to treat.) This vaccination drive will take us about five days, providing our vehicles hold out! Some days, we can only laugh about it; other days, well....

Martha left for school today. Gene carried her and two boys from here to Lutheran Training Institute, about a 30-minute flight, on his way to pick up an evangelist in the bush. On Sunday, we will take John to Grasssfield, about 100 miles from here, where he will go to a Catholic boys' school. It is also an excellent school. So Poliakah remains and will enroll in beginning school on Monday, here at the Phebe Campus school. It seems like we're starting all over again. If God blesses us, we will get the two older ones through high school.

Dearest Mother and all,   **March 2, 1975, Phebe**

Another week gone by and we're still plugging away. Unfortunately, we have so little time to devote to pleasure or relaxation. Harold left today for Lamco, where he will have some motors repaired.

He will take John and his things to school, which is near Lamco. Harold will sleep with some friends there and take care of his motor business in the AM and then drive back here in the PM. It is a four- to five-hour trip each way, too long to do in one day, the roads being what they are.

Harold will bring one of James Kekula's little girls, Maria, home with him when he returns from Lamco tomorrow. (James was one of Harold's best friends when we were living at Gbedin.) Marie is about Poliakah's age, can't speak English yet. Both will be in the first grade.

We decided it would be better to have two little girls rather than one, for company for each other. Poliakah is quite helpful, can wash dishes, and is quick to learn.

I have been trying to make a dress or two for the two little girls. I can zip them up pretty fast, since they are just made from lappa cloth, and the quality of sewing expected here isn't all that good. I made two yesterday and one this evening. They will wear uniforms to school, a blue cotton skirt, and a white T-shirt so that will be easy.

One of our neighbors has a cinnamon tree, so Harold brought me a branch of it. It is so fragrant. I haven't tried to dry any of it or beat any yet.

Last week, I found some little black seed pods, about one-half inch long and less than one-fourth, inch in diameter at the market. They are black peppers. We finished drying them and beat them in the mortar. Now we have about a half cup of black pepper for 5 cents. The pods are green at first and look like a miniature bunch of bananas. The people sell two or three clusters for 5 cents.

Very little food can be bought cheaply any more in Liberia. Prices have gone out of sight, but the average person earns less than $100 a month. Some here at the mission earn only $50 a month. I don't know how they manage. Of course, nearly everyone makes a farm for the market.

Dearest Mother,   **March 8, 1975, Phebe**

Today was our monthly meeting for county health workers in a town called Naama, about one and a half hours from here. The meeting was called for 10 AM, but it actually started closer to 12, a typical start here in Liberia. Of course, the interminable speeches don't help any to finish things on time. The horn players and drummers entertained us, which was quite enjoyable.

I left Harold at home trying to get a bus started. Vehicles are always in need of fixing here. We met in a school building. Many of the town people were present as usual. There were many women and little kids, and we aim part of the program to them and to the midwives. Today, it was about "stuffing," as it is called here. A common practice is to lay the baby down across your lap, and with one hand full of water (or food) hold the baby's nose with the other and force the child to swallow. It's a good way to kill a baby by strangulation or to give it diarrhea or pneumonia. We talk all of the time about feeding with a spoon and cup and still have to continue. Even if a new young mother wants to use a spoon, the old ladies often won't allow it. The reason for stuffing, they say, is to get the baby's stomach so full it won't cry.

We now have another school child, an eighth grade girl, who comes to stay with our girls and help me in the evening. She needed school help, so she is helping us for the help we give her, which is uniforms, tuition, registration fees, and copy books. School costs are quite high this year.

Dearest Mother,   **March 11, 1975, Sanoyea**

I'm sitting in a village clinic while some of the mobile team assists the clinic staff in operating their first under-fives clinic. It is bedlam periodically, as some of the tots reach the immunization nurse. Of course, some start screaming as soon as they enter the room, clinging to their mothers' skirt and peeping around the safety of her legs.

Two of the new Peace Corps volunteers and one of our former mobile team workers have been assigned to this town of Sanoyea. We decided to come to see how things were going and surprise Henry, who was a fine member of our team.

The clinic building is quite large, since it is a former Lutheran dispensary, just turned over to the government, after many years. There is room for patients to stay overnight and to deliver patients and ample room to teach and to treat the people. Today, their first clinic day, is well attended. And whenever you have about 50 little kids in a small area, you have lots of confusion. The people are constantly talking, always quite loud, and added to this are the piercing screams from kids as they are confronted with the nurse, the scales, and so on. They are fearful, which I guess we would also be at such strange surroundings and experiences.

One of the volunteers, Chris, is a practical nurse (LPN), very serious about her work and quite fearful yet, when kids come in pretty sick. I think she will do well. Henry, our former worker, is a physician assistant, about 35, very competent and honest, and was sent to work with Chris. There is another health volunteer here, Barry Hansen, a young health educator. He is also serious about his work and is interested in learning more.

I'm looking forward to working with this group since they should be able to do a lot of the kinds of things I send the mobile clinic to do. For example, they hope to vaccinate everyone in all the bush towns and try to hold clinics in nearby towns, as well. Sanoyea is about an hour and a half from Phebe, toward Monrovia. They hold under-fives clinic on Tuesdays, OB clinic on Thursdays, and general clinic on the other mornings. There is an RN here, too, and a midwife, both Liberians, so they have enough staff. One woman had delivered yesterday, and was still here, and there is also an eight-month-old baby (with her mother), who came yesterday with a high fever, vomiting, and diarrhea. The clinic staff were glad we had come to advise them about their problems!

We brought our lunch, so when all the patients are gone, we will have a little picnic and then meet with the staff to talk about their plans. One of my responsibilities is to try to improve the work being done in clinics, so this is one way to do it, go and work with the people to see what their problems are and then go from there. I also have a Peace Corps RN, Donna, assigned to outreach and have given her the job of setting up classes for the physician assistants who run the clinics. She has also taken over the monthly newsletter, which is a big help to me. She is a nice girl, about 24, very capable and cheerful.

Sunday, Phebe. I suddenly got very busy, so didn't get back to this. We all worked until 3:30 PM, had 62 little ones altogether, so it was late before we reached home. Now, we've just returned home after four days in Monrovia, where we were taking care of the usual kind of business in the city, picking up vaccines, supplies, talking to Ministry of Health people about public health matters. Harold had all kinds of things to "run behind" ["deal with"], finding parts for vehicles, getting supplies for people, and various other things to see to. It's always a "hurry up and wait" day, and then shopping for our month's supply of groceries and such. Prices are fantastic here, too, not only groceries, but everything else. We've practically eliminated sugar from our diet, not that that hurts us, really. I bought two pounds of sugar for $2.20.

When I got back here, I learned there had been a report of cholera in a town in the bush, about 30 minutes by air but a two-day hike from here. So yesterday, two members of our team went by plane into the bush, carrying IV fluids, vaccines, and supplies to take rectal swabs of suspected patients, and were left there. The pilot brought back the rectal swab specimens, and cultures were made. We are still waiting for that report. Our two fellows had to remain there and will come back tomorrow. The pilot couldn't get back there today because of other scheduled flights.

It will most likely prove not to be cholera. None of the towns we've checked out after such a report have proven to be positive, but we always have to check. The reports are always so exaggerated. For instance, I had a note from the Peace Corps nurse who works with me that the town we will visit tomorrow had sent a message that plenty people are sick, and some have even died in the past month. To my knowledge, no one has been admitted to the hospital from there, but at least we will go prepared. We will also check out every person who has been purported to be or to have been sick and check graves (usually they can't show you any!) We have such a small staff for all of these different things that managing assignments is tricky.

Dearest Vikki and Gill,   **March 19, 1975, Monrovia**

Harold bought me a combined Christmas and birthday gift. It is an African cross of gold filigree, on a long gold chain (18 carat gold). It is called an Agadiz cross, made by the Tuareg tribe, a tribe in Mali. The cross is about two inches long, very beautiful.

The weather is so hot just now, and humid. Everything is so parched looking, nothing green. It is quite ugly, although leaves are beginning to come out a bit. There is a gardenia bush by the hospital, and Harold often brings me a blossom.

Dearest Mother and all,   **March 24, 1975, Phebe**

We spent our 35th anniversary in Liberia, a little over a week ago. Amazing, isn't it? Lately, things have been very difficult for Harold, and he is having second thoughts about his work here. Actually, it is nothing new. It just seems like it's going from bad to worse. He says, "Maybe I'm just homesick." But I don't think so. Trying to patch things together can go on just so long. So many things were left undone for so long, and also, things deteriorate very fast in this climate. The x-ray tank, for example, is a mass of rust and will have to be replaced some way. The refrigerator in the morgue is about to give up the ghost—that's awful, isn't it! It goes on and on, and always personnel problems daily.

Well, so much for that; on to other things. Yesterday, we went to Ganta to "witness," as they call it here, the nursing graduation. These were students that I had as freshmen, so it was fun to attend. Also, Vera Hughlett, one of the instructors, is a good friend. We drove a VW bus, which we can rent from the mission for 12 cents a mile, and had it full of people, including our two little girls.

We went on to Gbedin, as usual, and had a pleasant and rather nostalgic time. People are always so glad to see us, and it's so good to see people we are fond of. So many of my former clinic clients were there, and they bring their babies to be seen, and we catch up on a lot of news.

When we were about half-way home (it's a 60-mile trip, one way, and two hours), suddenly, the motor died—out in the sticks, with little traffic, and of course, no gas stations. Harold soon diagnosed the trouble, which was spoiled distributor points. There was no town nearby, no garage, no spare parts, no flashlight, no matches. It was 6:30, a half hour until dark.

We immediately cut palm branches and put them on the road a short distance before and back of the car, the standard sign of trouble ahead. We were on a curvy road, just below a hill. Harold searched around for something he could use to fabricate the part he needed, but there was nothing in the car he could use.

One of the nurses in the car had a little sewing kit with a spool of thread and a tiny knife. Harold found a stick and whittled a little piece of wood to put in place of the plastic cam that had broken. In the meantime, one of the Peace Corps kids with us flagged down a big transport truck. Harold paid the driver to carry the boy to Phebe to get another car to come and help us.

But believe it or not, Harold's piece of stick and string worked, after a lot of adjusting by lantern light. (We had walked up the road to a little village and borrowed a kerosene lantern, which Harold set inside the engine area to give him some light.) We finally got home around 8 PM. We had overtaken the truck that had given Bob the lift, so it would have been a long wait for help. This morning when he took the piece out to be replaced, it was hardly worn, the thread still intact. I told him he was living up to his name—Mr. Wizard.

Maybe you would like to know what kind of diet we have. Today was rather typical. I'm sure if it were just Harold and me, we might eat more kwi food, but with three or four kids eating with us on a fairly regular basis, we stick to country food because of the cost. For breakfast, we had oatmeal with powdered milk and grapefruit, which we usually get for the picking. For lunch it was boiled eddoes, which are a starchy tuber something like a potato, and margarine, pineapple, and some cheese. For supper, we have big plate of rice with ground pea (peanuts) soup with fish. We use the fish head, bones, tail, and fins. Harold fillets it. We boil the fish with tomato paste, onion, chicken bouillon cubes, salt and hot pepper, and about one-fourth cup of peanut butter.

We get the peanuts from the market, parch them in the oven, and beat them in the mortar to make the peanut butter. Oh yes. After they are parched, you rub them in your hands to "loose" the skins, and then fan them in a fanner to blow away the skins. Anyway, it's a good source of protein and makes a good soup. We also had boiled green beans, a treat since they aren't easy to find in the country.

Lately, since the rains have begun, the termites, called "bug-a-bugs," have been flying early in the morning. These are tasty morsels to the people here and quite an exciting activity for a few days each year, when the people gather them. The people get up soon in the morning, 4:30 to 6:30, light a torch or a lantern, set it in a small hole, and wait for the insects to flock to the light. The wings fall off, and the bugs fall in the hole and are harvested. Our two little girls caught them this morning, parched them in a frying pan and ate them. Now Martha has just returned from Gbedin with a plastic bag, maybe two cups, of parched bug-a-bugs that someone there had sent to Harold. She also brought a paper carton containing bugs that she caught this morning, enough to fill about a three-pound coffee can. She will parch them in the oven. I suppose Harold will eat some, but, "myself, I can't able." The Liberians love them and gather them by the gunny sack-full. Actually, they are a good source of fat and protein. Harold says, "I like them."

John and Martha, home for vacation and helping in the kitchen.

When the bug-a-bugs are flying (they look like big flying ants), the big frogs or toads are hopping all about, snapping up the insects. Also, many ants come out, some up to an inch long, and carry off the bug-a-bugs. Sometimes, the load is bigger than the ant that is carrying it.

There are millions and millions of ants, and many different species. Some are only one-sixth inch long; some are as long as an inch. Some, not large, have a wicked bite, actually a pinch with their pincers. We always have ants in our kitchen, always have to keep sugar tightly covered.

One time I left a chicken on the drain board to thaw. When I came home, not only was it thawed, but it was invaded by hundreds of ants. Now I just tap on the container or drain board and get them to leave, where before I would have been aghast.

Dear Vikki,   **March 29, 1974, Phebe**

Our house is like a three-ring circus this week. Martha has been home for a week for Easter holiday, and John came Thursday afternoon and will go back Monday, plus the two little girls, plus the kids' friends in and out. None of our friends here at the mission have any Liberian children, although a couple of families had a high school kid with them at vacation time. At times I think we must be insane; it's a lot of work, palava, expense, but on the other hand I don't know what else we'd be doing with our time or money!

We do hope to get John and Martha through high school before going back to the States, or close to being through. As far as what other mission people think about our having children, I don't ask, because I don't think it's anyone else's business, although you can pretty well tell without asking.

The flowering trees and shrubs are beginning to be lovely; jacaranda, jasmine, crepe myrtle, plumeria, allemanda, hibiscus of all kinds, at least six different ones in our yard, mimosa, poinciana, bougainvillea, orchid tree, gardenia. Many of these have been planted here on the campus; they don't all grow here naturally.

Someone just killed a snake in one of our trees. An emerald snake, harmless according to the book, but to the people here, there is no such thing as a harmless snake. A little while ago we heard a lot of commotion about half a block from here—too many trees between to know what was happening so the kids all ran to see what all the hollering and sounds of beating were. A dog had chased an iguana in from the bush near where some men were working. It was over three feet long, black and yellow. The men "knocked" it on the head and killed it, but before that they said it was beating the dog with its tail. The men divided the thing each one getting a portion. One fellow came by our house with three sections of the tail, his share. Each piece was about five to six inches long. Apparently he will cook it skin and all in soup. People say "guana is sweet"—they hardly pronounce the "g," more like "wauna."

Dearest Mother,   **April 6, 1975, Phebe**

It's raining in torrents, hard enough to come all the way into our house, through the louvers. It's so refreshing when the rains come. People say the rainy season won't come for two more months, but it has been raining practically every day for the past three or four weeks. Things look so fresh and green now.

I don't think I've mentioned any of the obstetrical emergencies we've had here at Phebe. There is hardly a day that goes by that an emergency C-Section isn't done on women who have been in labor for days. So many times the uterus is already ruptured, due to country medicine they've been given, long forced labor, living far in the bush, etc. The old country midwives have so many traditional practices that have been handed down and which endanger lives.

In the US, a ruptured uterus is hardly heard of, but here it is too commonplace. Sometimes the baby is transverse, maybe arm presentation, sometimes breech. The woman is carried from far in the bush, then put in a taxi or pick-up truck, and jounced for miles to Phebe, many times just too late.

One of the things we are trying to do is to start to teach the old midwives, but there are so few qualified people to do it. And trying to persuade people to change their practices of a lifetime is next to impossible. Some younger women do go for midwife training, but it's hard for them to become accepted by the old ladies when they go back to their villages. We've managed to get a couple of trained midwives on the payroll to work in health posts with three physician assistants.

Did I tell you I've been sewing a patchwork coverlet? Anyway, it is nearly finished, just need about four dozen pieces. It is double-bed size, will be backed with Liberian lappas.

Lately, there are so many flying insects every evening that it is hard to be in the house at night with the light on. The table is speckled all around me just now. Ugh.

About your possible trip to visit us. Unless you have a preference, July or August would be a good time, weather-wise. It's the end of the wet season, the nights and mornings are cool, the rain is quite refreshing, and it doesn't rain all day, and of course, it isn't chilly.

Dearest Vikki and Gill,   **April 16, 1975, Phebe**

We've just returned from Monrovia after a three-day stay. I had to meet with the Minister of Health, along with a delegation from Phebe, to discuss the financial needs for the next three years. We stayed to do some shopping and to take delivery of a new UNICEF VW bus for our public health program, but as usual, there were delays. So I drove the car back, and Harold stayed to get things going. Finally, he flew back with the plane and then about an hour later they released the bus, so someone else drove it here, a typical experience.

It's quite warm and humid just now, and in Monrovia much more pronounced. It's always nice to get back up-country. The roads are surprisingly good right now. I drove 45 MPH most of the way—astounding!

While in Monrovia, I went to get my hair cut. The usual hair-cutter was gone, so I took a chance. Now my hair is about one inch long all over my head. What to do. It will grow out eventually!

We finally decided to take the little girls back to their homes. We were having a variety of problems we hadn't anticipated. They didn't get along too well together, were from different tribes. And both were from different tribes than Kpelle, the main tribe here. The tribes are very clannish, even though a variety of tribes are represented here at Phebe. The little girls were being sassy to adults passing by, too, who took offense, almost to the point of taking us to tribal court, which they call suing.

Liberian people love to sue each other. It's a good way to make money! Harold and I both have to be away so much, and it wasn't good for them to be alone, and when I get home at night, I'm usually so tired it was too difficult to care for everything. I decided that my mental health was more important than a relationship with their families, and told Harold I couldn't handle it any more.

Dearest Mother,   **April 16, 1975, Phebe**

Phebe's Ladies Auxiliary was meeting at my house at 3:30 today, so it was necessary to get home in time to bake some cookies and make iced tea, etc., before people arrived. Community women are members, some from Cuttington College, from the government farm, from Phebe Campus, and from the Baptist Mission nearby. Actually, it is primarily educated women, not tribal women, who are generally working on their farms all day.

I finally finished my patchwork coverlet. It grew to be quite large, almost a king-size width. It has a colorful lappa for backing. The whole thing looks quite gay, almost too busy looking. I think we will enjoy it, though, because of all the memories inside.

Dearest Mother and all,   **May 4, 1975, Phebe**

Phebe Hospital is celebrating its tenth birthday this month. A special day is being set aside for a program of some sort, with a little flyer being put together to commemorate the occasion. This year July 26, Independence Day, is being celebrated in this county. Government employees are required to voluntarily (ha, ha) give a month's salary to do all the projects. Phebe employees have been asked to do the same, but the county superintendent has said the money can be used at Phebe. So all agreed to put the money into building a new out-reach/outpatient building, separate from the hospital.

The plans started out quite modestly, but like anything else here, grew to be quite grand. Harold will have to see that the thing is built, with his limited crew and his oversupply of responsibilities, inflated prices, incomplete and vague plans—oh my. He may tell the doctor that he can't take on another job, but I don't know how that will go over. The superintendent stopped by during the week. The project had just been decided on a week ago, and he asked Harold why he couldn't see any construction yet!

More trees are blooming now. The cassia trees are flowering. They have big clusters of pink blossoms, something like an apple blossom, only much larger. The trees are masses of pink. With the brilliant red of the flame trees and the lavender of the crape myrtle, the surroundings are gorgeous.

It's Monday now, and as I came home from work, I discovered we had company. It was Adama. She came to stay a couple of days, loaded down with her wares. She had a lot of fabrics, tie-dye, batik, beads, snake-skin belts, and the like. She carries the whole load, about the size of a full gunny-sack, on her head. We invited some of the people here to come in and look at her things.

Adama is Muslim and has strict food taboos. She can't eat pork, chicken, or beef unless they are killed and bled in a certain prescribed way. We had palm butter, with chicken, and when she learned I had bought the chicken already killed and dressed, she couldn't eat it. So I opened a can of sardines to put on her rice, and she was satisfied. Muslim people pray five times a day, kneel on a mat facing the east, and go through a set of prayers. She said a woman can't "pray God" for 30 days after she gives birth, and she can't pray God during her period.

Dearest Mom,   **May 11, 1975, Phebe**

We're getting ready for Phebe Hospital's tenth anniversary, which is scheduled for May 25th. I'm making display posters about our department and also have to do a program for the Medical Association, which will meet here the day before. We, that is, the people who work in our outreach department, will do a panel discussion on our work.

Yesterday, we had our monthly health meeting at a town about 38 miles from here. It was off the main road on a narrow, very bumpy road through the bush. We took two busses and Dr. Gwenigale's station wagon, and had too many of the town people to carry home, so had to do it in two trips. I came in the last bus and the last half hour it started to rain. Before we reached home, the rain was coming in such torrents that I could hardly see to drive. Also there was a rattle-bang noise from under the bus. When I told Harold, he thought it was the shock absorbers, and said it was OK for the driver to make a trip to Gbarnga (eight) miles. Well, he never made it home from Gbarnga, something happened to the transmission! I would have hated to break down on the road in that downpour. So Harold had to go this morning and fix the bus enough to get it back to Phebe.

Dearest Kids,
                                                          June 1, 1975, Phebe

I'm sorry to be so slow to write—have been out of the mood to write to anyone, have had lots of things to sort out in my head. Anyway, I seem to be "back on track," so will get caught up now. There always seems to be so many distractions and problems, that if I'm not tired physically, I'm nil mentally, by the time evening comes.

Today, I did a bunch of sewing. Made a reversible wrap-around skirt, the second one I've made. I really love the style. This one is purple and white wax-print on one side, and green and purple and white tie-dye on the other. I also made a white blouse with binding around the arm and neck to match the tie-dye. I've just about finished a pantsuit of yellow, orange and white plaid, which I had started at least two months ago.

On Thursday, we are taking off with Geoff Thompson for the beach in Monrovia for five days of relaxing and a bit of business. We will stay at the ELWA [*Hospital*] guest-house, which is right on the beach. I need to see them about some radio health messages we're trying to write for them to translate into dialects, (one- or two-minute spots). They are primarily about caring for children so they won't be sick.

Lately, we've been having little frogs in our house at night. They hop around and hide in corners. And just now, Harold tried to chase a huge spider (an inch long, with legs over two inches in length) out of the living room. He wouldn't kill it; he says they eat cockroaches. When he pushed it with the broom, it just hopped along, rather than walking, quite high hops, in fact. It was really creepy to me.

Dearest Mother,   **June 1, 1975, Phebe**

The big celebration [*Phebe Hospital's tenth anniversary event*] is over. It was quite a success; at least, it came off on time. They even had the ground-breaking for the new outpatient building. Now people have started working on that. Harold was able to get some of the Peace Corps guys to come and do the needed surveying, lay out the building, and do better plans. One of the fellows is a civil engineer, and one is an architect, so we couldn't beat that combination.

Yesterday, a new doctor arrived. He and his wife were here five years ago for six months and have now come back for three years. We can really use another medical man. His wife is an RN and will teach in the nursing program. They seem like good people. Then on Monday we're having two visitors from the Christian Medical Commission who are coming to look at possibilities for financial assistance. Sometimes, it gets a bit wearing, having so many guests. When new people come, or visitors of some importance are here, they are given meals for three days, breakfast at one place, lunch at another, and so on. We all take turns cooking for them, but you can't just run out to the store if you run out of something. Finding vegetables to cook is a problem, unless one likes eggplant, okra, and sweet potato greens! There is very little variety at times. Once in a while in Monrovia, we can get dehydrated green peas and beans, which are quite nice. Well, fortunately, we can manage without too much difficulty. Right now, mangoes are in season! We have two trees in our yard, and if we can beat the neighbor kids to them, we get some from time to time! Little boys take long sticks and beat on the trees, spoiling a lot of the fruit before it is even ripe. What to do.

I flew to Zorzor this week for a meeting. We were quite low due to overhanging clouds. It's fun to look down on all the little villages, patches of two or three huts in among the trees, tall trees all around. People are "burning their farms" now, and in the 30-minute flight, we saw dozens of fires. The sky is hazy this time of year because of the farming time. They slash all of the bush, and then set it afire. This year rainy season came soon, so people are having a hard time getting the burning done.

Dearest Kids,   **June 15, 1975, Phebe**

Friday when I was out with our Mobile Clinic, we were asked to stop in another village to see a sick baby. We found a little boy, about one and a half years old, so anemic we couldn't even measure his hemoglobin (less than one gram), burning with fever, shivering, obviously malnourished; his little arms and legs were like matchsticks. We told the people he was too sick, but we could try, so the mother picked him up and got in the bus with us.

We had a couple other stops to make in towns to do some immunizations, so we sponged the baby with our cold drinking water and gave it sips of water. When we reached the hospital, it was next to impossible to even get any blood to check its blood type. The mother was the wrong type, so we had to hunt around for blood. In the meantime the doctors were trying to get into a vein with a saline IV, which took ages, the baby's breathing getting worse. They were giving it oxygen and suctioning it; there was a lot of fluid in its lungs. Two doctors, nurses, and nursing instructors were all working, trying to keep the poor little thing alive, but he finally stopped breathing about 6 PM.

I had picked it up in the village around 1:15. It seems so senseless for people to be so careless in the care of their babies. It was obvious that this baby hadn't been fed decently for months, and then finally when it's too late, they come and ask you to help. It's just so traumatic for me. We used to hold clinic in the town where this woman lived, trying to teach about how to keep their babies healthy and well, but none of it worked with her; she never came when we held clinic there.

Dearest Mother,   June 15, 1975, Phebe

Weddings are one thing that doesn't happen here. Only kwi people, "civilized" and Christian people really have a wedding ceremony. The tribal people have a different way, which involves paying some kind of "bride price" to the father of the woman, and then perhaps the family cooks rice, etc. Many times, the money isn't paid for months, so the thing isn't binding until it is.

Marriage arrangements are often made when a girl is just a baby; actually, the father is just selling his child, usually to an important man, thus taking out insurance for his own future. I met a chief recently who had given his young daughter to President Tolbert (when he was still vice president). Now the girl is grown and has had a child for the President, and "the Old Man can do anything, no palava," with this tie with the President.

This week we will know whether we are to go to Zorzor, or stay here. If we do go, it will be in the latter part of July, which will give us time to wind things up here and for Harold to break in the new man. Also for us to have a week of rest someplace, probably on the beach at ELWA, near the airport. They have an inexpensive guest house there. I do dislike the process of moving. It is such a chore. And the house will be smaller, only two bedrooms. Maybe we will have less company then!

Last evening we went to Cuttington College to hear the Music Department's concert, which was fine. They sang quite a few African songs using native drums, some spirituals, as well as standard choir numbers. I really enjoy African music, there is so much rhythm and beat, and the kids sing with a lot of enthusiasm. Such concerts are few and far between, up-country.

Dearest Mother and all,   **June 25, 1975, Phebe**

Our transfer is final, so within a month or two we'll have a different home, about three hours further in the interior. It will be quite a different life—fewer expatriates, smaller, less convenient home, but a less harried atmo-sphere from all reports. There is only one doctor (here there are five) even though the hospital is larger. It is run entirely differently. This one is fairly sophisticated, western style. Zorzor is a bush-type hospital, has a large TB quarter, leprosy quarter, and orphan quarter, where babies are cared for, for two to three years, when mothers die in childbirth.

I will be working with their community health program with the Liberian nurse who is in charge. He and I are working on a joint project already, trying to do some scripts for health teaching via radio, and we get along fine. There is always a job to do, no matter where you go. Harold may find himself busier than he expects since he will probably be expected to at least supervise maintenance in other Lutheran church stations. Knowing Harold, he will always find more to do than people expect of him.

Over the weekend, we had extra people as usual. One girl, Oreta, from Gbeden, is now living near here and was about to go into labor so she came for a few days (had a baby boy this morning). A girl from the University of Minnesota knocked on our door Friday eve, on her way up-country for a 10-week study and work project. Friends in Monrovia had sent her to us so she stayed until Monday.

This is typical. Often people come to spend time, a day or a week or a month, with the outreach program. We've really earned a reputation in the past few months for doing a good job in public health so people like to come and observe. We do have a long way to go, and it isn't easy. I have to be a stern task master because it's so natural for people to let down, start to come late, don't examine patients carefully, get careless about records. But we get along together even though we have to "make palava" every once in a while!

The past week we put on a big vaccination push in Gbarnga, the county seat which is eight miles away, for publicity mainly for the county super-intendent prior to the 26th celebration. We went three evenings from 3 to 7 PM and gave over 5,000 immunizations to children and adults. We gave vaccinations for measles, TB, smallpox, diphtheria, tetanus and whooping cough combined; and vitamins for pregnant women. Each evening a few students came along for the experience, and our regular team members. Talk about hectic and noisy—babies yelling at the top of their lungs. Quite an experience. It does sound like bragging, but since I've been here, this county has continued to give a third of all the immunizations given in Liberia, and there are eight other counties.

Dearest Vikki,   **July 6, 1975, Phebe**

Things are going OK here. We're about to go for a week's vacation. We will have to spend the week in Nimba since there is no housing for us on the beach in Monrovia. Anyway, we can "sit down" for a while and rest.

We will be living at Zorzor from July 22nd on. Our house is much smaller than this one but kind of cozy and quite convenient to the hospi-tal. Harold is looking forward to the change. Henry Zawolo will be work-ing there. Harold got him a job as farm manager at the hospital so it will be fun having him there.

Alfred, our house man, wants to come with us, so we won't have to hunt for a new person and have to get used to that. We visited Zorzor last week and checked things out. People are anxiously awaiting our arrival, which is a good feeling.

Dearest Mother,   **July 15, 1975, Nimba**

Our week's vacation is soon coming to an end and we will be off for Zorzor. Saturday morning we finished packing all our household things, stored them in one room of our house, tossed some clothes and food in the car and took off for Nimba for a rest.

We're in the church vacation house with three young people—a teacher and a nurse from Phebe and Geoff Thompson. It's been a restful time. We can cook here, there are stores, a swimming pool, a recreation center where people do weaving, tie-dye, and batik work (they also do a lot of Rya rug work), also show movies (and there was a good movie), and we have friends from Peace Corps days nearby. So we've had a good time.

Today Darlene, the teacher, and I spent the afternoon at the pool. Both of us got sun burned, but the water is so nice—a real treat to be able to swim. Then we went to visit a Methodist pastor and his wife and family who are from Gbarnga. They had invited us for pizza, and we had a lovely evening.

You asked why we were going to Zorzor, and I realized I hadn't really taken time to tell about it. Zorzor had made a request for a maintenance engineer to the mission people in New York. They had had one a year ago but thought they could manage with the Liberian who had been trained. This didn't work out.

There is a maintenance man at Phebe (had been at Zorzor until last year) who with his wife had been hostel parents at Phebe, taking care of missionary kids. This has been too much of a responsibility for his wife—they have four young kids—and they have to leave that job. They can't go to Zorzor because he and the man who is now there didn't get along too well plus if they went, their children would be staying at the hostel to attend school (no school for them up there). So it appeared that one solution would be for us to go to Zorzor, and Jerry and his wife to move into our house, and he could take care of the maintenance work at Phebe. We offered to do this.

Another factor was that I was ready to turn over my work to a missionary who had come out to do public health work so this opened the way for that. I had been really praying for direction, Harold too for that matter, and we both feel that this change is what God wants us to do. Actually it should be a much less difficult job for Harold. The hospital is not built on Western standards, and while they have a lot of patients, more than Phebe, the whole set up is simpler. There is also a public health program, which I'll be involved with but will merely assist the Liberian nurse in charge. Maybe I'll have less than a 10-hour day, I hope! There are very few expatriates, which pleases us. We're feeling good about the move—expect much less strain than we have at Phebe. Also less company, since we won't be on a main road, although people do seem to find us! We have so many guests for meals and for overnight stays that sometimes it's quite wearing. Fortunately Alfred, our house man, is excellent.

I'm looking forward to some time to do some sewing—haven't been able to sew for quite a while. I'm going to attempt to make some trousers for Harold—got some denim and some knit—and will see how it comes out.

Our house will be quite different—small, with two bedrooms. We will have to boil and filter our water. There is no window glass—only screens, which I prefer, since we need the ventilation. Apparently it gets quite a bit cooler there than at Phebe, which we'll enjoy. Hopefully this will be our last move while we're in Liberia.

Dearest Mother, **July 24, 1975, Zorzor**

Well, here we are in Zorzor, trying to get settled. What a job. This house is so much smaller that finding a place for things is quite a challenge. Fortunately, John is home from school, and Alfred, our houseman came with us, so I don't have to do all the work. Harold and I had a chance to fly up, while the truck carrying our things, and the guys and the dog and the parrot, went on ahead.

In this house we have a gas stove. The oven doesn't work, so Harold has spent a while trying to find out what to do to it. There is no way to get parts. Also, we have to boil and filter our drinking water again. He bought a different kind of filter, which disinfects the water, too, and hooks into the water pipes. Again, it was quite a task to get it going. Now, we will have to get the water tested at the hospital lab to make sure it's OK. The filter cost $75, so I hope it works. Boiling water with the gas stove is very expensive, so the filter should pay for itself. The water here is so full of iron that it is quite discolored.

We have a bath fence out back of the house. It is made from bamboo poles—a circular fence with a bamboo bench inside and gravel on the ground, where we can take a small tub of water and have a "bucket bath." It is really enjoyable, although Harold prefers a bathroom. He will concoct a shower there for himself.

The windows of this house have only screens and heavy wire grill, no glass. On the outside are country mats, rolled up and held in place with a forked stick. You let them down when it rains. The weather is much cooler here, in fact, I've had to wear a sweater today, and in the evening it is quite chilly. We are closer to the mountains, which accounts for the lower temperatures.

The doctor who is in charge of this hospital is from this area. He graduated from the University of Washington Medical School. His wife is from Kenya and graduated from the School of Social Work and did graduate work at Pacific Lutheran University. It is a small world, isn't it?

There are very few Americans here. There are three RNs, and one couple, a farmer and his wife, who will return to the states in September. One of the nurses will return in September, one around Christmas. One of the problems one faces when living on a mission station, such as at Phebe, and here, is that you are forced to live fairly intimately with the residents on the station, and often there are some you wouldn't choose to be friends with anywhere else. One of the nurses here is very lonely. She is in her mid-40s, very overweight (must weigh 300 pounds), and talks incessantly. She was so glad to see us arrive. Our house is near hers, and she has practically killed us with kindness. I will try to be her friend, but I'm afraid it won't be easy.

Now we will have to get used to where to shop for produce. Fruit is very hard to find anyway, but especially this time of the year. So far, we haven't seen any. I'm going to send John out tomorrow to look around. People say that sometimes someone comes around to sell different things, like bananas, pineapple, and greens. So I'm sure we will make out.

I don't know if I told you that this hospital is where they had the trouble with Lassa fever a couple years ago. Apparently, most of the cases came from Guinea, which is very close to Zorzor. In fact, many serious cases of other things, such as OB emergencies, come from there, where the medical care is very minimal.

We were saying before that we wouldn't have so much company here, because our house is so small, but here we are with John and Alfred, and now Annie Dolo, a girl from Gbedin, just knocked on our door to spend the 26th vacation with us. We will have to put her on the couch. She is a youngster who used to work for me, washing dishes in the morning and sweeping the floors and dusting. In return, I paid her school fees, gave her cloth, and taught her to sew. Her father wanted her to "stay by me," so she would learn to care for a house and not "go walk about" and get into trouble. We told a lot of our friends from Gbedin and Phebe they would be welcome any time, but really thought we were far enough away that not too many would come! Well, we usually enjoy them most of the time. But at times it can get pretty hectic.

The church plane arrived a bit ago, carrying a patient and also the mail bag. Mail is so welcome and no doubt will arrive less often up here, since there are fewer people to go to Monrovia (much farther), and we're not on the beaten path.

Saturday. It's Liberia's Independence Day, so things are very quiet. Harold took Annie out for a motorcycle ride to deliver some mail. John and Alfred went into town to a football game (soccer), and here I am, talking to the dog and the parrot! Harold thinks the parrot says "Hello," but I think you have to use your imagination!

There are many trees around our house. So far, I can't recognize the leaf trees. There are palms of different varieties. Out of the back window, it is quite brushy, "bush" we call it here. There are no houses behind our house for some distance. At Phebe, we had a lot of flowers and flowering bushes, but there doesn't appear to be so many here. I will get some gardenia, jasmine, hibiscus, and bougainvillea cuttings the next time I go to Phebe and try to get some started here. I do enjoy the blossoms. John started a small garden for me yesterday, parsley and lettuce. I don't know how it will do in this cold and rainy time, but it won't be much of a loss, just two packages of seeds.

Tomorrow, he and Alfred will go and cut some bamboo and make us a new bath fence. This one here has a lot of cracks between the poles and is kind of short. I'm also going to have Alfred build a palava hut for me. It is a thatched-roof hut with a dirt floor, and maybe, short side-walls where we can hang our hammocks. At Phebe, we had a screened piazza, quite large, where we had two hammocks hanging, but no way for that here.

I have wanted a "kitchen," which is the other word for the hut, ever since we came to Liberia, but Harold never agreed; this time he decided it would be OK.

The posts are made of a kind of stick that will always sprout. This way, the bug-a-bugs don't eat them. The framework is made of sticks tied together with rattan (a vine), and then the lower walls are daubed with clay mud and rubbed smooth. The floor is made the same way, daubed, that is. The roof is also made of sticks tied together with rattan. Then palm branches are tied on in layers. Such a kitchen is a work of art. I always sit in one and marvel at how cleverly they are constructed.

I tell Harold such a hut is really for his benefit, because then he can come home and lie down in the hammock and rest when he has had his lunch or when he has finished work. People will construct one for $10 or $20, which includes the material. They make a cool place to sit on a hot day, and a breeze can always blow through, too.

One thing I'm just realizing is that with our house so close to the hospital, we will always be aware when deaths occur because the people always wail so loudly. And there are so many deaths, since people wait so long before they bring a sick person to the hospital, and often it's too late. I've heard people say, more than once, they won't come to the hospital for kwi medicine, because that is where people die.

Ruth and Alfred building the new bath fence.

Dearest Mother,   **August 3, 1975, Zorzor**

This has been quite a week or two—so much company, along with our trying to get settled, and trying to work out routines. Because of the 26th

Celebration and school holiday, we've had our school kids home—three of them.

Then Henry Zawolo, a friend from Gbedin, arrived Wednesday with his brother. He has been hired as manager of the hospital rice farm. Being a stranger, the farm manager, and of a different tribe, he has "caught hard time" finding a place to live. Consequently, as his only friends here, we have had him staying and eating with us. Now, Harold has found a couple of beds and an empty room by the shop, so they are there, but eating with us and spending time here. Hopefully, a house lead will enable him to move into town on Tuesday or Wednesday, poor guy.

We tend to think because we're Americans and we are different, we have a hard time being accepted. However, one tribe is very suspicious of a man from a different tribe and is slow to include him. It won't be easy for Henry, learning to be boss over Loma people, who don't like another tribe to be over them. His girlfriend is a trained midwife, a good friend of mine. We used to spend a lot of time together in Gbedin, so it will be nice if she comes here, too.

Along with all these people, a new Peace Corps couple, about our age, was sent for a three-day stay with us, so he could see the rice project. They are farmers from Pennsylvania. We enjoyed having them, except it is time consuming and extra work, especially arranging sleeping space. Martha ended up sleeping on the floor one night. And along with all these things, there was a big wedding in town in the Lutheran Church. One of the men from Phebe was marrying a local girl whose father is a "big man" around Zorzor. You can't imagine all the fixing up that went on. This meant lots of extra people in town and at the hospital, which also involved more sleeping space!

It was a really nice wedding. The father had the church painted inside and outside, even the floors. The church was decorated with palm branches, two or three arches made with braided palm branches with flowers tied to them.

The bridesmaids were dressed in long turquoise sheaths, over which were Mandingo-style open-work nets of the same color. The bride wore the same style gown, only in white. The little flower girls and ring bearer were in pink, same style. All, even the bridesmaids, carried fruit, the little girls a pawpaw and the bridesmaids little round rice baskets holding oranges and bananas. All wore matching head-ties. One little girl scattered rice on the floor just in front of the bride and her father. Later, there was a reception in a hall in town.

One highlight was a fantastic wedding cake, made by two of the missionary nurses here. It took 16 recipes of a regular cake, was three tiers high, each tier separate, and four other layers placed evenly around the three. They never cut the cake while we were there, and we stayed two or three hours. I think the party went on most of the night, so no doubt it was eaten some time.

Another wedding highlight was the native music and dancing. About a dozen and a half women who are members of the Sande (women's secret) Society, performed. It was something special to watch. Most of the women are old, although there was one young girl about 12, and one woman about 18 or 20. Some of them were at least in their thirties, I judged. But could they all dance.

Some of the dances seemed to depict planting and harvesting. Some were similar to the hula. They wore skirts made of black string attached to a band of country cloth. Around their hips were many strings of beads and cowry shells; most had a leopard tooth or two attached, also, in the back. Around their necks they wore a kind of collar, joined in a kind of V, which was made of country cloth, with a shell or a tooth dangling. Each held in her right hand a leather hand-piece on which were at least a dozen brass bells and in the other hand, a braided leather whip. Both of these objects were shaken constantly while they danced. One old lady, dressed in a lappa suit, seemed to be the leader. She usually danced "small" and called out words from time to time; then the dancers would change their actions.

The music was made by about 10 to 12 women who had either a long animal horn (actually a piece of it), on which they beat a steady rat-a-tat, very rhythmic. Some had gourds with seeds strung around, as noise-makers. These were rattled and flourished, making quite a racket.

Dancing is such an important part of life here. When a baby begins to walk it starts dancing, as soon as any kind of music is played, or just tapped out with hands on the side of a can or a pot. Men are excellent dancers, too.

It was quite a day. Harold wasn't feeling too well, so we didn't stay too long. He's had another light case of malaria, so has been under the weather and not too ambitious. It takes one a little while to perk up after a bout of malaria, which leaves us feeling washed out. For some reason, I've never had malaria and actually, have 10 times as many mosquito bites. Perhaps I have more resistance.

This week we are going to Monrovia to buy a car. Here at Zorzor there is no transportation except for your work. Any other use necessitates paying 20 cents a mile for use of a hospital vehicle. This is really high for us, since most trips are 50 miles or more. To Monrovia is 170 miles one way. We can buy a car through the church and then sell it when we leave. Harold's bike is fine on the station, but we can't travel on the motor roads with it.

Your box of dolls arrived yesterday. The dolls are darling. Martha was here, and she spent a long time dressing and undressing each one. I told her she could take one back to school with her and also one for her baby, Vikki, and one for Poliakah. So she took another long period of time to check out each one for herself and carried it in her arms when she took the taxi back to school. Big girls really like to play with dolls and have never had one of their own.

On Tuesday, a member of the wedding family brought us a piece of wedding cake, all wrapped up in paper. Apparently, the custom is to not cut the cake at the reception, but to divide it later in the week and carry it around to the guests. I have no idea how they decide who will get it, since there were from 200 to 300 guests!

Thursday. Your good letter just arrived, so I'll write a bit more. We are expecting to go to Monrovia today for the car business. Gene is expected to bring the Bishop for some meetings, so we will return with him in the plane. He was supposed to come yesterday at 10 AM. We sat at the airfield and waited. We could see the rain far away, and sure enough, it was too bad at Phebe to be able to take off. It moved up this way, and then he couldn't land here. He tried three different times. Finally, at 5 PM, we gave up. Now he radioed he would be here at 11 AM, so we'll try again. This is quite typical. Dr. Andy Cole's wife (he's the Liberian hospital director and surgeon) was also trying to go to Phebe to await their baby's arrival. They were expecting to do a C-Section. She has had two already, and both babies came a month too early, so they were quite anxious about this one. She was planning to stay with Dr. Gwenigale, at Phebe, who would do the surgery. Wouldn't you know, she went into labor in the middle of the night, and Dr. Cole had to take her by car at 3 AM to Phebe. The road is pretty bad too. She had her surgery and got a fine big boy. Actually, I don't know if it's big, but at least it's OK. Their other two are girls.

Dear Vikki and Gill,   August 10, 1975, Monrovia

It's a rainy day, or actually, a rainy week. More rain has fallen these past few weeks than in the past 10 years. The streets are under water in many places. We're in Monrovia, in the process of buying a car. I think we should be able to get it Tuesday. There is a lot of paper work, so what began as a three-day stay is turning into almost a week. It will be a Datsun, a hatchback, which is the only kind of car available now, except a VW. The church buys the car, duty free, and then we make a monthly payment to them. When we leave, we can sell it easily, since this kind of car is very popular for a taxi.

Harold and I are reading *The Palace Guard*, all about why Watergate happened. It's hard to understand how the people had such control and were able to manipulate so many people and the general public, ourselves included, could be so unaware or unconcerned about where things were going.

Dearest Mother,   August 11, 1975, Monrovia

We're still sitting down in Monrovia, awaiting the paper work to be done on our car. Perhaps it will be completed by tomorrow, and we can take off for Zorzor. Harold has been busy chasing down necessities for the hospital. It's quite a hassle because you can't just go to a hardware store (there aren't any) or supply houses and expect to get all on your list. It means a lot of running around, waiting interminably, and no doubt, trying something else, or trying someplace else. Traffic in the area is like rush hour on the freeway, horns honking, pedestrians darting in and out, always being on the lookout for rogues if you leave things in the car. Well, that's Liberia!

(We are beginning to make plans for a trip to Scandinavia around Christmas time. The Bong Mine people have a cheap charter every year for one month, so we will try to get on it.)

We've been astounded at the number of blind beggars we see on the streets in Monrovia this time. Begging isn't a Liberian practice. The crippled beggars we see around doorways are mostly Muslims, however; apparently many blind people from Mali have moved in here now. They wander around with a small child leading them and go in and out of shops, begging.

One important cause of blindness is filariasis, caused by a small black fly whose bite results in a tiny worm eventually hatching in a person's tissues. It can attack different parts of the body, like your skin, and also in one's eyes. Eventually, without treatment, blindness results. There is a lot of filariasis here, but not all that much blindness yet. So many of the diseases here in Liberia are due to water-borne parasites and mosquitoes, but so far there is no organized program to do something about it. They are still only trying to treat the diseases rather than getting at causes.

Dearest Mother,   **August 18, 1975, Zorzor**

Tomorrow it will be one month since we came here to Zorzor. I think things are going to be OK. The water does take some getting used to. My dishtowels, sink, etc., look brown most of the time due to the high iron content in the water. I may get so I like the color, but just now it's pretty ugly.

Harold has one crisis after another, it seems. He's been working a good part of the day on the generator. Last night there was terrific rain and a lightning storm, which damaged the power plant, and so far he hasn't found the problem. Without testing equipment, it is very difficult. Tomorrow a testing device should come by plane so we will see. He had to get up at 1:30 AM and close our shutters because we were getting rained on in our bed! Then the lights went out, so he had to get up again, get dressed, and go out in the downpour with a flashlight to the power house, which is a half mile away.

Yesterday in church, a young blind Liberian man gave the sermon. He's about 19 or 20, a senior in a school for the blind in Sierra Leone. (There are no services for the blind in this country.) This fellow became blind due to filariasis [*an infectious tropical disease caused by thread-like filarial nematodes*]. Anyway, he decided he wanted to get an education and come back here and try to do something for the blind here. He is a top student. He's led his class since going to Sierra Leone and is going to graduate in 1976. The President of Liberia is so impressed with the boy that he said he will pay for his college education where ever he wants to go. His name is Sakwei, and he wants to become a minister. The people here who are helping him want him to go to school in the States.

I'm working with a young Liberian nurse who is now the director of the public health program, here. It is similar to the one at Phebe, although he also teaches in the practical nurse and midwife programs. He's having a hard time getting everything done because he is so disorganized and fritters his time away. I'm going to attempt to help him be a better administrator, so he can get everything done that he is supposed to. Right now, I'm team teaching some public health classes with him for first-year students.

We like our new car. It is a burnt orange color, four-door, two-seated Datsun, much easier to ride in than the trucks we usually use. Right now, the roads are particularly bad because of so much rain—deep ruts, churned up mud in spots where your car can get "hitched" before you know what happened. Fortunately Harold knows how to handle a vehicle.

Yesterday we went to a little town about 12 miles from here, named Borkeza. It is the town we visited the first week we were in Liberia and the first market we went to. Zorzor does not have a good market, so we decided to go and see what the market was like there and if it was like the market we remembered visiting more than three years ago. Actually, it was a much bigger market. Everyone had their produce spread out on sheets of plastic on the ground—just a sea of people and produce. We had to weave our way in and around, step over kids, piles of vegetables and fruits, etc.

Markets are so fascinating and fun. We bought a pumpkin (actually a squash), some tangerines, three for 5 cents, limes for a penny each, bananas, two pineapples, 20 cents and 50 cents, three coconuts, collard greens and sweet potato greens, plantain, peanuts, an eggplant, and a fish. This, along with rice and some kind of meat (right now we have some "cow meat" and chicken) will make our dinners for the next week. Market things are about four times higher than they were when we first came to Liberia. Food stuff is fairly economical for us, but kwi food is sky high. Coffee is $2.50 a pound, and so on. Fortunately, we like Liberian chop. And it's much simpler for Alfred to cook Liberian style. I cook if we are having kwi food. His family stayed in Bong County, and he rents a room in town here. But not being acquainted with Loma people (the tribe here), he'd rather stay with us than alone in town. I hadn't bargained for a full-time person, but guess it will work out. It isn't easy for a person from a different tribe to get to know those from another tribal area. Alfred is Kpelle;

there are some Kpelle people here, since the lower half of Lofa County is Kpelle.

We have a dog, a Basenji, such a nice, well-behaved animal. She was owned by a Lutheran pastor from this area who went home. We named her Subah, a Loma name, which we were told was her name. When we came here, we learned Subah was a "human being name," and it was bad to call a dog by a human being name.

We did some checking and found her name must have been Supahveh, which means mixed colors (she's brown and white), but now we're having a hard time breaking the habit of calling her Subah. She became very attached to me almost immediately and doesn't want me to get out of her sight. She goes to work with me every day, lies down in our office, which is a separate little hut. If I'm going to class or into the hospital, I have to make sure she is in our house with the doors shut. Harold wanted a watchdog, but she never wakes up at night if someone comes to the door. He doesn't mind all that much.

Another day. We are staying with our friends Elsie and Ray Minge at Phebe overnight, and then on to Monrovia tomorrow for the car checkup. He is a surgeon from Minnesota, here for a three-year term. They are about our age or a bit more. They are delightful, and fine Christians. She remarked, as we were making up our bed, (we arrived about 8:30, but they welcomed us even though they didn't know we were a coming, since we had no way to notify them), about how close relationships can be out here, with people you've never known before. Perhaps it takes the place of families, but friendships mean so much, and seem to endure even though we later must part. She told me she was so glad we had stopped and stayed with them, and were willing to share ourselves with them. We too look forward to our friends coming and taking the time to stay and visit and, especially, feeling free to just stop in and ask if they can stay all night.

Dear Vikki and Gill,   **August 21, 1975, Zorzor**

We are enjoying our new car, especially the gas mileage. We filled up the tank when we left Monrovia, have driven 270 miles, and the gas gauge still registers more than half full. We have to take it back to Monrovia for its 500-mile check, and it is 180 miles there, which means another trip in a few days. Selling it before we go should not be a problem. People want to buy Harold's motorcycle and his car, because they know he takes good care of his vehicles.

There are many more crafts done here than in Bong or Nimba counties. Country cloth is woven in a town about 20 miles from here. The lepers and TB patients do a lot of basket work, many very beautiful. Hammocks, too, are made locally. We just bought another one yesterday, which we will hang in our little piazza. I call our piazza the bird room because that is where our parrot sits on his perch. He is quite noisy at times.

Pottery, too, is made in a nearby town, country pots which the people use for water. I like them as hanging flower pots. They look nice with macramé hangars. I hung Mali beads on some of the strings. Another thing that is made here is a small, low stool, about six to eight inches high, called a palava stool. It is carved from wood, with the seat carved with a design that often tells a story. Most country houses have at least one such stool, which is brought out for guests to use. The Loma people here seem to be much more interested in design than are the other tribes we've met.

I'm trying to get started on a new job, and finding it much nicer to stay at home. There are so many things I would like to do that I couldn't do this past year because of so much job pressure—cooking and sewing for example. Several projects are developing though, so I'll probably be wound up again. The man I'm supposed to be assisting is so disorganized it's hard to know where to start!

Dearest Mother,   **August 21, 1975, Zorzor**

It's been a long day, with a lot going on. First it was church. Today a Liberian country man preached. Fortunately we could "hear" country English so we understood his sermon, which we enjoyed.

Then we went to a town called Wozi, about 16 miles from here, six of which were a single track road in the bush, which follows the original foot path up and down and around. We took a pickup, which was good since there were many spots that were mired down due to the rains. We drove through coffee and cocoa groves; cocoa is being harvested now. The pods are about the size of an acorn squash, growing right on the trunks of the trees, rather than on the branches. We had made the trip to Wozi so Harold could change the shortwave radio from one building to another. There is a Lutheran Loma literacy center there, where they are translating the Bible, and Harold is supposed to do repair work there as well as at other Lutheran mission stations, besides caring for Zorzor Curran Hospital's problems.

When we reached home, about 6 PM, we found Adama, our Mandingo friend from Ganta, had arrived for a visit. She came with all her trading goods—lots of tie-dye cloth and beads and such. She had just come from Ivory Coast. She always brings me presents, and I, of course, give her something when she leaves. Once I gave her one of my bone china cups, which really pleased her. Tonight she brought me a pair of sandals, two pairs of beads, two pairs of earrings, a leather bracelet, and a batik wall hanging.

She gave Harold—she always calls him Mr. Johnson—a leather wallet on a leather thong to wear around his neck inside his shirt. I'm going to give her one of your dolls for her children. She will stay a couple of days. I usually let people know she is here so they can come to the house to see her things.

So with a "stranger" in the house I had to get busy and cook rice and make a bed. I said to Alfred when we were cooking, "Our house never has a chance to get empty." He said "That because you have good way." He's so funny. One day I told him I didn't like to bake plenty of cookies and cake because it could make Harold too fat. He replied, "Myself, I'd like to be fat a little bit." He's so "dry," which they say here for "thin."

Dearest Ones,   **September 4, 1975, Zorzor**

Our dog is in heat now and Harold wants to have her bred to another Basenji. What a riot, trying to keep her inside with all the traffic through here! Saturday he'll take her to visit a woman who lives in the bush about 20 miles from here, at Wozi. She has a pretty male dog.

We finally moved our parrot outside. He was so messy, and Harold fixed up his cage and hung him in our back porch. He seems to be happy there, still makes a lot of noise, though. Then we hung the hammock in the piazza, put up a bunch of hanging pots—country pots, with palm-thatch ropes—in the windows. The piazza is a screened porch, a nice place for sitting and relaxing. It's actually a very small room but quite cozy.

Dearest Judith and Ciam,   **September 9, 1975, Zorzor**

It's raining and lightning, the tape player is resounding with the Blues Project, Harold is reading *Zen and the Art of Motorcycle Maintenance,* the dog is curled up beside me, and I'm trying to get into letter writing. Keeping up with correspondence has been a real problem for me, because if I'm feeling "some kind of way" about what I'm involved in, that can pervade everything I write.

In the town we went to today, the people were all busy weaving baskets, bags, and mats, and one man, even, was weaving country cloth. There is a craft shop here in Zorzor jointly operated by the church and a Peace Corps volunteer. Also, the Lutheran Church in Monrovia has started a craft shop. They sell country crafts and are learning to do batik work, using African masks as the major design. There is also a tie-dye co-op sponsored by a Peace Corps volunteer with assistance from the United Nations. I think they also sell country crafts.

This area where we are today is very involved with weaving bags and cloth, and since the crafts shops have started, the shop operators have

Airing mattresses at Curran Hospital, with women cooking for their family members who are patients.

been going around to towns and villages to encourage people to make things to sell. There seems to be quite a revival of the work. Formerly, people just made what they needed to use, or made a bag or a hammock now and then, and hung it by the road to attract a few passersby. Now, even women are weaving rice bags, and school boys, too, have picked up the knowledge and are quite consistent about producing.

There is a TB quarter and also a leprosy quarter here at the hospital, and these people are quite busy most of the time weaving and carving. Almost everything carried to Monrovia will sell, because of the tourists and the expatriate community. Prices are much higher these days, but not inconsistent with prices of everything. One little boy here brings me woven bracelets for 10 cents each. I've bought a dozen for the church shop.

Thomas Konie is the RN I'm working with in the community health department. We've decided I will work with students in the out-patient department, helping them with nutrition counseling that is supposed to be done with all mothers who bring a child to the pediatric (under-fives) clinic. Also, I will be working with the mobile clinic staff, trying to improve their work. People tend to let down when they're not supervised. I'm trying to do some radio scripts, and also help him to get organized so he can make better use of his time.

It's been interesting to discover that the community health program here, which started a year before the Phebe program and which I used as a model, is not the fantastic program I was led to believe. In fact, my activities at Phebe, which I left operating as stated in our list of objectives, is actually a better all-around program because we were doing what we said we were going to do, while I've learned that this program has either not gotten some of their things off the ground or they have backslid. I was striving to catch up and now discover we were way ahead! It took a lot of energy and determination, and now, no way to know how things will go with new people at the helm.

Oh yes, I have another activity, learning to type. Here at Zorzor, there is absolutely no one to type for me. It's the first time I've been in this predicament. So four months ago, in Monrovia, I found a manual called *Typing Made Simple*, a kind of programmed approach. So far, I've been quite consistent in doing each lesson as directed. When Thomas goes home at 4:30, I start, and spend two hours. So far, I have completed 13 lessons and fully expect to become a passable typist, at least to do the business letters and reports necessary for my work.

Harold is hunting a frog right now. He opened the door to let the dog out and a frog jumped in. It's the funniest specimen, a thin body and big hind legs and can jump like everything. In fact, he took a "helluva" leap, and now Harold can't locate him. I hope I don't with my foot.

We have two little boys who visit us all the time—mostly looking for food. They live in the orphan quarter but have parents. Peter's mother died, making him an orphan who was raised here. Then his father remarried, had several more kids, and in the meantime got a job at the hospital. The stepmother doesn't like Peter so he's mostly had to look after himself. He's eight years old but is no bigger than a five year old. His brother, Flumo, is about the same size. They come every day soon in the morning and get some biscuits from us. No matter when they come, they say "Morning." When we drive, they seem to spring from nowhere and are there to carry our things.

This evening, Peter came to the door carrying a huge cucumber on his head for me. It looked like a big pawpaw and must have weighed a pound. I have no idea where he got it; it's so mature it probably won't taste good. At least it was a present. We gave him and his brother some ground peas. Later, Flumo and his little sister came to the door. It was pouring rain, and they hadn't a stitch on, which is a common sight, especially in the villages. There's not much need to wear clothes, and it's a good way to take a bath!

Dearest Mother,   **September 12, 1975, Zorzor**

I'm involved in another project, trying to get a coordinating organization going for mission-related health programs. I found myself becoming the secretary and coordinator of the whole thing, almost by accident. So along with the trip to Monrovia for the car check, I've been up to my ears in conferences and planning meetings and such. Anyway, it's a much-needed agency, which could make it possible to buy drugs in huge quantities at low cost, etc.

I have to describe a trip we made to one of our clinic sites, in Zolowo. Leaving the hospital in the morning was something like a Marx Brothers movie. Nothing comes off in the same sequence twice, and things that should be done first, like filling the gas tank, are thought of last. Loading the motorcycle, which we were to deliver on the way home, became another comedy. We were finally all aboard, but then we had to stop in town for someone's things, who I then learned will stay in town, and then we were finally off at 9AM, the time we should be nearing Zolowo.

It is a 19-mile trip. The single track road winds through the bush up hill, then a short level run, and then down, to the rain puddle—mud

and mire—at the bottom, then up the hill. Halfway up, it becomes gran-
ite rock, jagged boulders, which we bounced over. Most of the hills are
creased with vertical gullies, carved out by the torrential rains gushing
down. The gullies twist and turn, finally veering off the side into a ditch
where the water can run off. A mile from a town called Salayea and five
miles from our destination, Zolowo, we rounded a corner and came to an
abrupt stop. The road appeared to be washed out over a culvert that had
rotted and broken away. Our Toyota 4x4 had too wide a wheel base for
the driver to chance it. The all-night rain had made the road so soft that
the pressure from the tire made more of the road break into the flowing
water, two feet down.

We all were out of our vehicle by now, everyone giving their opinion,
but not coming to a decision. Personally, I felt we couldn't chance it. Soon
a loaded pickup approached from Zolowo down the steep and winding
track; it appeared to rock from side to side, its top was loaded so high.
Inside it was loaded to more than capacity. The driver, a Mandingo as is
ours, and his companion alit, shook hands all around, and looked over the
situation. Then he said "Reverse your pickup; I'm going to cross." I was
afraid to watch, but believe it or not he gunned the motor, and rrrmm, he
bounced over, no palava. So what to do; we too must try.

Afraid to even watch, let alone ride in the pickup, I decided to walk up
the hill. The rest of my team clambered aboard with my fool-hardy driver,
and as I looked around, away he came, his rear wheels left the ground as
he cleared the hole. He didn't stop until he was half way up the hill. "Well
anyway," he said, as the rest of the people clambered aboard, "now is all
right; we made it. By tonight it will be worse. If the rain comes again, I
don't think we will able it." The rest of the drive was OK; some places were
good, some not so good. At least there was no traffic on these roads. Some
of the people walking at the side of the road called to us, "The people are
waiting in town for you."

It was about 10:30 by the time we reached Zolowo. It turned out to
be a long day. We saw and treated a total of 1,100 patients, so it was after
4 when we finished. Then a man had cooked for us. He was a teacher in
the school whose nephew was on our team today. He was one of the physician's assistant students from JFK Hospital who are affiliating in Lofa
County for two months. The teacher cooked rice and two kinds of soup—
palm kernel oil with bush hog and river crawfish, cooked *topagee* style

(using country soda, which results in a rather pungent mouth-puckering flavor; it takes some getting used to). Also potato greens and bush hog. It was all quite tasty. Some of our fellows ate from a common bowl with their hands, but spoons were provided for us.

At the entrance to the town of Zolowo, there was an arch over the road, built of two upright sticks with a crossbar. Suspended from it was a net-like formation of palm thatch holding a head of palm nuts. I asked the team nurse what it was. He replied, "For sacrifice." "Who can do so?" "A person in the town. For the town," was his reply. "When they can take it down?" "When the time come, it will go away," finished the conversation.

The six miles back to Salayea took a good 45 minutes. They found the hole even worse than in the morning. So again we all alighted from the truck, and our driver made the same kind of crossing as in the morning. Then we had to take another branch of the road to get to Tinsu, where the leprosy worker who travels with the mobile clinic with his Suzuki would get off with his medicines and supplies.

Tinsu was a fairly large town only four and a half miles away but the road there was little more than a foot path. Then it would turn into a two-path road, again winding around and up, looking at times as though the road would fall away in a sheer drop, then as the truck crested the hill, the road is steep, full of gullies and boulders, and at the bottom, a stream with a bridge across, the bridge being constructed of logs laid vertically, just a bit wider than the vehicle's wheels.

So we finally reached Tinsu, where we must delay while the people go for the chief. Then we learn he has gone to Zorzor and failed to pass the necessary information about the planned leprosy survey along to the acting chief. Well, never mind, it appeared that the town people agreed. So the motorcycle came out of the truck. Quite a process with all kinds of advice and help, and by this time as well, hordes of little kids appeared. It was a toss-up which sight is more absorbing, the white woman or the motor bike.

By the time we finally got back to Zoror, it was 6:40 and coming to be dark. The drive from Salayea to the hospital is only a matter of 12 miles, but there was another stop in Sukaramu, on the road, to deliver medicine to the clinic for a tuberculosis patient there.

And nothing is as simple as just handing it over to the clinic worker, with directions clearly written. No. The four packages of medicine had to be inspected, counted, discussed, and marked, before everything was clear.

Dearest Mother,   **September 28, 1975, Zorzor**

This has been a nice relaxed day for a change. Today I actually had time to work on the pair of trousers I'm trying to make for Harold. So far I've spent hours on them, just making two back and two front pockets! Well, just so they fit when I finally finish them.

Someone must have just died in the hospital; there is a lot of loud wailing, probably a child, since it sounds like it's from the pediatrics area. We live close to the hospital so really hear it a lot.

Today the male dog arrived, with its owner of course, so Subie was bred. Wouldn't you know Harold started to figure, afterward, when the babies will arrive and it's three weeks before we leave for Europe? Now he'll have to figure out what he's going to do with her. Of course Alfred could stay but we wanted to let him go home to be with his family; it would be lonely for him to be all alone here.

Today a letter came from my former students at Ganta Mission asking me to be their graduation speaker. I was really pleased, surprised too, even though it means an extra thing to do. Well there's plenty of time— it's not until March.

Dearest Vikki and Gill,   **October 3, 1975, Monrovia**

It was interesting to hear about your possible C-section, with a breech presentation. I wasn't aware that doctors were no longer choosing to deliver them as usual. Here, they are delivered by midwives, as are 99 percent of the deliveries.

Two of the American nurse midwives who have been here 10 years and who have been teaching midwifery all that time have developed a method of turning a breech. They have the patient assume the knee-chest position for five minutes every day, and usually the baby will turn and remain in the proper position.

I learned this while still at Gbedin and practiced it with my prenatal patients and have checked many prenatal records since, while at Phebe. It really works. I've been behind these two gals to document their observations, and at Phebe they've set up a system so that the nurse there is to be called to check every breech and to follow them up.

We're in Monrovia again for some meetings. I may have mentioned an organization I've been involved with, getting all the church medical people together for better coordination of effort. We met all day today and will tomorrow, too. Harold decided he should come too—you know he really gets lonesome when I'm gone—looks so woebegone, poor guy. So he and Dr. Cole came together in our car. Harold enjoys him a lot, and they seem to be very compatible.

When I reached Gbarnga in the taxi, John was waiting on the same corner where we stopped, trying to get a ride to Zorzor. He had a long weekend and was coming to be with us. He saw me in the taxi and ran across the road and spoke to me. Was I surprised to hear his voice! So he went on and stayed with Harold that night and then with Alfred, since he had a bunch of studying to do for national exams in late October.

He seems to be doing satisfactorily this term, and if he passes, we'll send him back next year. The Brothers have been good for him; they have very high standards and strict rules and do operate a good school.

Dearest Mother,   **October 6, 1975, Zorzor**

We just got back Saturday night from four days in the city where I was very involved in an organizational meeting of heads of medical missions in Liberia. It was really gratifying that we actually got the group organized, drew up a constitution, and laid out a plan of work with actual dates when things will be done. I can't believe it yet. Of course there's a lot of work yet for follow up.

We're investigating sources for less expensive drugs, for example. This thing has been on again and off again for five years but this time it worked. For one thing, the principal people there were Liberian doctors, not just missionaries who tend to like to "do their own thing."

We are so fortunate to have such fine young Liberian doctors and leaders—three particularly. Each one heads up a mission hospital. They're under 40 and have received their college and medical training in the States; one is a board surgeon, and one has some surgical residency done already. Getting their education has been a struggle but was made possible by missionaries.

They're fine, Christian people and excellent doctors, with a lot of concern for their people. So that's one of the good things about our work. Dr. Cole, the young man in charge here, lived in a town way up near the Sierra

Leone border. When he was 11½ years old, his older brother in Monrovia sent for him to come there and go to school. He had never attended yet—no school in his area. So since there was no road, he and two companions walked through the bush to within 40 miles of Monrovia where they met the motor road. This took seven days, sleeping in villages at night. He was sent to the Catholic school and completed through the twelfth grade in 10 years. (He never went home for eight years, at which time the road had been put in, and he could go by car.)

Then he started at the University of Liberia but soon was told about a scholarship possibility. He and 55 others took the exam. He was in the top 15. Then they took another exam, and he and one other were selected to go and study in the States, what and where they wished. He wanted to be a doctor and go to a Catholic school. So he was sent to Gonzaga and then on to the University of Washington medical school.

Later he spent a couple of years in surgical residency and just came back about one year ago. He said if he could do what he'd like most to do it would be to stay and practice in the States. But he is very matter of fact about the belief that he has a debt to humanity and feels this is where he should be, at least for a while. Hopefully he'll get to go back eventually and complete his work for full surgeon status.

In the meantime, he's running this place, supervising the public health in the district, doing all the surgery, on call all the time, trying to do what needs to be done on too little money and shortages of so many necessities and doing a good job, quite cheerfully most of the time.

Dear Vikki and Gill,   October 9, 1975, Zorzor

Today we had our monthly meeting of health workers in the Zorzor district; we did the same thing in Bong County. Anyway after the usual health discussion—today the topic was sanitation, and a great deal of talk was about toilets, getting people to build them and use them—then we all eat together. This is called entertainment.

Since our hospital was hosting the group, we were responsible for the food. I don't know how many pounds of rice they used, but it amounted to about a wash tub full when cooked; they had a goat, six chickens, and some fish and made two soups, one with collard greens. We had three cakes, some doughnuts, and two cases of Fanta. Nothing was left! All the little kids, like from the orphan quarter, flocked around the table as soon as the adults left and picked up everyone's bones and scampered off with their hands full.

Dearest Mother,   **October 16, 1975, Zorzor**

It is still raining these days, quite hard, even though people say dry season should begin. Gene said the field was so wet yesterday morning that his plane sank to the axles when he pushed it out of the hanger.

He was due in here yesterday but never made it; came today instead. He was carrying a trio of people into a bush village which is an eight-hour walk from here; when they got there, about 15 goats were on the field, despite his frequent threats to stop flying if they don't corral the goats. Consequently he brought the people back, a woman whose baby had been in the hospital here and the clinic nurse. He doesn't have a lot of patience.

Martha is home this weekend. John is due, too, but so far we haven't seen him. He had a long way to go, usually involving two or three taxies so it isn't surprising that he is late. Martha can always get a ride from Lutheran Training Institute without trouble.

Martha, Alfred, and I made pizza tonight, quite an undertaking but it always turns out fine and is a nice change from soup. Lately the market has been so poor—hard to find greens and seldom can see palm nuts, so planning meals is more of a problem.

This afternoon while we were making pizza, Martha was standing in the back door watching the puppies and suddenly yelled "snake!" Alfred and I ran out, too, and saw a green snake slither off the porch, through the grass, and into a mass of Wandering Jew growing over a stump. He grabbed a rake, she the mortar "pencil" (pestle), and I the grass whipper.

By this time the snake was out of sight but Alfred kept beating on the plants and raking them off the stump, and finally the snake darted away on the other side. (This was just at the edge of our back porch where our puppies live.) Martha yelled and started to beat on the snake, Alfred joined in, and I just jumped around—my grass whipper was much too short to do anything. She killed it after a few blows. It was about two feet long and looked like a mamba, which is poisonous. Actually, it was a pretty, dark green, velvety-looking thing.

With so many trees around, we do have a lot of snakes. I never think of looking in the trees when I'm walking under them, and that is where a lot of snakes "hang out." I figure if I don't bother them they won't bother me!

Dr. Cole has gone to Ghana for two months for some administrative training so the Ministry of Health sent two doctors to stay while he is gone. We've decided we would be better off without them. One is a Pakistani who studied in the States the last two years. Has little respect for nurses, comes late, goes early, and often won't come when called in the night. The other is a Nigerian who graduated from the Monrovia Medical School and must work a year for the government. As a student at Phebe, he was lazy and isn't much different here. He keeps the same hours as his friend. It is really difficult to work under such circumstances and the morale of the nurses is terrible as a result. But we'll manage someway.

Dear Vikki and Gill,   **October 19, 1975, Zorzor**

Lately I've been so involved in sewing for Harold. Finally finished the pair of trousers; what a lengthy job. They look pretty good but it took me about three straight days to make them. Have also been making three shirts for him at the same time, doing "design" stitching with the Elna machine. And I've spent about as much time ripping it out as putting it in, once because I'd stitched on the wrong side of a collar, another time because it puckered up too much. I can never find a shirt at a tailor shop to fit Harold because they're always too small through the shoulders and under the arms.

We've been reading Psalms each morning after breakfast. There's no bible study group here at Zorzor so Harold and I have our own "part of study." One would assume that on a mission station there would be quite a religious emphasis, but people get pretty involved in their work, and the atmosphere is the same as you'd find in any hospital set up. There's very little "spiritual food" unless you have it yourself. Actually the Christian community is pretty small, since most people are animistic. (Ancestor worship is much more important than Jesus Christ.)

Yesterday Donna Hutten came via taxi to spend the weekend and went home in the plane today when it brought the doctor back from a trip into the bush. Donna is a Peace Corps RN who came to Phebe last fall to work with the community health department. She and I had the neatest working relationship. She's a fairly new RN—had worked one year and was assigned here as a leader of a group of five other health volunteers in Bong County. We were very compatible; she could pick up a project I was on and carry it on. We often wrote reports in tandem; she'd do a piece, and I'd do a piece, and when it was put together it would fit. I hated to leave her at Phebe but she is really needed there, could have replaced me with no problem except there was another missionary there who was supposed to do the work.

Dearest Mother and all,   **October 24, 1975, Zorzor**

Another week gone by; we've done so much running around it's whizzed by—spent three days in Monrovia on CHAL business while Harold "ran behind" some well digging pumps. Then the next day took off for Cuttington College where I presented some material on visual aids to a group of new health volunteers.

We stayed overnight with the Austins at Phebe—they are the hostel parents and used to be our neighbors at Phebe. Jan Olson, the Peace Corps volunteer who works with me here, came along and helped with the lesson.

Yesterday we took off for Sanniquellie, which is about 150 miles away, to check up on John who had written that he was in a taxi accident and had broken his left arm. While it should be dry season coming now, we have been having an unwarranted amount of rain—steady downpour so that the roads are just awful.

On one hill in Nimba County we met a line-up of about six big trucks that had been there since in the night. A semi was jackknifed in the middle of the hill, a big transport truck was in the ditch on one side, and a VW bus was in the ditch on the other side (this is a two-lane dirt road). Fortunately there was just room for Harold to pass between the two big vehicles, with some people pushing a bit—our car is quite small, as you know. When we came back later in the afternoon, the semi was still in the road on the hill with parts of the motor strewn around and a couple of legs sticking out of the under-hood area.

Dearest Vikki and Gill,   **October 25, 1975, Zorzor**

Today we'll go to try to find a well digger and try to get him to come and dig a well and toilet for the TB area and the orphan quarter. He has two pumps donated and some money for the digger so maybe that can get done. We've been on it for months.

Tuesday. John came home last night late. He had been in a taxi accident a week earlier—the taxi was speeding—his upper left arm was broken so they took him to Lamco hospital where he was given a cast. About three days later, his people heard about it and arrived from the country, crying and carrying on. They took him back in the bush where the "bone doctor" removed the cast with a bucket of warm water and put on a bamboo splint—too short and not firm, country mud, etc.

When we finally got a letter from him, we wrote telling him he must get back to school and come here or to the Lamco Hospital and get fixed properly. This gave him a chance to leave, and he took off in the night, reaching here 24 hours later.

Doctor Gwenegali, at Phebe, took an x-ray and said it was in good position and just used a sling and bandage. So he's staying here a couple more weeks and then will get back to school—it closes in early December. It's nice having him home for a while.

Dearest Mother and all,   October 31, 1975, Zorzor

We're planning our first Christian Health Association meeting for December, and I have all the arrangements to make for that. It will be in Monrovia. I hope a new secretary is elected then; they'll have to by May anyway.

John is home for a couple of weeks with a broken arm. Yesterday one of his friends from Gbedin came to spend the weekend. He used to be Pearmines' houseboy and helped in our house too. He's a tenth grader at St. Mary's in Sanniquellie. He left this AM.

In the afternoon John and I cooked fufu and peanut butter soup for Sharon and Kathy—they'd never eaten it. Since Alfred is at his home for the weekend, most of my time was spent in the kitchen! Washing dishes is a real job when you have to heat the water in a bucket, carry it in, etc.

Thomas Konie had another tragedy last week. Another one of his sons died from sickle cell anemia. Three months ago, a son died from Sickle Cell and a week later his mother died, and now this one. Too sad.

People's extended families are so large that there's always a member of the family sick or in need, so nurses are often much too distracted from the main job. Difficult to deal with these cultural things, having been so imbued with our different standards.

Dearest Judith and Ciam,   **November 2, 1975, Zorzor**

I'm trying to sort out the medical stores and set up a system for stock control. Nothing has been done there for about two years, and you can't imagine the shambles. We're trying to reorganize the mobile clinic activity; morale is very low, fees are being "eaten," record keeping has been nil, etc. I'm also trying to put together a proposal for funding for a child nutrition rehabilitation center. So there are not enough hours in the days!

We are excited about the possibility of you and Ciam coming to visit next summer. It sounds as though Mom will come to Denmark to meet us, and perhaps come back here with us.

We've killed three snakes around our house lately, none have been poisonous, but they were pretty ugly. One was a boa constrictor about three feet long. Of course, people here think all snakes are poisonous; however, they eat a lot of snakes. I've never tasted snake, but we had porcupine yesterday for the first time. We didn't know what it was when we bought it from a girl walking on the motor road. She only knew the Loma name, but Alfred knew it when he saw the skin.

Dearest Mother,   **November 7, 1975, Zorzor**

The children left for school today. John with his arm in a sling with a wide bandage wrapped to keep his arm immobile against his side. The doctors say they don't usually put a cast on a fractured humerus, just immobilize it in this way. He must keep it in a sling for another three to four weeks. Martha took the nursing test Saturday—will learn Monday or Tuesday if she passed. Then of course she has to pass the tenth grade before she can enter the nursing program. We dropped her off at LTI on our way to Monrovia. I hate the trip—it's so long—but had to come to make some arrangements for the CHAL meeting next month and Harold needs more parts, etc. If he doesn't go himself, he always gets sent the wrong thing.

Thursday was Liberian Thanksgiving. I baked chicken and stuffing— had to borrow some sage—and Martha made pumpkin (actually squash) pie, the first time she had tried. She likes to bake and learn new things and does it well. Of course, we had rice, too, for the Liberians—it wouldn't be a meal without that.

Gladys left this week so we inherited her "yard man." He is an old crippled fellow who kept her flowers nicely, and every day he had rice and soup there. She was worried about what would happen to him and his little girl so we said he could clean around our flowers, and Alfred would give him rice and soup at noon each day. He has a little girl about four years old named Mami. She spends the day with him.

Dearest Judith,   **November 11, 1975, Zorzor**

Just now I'm sipping a papaya drink which I just invented today, pawpaw [*papaya*], ice, sugar, and lemon juice in the blender, quite refreshing and very pretty, kind of a tangerine color.

This has been an interesting but hectic few days. A few days ago the nurses went on strike—were off for two days—over a problem about back pay. At the same time Gail Thompson, our friend from Cuttington, came for Liberian Thanksgiving and stayed three days. Then Sunday two friends from Peace Corps days in Gbedin came to drop off three health volunteers who were coming for some training with Thomas and me. They came back last evening and stayed until noon today.

This evening Daniel Suah, Harold's friend from Foya, stopped in for a visit. He was a mechanic in Gbedin when we first came over. Harold taught him a lot and recommended him for a job at Foya with an Israeli company. He's Mano, but also speaks French, having been raised and taught in Guinea. He's worked his way up since 1972 and now is manager of the project there, a big rice project, with his company responsible for all the land clearing, planting, and harvesting.

Harold is so proud of him—he always calls Harold his old pa and thanks him so much for his help.

Dear Vikki and Gill,   **November 15, 1975, Kakata**

We are at Ming Ho's house in Garma. He's returned from Taiwan for another two years and is now at Kakata, about 40 miles from Monrovia. We're going to stay this evening and go on to Phebe tomorrow. He's so much fun and was so happy to see us that we decided to stay all night.

We have to be in Monrovia for two days for a meeting of the Christian Health Association of Liberia, a new organization I've been involved in getting organized. I ended up getting elected secretary/treasurer. One of the reasons why we wanted to form the organization was so we could set up bulk purchase of drugs. For example, buying in a group from overseas, we could get aspirin for about $1 a thousand, chloroquin for $6 to $8 a thousand instead of $12 a thousand, etc. Now we have to get a grant proposal together to try to get a donation to get a building and the initial purchase. Lots of work; maybe by the time we leave we'll be in business.

We're cooking lobster tonight. Harold found some at a roadside fish market in Monrovia. He put them on the floor of the car, took them to a friend's freezer, and then today we put them in a bucket with some ice and brought them to Ming Ho. He'd never cooked them before and neither have we, so we'll see what happens.

Dearest Mother,   **November 15, 1975, Kakata**

We are staying overnight with a Chinese friend at Kakata. He was our neighbor at Gbedin and has recently come back to Liberia with an agricultural project. (I taught him English when he first came.) We've been in Monrovia for some meetings and will go on tomorrow. Now he's cooking for us; in addition to lobster, he's killed a chicken and is preparing fish and pork, cabbage, green beans, cucumbers. It's always a feast; no way to get them to cut down. He's a really good cook.

The weather is getting pretty warm now. Fortunately in Zorzor it never gets as warm as near the coast. The altitude is higher, so both night and day it's nicer. Rains only come about once a week. Consequently, we must carry water from the well (about a block away) for laundry and baths. Good we don't have a big family. Alfred and Wilmot, the boy who works in our yard, carry the water.

Our big kids have finished school now. Ninth graders have to take national exams so they did that on Thursday. If they passed they can go into the tenth grade. John was baptized into the Catholic Church. We were so happy he did this. (He changed his name to Jacob when he was baptized.) Martha was baptized at Easter and has been taking catechism since then. Both of them have been improving all year. Martha will work in the hospital during vacation, and John has a job on a farm near his school, working for a former Peace Corps fellow, a friend of ours.

Dearest Vikki and Gill,   **November 23, 1975, Zorzor**

We're really ready for a vacation, especially so since we'll be meeting Mom. We got her on the Bong Mine Charter back to Liberia with no problem so it looks like we're all set.

This work is really frustrating—so many things have been badly mismanaged for years. And while trying to improve methods is expected on one hand, getting the people in power to really mean it is practically impossible on the other hand. Every other day or so Harold comes home fuming and the next day tries again. One doctor, a missionary, ran the place for 10 years in a very authoritarian way. He's now working for USAID in the county with a special rural health project and stays here and is still running the place.

On the other hand Doctor Cole, a fine young man and competent surgeon, is really the medical director but he doesn't want to be the administrator and has committees to make decisions. Trying to get a decision on really serious things is next to impossible. He refers it. So Dr. Mertens, the USAID man, goes on making his own decisions. Impossible situation for people who are responsible for departments because they can never really have the authority they need or expect to get the backup they need. It isn't too bad for me because I'm not in charge of anything and also because it's fairly easy for me to do what I want to do and defend my stand if necessary. Well, we keep on trying!

Martha is with us this month, working as a volunteer at the hospital. She'll go to the country when we leave. It's nice having her. She's doing some sewing for the children in her family and helps around the house.

Dear Vikki and Gill,   **November 29, 1975, Zorzor**

Lately little kids have been bringing avocados to the house, big fat ones for 1 cent each. What a bargain. They also bring pawpaw—3 cent, 3 cent, like that. It's next to impossible to find vegetables, though, except collard, cassava, and potato greens.

Last night we had five men from the Ministry of Health for dinner, three Liberians, an Indian, and, a Turk. The two latter were WHO [*World Health Organization*] epidemiologists. Tonight we had Dr. Cole, his wife, and three little tots for dinner. I was just looking at the calendar and saw that we had dinner guests each day for 14 days, and overnight guests seven different nights. We've been talking about starting some kind of a fee system, because a few of us have people so much. (I had the group for breakfast this morning, too.)

Tomorrow Harold will fly to Monrovia for an overnight stay. He has to try to line up a Chinese rice specialist to come here and operate the hospital rice farm. He has such good relationships with the Chinese that he's the best person to go on such an errand. He has to come back as far as Phebe by taxi and then the rest of the way by plane again. It will be the first time I've stayed alone here at Zorzor.

Lately I've been swamped with all kinds of writing assignments. A proposal for a Nutrition rehabilitation center—the mission board will give us $6,000 for it—and a proposal for a new carpentry area and improved maintenance shop. Also had to produce the mimeographed Christmas letter and several different letters for our new health organization. It all takes me so long to do because I'm the typist and mimeo person, too.

Christmas Letter   **December 4, 1975, Zorzor**

We want to share some pre-Christmas thoughts with you and let you know we are still alive and well here in our part of Africa. Soon it will be a year and a half since we came back to Liberia. Some days we're sure we've been here forever; other days we are apt to say "Where has the time gone!" Some days...discouraging, frustrating, other days we can feel good about being here.

There is so much to be thankful for. We're blessed with good health, good friends, a chance to serve where we can use our skills, the love of Jesus Christ. Yes, there are many more blessings, being able to meet people from many different countries and walks of life and to share ideas with them; having a second "family"—our two Liberian youngsters who are now in tenth grade; looking forward to Christmas with Mom in Denmark, our first holiday together in five years. It's nice to have such things to hold on to, on "those" days. Changes come so slowly here—don't they anyplace? But looking back three or four years, we know things have improved and we can't help but be hopeful about the future.

Every once in a while something happens to remind us that our time and efforts haven't been wasted. My work at Phebe Hospital last year with a measles vaccination program was a positive experience. Measles is one of the major killers of little kids in Liberia—in most West African countries for that matter. This came as a great surprise to me when I first started to do health work here.

A year ago, from September until the first of the year, with vaccine supplied by the Ministry of Health (actually UNICEF), our seven-man team immunized around 16,000 youngsters under six years. In case this doesn't sound like such a fantastic number, picture how we got around— by VW bus or Land Rover in either a cloud of dust or mired in mud; or walking and head-loading supplies on bush paths; or when the distances were too far in the bush, going by the church plane, sometimes sleeping in the villages.

But the satisfying part of it all was that we did not see measles during the usual measles time, January to June, as in previous years and as the rest of the country was continuing to see.

Now here we are at Curran Lutheran Hospital in Zorzor, starting with pretty much the same kind of situation that we've met with in our other two assignments. There are so many needs, so many things to do that it isn't easy to know where to start. And obviously many of them can be better done by others. We are in hopes that with God's blessing we will be able to help work out some of the problems in the next year or so.

Ruth and her mother, Signe Hanson, visiting a patient.

[*Ruth and Harold traveled in Scandinavia for a month, visiting their relatives. Ruth's mother joined them there and returned to Liberia with them for a month's stay.*]

Dale Veeneman's wedding party. From left: Ruth, Ben Newlon and friend, Marlene and Mike McFadden, Rich White and his partner Mirando, Dale Veeneman, and Harold.

1976

Dearest Mother,   **February 5, 1976, Zorzor**

It all seems like a dream, our being together for five weeks and your being here. The time passed so quickly, and so much was going on, that as I look back on it now, I feel like I was in a whirlwind.

I really missed you after you'd left—found myself quite "down in the mouth" for a while. I hope your spirits haven't suffered. It meant so much to us to have you, dearest mother.

We're back in the harness again. So much work to do after more than a month away. Thomas hadn't done the monthly newspaper so we had to get that done—write a couple of articles for it, mimeograph, fold etc. Then graduation for the LPNs and midwives took a weekend.

Now we're trying to do the 1975 year-end report—two months late, and the 1976 year plan, laying out what we expect to do this year. It's hard on me to wait for Thomas to take the lead. It would be so much easier to go ahead and do it myself but he has to learn to manage his time and take the responsibility for such things.

This week we've had visitors from the Ministry of Health Family Health Division, two RNs, a health educator, and a WHO doctor plus driver. They stayed two nights, one here with us. Martha had to move to the couch. She's been attending vacation school.

Yesterday I finally sat down and made a dress for myself—the first in several months. Starting the 15th, next weekend, I'll be staying at Cuttington College for the Bong County Health Planning Seminar. I hate to be away for a week but guess we can stand it.

Dearest Vikki and Gill,   **February 7, 1976, Zorzor**

My friend Nyarinda (the Kenyan woman, married to Dr. Cole) has been telling me how difficult her two-and-a-half-year-old boy has been. His name is Omandi, a bright cute child. She also has a seven-month-old son, a chubby cheerful baby and a four-and-a-half-year old daughter. She has an MS in social work from the University of Washington and understands child development but really keeps busy with three tots. Also teaches at the teacher training institute four miles from here.

We're back in the "harness" again here. So many projects to work on. Today we went for a motor bike ride around the area. It's nice to get out of the house and hospital.

Dear Vikki and Gill,   **February 12, 1976, Zorzor**

We have had a lot of people in and out. Poliakah is with us again so there has been sewing to see to, too. Then I've been trying to prepare a speech for a nursing graduation at Ganta, which also takes me a long time to accomplish. That graduation is next weekend, on Sunday. The day before is a meeting of our New Christian Health Association, at Phebe.

So we are combining the two events, and Harold will go along and go on to Gbedin to visit friends while I'm at the ceremony at Ganta Mission. The kids who are graduating were students of mine while I was still in Peace Corps.

Today the President came to Zorzor for the inauguration of the first town mayor. There was a lot of celebrating going on, country bands, dancing, many people in town. People really turn out.

As a result of all the extra people around, our house was like a revolving door. Dale Veeneman, his girlfriend, and another Peace Corps volunteer arrived for lunch, two nurses from Phebe arrived for the weekend—will sleep at a different house—a nurse came in to press her dress for the occasion, a representative came by to get ice cubes for the party, the director of nurses ran over and asked me to drive her into town to the celebration to find the doctor because there was an emergency surgery—

all this between 11 and 2 PM! Then Nyrinda came later and picked up Poliakah for a hot dog roast—a new experience for her—so Harold and I are alone for a quiet evening.

It's been raining off and on today, making a nice cool time. They graded the roads in town yesterday because of the visitation. Now with the rain and the additional traffic, the roads are a mess, full of mud and deep ruts again.

Not long ago, four o'clock like that, a woman was brought in from an auto accident in which a tree fell on the taxi, killing her husband and injuring others in the vehicle. A man was clearing farm [*clearing away bushes and trees to plant rice*] and sawed a tree down, letting it fall toward the road. People are very careless. That is the second such accident in this area in less than a year. In the first one, the tree blew down in a bad storm.

Did I ever tell you that there is a very high incidence of twins in this country? On Tuesdays we see around 200 children, and there are often a half dozen sets of twins—in fact more, probably, judging by the names, but only one is still living quite often. People have the belief that twins are apt to join together and kill a parent, or maybe one parent or the other will be caused to "go crazy" by the twins. They also believe that one twin baby will say to the other, "Well I'd better go back now, so everything can go to you, and you will be strong." I'm sure people have to find some explanation or justification for so many dying.

As a result of such beliefs, people tend to care more for one baby and actually neglect one to the point that it will die. I've noticed so often one twin will weigh one or two pounds less than the other—these are very young infants where a pound makes quite a difference. Before long there is just one child left. So often when you ask where the other baby is, the people say "it went back."

We have a cement walk from the parking lot to our house, about 300 feet long. On each side of it is a row of amaryllis with orange blossoms. They are simply beautiful right now, masses of blossoms all along the path.

Not much more than a month ago, they looked like dried up old bulbs, and I was thinking of taking them out and replanting them. Then they began to grow again, and within a week there was an explosion of blooms.

Dearest Mother,   **February 16, 1976, Suakoko**

While the meetings are going on I can take time to do some writing. Discussions tend to get off track, and my attention can wander very easily. I'm at Cuttington College for seven days as a resource person at the county health planning seminar. So far all the people who were invited have shown up—about 50 health assistants, midwives, health inspectors, nurses, etc. There are eight of us on the staff—two from the US from the planning organization in New York. It has been fun to come and see old friends and acquaintances whom I worked with while at Phebe.

I rode down to Monrovia with Dr. Mertens on Saturday just behind a Phebe vehicle that had four flats between Phebe and Monrovia. We stopped every time, took the people to a town, waited for patching, went back—what a day. It took us four and a half hours to get there instead of the two it should have.

We stayed with the Minges on Saturday might, and Martha stayed with Darlene. She and Harold came with me on Saturday and then went back on Sunday. The Minges will be leaving for home in two months. We'll really miss them.

We haven't had mail delivery for quite a while. Gene hasn't been up for more than a week, and people haven't been coming by. We did hear from Judith though, who said she and Ciam will be coming the last of May.

Last Friday we went to Ziggida to see the boys coming out of bush school. This is the first one held in 14 years for the Loma boys. In seven years one will be held for girls. In the morning before we got there, the boys had been brought into town—over 500 of them. Even little boys two to three years old were there, and on up through high school age.

All the boys were dressed in brightly striped robes made of the country cloth. The robes came nearly to the ground, were open on the sides. Over the shoulders each wore a scarf of some sort, knitted or crocheted, or a striped towel. On their heads they wore a kind of "stocking hat" made of country cloth, fringed by the face, nearly covering the eyes. All wore new shorts and shirt underneath and were barefooted. A bright piece of cloth was tied around the head.

Mats were spread in front of a house in several parts of the town, and all the boys in that quarter were seated there. It was amazing how nicely all the kids sat there in the hot sun and then they walked around single file to the next spot they were to occupy. Women would come dancing in a group, singing, playing sashas (gourd rattles); someone was beating a drum. People would give coins to some of the children. One man who must have been an official dancer was wearing a country cloth belt adorned with a bunch of little brass bells.

He jogged around from site to site, danced for a while, jogged on to another site. One big tall man told us he was the official warrior. He was carrying a spear and posed for Harold to take a picture.

It is believed that the children don't know anyone—not even their families—that they have been reborn "out of the devil's belly." They have to be taken around the town and introduced to everyone, shown where they live, even how they eat rice!

We met the boy who carried us around Konia the day you were there. He came up to me and asked about you and asked me to remember him to you. Then we stopped at the store in Konia on the way back, and there we met a couple of other people who had met you when we

Boys just back from bush school.

stopped at the clinic there. They say, "How is the old lady? She gone back now?"

It has begun to rain, surprisingly; it is too early for rainy season. Maybe it's a false alarm. It's thundering, lightening, rain is pouring down, and wind is blowing so hard that all the windows and doors in this big classroom are banging and swinging back and forth. It's so noisy we can hardly hear the talking, what with all these noises. Last night, too, it started to thunder and lightning, and all of a sudden the lights went out on the campus. It was about a half hour before the people got a generator going. This is going to be a long week—from 8 AM until 10 PM, Sunday through Saturday.

Dearest Mother,   **February 23, 1976, Zorzor**

I'll have to tell you about Harold's adventure today. He had to go to Suakako to do some work so he took Alfred along so he could visit his family. After they had passed Gbarnga, they saw an iguana, about two and one half to three feet long, run across the road. Harold stopped quickly, and Alfred took off after it—it had run into the grass at the roadside. He was about to catch it when a pickup drove up, stopped, and a man leaped out and snatched the iguana and then jumped back in, and they drove off. Alfred had objected but it didn't make any difference. He was too vexed and so was Harold, who had been too far away in the car to do anything.

They drove on, behind the pickup. After about two miles the pickup stopped. Harold stopped. The man got out, carrying the thing, which had already been killed. They were Mandingoes, and they always kill an animal by cutting its throat, so it will bleed properly, which is what they had done to this one. When Harold and Alfred reached the pickup, the men held out the iguana and said, "Here take it. We don't want you to sue us." Harold brought a box and put the iguana inside. Apparently one man in the car had persuaded the others that they had done a bad thing and could be taken to court.

Anyway, Harold gave it to Alfred's family. So his wife cooked potato greens and iguana soup, and Harold came and ate it with them. The way they had prepared it was to burn the hide off in the fire and then stew it with the greens. He said it was tasty, like chicken or fish. They were really laughing about the whole episode when they came home this evening.

Last night John and Poliakah arrived about 8 PM. He will stay for a week and have to leave for school next Sunday; it starts March 3rd. (His name is Jacob now, not John, since he was baptized. I can't remember to call him Jacob, though.) We will get Poliakah enrolled in the first grade here at the mission school. Today John has been working in the yard, digging up flower beds, transplanting bushes, and such.

He really enjoys gardening. He worked during vacation in the rice field and vegetable garden at Lamco. He earned $1.50 a day and said he made $90 during the two and a half months that he worked. He paid his room rent, bought food (not rice, his ma furnished that), paid the taxi fare for the two of them, which was $10, and managed to save $20 after buying shoes and a couple of shirts. We were quite proud of the way he had managed. Gary O'Neil, the man in charge of the farm, told him he could have a job there next year.

It was so good to get back home after a week away. I stayed in the dorm and ate in the college dining room. It was an interesting week, and I think will be useful. But I don't really enjoy being away from Harold. He spent most of the week in Monrovia on hospital business, visited with friends in the evenings, and managed OK.

Dearest Vikki and Gill,   **February 27, 1976, Zorzor**

It's been nice to get back home after a week at Cuttington. We went to the 4th of July celebration on Saturday at VOA [*Voice of America*], down near Monrovia. Every year at this time, the American ambassador puts on a big celebration for the American community in Liberia. Since rainy season hampers car travel, they celebrate it around Washington's birthday. I haven't seen so many white people gathered together since we were in Europe. I felt downright conspicuous, used as I was to blending into the surroundings in an all black population. They served all the hot dogs, Fanta, and beer one could wish for. This is the first time we've ever gone, and went mainly this time because Harold was already in Monrovia on business and I was at Cuttington College, so we could meet there.

Today, Harold came with me to a mobile clinic site to take pictures of the activities. I've had to do a report for some people who gave us a Jeep for our community health work, and they wanted pictures, too. I had gone to help Harold, but there were so many children and so few workers that I ended up doing all the immunizations—measles, DPT, and TB. When we finished, someone sent food for us. It was rice with topagee soup—a greens and dried fish soup made with soda and palm oil. Harold really enjoyed the day. We worked in the town and then in a small village on the way home. He's been wanting to go to see a clinic so this was a good way to get him there.

We have a young nurse from Stanford here for six months as a volunteer. She has had experience in emergency room work and is setting up our emergency room and helping in surgery. Her name is Mickel; everyone thought she was a man before she arrived! She is a nice person, from

New Orleans. There is a group called Vespers, run by a Dr. Honey in either the Bay area or Los Angeles. They help medical people go to a developing country to work as volunteers by making the contacts and paying the travel cost. The nurse or doctor themselves take care of their other expenses, and the hospital supplies a room or apartment. We had three nurses at Phebe before.

John, Martha, and Poliakah are all here now for a week vacation before going back to school. So we're busy with sewing and getting school supplies, etc. We're trying again with Poliakah; think it will be OK with only one child. She hasn't had a chance to go to school since leaving us, and her parents are so anxious for her to have some schooling and also to get her out of the "devil" business.

I think I told you that she had been selected as the devil's wife on the basis of a dream when the ma was pregnant with her. If she stays in town, she must participate whenever the country devil comes into town. If she is far away from the town, the parents just say she's gone away and they can't do anything about it. So we're trying again. Now we went shopping for uniform cloth—royal blue cotton skirts and white T-shirts—and must be ready for school Monday. Poliakah likes school and likes to try new things so we'll see. Alfred is here all day and into the evening so that's a big help.

I saw Oreta recently, while at Cuttington. She has a cute healthy-looking boy. The father has another girlfriend now. Oreta says when the boy walks, she will leave him with Robert and go home to her ma; the baby belongs to the father, legally.

Dearest Mother,   **March 2, 1976, Zorzor**

Your welcome letter was delivered today so I shall sit right down and reply. I read it while I was eating lunch of yogurt, pawpaw, pineapple, and butter pear, and wished you were enjoying the meal with me again.

We have another new RN now—a volunteer through Christian Brotherhood Exchange—she's from Pennsylvania and will stay for one year. Mickel, the other volunteer, is moving into the apartment where Kevin was living. He just left, and Harold is trying his possible best to get two other apartments renovated. The church truck has been "spoiled" for about two weeks so his ceiling tacks and nails and other building items are still in Monrovia. He made a quick trip down and picked up the roofing nails because the rains had started, and he was worried about ruining the interior that was still usable.

Poliakah was happy to be back. She and Alfred get along fine and she has jobs to do here—really willing to work and happier being busy. I think, with only her, we should get along all right. She is a sweet little girl, very anxious to please and learns very quickly. It's surprising how quickly she learned English. She has a gift for mimicry and can pronounce words almost as we say them but has no idea what many of them mean. Harold really enjoys having a child in the house.

On Monday we got her started in Grade One at the Lutheran elementary school. We're going to shorten her name for school. It's hard to spell and not a name that is known in this area. So she will be Poli Jacobson at school. She's grown quite a bit since we last saw her. She's about the size Ciam was when he came here in 1973. I've sewn her two dresses and now must make uniforms—actually only skirts, because they wear white T-shirts instead of blouses.

There is a Chinese agriculturist living in Gbanway, about eight miles away. He's supposed to advise the farm manager here about the rice farm. Today he came to visit Harold and brought us a bag of icicle radishes. Maybe he will try to grow vegetables here. We'd be happy about that. He and Harold are going to have a meeting with the head of the Chinese agriculture mission in Monrovia tomorrow evening about the prospects.

Dear Mother,   **March 5, 1976, Monrovia**

We're going back up today—have done what we came to do—shopping, hunting supplies, meeting, etc.

We were shocked beyond words to learn after getting to Monrovia that Jordan and Beth Holtam are leaving by the end of the month. He works for the United Nations as an agriculturalist, and his present appointment was ending in March but since his local development work wasn't nearly finished it was assumed he'd be renewed. However United Nations has cut out half their program people here because of lack of funds, and suddenly the Holtams are leaving. They've been here 18 or 19 years so it's going to be a real adjustment for them; he's only been with United Nations two years. He was the first person we met from Liberia. As the agriculture program officer for Peace Corps, he met us in Philadelphia and came over with us and has been a real friend since then. We will miss him and Beth.

That's one of the sad things that you experience here, saying so many goodbyes. Well next year it will be us, and that will be hard, especially to say goodbye to some of our Liberian friends and our kids, whom we'll probably not see again.

[Letter from John (Jacob) to Ruth's mother]

March 8, 1976, Carroll High School, Grassfield, Yekepa, Liberia
Dearest Gramma,

It is a pleasure to write you these words of mine. How are you since you left Liberia? Hope the Lord is with you always. About me, I am fine with health and school. I really enjoyed your stay in Zorzor. I felt very much happy spending times with you.

We are now back in school and everything is fine with us. I went again to Zorzor and visited for one week and came to school on the first of March. I guess this year lessons will be alright because this is my second year.

I am in charge of a whole house and I have five boys living with me in the house. So I have a part to play in the school affairs. I am also on the rugby team. I think you called it American football. It is a very rough game, and the team members need more exercises to make them strong.

We are having Jesus Christ Superstar playlet, and I invited Ruth and Harold to come and see this fine play in Yekepa—Lamco. I'm taking part too. I will also be playing on the school volleyball team this year, and we will go to play Martha's school team in Zorzor.

In my class there are all together 40 boys in the tenth grade class. There is really a competition among us in study. Because each one of us is trying to get the highest mark in class, so it is really rough!

I remain so far. May God bless you all days and nights. Your grandson, Jacob Saiwhy

Dearest Mother,   **March 12, 1976, Zorzor**

Today the President came to Zorzor for the inauguration of the mayor, the first time Zorzor had had a mayor. So there were lots of people in town and around. Country bands, dancers, sight-seeing groups. Dr. Cole had an audience with him, to talk about his money problems—the Ministry of Health has never paid his salary as they promised they would do but have left it up to the church to pay him.

Harold is finally getting his helper, the man he's been trying to hire for a few months as a counterpart, who will eventually replace him. He's feeling pretty good about that.

Our parrot is beginning to talk much more. He says my name constantly, also his own, Hugo. Even laughed last night, really entertaining. He and Harold make funny sounds at each other. Harold smacks his lips, and then Hugo does.

Poliakah seems to be getting along fine. I've sewn her uniform skirts and a couple of dresses, so easy to do with a person so small. She's trying to learn to print letters and just now is seeing everything in reverse, when she writes them. But she's trying hard.

Dear Judith,   **March 1976, Zorzor**

A pastor who was here many years ago painted a picture of Christ (I really have forgotten exactly what the picture is) on the wall of a church—the first Lutheran one in Liberia. The people are now attempting to restore the building as a special historical spot. They held a money-raising rally some months ago.

Margaret [*Miller*], the missionary's daughter, is a linguist who has been here 20 years. She lives in a small town called Wozi. When we took Mom there to visit, Margaret told us about wanting to have the painting restored. And always wishing the mission board would send an artist sometime. When we told her you were coming and that you are an artist, she wondered what the possibility would be for you to take on the restoration project. I replied that I could only ask you. Wozi is in a different part of the country—out of Monrovia. The painting is done in oils. If you think you'd like to take it on, you should bring paints. I can find out more about it, the size for example, if you'd like to try. Just let me know.

Dearest Mother,   **March 17, 1976, Zorzor**

Two of the nurses have just gone home after having pizza with us. Alfred has gotten pretty good at putting it together. While I'm sitting here writing, Hugo, the parrot, is speaking my name over and over. It's so funny to hear it all the time—like I should answer him.

Did I tell you about the invasion of grasshoppers we've had? They destroy so many plants; our collard greens were nearly consumed. And a lovely hibiscus bush by the hospital was completely stripped of its leaves.

Now new ones have come out so it didn't seem to have hurt the bush. Last week in the market I saw grasshoppers fried in palm oil for sale! Thomas said they're very sweet to eat.

Poliakah seems to be doing all right at school. She is a happy little girl. When she first started to print letters, she made them all upside down, backward, or lying on their side. Now this week she's making them correctly.

We've had our usual share of company lately, last week overnight guests for two nights; Sunday and Monday, Peace Corps friends from Gbarnga; and today Dr. Nickerson and another doctor from Phebe for lunch. I'm fortunate to have Alfred to help or I could never manage.

Tomorrow I'm driving the mobile team to a town to meet with the town elders about starting a clinic there. That's always kind of interesting. This town had a clinic for a while but it was discontinued because the chief wouldn't cooperate. So now we're trying again, since they have a new chief.

Here it is a week later and I just found this letter—after my resolution to write on a regular basis. Sorry, yah. Today the first clinic was held at the town I mentioned above, and many children were there. The team was happy about it.

Dearest Vikki,   **March 24, 1976, Zorzor**

I'm lying in bed trying to recover from an attack of malaria which caught me Sunday night. I'm over the worst of it but still have dizziness which I suspect is from the chloroquin used to treat it, and weakness. People are so nice when you need them, doctors and nurses come in all day long to give me medicines and see what they could do to help me. And friends came to say "Neh my, yah."

Oreta, a friend from Gbedin, is here this week. She has a baby boy now, eight months old, from a different man so has been with him in a town near Phebe. He has a new girl friend he has "pregnated," and Oreta won't accept this. So there's been plenty of palava in the house, and she's ready to leave and go back to her mother, maybe without the baby since it's for the man. She's really cross and irritable with the children (her five-year-old daughter is with her), I suppose because of her dissatisfaction with her situation. And since I've been in bed all the time she's been here, it hasn't been the best situation here. What to do. I'll help her sew some clothes for herself and the children before she leaves and try to send her back when she's been here about a week.

We left here early Saturday morning to reach Phebe where the Christian Health Association was meeting (I'm secretary). Then in the afternoon Harold and Elizabeth Mulbah, director of nurses from here, and I went on to Ganta. We had a pleasant time, seeing lots of old friends and enjoyed being with the two nurses, Vera and Loretta, who run the nursing program there.

Sunday I gave the graduation speech at Ganta Mission Nursing School. It seemed to be well accepted. I talked about expectations of the nurses but more especially of the public's expectations of nurses.

John is typing his letters to us this year. He took typing last year for one semester, so we're pleasantly surprised that he can do well enough to correspond. He seems to be doing well in school, seems quite serious about a good record and does like the Brothers who run the school. The school is run like a British boarding school. They have a rugby team too, which John plays on. In April they're putting on *Jesus Christ Superstar* so we'll try to go. John is in it too.

Dearest Mother and all,   **March 28, 1976, Zorzor**

It's Sunday morning and we're waiting to go to church, so there's time to do some writing. It's a lovely morning, cool but not cold. Things have grown up a lot in our back yard now so it looks pretty nice with all the trees and vines. We're the only missionaries here this weekend; everyone has gone away for visits or meetings.

Harold went yesterday, too, to take Oreta home, so Alfred went with him to visit his family. Poliakah and I stayed home and really cleaned house. Alfred is so good but he never sees the corners. So when he's gone I go at it. Poliakah did the kitchen; she really enjoys helping. Then in the afternoon I sewed, made a dress for her from an old one of mine, and a shorts and top outfit for play from material that used to be on our sofa cushions and was still OK.

We have a new pastor right now, Tommy Luciny. He's Geisi tribe, a really wonderful young man. He recently completed his theological studies (three years) at the seminary in Gbarnga, one of the first Lutherans to graduate. He's such a joyful, articulate man, so happy to be a Christian and pastor that it's great to be around him. He's also teaching religion to the student nurses, thinks it's a real privilege to be able to. He comes to the house often to visit.

His wife, Yata, is fine, too, and three little girls. Last year his diabetes was healed through prayer. He'd been taking insulin for several years and believe it or not he was able to stop taking it. He had tests for several months afterward, and the doctors were finally convinced that his diabetes is apparently cured.

It took me nearly a week to get over that malaria attack—didn't realize it could lay me so low. But this week all is well again. Harold is doing fine, says he's never felt better. He's trying to get his carpenter shop built, even though the mission board turned down his request for funds. He says he'll go ahead on faith and build it small, small because money and supplies seem to come in. He's determined to construct something where he can keep tools and materials—lumber, tools, and such—under lock and key, because they always seem to "walk" away, and he'll save them a lot of money if he gets it up—then the people will say, "Of course, just what we wanted, didn't we say so!"

A patient died the other day who had come from another area, so the body had to stay in the hospital until the people came the next day. Then when they came, they dressed her, and different members of the family had to talk to her, to tell her certain things, to beg her spirit not to come back and hurt different members of the family. I'm not sure if they made sacrifices but expect so, because this is often done—feeding the spirits. People are very afraid of the spirit of a dead person, think they will come back and take another person with them—in other words, that person will then die.

Dearest Mother,   **March 31, 1976, Zorzor**

Today we went to Wozi. Harold had to go in to check on a spoiled car and refrigerators so I decided to go, too, and visit Yella Quaqua, the Liberian linguist who works with the Loma literacy program.

Thomas and I have been trying to get our radio messages finished so we can get the broadcasting started. I decided to have Mr. Quaqua critique the ones we've (actually I've) done—three so far, each one minute. He will translate them for us, and then they will go to the Loma, Kpelle, and Bassa reporters, for starters. We're hoping to reach the illiterate people living in bush towns—road towns, for that matter, but primarily people who can't read. I certainly find myself dabbling in things I've never thought of before!

This weekend we're taking a short trip to Foya. Harold has been wanting to visit Daniel Suah, his friend from Gbedin who is managing the mechanical end of an agriculture project at Foya. And I need to visit a Catholic mission in Voinjama and a Swedish Pentecostal mission in Foya for the Christian Health Association. So we're combining business and pleasure. Poliakah will go with us. Daniel is Mano and Poli can speak Mano, so she should enjoy the trip. We'll find someone to stay with if Daniel hasn't room—the mission, the government guest house, or Peace Corps there.

Dearest Judith,   **April 2, 1976, Foya**

Just now we're in Foya which is in upper Lofa County, just next to Sierra Leone (where the cloth market is) We came to visit Daniel Suah, Harold's good friend from Gbedin days. We brought Poliakah with us, and Daniel put us up in the guest house. He was so glad to see Harold, embraced him, just beaming. He's a really sweet guy.

Tomorrow we will go to the market here in Foya and then will go to Bolahun, a town off the main road about 30 minutes from here, where a lot of country cloth (hand-woven strips) is made. Harold wants to get some instead of waiting until we're ready to leave here.

Harold finished *Zen and the Art of Motorcycle Maintenance* this weekend. He really was entranced since so many ideas expressed were just like his, had to read much of it aloud to me and also write some comments down. He's really turned on to reading different things, something he would never have done at home.

Dearest Vikki and Gill,   **April 6, 1976, Zorzor**

Well, the time has passed too quickly since I last wrote. As usual we're always busy doing something.

Yesterday while we were eating lunch we saw a long green snake on the tree outside our dining room—three to four feet long. Harold ran out and grabbed the garden rake and started to hit it, and it slithered around the tree; he chased it, kept hacking at it but it finally got into the bush at the edge of the yard—actually only a few feet from our house. We see quite a few snakes around here—usually in the trees. They like to hang around in palm trees and catch the birds that come to eat palm nuts or that make their nests there. They're really clever the way they can go right up the side of a tree.

John's school is putting on *Jesus Christ Superstar* in Monrovia this coming weekend (he's in it) so we are going down to see it—have to go for shopping and Harold always needs parts and such for his job.

Dearest Mother,   **April 9, 1976, Monrovia**

We've been out of stamps, no place to buy them in Zorzor so I think I'll be mailing about three letters at once. We came down last night to Monrovia for business and then learned today is a holiday—Fast and Prayer Day—and nothing is open!

Actually it was rather nice having a day we could "sit down" and relax. We are staying with Geoff Thompson. Geoff has a cook whose specialty is French cuisine so he's planned a special dinner for us. He wants us all to stay here with him when Judith and Ciam arrive.

It's been fun to stay with Geoff. He has a nice big house in town, nicely furnished, has a lovely yard with lots of exotic flowers. Before I leave today I'm going to take some cuttings—gardenia, hibiscus, others I don't know the names of. Geoff has a new job, for at least one year, with the United States Education and Cultural Foundation, some part of USIS [*US Information Service*]. He gets a good salary, a car and driver, and the house and enjoys the work.

On the way down yesterday we stopped to see Ming Ho, who loaded us up with "yellow melons." Rather small yellow fruits looking something like a fat cucumber and tasting like casaba melon—a bit crisper. He raised 5,500 pounds of watermelon in March. Sunday on our way home we'll have lunch with him. He's such fun.

We went to a church to today that is situated in the original area where the returned slaves settled in the 1800s. There are many old United States southern-style houses there, commonly called AL [*Americo-Liberian*] houses. They are generally built up on piers and have many windows all with shutters. Most are quite dilapidated. They are so different from the usual country house.

Triplets were born at Curran this week. Even having twins is close to being a tragedy for a country person so you can imagine what three babies at once would be like. The lady is from Guinea, where life is very hard, so it's kind of sad. They're fine looking little things, two boys and a girl, all between four and five pounds.

Dearest Mother and all,   **April 14, 1976, Zorzor**

Flowering trees are so pretty now. The crepe myrtle is a beautiful lavender mass, poinciana a brilliant red, and on the ground is a red carpet from the fallen petals. The jacaranda is a lovely blue and below it, too, the ground is carpeted with petals as long as there are blossoms on the tree. Poinsettia bushes, too, are a bright red now, and always there are lots of hibiscus and bougainvillea. The little hibiscuses we set out have begun to send out new leaves, so a few months from now they should be fine.

John is home this week for Easter vacation and is doing a lot in the yard. He likes gardening so it's quite a help for Alfred who is usually quite busy and not too aware of what to do about flowers. When we were in Foya, we bought a chicken-carrying basket at the market for 50 cents. It's made of bamboo strips and woven in a kind of open-work pattern. I found three little plastic cups in which John will plant trailing plants—wandering Jew, a philodendron, and something else. Then he will put the pots inside the basket, and we'll try to train the plants to creep out of some of the spaces. It will hang in the piazza above the hammock, with some country rope.

Dearest Vikki and Gill and all,   **April 14, 1976, Zorzor**

We are just enjoying a refreshing rain. It is always nice in the evening when the wind begins to blow and the rains come—cools us all off so quickly. We have John home now for a week—nice to have him here. He likes to work in the yard so he's setting out some cuttings I brought home from Monrovia.

Last evening he was "carrying Alfred half-way" and slipped and fell and cut his chin—just below his lip. We took him to the emergency room and had to have four stitches put in. It's a bit swollen today but doesn't hurt and should be ready in a couple of days for them to come out.

Alfred has developed a hernia so we'll have to have it repaired around the end of the month, when his wife can come and stay to take care of him in the hospital. When Dr. Cole stopped in to check it, he said to Alfred, "Is the hernia getting big small." I really like Liberian expressions.

This has been quite a week—dangerous in fact to live here! First John's fall, then the next day he was up on the roof, which is corrugated tile sheets, to sweep leaves and branches off. Our water comes from the roof so it helps to have the junk off. Anyway he slipped and fell head first and made a huge hole, crashed into the attic and cracked the ceiling but fortunately a cupboard in the kitchen stopped him.

About that time I got a catch in my back and have had a time getting up and down. Yesterday Harold juked himself while working, cut his wrist and had to have a few stitches, this morning Poliakah has a bad cold and had been in bed all day, with a fever. It sounds like we've been jinxed doesn't it. Martha just arrived from a few days with her family in Gbedin. I told her, "take time, yah" so nothing happens with her!

We finally butchered the goat so yesterday John dug a small pit, put a cement block on either side and a grill on the top, and we had a barbecue pit. Then we made shish kebabs using pieces of marinated meat, green pepper, onions, and summer squash. It was really good and fun to do.

Dearest Judith and Ciam,   **April 14, 1976, Zorzor**

We finally got to the church to see the painting—when we were in Monrovia last week. It is about 30 to 45 minutes from Monrovia, a quaint little church, quite interesting style. The picture is about ten feet long and six feet high above the altar. It is on a rubbed cement wall, done in oils, a scene of the crucifixion. It has been damaged from the rains—there are a lot of white smudgy spots on the painting from leaks. It doesn't have to be repainted in entirety, mostly patching the spots and, I think, generally brightened up.

The entire thing seems quite too dark to me but having never seen it when it was new, I may not be correct. The sky is done in dark greens and browns—looking very overcast, which fits the mood. Bishop Payne would be too pleased to have the picture restored. In the foreground are recognizable figures some brighter accents, a little red in their garments but mostly it leans toward very dark greens and browns.

Dearest Mother,   **April 18, 1976, Easter Sunday, Zorzor**

Our day was nice. Church service was at nine, and then Gladys had brunch for people on the station. Later in the day Martha came home from visiting her parents at Gbedin so our whole family was here. A few people stopped in from time to time, a nice restful day. Fortunately Harold wasn't called so he could even take a nap.

At church this morning when the service was finished the pastor had a special prayer ceremony that was quite touching. One young man, an LPN who was working on the mobile team, was transferred into the hospital because he was having problems with drinking and depression. He's really gotten quite bad and talked about suicide.

Pastor Tommy Luciny, the young Liberian I've written about, is quite an effective counselor and has been visiting with David (the nurse). He asked him to come to church, which he did, and he took communion, and then when the service was finished Tommy told the congregation one of their brothers was having trouble with drinking and other things. He asked them to pray for him when they leave and then asked David to come up to the altar and kneel there, and friends who wished would come up with him and pray for him. Several people came, Elizabeth Mulbah and Deanna, among others. This is the first time I've seen David in church since I've been here although he is a member. It would be so fine if Tommy could be assigned here permanently as the pastor. He loves to work in the hospital as chaplain, too.

Poliakah is busy trying to write her ABC's and numbers. She seems to be coming along all right. John, too, is doing fine in school and is well liked by the Brothers. Martha is finding some subjects quite difficult this year. We'll have to see.

Dearest Mother and all,   **April 23, 1976, Zorzor**

You would have laughed at Harold and me the other night. I had developed a bad back—severe muscle cramps and couldn't bend over. Harold had cut his wrist while at work and had to have it stitched up and couldn't get it wet. We decided the only way we could get baths was to help each other so we got our tub of water in the bath fence and what a hilarious time. Getting my feet washed was a riot, with Harold with one hand.

I'm teaching class every day now and also supervising freshman students in the out-patient department. In addition, Thomas is on vacation for a month so I'm in charge of the department and I'm also trying to "shape up" the people on the mobile clinic team. Then a few afternoons a week I'm helping to get the medical stock department sorted out and a system organized. That's really a full time job.

Dearest Mother,   **April 30, 1975, Zorzor**

Thomas is off for a month vacation so I'm in charge—trying to catch up with a lot of things that have been put off for a year. Yesterday Dr. Cole and I went to a meeting in Voinjama, about a two-hour drive north of here.

I had to drive our car because his was being repaired. It had rained the night before so there was no dust but pretty muddy in spots—and bumpy and with deep cracks across at the bottoms of most hills where water has washed across. I never like that drive because there are very tall trees along the road and most of the brush has been cut down for farms. In heavy winds limbs and entire trees crash down on the road; two times in the last year they have landed on cars. If it starts to blow, we stop in an open place and wait until the wind dies down.

Alfred will have his hernia repaired next week. His wife will be finished with her farm work by that time and will come Sunday to stay with him. Each patient has to have a caretaker to take care of their physical needs and to cook for them. The nurses do the meds and treatments only, and I don't have time or inclination to do it.

We have arranged for someone to carry water for us, and Poliakah will do the dishes—my biggest headache—and help cook dinner. She really likes to cook and can do the rice and some soups pretty well. She also loves to make French toast or fry pancakes. We're trying to teach her as much as possible and are in hopes that someone else will be willing to keep her for the next year or two (after we leave) until John gets out of school. I'm sure he will want to keep her in school then, and she will be a help to him in the house, too. We're praying for a Christian family to take her.

We now have one chicken (a hen). Pastor brought it to us a few days ago and Harold decided to keep her and try to get some guinea eggs for her to set on. So we've had her tied with a string on one leg, and she seems perfectly happy. And yesterday she laid an egg! She's small, kind of like a banty. Alfred will bring guinea eggs back from Gbarnga when he comes Sunday; they're sold there for about 10 cents an egg. Harold has been wanting guinea hens "ever since."

Dearest Judith and Ciam,   **May 8, 1976, Zorzor**

Just a quick note to say—we're counting the days! Do hope you have an enjoyable trip, and that the customs in Monrovia won't be too much of a hassle. They're usually pretty much OK but just take time. Out house has been like a zoo lately. Alfred's wife and little three-year-old boy are here while Alfred is in the hospital with a hernia operation. Yata, Pastor Luciny's wife, comes to help me, since Paye, Alfred's wife, can't speak English, only Kpelle, and Yata is Kpelle. Also Paye has never cooked on a kwi stove but wants to help. And on top of that, I'm gone most of the day.

Yata has three little girls, three, five, and five months, really little dolls. The baby is a darling plump little girl with shiny black skin and little tiny plaits all over her head. They take beautiful care of her. Yata learned home crafts while Tommy was learning to be a pastor—three years—so she can sew and knit and crochet very nicely. We're very fond of her and Tommy. A little girl, Esther, who is the daughter of a friend, also stays with them. She's about Poli's age (10 years old, or so), and is in the second grade. They are friends and visit back and forth.

So since Yata is cooking for us now, we have them stay to eat, including Tommy Luciny. So each night for dinner, we are twelve, six adults and six children. It's fun but gets hectic and what a mess.

Dearest Mother,   **May 13, 1976, Zorzor**

This has been a bad two weeks. Harold has been ill since the first of the month. Alfred had his operation so I had no help. His wife and three year old were here—she can't speak English, just "one-one" [*only a few words*]—and Thomas has been on vacation. What a hectic time. Harold first caught a cold then came down with malaria, which often happens if you're already down with something, then before the week was over he got the flu, and then developed bursitis in one shoulder. He's been miserable; now that he has been diagnosed and put on cortisone, it is improving but slowly.

Alfred stayed in the hospital four days and started back to work small-small. His wife helped him so he didn't have to lift anything. Thomas should be back to work sometime next week so it looks like I'm going to survive.

The bishop was here for lunch yesterday and told Harold he could go ahead with his shop construction.

It's beginning to rain now—quite heavily in the late afternoon and night. Our flowers are beginning to bloom now—some bushes were looking dead and now have perked up and burst into bloom.

Remember how the grasshoppers demolished the bushes just a short time ago? Now a hibiscus bush that was devoured is fully in leaf again and full of lovely blossoms. It's hard to believe how things can grow here; vegetation is quick to overtake things.

Dearest Ones,   **May 13, 1976, Zorzor**

Prices are getting higher here. Imported food is ridiculously high. Market things are still reasonable, in fact quite cheap. For example grapefruit are two for 5 cents, avocados one or two for 5 cents, mangoes 5 cents each, pineapple, medium size 25 to 30 cents. On the other hand coffee is $2.50 a pound.

It's really nice that you can make your own baby foods—so much more healthful, I'm sure, and of course less expensive. We try to teach all the women to start serving rice porridge by four months, by six months add peanut butter to it, as well as pounded dry fish, greens, and other vegetables and to feed the baby three to four times a day. It's so hard to convince them that their children will stay well if only they are fed adequately.

Dearest Mother,   **May 16, 1976, Zorzor**

Harold is improving. He is trying to work a bit each day. Dr. Nickerson prescribed specific exercises, which seem to be helping. We're fortunate to have good medical care so convenient and free.

Thomas came back from vacation today so things should be easier now. He will take over the main part of teaching, which will be a relief. Classes every day does push me, since I have so many projects going. We have another volunteer nurse; she will be here until December. She is a very competent cardiac nurse who is on her own except for her travel expenses and $40 a month for food. And of course, her apartment is furnished by the hospital. It's surprising how many such persons come, support themselves, and make a wonderful contribution. She is helping on adult ward and doing clinical instruction and in-service for the graduates.

Dr. and Mrs. Minge are gone now, and Darlene will leave in three weeks. Our favorite people—hate to say goodbye. I'm sitting here at the dining table, it's late in the evening. Outside the cicadas and many other insects are singing and chirping—a constant high sound. Intermittently comes the voice of some little animal fairly close by—A HOOooo. Haven't any idea what it is. Then farther away another animal is sounding off—kind of a harsh hoot—it's a tree animal of some sort that "talks" every night, getting closer and closer until it passes and then fades away.

Dearest Mother and all,   **May 26, 1976, Monrovia**

Today is the big day, and I woke up early too excited to go back to sleep. Wondering if Judith and Ciam will be on the plane, and so on. We are off to Geoff Thompson's where we'll all stay until we go up-country Friday.

One young man from a seminary in Chicago came to Liberia to do his internship—spent nine months here last year. While here, he helped teach in the seminary for Liberian pastors, which is located in Gbarnga—it's a joint Lutheran, Methodist, and Episcopal program. Our pastor at Zorzor graduated from there last year—a fine fellow with a good theological background.

Lebanese traders here collect silver dollars, which country people bring in from time to time, hoarded in their homes. Blacksmiths make bracelets from them, too. Some I have seen are quite old. We've bought a few bracelets, some as low as $2, and one for $10, which was quite heavy. Some of the bracelets have been made from shillings from Sierra Leone and from Guinea silver coins.

Work has finally begun on surfacing the road up-country. It's doubtful whether it will be finished before we leave but at least it's started. An Italian company is in charge and is busy straightening curves and filling just now.

Dearest Vikki and Gill,   **June 6, 1976, Zorzor**

Your letter arrived today. Mail is irregular now since the pilot has gone home for a three-month vacation, and there isn't all that much automobile traffic either going or coming.

We were so glad to receive Judith and Ciam. They arrived on time but not their bags, which meant another trip to the airport and a longer stay in Monrovia. Their bags came two days later, so no palava. Since then we've been here in Zorzor, and this week will take a couple of trips—an overnight trip to the bush tomorrow, but sleeping in a kwi house, and then on Thursday going on up to Foya and to Koindu in Sierra Leone for the cloth market. It should be fun because Daniel Suah will put us up. And also Tommy Luciny, our pastor, will go along and take us to his people in Kolahun and then go on to Foya with us, where his mother does batik work. We'll stay about five days.

It was fortunate that this week was a school holiday for John so he was home the whole week. He and Ciam had a good time together. John and Martha have decided to call us mom and daddy instead of Ruth and Harold. He is doing quite well but Martha is having a hard time this year.

Today we all went to church in Fissibu, a town four miles from here, where Tommy was invited to preach the sermon. Most everything was in Loma since the entire "audience" was Loma with the exception of us, plus Tommy doesn't speak Loma—he's Geisi—so there was a translator. Then there was communion, and also some business matters to discuss. The singing was very different; one person sings a sentence, then the rest come in on a chorus; this is repeated over and over, very nice. They also use a Loma song book, and since the words are written phonetically, it was easy to sing along. They also asked Harold to tell "what news from there," so he made a few comments.

Dearest Mother,   **June 13, 1976, Foya**

Here we are in upper Lofa County, having a nice time together. We just came back from Koindu, which is in Sierra Leone, where we went to buy cloth. There is a big market there, produce as well as cloth. We bought a lot of the tie-dye material for a variety of people who had asked us to shop for them. Now Harold and two of his friends have gone out to view the agricultural project here, which they have been developing. Yesterday we went to the market here in Foya then drove to Bolahun, about 15 miles away, where country cloth is sold. There is a big "monkey bridge" [*built of vines*] on the way, which Judith and Ciam could cross—kind of scary since they sway around but actually are quite safe. The water is high under it. I can't imagine crossing it with a head load and baby on my back!

Tommy's father is the district commissioner here in the Bolahun area and invited us to stay one night with him. A district commissioner is next to the county superintendent, who answers to the President. He is responsible for the chiefs in his district. He has an immense three-story home and office combined, on a high hill overlooking the town. We were given the top floor—the apartment usually set aside for the President and other "big people."

On the way up one of our stops was to buy a monkey, which was hanging by the side of the road—by neck and tail—dead, of course. We bought it to give to Tommy's family. It was black with an orange seat—quite good sized. We were afraid they'd cook it for us but his father—he's called Honorable—said that it wouldn't be fitting to cook meat we had carried there. He'd provide the food for us! They killed a goat for us and treated us so well.

Later we drove to Tommy's "born town" and met many of his relatives who also welcomed us. The people just love Ciam, and of course, he meets them so nicely, too. One man climbed a coconut tree and picked coconuts for him. Here, they use a "climber" something like a telephone lineman uses. It is made of vines and rattan.

Some of the people in the village had a hard time sorting out our relationships—thought Judith and I were Harold's wives and Ciam his son! Tommy's father has many, many wives—maybe doesn't know how many! Or how many children. It is a great responsibility for him to see to all their welfare. And he can't play favorites!

Tommy's mother lives here in Foya. She makes batik materials from country dye—uses a wood she gets from the forest, which produces indigo. Unfortunately, she didn't have cloth to work on while we were there, so we couldn't watch the process.

Tomorrow we'll start back to Zorzor. It's a three-hour drive but we'll take much longer for a variety of stops.

Dearest Mother,   June 1976, Gienple

While we are resting here in Gienple, John's town, I can do some letter writing. We walked in yesterday—about a two-hour path trip. Each of us carried a small load—a sheet and towel and small gifts. We have been treated so nicely and received gifts, too, among them a chicken and a guinea fowl, along with two other roosters we were given in Gbedin. Friday, we'll have quite a bit of livestock to carry back in our little car! John is cooking chicken and rice for our "breakfast" and then we'll start back on the trail.

Dearest Ones,   July 11, 1976, Zorzor

It seems as though you have been gone for a long time and actually it's only four days! Once we got back here, we were back "in harness" with things waiting to be done. On Thursday morning we got up early and swept out the house and washed dishes and packed and were ready to go around nine o'clock. When we arrived here, we learned that not only had Thomas's mother died, but also one of his sons had died. The child had sickle cell anemia and apparently had a crisis. I was expecting to have to go out with the mobile clinic since Joseph Moore was taking some time off, which we owed him. However he decided I'd be too jammed, so bless his heart, here he came this evening ready to spend the week working and will get his time off at a later date.

Yesterday the Phebe nursing students came to play volleyball and soccer with our nursing students. Anna Kohdable and her fiancé James Sengita (my former counterpart at Phebe) came along to talk to Tommy and us about their wedding, which is now planned for the last of August. She brought the cloth, white brocade, for her dress, which I'm going to make and also cloth for two little girls' long dresses.

Yata is busy with her canteen business so doesn't have time for study just now. She is doing quite well and enjoying the work. Tommy said they have purchased what they need to keep the business going and are now ready to start paying off the loan. [*Harold and Ruth had helped Yata borrow some money to start a small business.*]

Dearest ones,   **July 11, 1976, Zorzor**

Thomas is away for a few days. Fortunately I came back the day after his mother died so I could take over his responsibilities. His mother was the oldest woman as well as the head zo woman [*like a chief of the women*] in his town. Consequently the burial business is very involved. They will have to provide a feast for at least three days for plenty of people. Of course, people do bring things, too, but it is a big expense for the family.

When a person dies and is buried, some of the family bring things to the grave, like a white chicken, kola nuts, etc., put them on the grave, and talk to the spirit of the person. Even Christians will do this.

The weather is quite chilly now, especially in the early morning and forenoon. Things are so damp; we'd like to start packing some of the things we aren't using, but are a bit afraid they will get too musty. Things mold so quickly. But Harold is getting anxious to start; so he rigged up an electric light to suspend in the barrel as it is being packed to try to dry out as he goes!

Our dog is in heat this time, and we don't want her bred—no good looking Basenjis around. We keep her on a chain, fastened to a chair leg in the house because there are so many people in and out and no one to pay attention to the dog. She can open the screen doors and go out so easily. Actually, I wouldn't mind having puppies again because so many people want one, and she did have darling babies last time. One of her daughters is at Phebe with a Peace Corps friend. She looks exactly like the mother, same color, markings, and her disposition is the same.

The dog was an adult when we got her and already well trained. People in this area—Loma people—eat dog meat. They say "it's too sweet." So we don't let our dog run around at night because she's fat and healthy looking and would disappear easily. Harold saw dog meat at the market recently.

Dearest Mother,   **July 15, 1976, Zorzor**

Yesterday we had some excitement here. There was a big snake—80 inches long—in a big tree just back of our house. Someone spotted it when he was looking at a bunch of excited birds in the tree, you may remember how high those trees are, and the snake was way up there. People shot at it with slingshots but finally one man came with a shot gun. He shot it and then it just hung over the branches. In fact before it was shot it shed its skin as it was crawling along. You should have heard the people exclaiming.

Later on in the evening one little man who works for Harold came with a ladder and climbed into the tree, shimmied up higher and then with a long stick poked at the snake, which finally fell to the ground. After it had been examined and exclaimed over and measured he picked it up and trotted off. He said it was for his cat but others said he'd cook it for his own soup. People say it is very tasty. I don't think I'll be trying it!

Now this evening again the birds were fussing up in the tree and Harold saw another snake there. I wonder how many snakes are in trees when I'm wandering along underneath! One thing is sure, I always look for snakes as I go into the bath fence to bathe. One day Alfred met a snake having a sun bath on top of the fence, just wound around the top of one of the posts.

Martha came home yesterday. Her term ended, and she has about two weeks off. She brought her report card showing she had passed so I gave her the beads you had sent as a reward. Today she was busy making neck-laces and earrings. She said the girls at Lutheran Technical Institute [*LTI*] want some and will pay for them, and she will take them to Gbedin, too, when she goes next week and try to sell some.

John will be home Sunday or Monday. We're apt to have a houseful next weekend, the 26th celebration, Donna and another health volunteer want to come for a few days, and Ella, Gail's former house girl, who now attends St. Mary's in Sanniquellie, wants to come, too. We'll have to make beds on the floor, I think.

I'm starting to teach pediatric nursing next week. With Elizabeth leaving, Deanna is really jammed, so I'm glad I can help out that way.

Dearest Vikki and Gill and family,   **July 19, 1976, Zorzor**

It's Saturday morning and Harold took Alfred and the girls to the market so it's great having the house to myself. This house is so small that it's hard to be alone and quiet.

It rained all night but now the sun is out. It always surprises me that the water disappears so quickly after a rain. I was on radio duty this morning and learned that the weather was bad all over the country. We have a clinic team in one bush town and Dr. Cole is at Foya, all awaiting the plane. They've been out since Thursday so it will be fine if the weather clears enough for flying. It always amazes me that the pilot can get in and out of some of the little airstrips in the bush. Judith went on one vaccinating trip by air.

Martha is home from school for a two-week break. She did all right this term, passed with an average of 74, which is OK for her. We're talking now of having her try to get into midwife training at the end of next term instead of going on into the eleventh grade. LPN and midwife training only need the tenth grade. Her grades indicate she couldn't handle professional nursing. She'd like to start midwifery now rather than after high school so in November she will take the pre-entrance exam. It would be nice to get her situated here, while there are people here that she knows.

We had a party this afternoon, and fortunately the rain held off until the party was over. A Peace Corps girl has been helping us here doing secretarial work. She ran the craft shop in town but was turning the work over to her counterpart, a young Liberian fellow. She is so full of nervous energy and begged me for something to do. Consequently she has typed and mimeographed for us—for all the instructors and doctors, as well. Just whizzes through any job. She is leaving for home in a few weeks, so today I had a cake and coffee party to say thank you. We had about 20 guests. I made a caftan from tie-dye material for a department gift.

Harold has had some health problems in the past three months. I think I may have written to tell you he had bursitis, didn't I? He had tonsillitis, flu, malaria, and some skin eruption, all one on top of the other. Then he developed terrible pain in his right shoulder, and they finally decided it was bursitis and treated him for that. It slowly improved about the time that Judith came. Then we discovered that a muscle over the shoulder blade was completely atrophied and couldn't work. Dr. Nickersen at Phebe said there was no way for it to ever come back because the nerve was destroyed.

However when we went to Ganta to visit Dr. Getty, a rehabilitation specialist who works with leprosy patients examined him and said they've been having success in reactivating damaged nerves in leprosy patients through the use of cortisone, and recommended that he try it. So Harold's been taking it since about the 28th of June. I think his muscle is a bit better, and he feels it is, too. He does exercise regularly. The unfortunate thing about it is that it is his right arm and certain motions aren't possible. So we'll have to wait and see how it goes (of course he works full time).

Dr. Cole, the Liberian doctor here, is leaving Wednesday for Akron, Ohio, for two weeks to make arrangements for a pediatric residency there. He was there for a year about 1974. Before that he graduated from Gonzaga and University of Washington Medical School and would love to go back to Washington, except residencies there pay much less since they are more desirable, and people are willing to go there for less money.

You can't imagine how cold the weather is now. We have to wear sweaters every morning and evening. Of course, the fact that we have only screens on our window is a factor; the wind really blows through three sides so there's no problem with ventilation!

Dearest Judith,   **July 28, 1976, Zorzor**

Our house is quiet tonight for the first time in ten days. There were at least eight at the dinner table every night. Martha's sister Oreta and little Vickie came soon after school closed and just left today. What with John and Poli, it was really togetherness. Plus extras for meals almost daily.

Elizabeth Mulbah is leaving Sunday for Iowa State so last night we had her and James over for dinner. Her mother has come to take care of the two little kids. I know it will be hard to leave when the time comes. Deanna took her place, in addition to teaching.

I took on the job of distributing medicines at eight and three—refills of things like penicillin, streptomycin, and such high-cost "shot medicine," which disappears very fast unless it is given to the floors with tight controls. I've also started the control system with drugs that move the fastest at first.

It's really a busy time—that task in medical stock, helping Thomas, and teaching two hours a day. Actually it's been nice to get out of the house once in a while, with our houseful!

Yata is doing fine—is now cooking rice and soups in addition to breads [*for her canteen business*]. And has already paid back $40. She's hired a helper, Korto, old man's sister, who was in the orphan quarter.

We drove down to Phebe on Saturday so I could meet with Dr. Gwenigale about CHAL (Christian Health Assn. of Liberia). We decided to go on Friday and stay overnight with the Austins, who take care of the children at the hospital. They seemed so grateful to us for staying. It was pleasant. They're Montanans, younger than we by 10 to 15 years, or more I guess. Have four children from first to seventh grade. Two are American black children they adopted when in the States.

By the way, I was told by a friend of Margaret Miller's that she was so pleased with your work on the picture. Said you did an excellent job. Harold now has the matte varnish, which we'll take with us the next time we go down so we can check the thing out.

Dearest Judith,   **August 8, 1976, Zorzor**

Poliakah went home. She was a behavior problem at school and not too dependable here unless I was home, and with our mixed up schedule, it didn't seem fair to her or Alfred to continue. John advised that she go home because she wasn't serious about school so he took her when he went. She was looking forward to going home.

I'm sending Alfred home in the afternoon, as soon as his work is finished, so Harold and I have the evening together. I do the cooking for us, and we have a relaxed leisurely evening, unless we have guests. Of course, that's kind of often but anyway the other evenings are OK.

Dr. Ruben Pederson, ELCA [*Evangelical Lutheran Church in America*] secretary for Africa, is coming in a week, at which time we expect to do some talking about next year. Dr. Getty, the doctor from Ganta who has been advising Harold about his muscle problem, wants to talk to Dr P. also, about what he thinks might be done, if anything, to improve his condition.

The Chinese fellow at Gbanway brought us some long white radishes, which I used for soup—peeled and sliced them, cooked in enough water for broth with three Maggi cubes [bouillon], small ginger root, and green onions. Tasty.

Dearest Vikki and Gill,   **August 8, 1976, Zorzor**

Already August. What a surprise. It's been a really nice Sunday. The bishop has been visiting Zorzor and preached today on the prodigal son. Then he came to our house for lunch! We had made palm butter and chicken and a lime chiffon pie. The bishop is Liberian, educated in the States.

Later Harold and I drove to Gbanway, a small town about eight miles from here, to visit a Chinese agriculturist. Harold needed advice about weeds. This young man came to Liberia in October and has been learning English since he arrived. Actually he speaks fairly well, with a limited vocabulary, but really had a hard time understanding what we were saying. He's advising the farm manager here on vegetables and rice.

Today the man who carried water for us—who is really "cracky"; he often talks to the wall—brought me two huge mushrooms that he found in the bush. They are about six inches across, brown on top. He finished cooking and eating his own and is OK. Other people told us they are "too sweet," so tomorrow we'll try them. I was apprehensive about wild mushrooms given to me by a rather strange man but we believe other friends!

Some strange things have been happening in this area. There have been a lot of unexplained deaths. What appears to be poisoning sometimes. A lot of shootings—like when people are hunting—at night, a man will be shot. The shooter will be arrested and tried. Three such cases have occurred just recently. Last week a child got its father's gun (loaded) and shot into a group of children, killing one and injuring several. Now the authorities have come and are collecting all the guns, and it is said martial law will be declared. People are really antsy. Lots of people depend on hunting for their meat and to have meat to sell.

Dearest Mother,   **August 16, 1976, Zorzor**

You should see our bath fence now. Most of the posts have sprouted and green plants are growing all around inside. They look something like orchid plants, only no blossoms. Tonight it was so pleasant there; it was just dusk, the moon is nearly full, all the plants and leaves are so pretty, a very pleasant place to take a bath.

We have a budding chicken flock again. A hen with six chicks, two white chickens—the twins, Harold calls them—another black hen and a big grey rooster. The only trouble with them is that they are so tame they hang around the back door waiting for a handout, so you know how messy our back porch is most of the time. And the mother hen dusts herself in the flower bed by the front door, so we usually have to wade through that dirt to get inside. What to do!

Did I ever tell you about Bana, Thomas Konie's little 14- year-old boy? We've been taking care of his school expenses this year so have become well acquainted with him. He's a small, "bright" [*light-colored*] child, quite good in school. He brings his papers and his grades to us to see. We soon realized his eyes weren't good. Even so he was promoted from the fourth to the fifth grade in mid semester.

We made arrangements for him to go to Monrovia to an eye special-ist during July vacation. He came back with glasses and can now see the blackboard and can see the books so much better. He's so proud of his glasses (we paid for them) and should do so well now. Marcia, the girl who was killed in Gbedin, had parents who offered to help educate Liberian children (through Peace Corps) but have never been able to work any-thing out. So I wrote to them about Bana and asked if they'd like to help this little boy get an education. I'm in hopes they will agree. We'll help him while we're here but our future is not too certain at this point. Bana is a twin; he's short and bright, and his sister is tall and black. They don't look a bit alike. She's like a little toothpick—so skinny.

Dearest Vikki and Gill,   **August 16, 1976, Monrovia**

We came to Monrovia to attend a program and dinner for Ruben Pederson, who is the secretary for Africa from the mission board in the States. He is retiring, and this is his last trip to Africa. We combined the trip with busi-ness for the hospital. It's always a rush though, trying to get everything done in time so you can go back. It's hard for me to be away with some of the responsibilities I have just now—teaching and trying to set up a stock control system for the medical supplies.

Did I tell you two of our Liberian friends are getting married on the 29th at Phebe? Harold is giving the bride away. I've made her dress and also dresses for two little girl attendants and tomorrow have to buy their wedding rings! I've never done that before. They gave me $25 for each of the rings, want gold bands, so I'll try. Every time I come to Monrovia I seem to have the strangest shopping list—things for others that take much more hunting and decision making than my own. I always say I'm not doing it again. And then circumstances are such that I don't seem to be able to refuse. What to do!

We also learned that one of our favorite Peace Corps friends here, Dale Veeneman, is getting married next Saturday to another volunteer. They're both nice people. We are coming to Monrovia for their wedding. Then the next week will be Anna's wedding. That seems to be our business just now—getting people married, that is.

Dearest Judith,   **August 18, 1976, Zorzor**

Just a quick note to tell you what happened today when Dr. Pederson and Dr. Getty conferred with Harold. Dr Getty said we should go as soon as possible to the States to have an exam by a neurologist to be absolutely sure the condition isn't progressive. He said there is a remote possibility there could be a tumor that is causing the nerve to be damaged due to pressure. This in turn causes the muscles to atrophy. So we will be leaving here within the next three weeks for New York. If all goes well we will be there no longer than three to four weeks (unless surgery is indicated). There's only about a 10 percent chance of that, according to Dr. Cole.

Dearest Mother,   **August 29, 1976, Zorzor**

It's getting late but I must write tonight because the plane may be in tomorrow to pick up mail. When we got back from Phebe, we found a bunch of letters someone had carried up from Monrovia including yours.

We left yesterday for Phebe for John and Anna's wedding, the Liberian nurses I've known since Ganta. Harold gave the bride away. Besides her wedding dress, I made the bouquets and cookies (other people did, too). It came off all right, which was surprising since none of the participants knew anything about a church or even a kwi wedding.

The missionary ladies at Phebe were not keen on helping because the two had been living together unmarried. (I told them they hadn't been living in Liberia long enough to know that was the way most people lived here!) And this was Tommy's first wedding ceremony as well. We didn't even know how to start to cut the wedding cake; it was lovely, made by one of the Phebe ladies—three tiers with flowers, etc. And all day it rained—just poured—then the sun would come out and be sunny and bright—then here came the rain again. We had to hold an umbrella over the cake to get it from the house to the church.

Tommy, Harold, and I slept at the Minges'. She played the organ. Incidentally, they decided soon after getting home that they should be back in Liberia. Also felt the luxurious life style of many of their colleagues was just too much and too foreign to their tastes.

Our dog is expecting again and wouldn't you know, she will have the babies while we're gone again. What a nuisance. We kept her in, took her out on leash every day, and then one day Harold said I think she's OK now and put her out. She promptly ran off and stayed *long,* and then later it became evident she wasn't ready to be loose. What to do. Hope she has cute puppies again.

Dearest Judith and Ciam,   **September 6, 1976, Monrovia**

Harold has an appointment at Columbia Medical Center on the same afternoon that we arrive in New York. No time wasted there, was there. When we finish with Medical business we'll go to Albany to stay with Rich and Evelyn.

We finally got away from Zorzor yesterday mid-day. What a circus. So many people come and sit down waiting to bid you farewell and you're trying to do lost minute things involved with closing up you house. Martha came for the weekend and was crying off and on, others were sad because they're convinced we won't be back. Since we were required to pack our things just in case, it looked pretty ominous. Harold had a lot of buying and other business to do for Curran so we left three days early—so nice to be away and have all that leave taking behind us.

We're going to Geoff's tomorrow to stay the night and then he will carry us to the airport Wednesday night—at midnight, yet. Well darlings, it's time to go wake Harold from his nap so we can go to the Mandarin for dinner.

Dearest Mother,   **September 7, 1976, Monrovia**

Just a few nights before we left, someone broke into our house again at three in the morning. They cut the screen and the heavier wire netting in one window and came in. Fortunately Harold heard the screen door as they opened it and got up, making too much noise so they fled. They were in the process of taking our Sony tape player, had it disconnected already.

The only other things taken were ridiculous—my toothbrush, can you imagine, a box of plantain chips, one of Martha's dresses and a matching hat, and two knit shirts Harold was going to use when he travels. They also tried to get into Deanna's the same night—made so much noise trying to loosen the rogue bars that she woke up. It's a challenge trying to outwit such people. We always try to keep things locked up, including our bedroom door. What to do—that's life in most developing countries.

[*Tests in New York showed that a muscle in Harold's shoulder had atrophied. He was given steroid shots to relieve the pain. While they were in the States, they visited Ruth's brother Rich and his wife, Evelyn, in northern New York State.*]

Dearest Mother,   **September 27, 1976, Monrovia**

Just a short note to let you know we reached Liberia with no problems. A good flight; we slept a bit. Geoff met us at the airport, took us home for breakfast, then we had a nap, and we were ready for palm butter and rice that evening. That was the first rice we'd had since we left home (Liberia).

It is good to be back here. Everyone was happy to see us and we're eager to get up-country and dive into our work to get it finished. This morning we will go for groceries—our house is pretty empty—and then take off for Zorzor. We had thought we'd stay in town a couple of days but then decided there was no reason to.

Dearest Mother,   **October 1, 1976, Zorzor**

Here it is nearly a week since we came back and it's almost like we were never away. We are back in the swing of things. Harold's projects came to a standstill while he was away. Now he's putting together what he needs to get the surgery remodeled and complete his shop buildings by the time we leave. It means another trip down for buying. You can't just send an order and expect to get it. Always have to "run behind it."

Deanna is leaving for a month's vacation so I'm taking over some classes for her—two days a week. Also a lot to do in medical stock to get the bugs worked out of our control system. I am also working with Thomas in community health. We're planning another bush vaccination drive for November; it takes a lot of work to lay out who will go where, what they will need to carry, how they will get there. I'm planning to go on at least one weekend trip with the team. The rains should just about be finished by that time so we can manage the paths. The streams get so full during rainy season that a person has to wade waist deep sometimes. That's not for me!

Dr. Cole left yesterday for Ghana for a two-month session for senior medical officers, all about administration. In the meantime we have a Pakistani doctor to take his place; he's a Liberian government employee.

Alfred is fine. He was so happy to see us back. Everyone was worried that we had left for good. We stopped to see Martha at LTI on our way home, to let her know we were here for the duration of our assignment. She will be taking the nursing exam next month—the pre-entrance exam for this school.

Another responsibility just now is a group of six physician assistant students from JFK hospital in Monrovia, who are here for a two-month affiliation. In Deanna's absence, I must orient them and meet with them off and on for ward conferences.

They live in a small dorm here, but a man is hired to cook for them. They rotate through all the services, and especially concentrate on OB, since it's about the only chance they have to do deliveries during their two-year course.

These boys are high school graduates and will be assigned to government clinics when they complete their course. They spend two months here and two months in a health center in upper Lofa.

Dearest Mother,   **October 3, 1976, Zorzor**

It's a rainy Sunday, but warm and not dreary. Today was communion, a joint service, preached in English and Loma. Betty McCrandall, a Peace Corps teacher, and Harold and I were the only white people there. There must have been over 100 who took communion; the majority were country people in lappas, head ties, or shorts and country shirts, and barefoot or with sandals. We felt right at home. I always wear a lappa "suit."

Yesterday we had a lot of excitement here. When we got up and went outside we found driver ants surrounding our house. I walked out to get some grapefruit, and my feet were attacked before I knew what was happening. You can't shake them off. You have to pull them off—they hang on with their pincers. Our puppies and Suebie were on the back porch.

Fortunately they hadn't invaded there—they could have killed the babies in a short time. There were streams of ants about one to two inches wide all around front and back. Harold and Alfred started spraying with the government DDT and kerosene, and it started to work. Finally they found their nest—Alfred called it their town—in the bush near our house. So they tried to burn it using old crank case oil. Since it was raining and had rained a lot before, it was too wet to do much good. A good part of the day Alfred and Harold worked to get rid of them. By this morning there is no sign of them; in fact they left their "town" in the bush.

Later in the afternoon I heard a lot of shouting and a bunch of men carrying cutlasses dashed past the house, with Alfred joining them. I thought they must have seen a snake or that some accident had happened. But instead they were chasing a small deer—not much bigger than Suebie. Fortunately it escaped in the bush but Alfred said it ran right past our porch and leaped the old stump there so he took off after it, just as excited as the rest. If they had caught it they would have killed and divided it among all who had helped catch it. You can imagine the little pieces that some get—maybe just one foot!

Dearest Judith and Ciam,   **October 3, 1976, Zorzor**

I've just come in from having a bath. The moon is three quarters full, it has a golden halo around it. No stars are out but the sky is a deep blue, and the trees are silhouetted deep black all around as I look up in the sky. The plants in the bath fence have grown so that it's woodsy inside it. The cicadas are shrilling and buzzing in all the tree tops—a very pleasant time of evening. Today was rainy but when it cleared up, it was so nice.

Harold has just left to take Nyarinda home. She is having trouble with a leaky gas tank. Andy has just left for Ghana for two months, she has a houseful of his relatives, all of whom have come because of money palava, and she is down to pennies until her check comes. Poor dear, having to deal with Andy's extended family is really a drag. Her children are so active, I don't know when she ever rests.

Tommy left today to go to Voinjama on church business so he will reach to [*stop at*] Kolahun to see his pa. Tommy has Tim Thomas's van now. Tim left right after persuading the board to fund a bush evangelical program. The Bishop told Tommy he should take on the evangelical program, along with the Zorzor parish. At least he has a vehicle. It's really much too big a responsibility to do "all two," as they say here.

Harold is a different person since we got back. He's finally resolved his problem mentally, I think. His arm is really growing stronger, even though the doctors say the muscle won't come back. Apparently other muscles have compensated, and he can do more. Mentally and emotionally too he's in a good shape.

Our puppies are so cute—five fat little sausages. They pile up on top of each other, roll off and continue to sleep. Their little noses and toes are so pink. Subie is a really good mother. She has a very quiet, calm nature, and her babies seem to be the same way. We will keep them for eight weeks and can enjoy them small before giving them up. Everyone wants them. We could get $5 easily for each one. Alfred will keep Subie when we leave. She loves him and he takes good care of her. We just give the babies away but he will sell his when she "borns" again.

Dearest Mother,   **October 12, 1976, Monrovia**

Harold is trying to round up materials for his building projects and I came along to take care of Christian Health Association business and just to keep him company. We came Sunday. It took all day because we stopped three or four times to visit friends.

This past weekend was parents' weekend at LTI. We went on Friday evening and watched the dancing—native-style put on by the school culture troupe and the town horn players. It was very good. Saturday we went to visit Martha's advisor and see the home economic exhibits and then went back in the evening for a play put on by former LTI students who attend the university here in Monrovia. It was a pleasant weekend. Many parents come and stay in the dorms. They also have a PTA meeting but I didn't go to that—figure the Liberian parents should go to that.

Dearest Judith,   **October 17, 1976, Zorzor**

Another Sunday has just finished. It is dark outside, the wind is starting to blow, and all kinds of night creatures are talking—cicadas, frogs, some kind of little animal, even.

It's been a nice unhurried weekend, although we both worked off and on. Martha came Friday afternoon, and we just took her back. She's turning into a nice young lady. "Caught hard time" with grade business—what an expression, to say she failed two subjects this grading period—but there is hope that she will pass. There's one more grade period before school closes December 6th. John was supposed to come for the weekend but never arrived—will have to wait to hear what happened.

Yata rode with us to Salayia. She had come to visit Martha just as we were leaving for LTI. She was really in a talkative mood—told us a lot about her home. She said when she was small like her little daughter, who is about four, she was given to a man to become his wife. Money was paid to the father for her. She stayed there until she was big—I guess until about 14.

The man had 15 women and was considered rich. As she grew up she decided she didn't want to stay and be his wife. She said, "If you don't agree, they can beat you—the other women—beat you, beat you, until you "tiyah (tired)." "Did they do so to you, Yata?" "No I ran away. One morning soon in the morning I got up, took my things, and ran away. I was running when I met Tommy. Then I stayed with him. I was looking for job—picking coffee—and Tommy told me to stay with him." I'm sure she was no older than 15 at the time, probably younger if she was about to be taken to his bed. I asked her what about the money her father received and she said, "I didn't know about money business. I just left." I really am fond of her.

We spent three days in Monrovia last week for Harold's purchasing, came back Wednesday. Tomorrow we go again so I can attend a CHAL meeting. We'll come back Wednesday. On Thursday we have to go to Cuttington College to teach a class Friday for the new Peace Corps trainees on visual aids. Traveling that much so far is not enjoyable. I would go by plane except Harold wants to take me. He's trying to promote some well drilling and can take care of that in Monrovia while I'm there and wants to visit around Gbarnga while I'm at Cuttington. It's nice to go together.

Dearest Vikki and Gill,   **November 7, 1976, Zorzor**

Do you remember Hubern Edwards, the man we visited in Zleh town? He is now director of extension for the Ministry of Agriculture and lives near Monrovia. We stopped to visit him today and had an enjoyable time. He asked about you and Ciam and asked to be remembered to you.

Wednesday, Nyarinda (Dr. Cole's wife) and I are going to LTI to do some wax printing. The dean of girl students is a Ghanaian lady who teaches home arts and does lovely tie-dye and wax prints. She told us we could come and do some with her. I'm really looking forward to doing it. She has all kinds of printing blocks and also a lot of different colors of dye.

Dearest Mother,   **November 11, 1976, Zorzor**

The days have been so hectic lately—medical stock takes a lot of time, I'm doing four to five hours of teaching a week again, and trying to get a CHAL meeting set up for December, lots of letter writing for that and people to call on in Monrovia, etc. Nothing easy like calling up on the phone.

We got a radio message yesterday that Donna Hutten, a Peace Corps friend from Phebe, and another person will be here to stay the weekend. Last night while I was preparing dinner—making some Chinese food— two WHO doctors from Monrovia arrived and needed a meal and a place to sleep. Fortunately I could stretch such a meal. Ming Ho had given us a lot of vegetables the day before—Chinese cabbage, green onion, cucumber, and Japanese eggplant, beautiful vegetables. So I've been having fun cooking Oriental style. We have a nice patch of ginger growing in our back yard, too.

Today Nyarinda and I will go to LTI to learn to do batik work. Mrs. Takiys, the wife of the principal there, is from Ghana and has many printing blocks. Nyarinda bought a lot of cloth (white cotton damask), and Mrs. Takiys has a good variety of excellent dyes.

Later. The batik went well. There were five of us so it wasn't possible to do a lot; we each did three yards. I dyed mine pink, and it turned out pretty good. Stamping it with the block, after dipping the block in melted wax, isn't as easy as it looks. There's just the right amount of pressure needed—just takes practice. After the New Year when school vacation is over, we will go again. I'd like to try a lot of different designs—maybe combinations of some. There are a lot of steps to go through in the batik process after dipping it in the dye. We cooked it in a pot of boiling water (over the fire, outside) to remove the wax, then rinsed, then washed it in soapy water, then rinsed, then hung it to dry.

We've had rats in our attic—but with a combination of traps and poison have managed to eliminate them. They were so noisy when they ran around and sometimes came down in the night and ate bananas that were in a basket on the counter.

Dearest Vikki and Gill,   **November 14, 1976, Zorzor**

Friday evening Rebecca Lama arrived unannounced from Lamco. She came to take the nursing test—a week late. So she won't have a chance for the course this year. And Martha didn't pass it either—quite surprising to me. So she will have to go back to high school and try again next year. We always seem to get the weekend guests!

Ming Ho had given us a lot of vegetables so I cooked a lot of Chinese food this time. One thing is a Chinese cabbage soup—made with chicken broth, green onions, some ginger (fresh), and garlic. It is quite tasty and a light soup. Then today I made it with cut-up roast beef with more cabbage, making it more like a main dish. It is fun to try different things.

Dearest Mother and all,   **November 20, 1976, Zorzor**

Well our rains have finished—almost. It's only rained two times in the past week. Now we can look for cool mornings and Harmitan winds [*dry dusty winds that blow along the northwest coast of Africa*], which bring a very hazy atmosphere due to the dust blowing here from the desert.

The past week has been too busy with a lot of frustrations. It will be nice to have Aris [*Swanson, a family friend*] here for a change of pace. My class will finish Wednesday for this term. I've been teaching public health concepts. Our vaccination drive is going to be over week after next— another task out of the way for this year. Today Harold and I drove to Killiwu, a town in the bush about four miles from here, to pick up a team that went out Friday. They were exhausted; the towns they walked to are on high hills, very steep ones. They also have to carry their equipment, although usually the chiefs give them a carrier to help.

A new couple arrived about two weeks ago—the Krabbenhoffs, who were here nearly a year ago. He is a farmer from Minnesota who came to help with the farm. His wife is a nurse although she's never worked.

Nyarinda is afraid that Amandi (the three-year-old boy) has hepatitis. Today they sent a blood sample to Phebe. I think his eyes are looking yellow. So is his urine and he's pretty listless. Keeping her children down is next to impossible so I don't know how she will manage with him if his tests are positive.

Yesterday, Tommy's baby was one year old so I had a party for her, invited the Cole kids and Lucinys and, of course, some followers came. Altogether there were about 15 plus adults. We had birthday cake and bananas and toffee (hard candy) and pawpaw, orange, and lime drink, made it in the blender with ice cubes. They sure liked it.

Dearest Vikki and Gill,   **November 20, 1976, Zorzor**

We just had a nice letter from Larry and Mary Pearmine. They are determined to have us come there. Harold thinks it would be OK. They say they have a house for us. It's the house they lived in when they first went back—an old two-story, cozy farm house at the edge of the cherry orchard.

Our puppies were fun but a lot of work. Fortunately Alfred fed them most of the time. Now we have only one left, and it will go to Monrovia with us Friday to a friend there. He's really cute and quite playful. The fourth one left yesterday, and the two romped all day. Then last night number five cried when his mother was in the house and he had to sleep alone. All the babies were white with brown spots—look just like Spot in Dick and Jane books.

I think I told you about the driver ants we had about a month ago. And our latest invasion was by *rats*. They were prancing around in our attic, and one night when John got up he saw five in our living room. We got two traps—caught one—and put poison upstairs. Within a week they were gone. I don't like rats. These were big, big.

Dearest Mother,   **December 5, 1976, Zorzor**

Since Aris came, I haven't written any letters—trying to keep up with work and visiting and driving around has put us in a bit of a bind. It's so nice to have her though. We've just returned from Ganta; we stayed at the mission for two nights, went to church there today; went to Gbedin to visit everyone yesterday.

On the way home today, we ate lunch with some Chinese friends—he's an old friend from Gbedin, now at Kpain and has a new wife, a pretty

Chinese girl named Chiu Shia. She can't speak any English except *hello* and *welcome* but hears small.

Nyarinda Cole is leaving this week for Kenya to visit her mother. She will take the three children; the baby is only 15 months old. I don't envy her the vacation, although it doesn't take too long to fly there, maybe five hours.

Martha came home today—their school term has now ended. She passed into the eleventh grade but will have to take French in vacation school since she didn't get a passing grade in that. John has to make up math. Both will stay with us this vacation. John will help in the hospital vegetable garden. We'll have lots of help around the house! Maybe I'll get them to practice their typing, too, since they will need things to keep themselves occupied.

Dearest Mother and all,   **December 12, 1976, Zorzor**

We've just returned from a weekend at Foya with Aris. We stayed with some people who work for the United Nations on a project to build furniture that has never got off the ground. They were Peace Corps volunteers when we were. They've invited us often but we never visit them so this time decided to stay there. They have no electricity or running water— have an outside bath fence and latrine but everything was fixed so nice— a big roomy house where we felt quite welcome. We had a chance to visit our Liberian friends too—fellows who used to work with Harold at Gbedin. Also took her to the market there and at Bolahun, 14 miles further, where country cloth is woven. No matter where we go, we always run into people who know us.

I took Aris on a bush hike to watch people cutting rice; it was quite a hike, about an hour, lots of mud and water to maneuver around, also some up and down hills. We rested at a palava hut where the people were cooking. Over the fire was a wire rack with some meat drying. I saw a rat, all black and dry, lying on its back with its mouth open, just a small thing.

Later when we came from the fields, the people gave us a bowl of rice with meat and greens soup, which we ate with our hand, joined by the two boys who "carried" us. Aris ate some; I told the boys to eat the meat. (It was too big a piece to be the rat!) Later I asked Aris if she had seen the meat drying on the rack, and she said she didn't realize it was a rat! She's a good sport—willing to try most things we suggest.

Dearest Mother,   **December 17, 1976, Monrovia**

We are in Monrovia to attend a meeting of CHAL. I've had to make all the preparations, send out letters and questionnaires, etc. My, I'll be glad when it's ended; it will be all day tomorrow, too. We'll leave as soon as it's over and try to reach Zorzor in the night. Aris stayed home because she had a cold so I don't want to stay down here any more than necessary. John and Alfred are taking care of her, and she seemed perfectly content to stay there.

It's awfully muggy here in Monrovia—hot and sticky. We're both glad we don't live here, more than ever now because theft, pick pocketing, street assault, and such is so much worse now than even a year ago. I always carry my money now in my bra when I go shopping on waterside. Harold puts his in his shoe! Quite a challenge, eh?

The CHAL meetings went OK. One nun told me it was the best meeting she'd ever attended! It was a real job to do everything. New officers were elected, and I'm no longer secretary-treasurer, praise the Lord. It was a very difficult job for the past year and a half.

The weather is very dry now—leaves are falling from some of the trees, others are turning red! Seed pods are bursting open too—great long ones, full of fluffy down or big seeds. Some sound like a gunshot when they pop open.

Did I tell you that Dr. Gwenigale's three little kids had whooping cough—including the one-month-old baby. The two older children had taken vaccine but the baby was too young for it—it's really dangerous for such a tiny baby. We've had a lot of pertussis the past few months.

Dearest Mother and all,   **December 25, 1976, Zorzor**

Harold and Aris are both asleep. We got up at 5 AM to go to church, met the congregations as they were walking about singing (in Loma), each one holding a lighted candle. We three joined them and for an hour, wound around, between houses, and gradually our group became larger, each new person getting a candle. By the time we reached the church, about 6:45 AM, there were about 70 people in the group.

It was just beginning to be daylight. There is no electricity in town, so besides each person's candles, there were just altar candles and the four Advent candles on a vine-covered hanging cross near the pulpit. The sermon was in Loma (there was translation) as was most of the singing.

There were only six of us non-Loma speaking people there; the rest were mostly so-so country people [*seemed mostly to be people from up-country*]. It was a very nice experience. During the service the sun came up, so beautiful over the housetops, pinky yellow with a haze around it.

We are all to go to the Krabbenhoff's house (he's the farmer here for four months) for dinner tonight. Andy Cole went to Voinjama for midnight mass and will be back for dinner too. Along with all our "strangers" there will be about 16 persons. Last eve we went to Deanna's for homemade ice cream and cake and Christmas carols. It has been hard for us to get into the celebrating mood—it never really seems like Christmas here, the weather is so different from what I associate with the Christmas season; there is so little of traditional customs we were used to, except by the missionaries, and it really seems out of place to me, here where Liberians have different ways.

A person has been assigned to the medical supply department to work with me. I must train him to take care of all the receiving of drugs and supplies, dispensing them, and also keeping control and account of them. So as time goes on I should be able to pull back from there. Then remains community health with Thomas, and I've already taken less responsibility there—mostly consulting when he needs help. Twenty new students are coming the 24th of January so Thomas and I will have to begin team teaching the community health and nutrition classes right away, in order to get them finished by the time our departure date arrives.

Ruth and Harold in 1977.

1977

Dearest Judith and Ciam,   January 1, 1977, Zorzor

Since Aris is leaving tonight, I am sending a letter along with her. Christmas at Zorzor was OK. On Christmas night we had about 20 people at one of the missionary homes, Americans, Liberians, and a Pakistani. Lots of good food, including turkey and pumpkin pie, and fireworks afterward. On Christmas Eve we were at Deanna's, again a varied group. Then on Monday, we had a bunch at our house for palm butter and rice.

Things are so-so here; so many problems at the hospital, basically financial, but which are due to poor management and theft. Both of us will be glad when it's time to leave, but thinking of saying goodbye to the children almost makes me cry.

John is staying home this vacation since it is the last time we'll have together. Also, he has to take math in vacation school to make up his grade. Martha is with her people but will come next week, since she, too, has to make up a subject.

Dearest Mother and all,   January 10, 1977, Zorzor

I'm so sorry to be so slow in writing—every day I seem to be more jammed. We did enjoy Aris so much, but found ourselves feeling like we were leading double lives, working and trying to entertain her. Where we live, it isn't easy for a person to go around on their own, as you know. Now, as soon as she left, Thomas went on vacation, leaving me with all that work. Graduation was yesterday, and we have a bunch of people staying with us. John and Martha both here for vacation school, Martha's sister and boyfriend and her baby—eight of us for meals. They will all be here for a week. Of course, then I'm expecting the ELWA (*Hospital*) community health team for a week. They are to spend time with our mobile clinic. Such is our daily life here!

Vickie, Martha's little girl, who was three in October, is such a cute little thing. Martha's sister, who is childless, takes care of her and treats her so well. Vickie seems so happy, plays by herself all day. Our Vikki sent a Snoopy dog that's about five inches high. So when little Vickie is here, she carries that one in her lappa. It's really quite comical to see the little wee girl with the big puppy dog bobbing along on her back.

She usually uses a rayon head tie as her lappa, and it's quite slippery. She spends most of her time getting the dog arranged and the scarf tied. Then it falls off, and she starts all over again and never gets vexed with it when it doesn't work. When she eats, we set her on a little low country stool. She sets her bowl on the floor between her legs and stirs and mixes with her spoon, oblivious to the adults who are eating at the table. It was fun having her.

Yesterday we graduated six midwives and six men practical nurses. It started one and a half hours late, a usual occurrence. The night before was class night. The class cooks and serves the faculty and friends. They also put on a performance, which was hilarious. One act was the story of Shylock, which they acted out, in modern Liberian characters.

We are getting another class of 20 nursing students next week, and still have 17 who have just finished the first year and received their caps and badges yesterday. So classes will begin again by the end of the month.

Nyarinda and the three children are in Kenya to visit her mother for at least two months. We miss her here since we spend a lot of time together. They and Andy will leave in June for the States so we will no doubt visit with them when we get home. They will be in Youngstown, Ohio, where he will do a pediatric residency for at least three years. So far, we don't know who will replace him here at the hospital.

Dearest Mother and all,   **January 17, 1977, Zorzor**

It's a pleasant Sunday afternoon and quiet after all our entertaining, although we are having three extras for dinner tonight. A new doctor and his girlfriend arrived today so they and Dr. Cole will eat with us. Since Nyarinda left, he usually eats lunch with us and dinner with one of the other families here. Most of the time he's at the hospital so spends little time alone.

The Porro Society bush school is in progress not far from here. The path to it is just past Deanna's house. There are several hundred boys there, some for almost a year, but many school boys have been going in ever since school has been out in November. Lately, the celebrating and dancing has been increasing, and boys are going almost daily. After they've been there about a week, they receive their new names, and the zos come into town playing and singing and calling out their names. We can hear them nightly, and are prohibited from going into town if the "big zo" is present; only men who have been initiated into the Porro can see him.

The boys will come out in two to three weeks. We are looking forward to seeing them. They start coming in the morning, and it takes all day for them to finish. We went last year to Ziggida when 400 boys came out. This one will be bigger. Thus is the first time in seven years that the Porro Society school has been held. Geoff says all of upper Lofa County is holding similar schools. It's just about the most important event in a family. Everything stops for it.

The children who are going now are generally just little things. Old Man, the five year old who stays with Deanna so much, has gone, and little guys, like three year olds, are taken, too. Of course, it's only for two to three weeks, but the way kids can get sick here, I'd really worry.

When Martha came from her home, she brought us a goat and a half bag (50 pounds) of rice, a gift from her father in Gbedin. (She brought them in the taxi!) Harold has the goat tied out in the bush by our house and plans to butcher it for a feast for the workers before we leave. He's pretty good sized, so Harold will have to get someone to help with that and with the cooking, because there will be a LOT of people. We'll serve plenty of rice with pepper soup; it's made like a broth, with goat meat, plenty of hot pepper, some canned tomatoes, and salt. People love it.

As soon as vacation school is over, about February 5th, we plan to take John and Martha to Monrovia to do some school shopping. We have never taken Martha and decided she should have a trip. We'll all stay with Geoff, which makes it financially possible. All of us staying at the church house gets pretty expensive. Then we must go to Foya to visit Daniel Suah one more time before his wife goes back to school in Saniquellie.

Dearest Mother,   **January 28, 1977, Zorzor**

Today has been very interesting. The boys' bush school closed today, "broke bush," as they say. And all the boys came into town 1,422 of them. Can you imagine all of those kids plus all the families and spectators in little Zorzor town?

The boys were all ages, from one year to adults. Many little tots, all ages, from two and a half to five years, were seated on mats, on both sides of the streets, lined up in a single line. It was quite a colorful sight, with all of them dressed in black and white country cloth gowns, a long drooping hat of country cloth, with a fringe around the face so the upper part of the face was covered. Rows and rows of big safety pins lined the hats. A bright terry cloth towel was used as a scarf, and many kids had head-tie cloth around the heads.

I learned that many mothers had sent head ties for this purpose so they could identify their own boys. There was so much dancing and music making, you can't imagine the celebration. Some of the boys have been gone for a year, so you can imagine how happy the mothers were to see their sons. It was hard to have enough people to work in the hospital today, since everyone wanted to witness the doings.

We've had the little goat Martha brought us tethered in the bush behind our house. Now today it broke its chain, and we've had a hilarious time trying to catch it. John, Martha, Alfred, and Yarkpowolo (who carries water for us) chased him through the yard, through the bush, laughing and yelling and falling down. Finally, after about 30 minutes, Alfred tackled him and caught a hind leg. Now, he's tied up again but objecting to it.

Soon after, while they were standing at the edge of the yard, Martha called "Snake!" And there was a green snake, about a yard long, coiled around in a tree, about head height. So the guys grabbed cutlasses and cut the snake in half. It was a green tree viper, a very poisonous snake. So now our excitement is over.

Two days ago, they caught a longer green snake in our front yard. People say during dry season, a lot of snakes stay in the trees to catch birds. Yarkpowolo (you know he's really unbalanced) says snakes can give him power. He says, "Snake power is too much." I don't know if he holds them in his hands or what, he just rambles on and on.

Dearest Judith,   **January 30, 1977, Zorzor**

Today, the bush school boys are turned over to their parents officially. Each parent must pay 50 cents per boy to the chief zo for the blessing. Then later a feast will be held for all the men and boys. No date is set yet for that. All the boys are around town in their costumes, but romping around like any other kids. Of course, it's not just boys who go into the bush school, some are just babies. One was just eight months old, but the mother is a member of the men's society—some kind of way—but can't participate in the women's society activities. So she could go into the school and continue nursing the baby.

Annie's little son, Varfly, who is about eight went, and so did about eight of her nephews. They were all so happy yesterday, dancing and singing and playing. Annie is so pretty. I'm really going to hate to say goodbye to her and Thomas, as well as Tommy and Yata. Tommy's diabetes has come on him again. So far, he's managing with pills.

The Harmitan lilies are blooming now. They grow so rapidly. One week they look like dry brown bulbs poking through the ground. The next week the lilies are in bud and blooming. I'm going to put a marking stick beside one just to see how many inches it grows in a day.

Dearest Vikki and Gill,   **February 5, 1977, Zorzor**

This week we heard some disappointing news. Liberia has established trade relations with Red China. Of course, you know there was a lot of money involved. Now, Taiwanese who've been here assisting with agriculture assistance programs since 1962 will be leaving.

We stopped by to see Ming Ho on the way to Monrovia and found him and his partner still kind of stunned, just waiting to hear when they will be leaving. The Taiwanese have been building a several million dollar sugar factory and planting thousands of acres of cane for it. Now all has stopped, since all the machinery is from Taiwan. The factory was due to begin operations in a month or two. I don't know what the next step will be, since there won't be replacements available.

Dearest Judith,   **February 11, 1977, Zorzor**

The ELWA village clinic team (six people) spent a day with us so they could go out with our mobile clinic. They will leave tomorrow. We put the boys up in the boy's dorm, and our kids cooked for them. A team of experts in immunization came from the Ministry of Health on Monday and left on Tuesday. They spent time in our community health department and were pleased at what we've been doing in regard to vaccinations. It made us feel good, since previously they've been hypercritical.

Two leprosy doctors, one of whom is an Irish nun, spent most of the week with us, reviewing the leprosy program. Now today, we're expecting Geoff for the weekend, plus one or two friends. Deanna has four guests from Monrovia for the weekend, and the Minges from Phebe came to visit the Krabbenhofts.

Dearest Mother,   **February 11, 1977, Zorzor**

This week has gone by so fast, although I can't say I'm sorry—so many things going on. Harold says our house is like a train station; the door is swinging all the time. This was the week when everyone came to Curran Hospital and to the community health department primarily, starting last Sunday.

On Monday evening we cooked for 21 people—the two doctors who came for leprosy control work, two other doctors (a Welsh man and a Turk), plus a Liberian immunization specialist who came for the purpose of evaluating our community health program. An American nurse from ELWA Hospital village clinics and the five young men who work in clinics with her were here for the rest of the week. Then Dr. Cole and Dr. Huda (he's Pakistani), the Krabbenhofs, and Joanne Braun [*a friend from the States*], plus our family. John and Martha cooked for them all every day.

Actually it was an easy evening. The guys made palm butter and rice, which people really like and is easy to serve. The only hitch all week is we have to do all the cooking over the fire in the back yard. Our gas tank finished Sunday, and there is no gas in the county for cooking. We have the electric coffee pot which I use to boil eggs, make tea, etc. We also have the electric frying pan. But to cook rice and soup, fry plantain, etc., all must be done outside over the fire. I'm fortunate to have all the help that I do. School hasn't started yet. It won't start for John until March, and Martha must be on campus the 21st.

Tomorrow when all of our guests depart, Martha and I will sew. She is trying to get school clothes ready. I'll make two dresses for her, and she will sew two. Both of the kids wear uniforms at school, so don't have to have a lot of clothes.

Actually at John's school, they only wear uniforms on special occasions, and on other days they wear just shirts and trousers that look "smart," as their school information sheet describes it.

Harold has turned over the responsibilities for the maintenance department to his Liberian assistant and now is trying to get special building projects completed. It will be interesting to see if the man will take hold and really be responsible. He's capable but not too energetic.

This time of year there are so many sick people in the hospital. During dry season, the water supplies are so bad, and there is so much sickness due to that as well as diarrhea from a variety of organisms.

Yesterday the boys butchered the goat. We will save it until April, when Harold will have a feast for all the workers. The goat kept breaking his tether and wandering away, so we couldn't keep him any longer.

Dearest Vikki and Gill,   **February 20, 1977, Zorzor**

It's hard to think of leaving here and saying goodbye to some of the people. And it will be hard on the kids to have us go. I wonder if US life will be too strange after all this time, for us to adapt to it. Our life is so different here. Of course, I won't miss some of it!

Yesterday, we were in Ganta, so we stopped to see Adama. She is about seven months pregnant and is feeling miserable. She said this is her last baby, said she will have a tubal ligation after she delivers. Also, says she will go to Mecca next year. Her husband, a big diamond buyer, has four wives. Each will have gone to Mecca when she goes next year.

Harold told her she should find a diamond for him to buy for me, to replace the ring he lost (my engagement ring). Adama says she should get a diamond for him at the price her husband pays the digger, since "we're her best friend." Ha. We'll see next month when we go for the nursing school graduation.

Dearest Mother and all,   **February 20, 1977, Zorzor**

Today Harold took Martha to school. Loaded her trunk and bath bucket, books, clothes hangers, etc., into the Datsun. Took Deanna and a twelfth grader she is sponsoring too. It's only 14 miles but getting there in a taxi with their loads is not easy. It's about a 30-minute trip one way. Tuition at LTI has gone up $100 a year since we started her there. It's now $450—this includes board, room, and tuition. John's is $400 this year at Carroll High. He will leave Wednesday, stay one night at Gbedin, and go into the bush to see his folks at Geinple before reaching school Saturday or Sunday. Getting John back to school takes some effort, since his school is 170 miles from here. He's afraid to go in a taxi since he was in the accident, but what to do. It is really quite dangerous to be on the road now because the dust is so heavy when cars pass. Visibility is so bad, a person has to drive so carefully, but the Mandingo taxi drivers don't care. Being Muslim, they believe that they have an appointed time to die, no matter what.

We're still cooking over the fire outside, have a little metal frame to set over the coals, just like camping! It's the way country people cook so it's really no problem for Alfred and the rest. But you can't just heat a pot of water without planning ahead. And do the pots get *black*.

I'm trying to train a new man to take over the medical stock department and what a chore. He can't subtract, and one thing he must learn to do is to keep a running inventory on all the drugs. Trying to teach him to subtract a three-digit number from a five- or six-digit number is, so far, an impossibility. But maybe two more months might make a difference!

Dearest Judith,   **February 26, 1977, Zorzor**

We're back at Geoff's; we seem to be making a habit of it. We came to Monrovia to tell the lumber company that Harold couldn't accept their offer. He's there now. It won't be easy to tell them because they really need him.

Yesterday, a good letter came from Mary and Larry, in Oregon, telling us that we are welcome on any terms. The house is empty just now—an old two-story farm house on the edge of the cherry orchard—and it's ours for as long as we want to stay and get our bearings or to stay and Harold work for them, part time or full time, whatever. It's such a good feeling.

John left for school yesterday. He planned to stay in Gbedin or Geinple for a night each place before reaching campus. He was so sad about leaving us. I know it's hard for him to know we won't be seeing each other again after we leave Liberia. We plan to go to visit him by the last of March, and talk with the Brothers about handling the school fee business for next year.

Dearest Vikki and Gill,   **March 4, 1977, Zorzor**

We still have dry season. It has rained only twice since the first of the year. We had two wells dug recently, paid for with the money Sonja [*Harold's niece*] sent—one for the orphan quarter, and one for the TB area. Now both are dry. Of course, that may be fortunate since the well digger is now going down further. So maybe next year the wells won't go dry. Harold managed to get two hand pumps and enough pipe for both wells from a Peace Corps friend who works with a construction project. Now what remains is the cement top, and then they can get the pumps set up and ready for use. Happy Day!

Yesterday we went to a town about 25 miles from here—six of those miles from the main road. We (the mobile clinic team) went for a district health meeting, which we do once a month, in a different town each month. The physician assistant has always seemed like a dud to me. However, yesterday, he showed us the fine, new clinic building that the town people have constructed on their own. We also walked about the town, shaking hands and being greeted. A lot of the town people came to our meeting. The town chief, garbed in his country-cloth robe and hat, was accompanied by a drummer and a sassa [*a gourd rattle wrapped in a net strung with seeds*] player, with three or four elders walking behind. Then when the meeting finished, there were a lot of speeches, followed by a troupe of ladies who came to dance. There were four little girls and about a dozen adult women. They never seemed to get tired, must have danced for 30 to 40 minutes, so energetically and expressively. Each wore a woven raffia band dangling with seeds just below each knee. Some wore a bra, some none, and each wore a short lappa. Even the little girls were excellent.

I hadn't wanted to go to the meeting (it's always such a long, tiring, and boring day) but was forced to because Thomas was away. In the end I was glad I'd gone. As usual, they cooked rice and soup for us.

Dearest Mother,   **March 4, 1977, Zorzor**

Thomas is going to the States for a family planning administration seminar, so I'll have his entire Community health supervision responsibility along with teaching alone. He will be in DC, and maybe a field trip to Chicago.

We are having an epidemic of measles, mostly centered in towns where the boys were in bush school. From February to today we've admitted to the hospital 33 cases, and several of the patients have already died. It's so sad since most of the children afflicted will develop kwashiorkor [*a form of malnutrition that occurs when there is not enough protein in the diet*] as a result of the severe measles and diarrhea. It's even sadder since we have measles vaccination drives twice a year and have been to the very towns where these children came from. Apparently the parents didn't bother to bring their little ones for vaccination. As you know, some of these villages are far in the bush, so it's not easy to get our immunization teams there but we do it.

The relationship of measles to the bush school is that hundreds of boys are together very closely over quite a period of time, and if one gets sick with a communicable disease, it spreads so easily and so quickly. Along with that, people are so slow to take their children for kwi medicine, and even more so if the boy is in the secret bush school, which means so much to the people.

We are expecting Geoff Thompson and his friend Svend Holsoe, for the weekend. Svend has been living in Liberia off and on since he was nine and now is nearing forty. He knows the people, little and big, and all the political overtones, so it's very interesting for us to be able to visit with him. His parents were from Denmark.

Dearest Judith and Ciam,   **March 7, 1977, Zorzor**

Another week is gone. May 1st is overshadowing everything—so much to do. Visiting and such become very important now. Geoff and his new little girl, Nyamah, who is about nine and is Ella's sister, spent the weekend with us.

He's leaving today for Voinjama to set things up in a Bande town beyond there for a visit from the American ambassador tomorrow, who will dedicate a school in the town, which a special embassy fund helped pay for but which the town people built themselves. It's been a pleasant weekend, nice to have him here. We always have fun together—visiting and reading. He's always interested in things we're doing, came to the hospital with me, walked about with Harold to see his projects, etc.

Thomas Konie is leaving tomorrow for Washington, DC, for six-weeks. He just learned he was going five days ago then had to get busy with visas, shots, and all that. It seems that is the way things are done here. He was to go a few months ago then things fell through with the travel money so when he actually goes he will believe it. He and Annie, his wife, came by last evening for a short visit. She is so fine.

Dear Mother,   **March 9, 1977, Zorzor**

Harold had to go to Konia around 8:30 tonight to help the pastor out. He had an accident around 6—rolled his truck over into the ditch. He was blessed that both he and his passenger escaped injury. Harold hated to go, since it's so hard to do things in the dark.

Our house is empty for a change. Alfred went home for a few days. Geoff was here since Saturday and left this morning for Monrovia. It's so nice to not have a bunch in the house. It seems like every evening there are extra people. Last night it was the blind student who was corresponding with Uncle Emil last year. He's leaving Friday for Florida State University, on a four-year Liberian government scholarship.

Tonight the chief from Zolowo, a town about 20 miles away in the bush, came with his son, Eddie, to visit with us and invite us to his home on the 19th of this month. Eddie is a good friend of Harold's from Gbedin who now works in Foya. Harold got him the job in Foya four years ago. We've been waiting to go visit him, so it was nice they came and made it official. The chief thanked us for Eddie. He said, "God is truly wonderful. Here you people came from so far away and reached to Liberia and helped my son." Of course, this was all in Loma, so we had to have someone translate for us.

The weather is extremely hot and dry now. The grass is brown and crackly and everything is quite ugly. The Harmitan winds are here again, along with smoke from burning farms. It's almost like smog, very irritating to the lungs and nasal mucosa. Our lips, too, are chapped, the first time here in Liberia. Because there is so much dust in the air the setting sun, usually a brilliant orange, is now barely visible, a pale apricot.

Dearest Judith and Ciam,   **March 11, 1977, Zorzor**

Nyarinda is still in Kenya, apparently trying to get a house built. Andy really misses his family. He spends a lot of time at our house, eats lunch with us every day and some dinners. He says Sundays are the worst, because that is when he misses four-year-old Omandi, who usually spent time with him then.

Saturday we expect to go to the town of Zolowo, six miles from Lutheran Training Institute, to visit the chief. The week after, we will go to Ganta for the Nursing School graduation, and on to Carroll High to see John. The week after that, to Foya to visit Daniel Suah and Eddie. After all this, maybe we can stay here the rest of the time. That will be Easter vacation when the children will be home for a week. It almost makes me breathless to think about it.

Dearest Vikki and Gill,   **March 14, 1977, Zorzor**

We are having a serious measles epidemic, have had 25 to 30 cases in the hospital since the middle of February, and many deaths. It is so disappointing since our vaccination drives are every six months. And still there are all these people who have not had their children vaccinated. When our teams go to the villages, after announcing their coming, many people will already have gone to their farms and carried their children with them. Now these children who have measles, and don't die, will end up with serious malnutrition, and stunted for years, both mentally and physically.

Harold and I are reading *The Final Days* [*behind-the-scenes account of Richard Nixon's dramatic last months as president, by Woodward and Bernstein*]. So shocking how such things could have been going on for so long, isn't it? And also that one man could gain so much power.

It has been so long since we've had mail of any kind. There are so few of us here now that there is very little traveling back and forth, thus the mail from Monrovia is very sparse.

Dearest Mother,   **March 14, 1977, Zorzor**

I'll dash off a quick note before going to bed so Harold can carry it in the AM. He and Joanne are leaving about 6 AM for Monrovia and coming back the next day. We're still without stove gas and having to use a fire outside for most of our cooking. Alfred was at his home for four days, so I just used the electric frying pan; cooked one thing, put it aside and started on the next thing. It worked, but I do miss baking. Of course, we could bake over the fire, too, but it would have to be a special pot to put the bread or cake pan inside. Then you put coals on top of it, too. Some of my Liberian friends bake that way.

Dearest Mother and all,   **March 20, 1977, Zorzor**

Yesterday was my birthday, and it was a different one. We had made plans to visit Eddie Robinson's father, who is the chief in Zolowo. The town is six miles off the motor road, in the bush. It's the town I wrote about before, telling about the harrowing trip with the mobile clinic where the road conditions were terrible.

We had made arrangements with another of the chief's sons, a Zorzor schoolboy, to carry us there. It is a typical bush town. Everyone ran out to see us when we drove into town, waving and smiling. The old chief, who says he's 80, but I don't think he's that old, welcomed us warmly as did his wives. There is always a lot of formal talk, presided over by an interpreter. Later we went to the home of the clinic nurse with whom I work. There they served us rice and chicken. The old man brought us beer, which he called our "cold water," which is a term used for either money or drinks at such an occasion.

Then people came in to visit us and brought us palm wine. The chief's wife gave me a bundle of Loma money. This is the old twisted iron rods that were used long ago before actual coins were available. It was made by the blacksmith, actually looking something like barbed wire without the barbs, about 12 to 15 inches in length.

The chief also gave us a goat, which we carried home in the back seat of our car. It's now baaing outside the door. Harold will butcher it tomorrow. It will be part of the soup we plan to cook for the hospital staff before we leave. We have another goat already frozen for that purpose. The children will be home for Easter vacation on the first of April, for about ten days, so they and Alfred will do the cooking.

Dearest Vikki and Gill,   **March 20, 1976, Zorzor**

We were given a little goat when we went to visit the chief in Zolowo yesterday. It is small but has a large voice, which it uses continually! He will join our other goat in the freezer for the soup we will cook for the staff in couple of weeks.

Last evening Joanne Braun (with Harold's planning help) had a birthday party for me—a surprise. It was fun. She had invited Liberian and Peace Corps friends as well as mission people, which was a nice change. Harold had bought a big watermelon in Monrovia, and she made it into a bowl and filled it with chunks of melon and bananas.

Dearest Mother,   **March 24, 1977, Belaqualazu**

Harold, Dr. Cole, and I are sitting in Belaqualazu, a town in the bush, waiting for Gene to come pick us up. We flew in this morning to visit the clinic. The nearest town is a three and a half hour walk away through the bush. Gene's nearly an hour overdue, so we are hoping we won't be left here for the night! Last week our clinic team was. They had been out two nights in two different towns and were to be picked up in the afternoon. Then the plane's gas was too low, and it was getting too late to get back to Phebe to gas up and come for them. So they slept out another night.

Dr. Cole had come with us to see patients that the physician assistant had screened for him. I came for clinic supervision, and Harold came just to see the town. The town chief gave each of us a chicken, to say thank you for coming. Another family cooked rice and soup for us, and the whole town came to meet us at the plane when we arrived. They will no doubt be at the plane to see us off.

It is so beautiful flying over the countryside. Gene flew quite low, so we could see people and huts and farms. We always look for elephants, but have never been fortunate to sight any. Sometimes they come to the streams to drink, but not usually in the heat of the day.

Later on, Zorzor. Well, we made it home that night, and here it is a whole week later before I got back to finish this. Life is so hectic just now. We left the next day for Ganta, where we attended the nurse's graduation. It was my last class there. They were freshmen when we left Gbedin. Then we went on to Lamco, a long tiring drive, to visit John, and make arrangements for his school fees for the rest of the year. We stayed with friends there, former Peace Corps volunteers; then drove back to Gbedin for a visit.

It was a strenuous weekend since the roads were so dusty and "washboardy" a good part of the way. Everyone asked about Ciam wherever we stopped, and all asked us to tell him hello when we get back home. We came home with a chicken that day too, a standard dash.

It is now beginning to rain in the afternoons and evenings "one, one," as people say, meaning "now and then, not every day."

Dearest Mother,   **April 2, 1977, Foya**

This is my day to try to catch up with letters. We came up yesterday to visit Daniel Suah and Eddie Robinson, former colleagues of Harold's at Gbedin. We are staying in the Agrimecho guest house and are being treated like special guests. The houseman cooks and does everything for us. Daniel is forever grateful to Harold for his position here and can never do too much for us.

Getting here took some doing. There had been a heavy rain the night before, and they had just graded the road that day. The road from Zorzor to Voinjama is very hilly, long curvy hills. About 20 miles from home, one long hill was totally impassable, cars and trucks were stuck every which way. So we turned around and went home for about three hours. By the time we reached there again the grader had scraped the mud off and moved the stalled vehicles, and we were able to make it. Fortunately, with mud and rain there's no dust. Actually the paving has begun and should reach Ganta by 1980!

Today we went to the market here. It is held every Saturday and is huge. Truck after truck comes from Sierra Leone with unbelievable loads and packed with people. The noise is fantastic, everyone talking at once. It's fun to go and look at country things and just watch the people. I bought three little fish baskets made of wicker, about eight inches high. Ladies tie them to their waist when they go fishing.

There was a snake man there. He had three or four *large* snakes, black shiny things, some about four to six feet long. He let them hang around his neck and slither around him. He was selling snake medicine and makes a lot of money—usually $1 per. Supposedly snakes won't bite you if you have snake medicine. It's creepy to watch them. We've been killing snakes lately, one hoodless cobra just by the front door a week or two ago.

Dearest Mother,   **April 8, 1977, Zorzor**

While everyone is still asleep I'm trying to get some writing done. Today is Good Friday. We will have a church service at 9:30. Then on Sunday at

Easter service Alfred will be baptized. Last night I made him a new shirt for the occasion, of a blue and white wax print. We have gotten a job for him at the children's hostel at Phebe so he's going to be OK.

For the two past months our hospital has been overloaded with terribly sick patients—measles, meningitis, typhoid. Dry season is especially bad for any water-borne disease because water supplies in villages are so poor and very contaminated as a result of the short supply. Andy works night and day, being the only doctor here.

The kids are home now, including an extra boy from Nimba, who is spending Easter with us. John is doing some typing for me, good for his practice and a big help to me. Martha, as usual, is sewing and made shirts for both of the boys.

Dearest Mother,   **April 14, 1977, Zorzor**

We're doing all kinds of "last things." Our house is looking bare now. We've sold some things and given some away and have nearly packed up all we want to take home. Everyone wants to buy things but fortunately two of our friends took all, and this has eliminated a lot of humbug.

Today we had a "feast" for the staff. Annie, Thomas' wife, and two other midwives and Alfred and Deanna's cook did the whole thing. The new students, 12 of them, did the serving and washing up. We cooked goat and fish soup and rice for about 100 people! Here's the recipe: 2 goats (both small, and given to us), a case of fish (about 20 pounds), 1 pound onions, 2 pounds potatoes, 1 package macaroni, 5 cans tomato paste, bouillon cubes (a handful), hot pepper. All this was cooked in an immense pot over the fire while another huge pot of rice (50 pounds) was cooking the same way. None of the goat was wasted; head, intestines, all were cut up and used. The girls stirred the rice with a long stick. Everything was ready by 12 noon. It was fun. The girls are so used to cooking for a large group, they never hesitated. And working outside is nice, no mess to clean up.

The children have gone back to school now, left Monday and Tuesday, and so we won't see John again. It was hard to say goodbye. We'll still see Martha at Lutheran Teaching Institute, since it's on our way. We've sold our car and will deliver it on our way down the 1st of the month.

Sunday. Alfred was baptized today. He was anxious to have it done before we leave. We had a little tea party for him after church. Did I tell you he has a job at Phebe as soon as he leaves us? People like him and several wanted him to come to them. Afterward, Harold finished the packing. I painted addresses on the crates, and Beard Beard, the Lebanese trucker, came and agreed to carry everything tomorrow.

Liberians call people who have a big mustache (as B.B. does) or a beard, "Beard Beard," actually "Beah Beah." Harold has a mustache, but people just call him the Old Man!

Carrying water in Sanniquellie.

Last night triplets were born, and the mother died; her uterus became inverted, and she hemorrhaged, just a young woman with one other child. It's really a tragedy because it's so hard for a baby to live if it's fed on a bottle. Now, the nurses are trying to figure out which of them can take the babies, one baby to a nurse. The hospital will provide milk. I'd really like to help, if I were here. They said Deanna could have one, but I don't know how she can do it.

Dearest Vikki and Gill,   **April 18, 1977, Zorzor**

Finally the packing is finished. Harold is just now nailing the lid on the last crate, all are addressed and will be hauled to Monrovia tomorrow. So we should be able to relax a bit. Except for daily work and my class, which won't finish until after next week. And we have one more vaccination push.

Dearest Judith and Ciam,   **April 18, 1977, Zorzor**

In two weeks we'll leave here. It doesn't seem possible. Hard to believe we won't be coming back. After six years, it seems like we belong here. John went back to school; it was hard for him to leave us. We all cried. We haven't said goodbye to Martha yet, since we can see her at Lutheran Teaching Institute. We'll go to church with her there next Sunday.

Dearest Mother,   **April 24, 1977, Zorzor**

Friday a Dr. Frame (whom you may have read about in the book *Fever*) arrived to do some sample collecting for his lassa fever research. We had to put him up, feed him, etc., for two days and set up his project in the hospital. He took blood samples from all employees and later will send results showing who has antibodies for the disease.

Then Saturday afternoon a dentist and his 12-year-old son arrived, to stay until Tuesday. He's doing a feasibility study to see about setting up a dental program here and in Upper Lofa. They are staying with us. Later in the day two couples (all doctors) came from Bong mine to see the hospital and stay the night. One was a specialist in tropical hygiene; all are from Germany. I had to get sheets and towels and dishes, etc., and get a house ready for them to stay in. In between, I've been trying to finish some sewing projects—a tablecloth for Geoff, a dress with design stitching for one of the girls in the DWME [*Division of World Mission and Evangelism*] office in New York, and a patchwork quilt for one of the triplets. So time flies.

Tomorrow the Bishop is coming with the DWME secretary for Africa who is visiting for a week. I could be busy all the time just being a hostess without doing any other work! This week we'll see the last of my class, about time! Today we went to Lutheran Teaching Institute to go to church with Martha. She seems to be doing all right, so far.

Dearest Mother,   **May 2, 1977, Monrovia**

People were so nice to us when we left, had a party with gifts at Zorzor. Saturday night we slept at Phebe, and the people there all gathered in our honor, too. Now we're in Monrovia for three days, and we'll leave late Wednesday evening.

Epilogue

January 1, 2011, Olympia, Washington

We'd looked forward to coming home. But it didn't take long before we realized that home wasn't where it once was. Not to say we weren't happy to be back, to see family and old friends. However, we realized very soon how much we had changed. Not only had we changed, so had everyone else, but we had all changed in different ways. It was soon apparent that we were very different people than we were when we left for Africa more than six years before. Our attitudes and viewpoints had expanded. And we soon knew that we would no longer fit in where we once were at home. Thomas Wolfe's premise "You can't go home again," proved to be so true in our case.

Our experiences and the life to which we had become adapted had drastically affected our attitudes, choices, and wants. Our life in Liberia had prepared us to be more economical and enhanced our awareness of other people's needs. Harold had gained self confidence and realized he could fit anywhere.

We had worked hard and traveled extensively but earned very little money in either Peace Corps or the mission. Actually, my work at the mission was all voluntary. Only Harold had received a salary. So now we had to get serious about earning a living, as well as deciding where we wanted to live.

Once again the solution appeared without our searching for it. Where we would live was answered by a letter from Larry and Mary Pearmine, Peace Corps friends with whom we had become close while in Liberia. When they returned home after Peace Corps, they had settled on their large family farm in Oregon near Salem. While we were contemplating our next move, Larry wrote offering us a place to "sit down" for a time. He offered Harold work on the farm in any capacity, a return to his mechanic trade if that was what he'd like, and a homey old farmhouse on the farm, as well. We loved the area, and these people were like family. We knew this could be home.

We immediately wrote accepting their offer. Of course, what I might do once we were settled on the farm still had to be figured out, but knowing that registered nurses were always needed gave me some comfort, plus I knew many people in the nursing profession. I would deal with that once we were settled in Oregon. I could always go back to teaching, I thought. But just as we had changed, the field of nursing education had also changed in the six years I was gone. Where once a diploma in nursing was a ticket for many nursing positions, now a Master's degree was required for the professional nursing that I once enjoyed and for which I had earned recognition.

So as Liberians often said, "Well, what to do." I would just have to go back to school. My old voc-ed friend, Art Binnie, now president of the community college in Salem advised me to check out Marylhurst College in Portland, where I soon found the kind of program I needed, and it was only 30 miles away. Less than a year later, I graduated with a BA degree.

Harold had settled happily into the work he loved, enjoying the daily challenges of helping to keep everything on the farm running. When Harold was finally ready to retire, in 1980, we decided to move back to Washington State to be nearer my elderly mother. I had already taken a job as executive secretary of the Washington State Board of Practical Nurse Examiners, where I worked until my own retirement in 1986.

Sadly, our Liberian son, John (Jacob) Saiwhy, was killed during the civil war. But we still have contact with Martha Sayeedeh, who calls occasionally, and her daughter Vickie Lakpor, who has been attending university in Atlanta, Georgia. Martha remained in Liberia and is a public school teacher. We know that Dr. Gwenigale is now minister of health in Liberia, appointed by the new Liberian President.

In the intervening years since we retired, we've participated in our church and community activities, taken care of my mother at the end of her life, and continue to treasure our relationships with old Peace Corps and mission friends.

Our six years spent living and working among the Liberian people remain one of our most invaluable, formative life experiences, one we wouldn't trade for anything.